ALDEBURGH STUDIES IN MUSIC

General Editor: Christopher Grogan
Volume 10

ISSN 0969-3548

Other volumes in this series:

1. *Britten's Gloriana Essays and Sources*, edited by Paul Banks
2. *The Travel Diaries of Peter Pears, 1936–1978*, edited by Philip Reed
3. *On Mahler and Britten: Essays in Honour of Donald Mitchell on his Seventieth Birthday*, edited by Philip Reed
4. *Britten and the Far East: Asian Influences in the Music of Benjamin Britten*, Mervyn Cooke
5. *Britten and Auden in the Thirties: The Year 1936*, Donald Mitchell
6. *The Making of Peter Grimes: Essays*, edited by Paul Banks
7. *Imogen Holst: A Life in Music*, edited by Christopher Grogan
8. *Benjamin Britten: New Perspectives on his Life and Work*, edited by Lucy Walker
9. *Beyond Britten: The Composer and the Community*, edited by Peter Wiegold and Ghislaine Kenyon

My Beloved Man

The Letters of Benjamin Britten and Peter Pears

Edited by

Vicki P. Stroeher, Nicholas Clark and Jude Brimmer

THE BOYDELL PRESS

First published 2016
The Boydell Press, Woodbridge

ISBN 978-1-78327-108-5

The Boydell Press is an imprint of Boydell & Brewer Ltd
PO Box 9, Woodbridge, Suffolk IP12 3DF, UK
and of Boydell & Brewer Inc.
668 Mt Hope Avenue, Rochester, NY 14620–2731, USA
website: www.boydellandbrewer.com

A catalogue record for this book is available
from the British Library

The publisher has no responsibility for the continued existence or accuracy of URLs for
external or third-party internet websites referred to in this book, and does not guarantee that
any content on such websites is, or will remain, accurate or appropriate.

This publication is printed on acid-free paper

Typeset by BBR, Sheffield

Published with financial support from the Britten–Pears Foundation

For Pam and Anne
With love and gratitude
V, N & J

Henry Lamb, Double Portrait (c 1945)

Contents

Plates

between pages 252–3

These images, of Britten and Pears in private life and at work, are all taken from the archive of the Britten–Pears Foundation.

1. Benjamin Britten (c 1942). [PH/4/82]
   Photographer: unidentified

2. Peter Pears (c 1940). [PH/2/12]
   Photographer: unidentified

3. At the Old Mill, Britten's home in Snape, Suffolk (c 1943). [PH/3/7]
   Photographer: unidentified

4. Publicity shot for recitals in Vienna, while on an Austrian skiing holiday with the Harewoods (March 1952). [PH/3/35A]
   Photographer: Studio Fayer, Vienna

5. On the train to Rome as part of a recital tour (April 1949). [PH/3/30]
   Photographer: unidentified

6. On tour with the English Opera Group (August 1947). From left: Britten, Pears, Joan Cross, Otakar Kraus, Lesley Duff and Anna Pollak. [PH/5/33]
   Photographer: unidentified

7. In recital, their television debut on NHK, Japan (9 February 1956). [PH/3/146]
   Photographer: NHK

8. On a picnic in the Suffolk countryside (mid-1950s). [PH/3/39]
   Photographer: unidentified

9. Playing recorders at Crag House, their home on the Aldeburgh seafront (1954). [PH/3/37]
   Photographer: Roland Haupt

Illustrations

Foreword

FIONA SHAW

All artists share a longing for what Yeats called 'the heart and the hearth'... the desire to be home, but blessed and cursed by the need to communicate with the world. These letters show how two huge artists who were so often parted, survived. There is no question of either of them changing their natures, one an extrovert performer, the other a quiet composer – scruffed necks pulled apart by their gifts which were their attraction – and both paying the price, dealing with the necessity of long parting with an unrestrained frankness that allowed them to be together, intimately creating a hermetically sealed world.

To read these letters is to climb up a wall and peer into the secret garden of two giants. You expect to hear the roar of their success and achievements but instead you read the timpani sound of their affections. It is the terms of endearments, the 'Honey buns', the 'My darlings', that remind us we have encroached on their lives. Many of the letters have our text message modernity and brevity. Some are like email as they send short hand requests for times of trains, whinging about touring and the disorientation of endless hotels, asking for scores to be found on top of cupboards, passing love from mutual friends. The quarrels too are immediately recognisable, reprimands for mistimed calls and bad moods, the vibrant, intense need to make up, and heart-stopping, delightful, random declarations.

It is astonishing that these men created a totally realised domestic relationship that has remarkable contemporary immediacy during a period when it was illegal to love someone of your own sex. To me their lives seem an act of huge integrity. It shocks us into admiring the clarity of their affections. Here we see the secret, brave counterbalance in this fulcrum of daily love as it beams light into the seam of desolate ostracisation that runs through Ben's work.

Letters are fragments. The act of parting and re-meeting which of course we never read would hold a different vocabulary. This throws up the interesting hunt in the mystery of creative invention.

In my experience of creative enterprise and relationships, new work is the art of pushing each other's abilities. Practical experiments occur in the rehearsal room, the piano room for Britten. However creation does not stop there and some of the best ideas happen quite incidentally – cooking or reading or chatting or travelling. They can emerge from the ordinary. In these letters, we hear the metronome of comfort, recognition, trust, and the beat of mutual assurance. This, I think, is the bedrock of the art they created. They knew what they were trying to do, before others did, because they trusted the previous beat. Britten praising Pears having listened to a radio concert must have been profoundly encouraging for the singer because he knew that Ben could hear him better than any critic or audience member. He understood where the performance came from. Creative relationships are built on witness.

At the end of the 'Rape of Lucretia', which I have had the joy of directing, Collatinus and Lucretia, two parted lovers who also survived on letter-writing, re-meet when it is all too late. Collatinus sings

> 'O never again must we two dare to part.
> For we are of one another
> And between us, there is one heart'.

This is undoubtedly one of the most beautiful sections of the opera, and I found myself thinking of it over and over as I read the later letters. The music has a sublime melding with the sentiment, so we can feel the composer's understanding of domestic love's fathomless depths. When the letters warn us of Britten's impending early death, his art allows us to foresee a reply.

They both acknowledge in these letters how grateful they are to have found each other and that the time spent loving was the best of themselves.

As Collatinus and Lucretia go on to sing in duet

> 'To love as we loved was to live on the edge of tragedy'.

Acknowledgements

We must first thank Pam Wheeler and Anne Surfling, without whom this, like so many other books on Britten, Pears and their lives and work, could not have been written. Having spent much of the last four decades indexing and researching the archive at The Red House, they know the collections better than anyone, and their patient contribution to this project – checking the transcriptions and drafts – has been immeasurable. The publication of the complete correspondence of Pears and Britten has long been a heartfelt wish of theirs, in part because they know it was what Pears wanted, and as such we dedicate this volume to them, in gratitude for the many years they have given to The Red House.

We owe a huge debt to our predecessors at the Britten–Pears Foundation (Library as was), whose expertise in sorting and dating the letters proved to be invaluable in the development of this project. Particular thanks must go again to Pam Wheeler, to Dr Philip Reed and to the greatly missed Rosamund Strode.

We are deeply grateful for the financial assistance of the BPF, and support shown by the Publications Committee, Dr Colin Matthews, Richard Jarman and particularly Dr Christopher Grogan and Dr Lucy Walker for their expert advice (and many thanks especially to Lucy for initially transcribing letters and guiding the project at its inception).

Several of BPF's wonderful volunteers provided vital assistance to the project, particularly Anne Bartholomew, who spent many weeks digitising the letters, making our task considerably easier!

We are very grateful to Dr Donald Mitchell, Dr Philip Reed, Prof. Mervyn Cooke and Jill Burrows for the scholarly achievements of the *Letters from a Life* series – an encyclopaedic edition of Britten's selected correspondence with an extraordinary amount of biographical detail which has been invaluable in the preparation of this volume.

Many thanks to Michael Middeke, Megan Milan, Rohais Haughton and the team at Boydell & Brewer for all their help.

Deepest thanks also to: Sally Schweizer, for answering questions and sharing memories about her uncle Benjamin Britten; Susan Phipps, both for answering specific queries to help with our chronology, and for providing permission for our use of Jack Phipps's photograph of the aftermath of the Snape Maltings fire; Nigel

Luckhurst, for allowing use of his wonderful photographs of Britten and Pears; Photographer Brian Seed, who made his striking and evocative images available for use as part of the archive collections at the Britten–Pears Foundation; Peter Hutten, for allowing the marvellous Aldeburgh photographs by his father, Kurt Hutton, to be preserved and used by the Britten–Pears Foundation; Philip Stuart, for his invaluable and comprehensive Britten discography; Jean-Pierre Surget, Archivist for the Orchestre de la Suisse Romande; Dr Johan Giskes, for providing information about Pears's concert performances with the Concertgebouw; Will Kerley, for providing biographical information about Basil Coleman; Henrietta Phipps, for allowing reproduction of the double portrait of Britten and Pears by her father Henry Lamb, and to Rebecca Burton, Collections Assistant, Harewood House, for providing the image; Ian Beck, for permission to reproduce the work of Reynolds Stone; Marian Aird, for all her hard work providing the General Index; and Fiona Shaw, for very kindly agreeing to write our Foreword.

We have made every effort to trace and acknowledge all artists, photographers and other rights holders wherever possible, but there are some we have not been able to identify.

All letters and diary entries by Britten and Pears reproduced in this book are © Britten–Pears Foundation.

VS

Donald Van Horn, Dean of the College of Arts and Media at Marshall University, Huntington, WV for financial support including sabbatical leave in Fall 2011; Colleagues in the music program for their support and kind words during this process; Melinda McCurdy, Associate Curator, British Art, Huntington Museum, Los Angeles, CA for information on Constable paintings in the collection in 1976; Justin Vickers for reading early drafts of chapters; and Mike Stroeher for his patience, humour, cooking and dog wrangling.

NC & JB

All our colleagues at The Red House for their patience, support and good humour: Amanda Arnold, Anna Hunter, Carol Scopes, Caroline Harding, Chris Grogan, Chris Milton, Jess Cowper, Judith Ratcliffe, Julia Mael, Jyoti Patel, Keith Nicholls, Kevin Gosling, Lucy Walker, Paul Cook, Rachael Welsh, Sarah Bardwell, Sarah Singh and particularly Naomi Sturges for all her sterling work looking after the reading room while we were busy deciphering handwriting.

NC would also like to thank Patricia Egan for being a good sounding board for ideas.

JB is very grateful to Jonathan for staying awake while looking at drafts and generally being a good sort.

Editorial Note

There is already an exhaustive reference text based on Britten's letters in the formidable shape of the *Letters from a Life* series – we have no interest in repeating the editors' considerable achievements in documenting the composer's life. Instead our focus has been on providing access to the joint correspondence of Britten and Pears, giving equal prominence to the latter for the first time. Our intention as editors has been to intrude as little as possible. It is a difficult balance, providing just enough information to illuminate the text without getting in the way of the narrative, but this is what we have tried to achieve. We have separated the 365 letters into eight chapters, drawing lines where there are significant events or large gaps in the correspondence. Each chapter has a short introduction to set the scene, and we have inserted interleaving text between letters within a chapter where there is a gap of longer than a few months, or an important change in circumstances which is not made clear in the letters.

In order to provide further detail but avoid breaking up the flow, we have included a Personalia and List of Works. These are made up of entries for people and works either specifically mentioned or implied by Britten and Pears in the letters – we have not included anything which only appears in the editors' text.

The Personalia is for close contemporaries of Britten and Pears mentioned in the letters, not for composers or artists who are mentioned because of their work, i.e. Bach, Schubert etc. (for these, see the List of Works). To avoid too many intrusions in the letter texts, we've included a First Names list – so if only a first name is mentioned, the person can be identified and located in the Personalia and no footnote is necessary. We have occasionally inserted text in square brackets into a letter to help differentiate a Barbara, Basil or John where we can.

We have not tried to provide a Personalia entry for every name mentioned in passing (particularly by Pears, who often lists scores of names of fellow performers, attendees of parties etc.). Our policy is that if someone is mentioned multiple times in at least two chapters, they are listed in the Personalia. This practice has led to some surprising omissions – Frank Bridge, for example, whose significance in Britten's life was considerable – but it was never our intention to provide a list of 'VIPs', merely to reflect the actual content and assist navigation of the letters. The Personalia gives their dates where we know them, and we have tried to give details about them which help explain their relevance to Britten or Pears, rather than a mini biography.

Where we have been able to trace further details on other 'passers-by' (i.e. those not in the Personalia), we have noted them in the text proper. Where a person mentioned has proved completely unidentifiable, we have said so. Nationalities throughout should be assumed to be English, unless stated otherwise. We have assumed that a reader will remember a note from earlier in the same chapter, and we have repeated biographical notes on a person's first appearance in any subsequent chapters.

In the List of Works, again to ease pressure on the footnotes, we have noted any 'artistic' work mentioned by Britten or Pears, including musical works, art, films, books, plays and poetry. We have given dates where possible and, like the Personalia, have focused on details which are relevant to Britten or Pears and their involvement with the work, rather than try and give an overall history of the work itself.

Our notes also contain citations for primary and published sources we have consulted – these are given as short titles in the notes and full details can be found in the Select Bibliography.

We have attempted to keep in all of the idiosyncrasies of Britten and Pears's writing, including misspellings and crossings out, to reflect the tone of the original letters as far as possible in print. There is often a breathless, enthused tone to their letters which comes from frequent use of dashes rather than full stops, which we have always tried to replicate in the transcriptions. Also, some misspellings are deliberate, part of a word game or in-joke, while others are simply due to rushing, so we felt it was important to present their text 'as is'.

Dating of the letters is in many cases a best guess – Pears in particular was not in the habit of writing dates on his letters, though Britten fortunately added dates more often than not. The detective work involved is not foolproof, and in a few cases we have had to take greater leaps of logic than in others, but we've made clear in the notes where we really cannot be sure that a letter is in its right place.

The letters are in order by the date/time we think they were written, rather than read. Often with the overseas post particularly this leads to 'bunching up', and a reply appears several places along. If it is not otherwise obvious, we have tried to indicate with a footnote where we can link a letter up with its reply.

Many enclosures are mentioned – often the letters are written to accompany post being forwarded on – but they do not usually survive still attached in the archive. Either they were efficiently filed at the time in the appropriate separate folder in the general correspondence (in the current archive this fills upwards of 500 boxes), or an individual piece was not retained by Britten and Pears in the first place. In the case of a small number of Britten–Pears letters which are referred to but have not survived, one theory we have is that they were carried around by the recipient until they deteriorated – the current fragile state of several of the surviving documents bears this out.

It is of course possible that further letters will surface which may fill some of the frustrating gaps, but for now we hope we have allowed Britten and Pears to tell their story in their own words.

JB, NC, VS

INTRODUCTION

Britten and Pears's 'personal and consistent' Correspondence

'your letters have been life & breath to me [...] My man – my beloved man.'
Britten to Pears, December 1942 (Letter 27)

Maintaining contact through their letters was of vital importance to Benjamin Britten and Peter Pears throughout their 39-year relationship. Towards the end of his life, on 17 November 1974 (Letter 349), Britten wrote a letter from Aldeburgh to Pears who had recently made his Metropolitan Opera House debut in *Death in Venice*:

> I've just listened to a re-broadcast [on the radio] of Winter Words (something like Sept. '72) and honestly you are the greatest artist that ever was – every nuance, subtle & never over-done – those great words, so sad & wise, painted for one, that heavenly sound you make, full but always coloured for words & music. What <u>have</u> I done to deserve such an artist and <u>man</u> to write for? I had to switch off before the folk songs because I couldn't [bear] anything after – "how long, how long". How long? – only till Dec. 20th – I think I can <u>just</u> bear it
> But I love you,
>   I love you,
>   I love you —— B.

Britten's appeal 'how long, how long' echoes the concluding cry in 'Before Life and After', from the song cycle of Thomas Hardy poems *Winter Words*, a work that he and Pears first performed together in October 1953 and which had become an established part of their recital programme. The phrase conveys a longing for the return of a mythical past, an ancient world that came before the corrupt one, an impression that Pears described as Hardy's 'most personal and consistent view of the universe'.[1] Removed from this context, it offered Britten a more intimate meaning and he employed Hardy's words to put across his more immediate longing – 20 December was the final New York performance of *Death in Venice* after which Pears would return home.

Britten's valedictory question was a familiar way for him to end a letter to Pears. A plea for his partner's swift return had become a frequent closing sentiment in his correspondence during their periods of absence from one another. What was different in this case, though, was Britten's awareness of the grave state of his health. He was suffering from a heart condition which surgery had attempted to correct the previous year, but which would end his life just two years later. From today's perspective, it is difficult to read Britten's letter without acknowledging a sense of finality. It has been highlighted by biographers as a summation of Pears's worth both as a musician and as a partner because it appears near the culmination of their life together. But it is only one episode in the narrative. Between 1937 and 1976 they exchanged at least 365 letters, cards and telegrams (all now held at the Britten–Pears Archive, Aldeburgh) which, when read from beginning to end, provide broad insight, a 'personal and consistent view', to borrow Pears's description, into their relationship.

Indeed, both men encouraged their story to be related either in their own words or in those of friends. As Pears told Stephen Greco of *The Advocate* in 1979, he hoped that eventually 'the climate [would] be right for publishing some of the most marvellous letters that one can imagine, that [Britten] wrote to [him]' so that their relationship would be described 'clearly'.[2] Pears had even planned to publish the letters in a book of his own, but that project remained unrealised at his death.[3] It had also been Britten's wish that his friend and publisher Donald Mitchell write his biography; the key motivation, he urged, was 'to tell the truth about Peter and me'.[4] After the composer's death, Mitchell and John Evans produced *Benjamin Britten: Pictures from a Life 1913–1976*, a pictorial biography that told Britten's story, but also documented his life with Pears. Commenting on the volume, Pears declared that it was not 'the story of one man. It's a life of the two of us.'[5] The purpose of this book is to allow both men to relate that life in their own words.

✠ ✠ ✠

The correspondence gives us access to the couple's thoughts about each other as well as a wide variety of other topics. They never originally intended their words to be read by anyone else, as some of their frankly expressed opinions clearly imply. Although a certain amount of insight may be gained into the genesis and development of Britten's music, more compelling is the detail that the letters give of day-to-day activities both professional and domestic, conveyed in sometimes clumsy grammar and frequently idiosyncratic spelling. Their personalities emerge through the often hastily written but usually legible, cursive script. The speed of writing is often suggested by the endless dashes that punctuate their sentences, appearing in place of colons or full-stops. They do little to hide when they are irritated with each other and certainly do not refrain from incidental spitefulness when referring to friends, musical colleagues or, particularly in Britten's case, when making derogatory remarks about other (usually English) composers. Their letters are also interspersed with occasional lightheartedness, wit and a shared sense of humour.

Both men were gregarious, enjoying the company of others either at home or on holiday, but they also highlight in their correspondence the reality that theirs was an intimate world of mutual dependence. Enid Slater, wife of *Peter Grimes* librettist Montagu Slater, discerned a natural bond between them, later commenting 'I thought this relationship [was] right […] this [was] absolutely perfect.'[6] She had visited them working and relaxing together at the composer's home, The Old Mill at Snape, in December 1944, their partnership now fully established. The correspondence shows a shared belief that, as outsiders together, they were often in opposition to the society in which they lived. 'We are after all queer & left & conshies [conscientious objectors] which is enough to put us, or make us put ourselves, outside the pale,' Pears asserted (Letter 276).

Pears's remark is a rare reference, made in hindsight in a letter of July 1963, to the stance they took during the Second World War. In the early 1940s, they had witnessed war raging in Europe from the relative safety of America. Britten's concern about his absence from England, particularly as the Blitz in London was underway, is seen in a letter to his publisher Ralph Hawkes in October 1940:

> I have been desparately worried, not really about what people are saying […] but about the fact that one is doing nothing to alleviate any of the suffering, that both of us again asked official advice on what we had better do. The answer is always the same – stay where you are until called back; you can't do anything if you do go back; get on with your work as artistic ambassadors etc. etc.[7]

As the composer remarked in his 1942 statement to the Local Tribunal for the Registration of Conscientious Objectors, his fundamental decision was to offer support to his 'fellow human beings' through his music,[8] a purpose fully shared by Pears. The correspondence shows Pears, especially, travelling between performance venues, giving recitals and reporting to Britten about where and under what conditions he had to sing. The Council for the Encouragement of Music and the Arts (CEMA), an organisation set up by the Government in 1940, supported orchestras throughout the regions, as well as the Sadler's Wells opera and ballet companies in London and theatres elsewhere.[9] The work Britten and Pears undertook for CEMA, while a condition of their registration as conscientious objectors, was all part of the committed belief that their music-making was important, and could help to relieve what they saw as the privation caused by war. As well as giving recitals together in the provinces they also performed in well-known London locations for wartime concerts such as the National Gallery and the Wigmore Hall.

In addition to their work during the war they remained committed pacifists throughout their lives. In December 1949 they gave a recital at the Community

The governments of the world have declared in the Charter of UNESCO: "Since wars begin in the minds of men, it is in the minds of men that the defenses of peace must be constructed."

One of our leading English writers, the historian of art, Mr. Herbert Read, has pointed out what the scientists and the military also in effect declare, namely, that with the advent of atomic and biological weapons, war and armaments no longer provide any defense. Power in the military sense has become an illusion and it is indeed "worse than an illusion —it is an hallucination which invites suicide." Herbert Read says that under these circumstances young Englishmen who agree to be drafted "are engaging in a gigantic conspiracy which can only end in the obliteration of their island home" and adds that "the case is not different for young Americans, young Frenchmen, young Russians—for the youth of any nation."

Not only is modern war completely irrational and suicidal; it is also completely immoral. Recently Rear Admiral Ralph A. Offstie, U.S.N., at a Congressional hearing, raised the question, in a denunciation of atomic and "obliteration" bombing, what people mean by "survival." He declared: "If we mean the survival of the values, the principles and traditions of human civilization, we must insure that our military techniques do not strip us of our self-respect."

In these circumstances the first act of sanity for any nation is to break with war. The first patriotic, sane, morally decent step for the youth—any youth of any nation—is to withhold himself from military service.

Once we have decided not to slip over the precipice into atomic war, we can train ourselves to use higher and truly effective means to resist evil and possible aggression. If our democratic peoples maintain a vigorous health in their economic life, in relations between the nations, in education and art, health will gradually be instilled into the whole community of nations. Gandhi has shown how nonviolent resistance can be "a living reality among the practical policies of world politics."

It is because we believe these things and have in our own country been connected with movements which promote these pacifist ideas that we gladly give this performance under the sponsorship of two organizations which in this country seek to advance the same cause—the Fellowship of Reconciliation and the War Resisters League.

BENJAMIN BRITTEN
PETER PEARS

Statement from the programme for a recital given by Britten and Pears at the Community Church Auditorium, New York (8 December 1949).

Church Auditorium, New York, in support of the Fellowship of Reconciliation and the War Resisters' League. With the dangers of the nuclear age now fully apparent they published their own pacifist manifesto (see illustration) in the programme. Although it is not mentioned in their letters to each other, they had clearly taken the decision together to make a joint statement, calling on the youth of America to 'withhold [themselves] from military service'. Music was one of the 'effective means' employed to convey their belief in unison, as 'firm-united souls' in Britten's setting of Francis Quarles's words of *Canticle I*, one of the works performed that evening.

Only brief glimpses of their impression of the war are contained in the letters of the time. Instead there are accounts of arduous schedules often made more difficult because of travel restrictions, reduced resources or poor conditions for performers, rather than a discourse on conflict and destruction. Britten's deeper impressions of the growing horror are found in the descriptions of London that he conveyed to their friends in America. In June 1942, for example, he noted to Bobby Rothman the 'terrible sight' of destroyed houses. 'I have been in several alarms', he added '& have heard lots of guns […] The sirens make the most horrible wailing noise, like hundreds of gigantic cats, & they always make my stomach turn upside down!'[10] Later in September he noted to Elizabeth Mayer that his and Pears's work took them 'all over the place, under the strangest conditions – playing on awful old pianos – singing easy, but always good programmes – & really [having] the greatest successes with the simplest audiences'.[11] The cumulative pressure of travel, less than ideal performance venues and the constant threat of attack inevitably take their toll and he invokes an even darker tone two years later as he describes again the damaged capital. 'It is indeed a strange time – like living in an H.G. Wells fantasy, with everything unbelievable until you meet it face to face, & then terrifying! […] We had a lot of concerts together around London (& Southern England!), & they had to be done under harassing conditions.'[12] Witnessing the devastation together, there was little need for Britten and Pears to write about it to one another. Strictly limited telephone communication at this time prevented direct contact and their letters often focus instead on the demoralisation brought about by sustained periods of separation. Pears performed in factory concerts and at numerous other engagements while Britten, at work in London and Snape, declared himself to be 'hopelessly homesick' (Letter 44) in Pears's absence.

The other aspect of their lives that made them both 'outside the pale', in Pears's words, was the isolation from society caused by their sexuality. The letters they wrote to each other make no concession to legal or more general criticism of their lives together at a time when homosexual acts were regarded as a crime. Even so, Britten and Pears realised they could not afford to be entirely open about their partnership, as Pears's caution to the composer to seal his letters properly might suggest: 'The last one flew the Atlantic wide open!' he warned on 1 November 1948 (Letter 100). They were aware of the scrutiny that surrounded them, that a decision to share a home together (officially Pears kept a London home while the Aldeburgh homes were always in Britten's name) and the true nature of their partnership would not go unnoticed. Interestingly, as public figures they seemed to escape for the most part formal censure or accusation for their lifestyle. Britten is said to have suffered the indignity of being questioned by the police in 1953 but was able to avoid the public humiliation suffered by other prominent figures such as actor John Gielgud, arrested the same year, and Conservative peer Lord Montagu, arrested in 1954, on charges of indecent behaviour and sexual assault respectively. Britten and Pears had both emerged from respectable middle-class backgrounds, were well spoken, cultured and invariably well presented in dress and general appearance. They were prominent figures on the concert stage, friends and acquaintances of nobility and royalty, and were themselves recipients of honours: Pears was awarded a CBE (1957) and a knighthood (1978), Britten the CH (1953), OM (1965) and a life peerage (1976), all in addition to a host of music awards, medals and honorary academic titles. Their letters show that, like other gay men, it was necessary to create dual lives.

Homosexual law reform was introduced in the United Kingdom in 1967, but in the decades leading up to the Sexual Offences Act, which legalised consensual sex between men in England and Wales, the threat of prosecution and, potentially, imprisonment was ever present. As Jeffrey Weeks observes, a gradual change in attitude began to be felt, despite obstacles such as anti-gay views promoted by some areas of the media as well as the campaigning of politicians such as Home Secretary Sir David Maxwell Fyfe who spoke against homosexuality in the House of Commons in 1953. Prejudice and basic lack of understanding, particularly when it was fuelled so visibly, did little to alter public misconceptions about same-sex relationships.[13] Britten and Pears had been together for seventeen years when a Home Office Committee chaired by John Wolfenden, Vice-Chancellor of Reading University, was founded to research and produce a report completed in 1957 on the law as it stood on homosexuality and prostitution. Although unafraid to share a home together, to withstand rumours, they were also discreet about their sexuality, choosing not to flaunt it. Nearly thirty years after Pears's admonitory remark to Britten to seal his letters, there was no need for this façade as their relationship was by then well known, yet 'The news announcer referred to Peter Pears as "[Britten's] close companion", to whom the Queen had sent a telegram', James Lees-Milne recorded in his diary after hearing of the composer's death. 'Quite right, but I thought what an advance this was, that the Queen should tacitly but publicly recognise a homosexual relationship.'[14]

✠✠✠

As well as showing the reader what isolated them from society, the letters also reveal a lighter side to Britten and Pears – that they shared a rather schoolboy sense of humour and did not take themselves too seriously. In Letter 221 Pears playfully reattributes a painting, reproduced on a Wagner museum postcard, to Mary Potter. It captures Britten as 'the Master at Home' surrounded by acolytes Imogen Holst, Pears and Stephen Reiss. A secret language in which the letters ARP are inserted before each vowel becomes an affectionate code to Pears in January 1972: 'Arpi, Larpove, Yarpu, & wish I were with Yarpu' (Letter 320).[15] They developed an intimate form of address, sometimes complemented on the page with small cartoons, as marks of affection. Mildly flirtatious phrases and some risqué references appear now and then, especially in the early days, but the letters are not remarkable for their racy content. There is a diversity of salutation and they greet each other variously as 'Darling Honey Bee', 'My Darling P', 'My own darling Poppet', 'My old honey-bun', 'Dearest B', 'My darlingst P', 'Dearest Bunch' or 'Poppety mio'. Although their time was taken up with rehearsal, business meetings or composition, they made space for the letters that enabled them to remain in contact. 'This is not a proper letter', 'Just a scribble' are characteristic opening remarks, signalling an understanding of their rushed schedules but also determining their easy form of communication. Pears attempts from time to time to try out his not always firm grasp of German – a language Britten learnt at school – in brief phrases. Even Pears admits his command of the language is not always convincing as he discovered during an Ansbach performance. 'I was nervous & made one ghastly howler in German' he confesses in July 1956 'singing "Lust" instead of "Last" but noone seems to have noticed!!' (Letter 202).

They could also turn a minor quarrel into a playful exchange. On 1 June 1942, for example, Britten in London 'having wasted a bob' on a telegram castigates Pears for missing a planned telephone call, beginning with an accusatory 'God – you blighter' (Letter 15). The banter here is enlivened by references that are designed to needle and spark a reaction. Britten mentions his meeting that day with Wulff Scherchen, the young German émigré with whom he was involved before Pears, hinting at his renewed attraction to him – the tongue-in-cheek tone is underlined through his repeating 'boohoo', alongside various insults 'blast you – why can't you be in when I want you', revealing his frustration. In reply, beginning 'Dear Sir', Pears accuses Britten of displaying his 'artistic temperament […] stifle it how you will – you old tree-shrew you! However, I gave such a good performance last night that all your Billingsgate is powerless to disturb me! So there' (Letter 16).

Pears's evocative metaphors also appear in descriptions of some of the places he visits. 'It is a charmless dump' he writes on a postcard from Bucharest in November 1973. 'They call it little Paris, a fair comment except that the food is not so good' (Letter 331). He writes colourfully of some of the lodgings he spends time in while giving CEMA recitals across the UK, for example in Letter 14 'I'm sure this is not bad really – a dreary journey, a frightful city, a bleak room, a landlady like the Ugly Duchess, no hot water, fire which won't burn, nothing but sausages till Tuesday.'

He and Britten of course both ventured to other parts of the world and the letters document their travels. Pears's accounts, in particular, are often punctuated with amusing, informed observations and he welcomes the opportunity to see new landscapes and comment on different cultures. Britten, despite his fondness for Suffolk, was an avid sightseer and we learn much about his appreciation of art and ancient buildings, particularly when he writes about visits to Italy: 'got into St. Donato (the Romanesque church) full of splendid things – wonderful floor like S. Marco' (Letter 303). This same letter mentions how work on the Church Parable *The Prodigal Son* (1968) goes 'very fast', an indication of how the stimulating environment helps him to compose.

The correspondence reveals tension as well as intimacy, the occasional examples of 'miserable tiffs, our nagging heartaches', as Pears describes them (Letter 20), in their exchanges with one another. Their letters highlight Britten's acute sensitivity, as the language that Pears employs when stating an apology suggests: 'I didn't mean to be cold last night, but it seemed to end up like that – v.v. sorry, my darling –' (Letter 116). 'I know we can't always be together & perhaps shouldn't always be together' he writes from Elmau in January 1961, insisting he is 'not complete' in Britten's absence, 'though I may be beastly and foul to that piece of me, I need him [...] to try and help him so that he may feel that I am part of him and can be of use to him' (Letter 261).

The cycle of quarrel and reconciliation, then, is sometimes documented in full, but there are instances where the correspondence can tell only part of the story. In the subjective exchange of letters between the two there are inevitably moments where we enter a conversation or find unexplained references to previous disagreements. In December 1942 Pears describes their relationship in a way that recalls the imagery of Sonnet XXXII of the *Seven Sonnets of Michelangelo* ('in two bodies one soul is made eternal'). He speaks of the 'seriousness' of their love, emphasising the 'great responsibility' of commitment to their relationship, remarking that it is based on 'a sharing of personalities – It's not just a pleasure & a self indulgence' (Letter 28). And yet he acknowledges that these personalities contain qualities that are also distinct from one another. In January 1944, following an acrimonious exchange, he draws attention to an observation made by the artist Kenneth Green: 'Don't judge me too hard. Kenneth said that we were as different types as could be, so perhaps we mustn't be too surprised if sometimes we differ – but it isn't very often really is it?' (Letter 42).

Another contrast is apparent in the ways in which both coped with the pressures brought about by work and illness. Britten's poor health in particular is a recurrent theme in the letters, ranging from minor ailments ('I have a cold to end all colds', for which he blames Covent Garden's David Webster, Letter 250) to more debilitating on-going problems such as bursitis, recurrent stomach pains which led to hospital treatment for diverticulitis in 1966, and endocarditis diagnosed in 1968 which marked the gradual path towards heart failure. There is reference to his need to rest, to visit medical experts in both London and Aldeburgh, as well as to delays or complete withdrawal from concert engagements. These prompted apologies from Britten, hoping to be 'adequate again' (Letter 247) or a more self-conscious comment in which apology and frustration are balanced against vulnerability:

> I am so dreadfully sorry I'm being such a broken reed at the moment – it is the bloodiest nuisance from every point of view. But I promise you that it is only a bad patch this, & I'll get it all coped with & promise to be a worthy companion for you from now on! (Letter 271)

The correspondence highlights the sometimes divergent paths on which their careers led them: the isolation that Britten felt was essential in order for him to work, juxtaposed with the constant series of tours and other performance partnerships that occupied Pears. The tone of Pears's letters also differs, suggesting the demanding schedules, the pace of travel as well as meeting friends whilst abroad that was all part of his touring life. Britten is sometimes all too aware of being a distant observer as his response to a letter of July 1957 indicates. Pears had written to him about a recital with Julian Bream in Wolfsgarten which was followed by socialising with the Hesse family. The composer responded with a list of social engagements in which *he* had been involved in Aldeburgh, pointing out: 'so you see, even the stay at homes have busy lives!' (Letter 212). Pears is not immune from venting frustration, showing occasional self-pity or complaint about annoying colds. Yet, there is stronger evidence of his sympathy and support, even a suggestion at one point that he consider relinquishing his own artistic life, that he 'should long ago have thrown my silly career out of the window & come & tried to protect you a bit from worry and tension, instead of adding to them with my own worries and tetchinesses' (Letter 272).

✠✠✠

The letters augment what other primary sources already tell us about Britten at work. Scene synopses, libretto drafts and heavily pencilled manuscripts explain the development of his music from sketch to fair copy, but his comments to Pears record when and how fluently his creativity flowed or, indeed, faltered, as seen in the concise evaluation of *Peter Grimes*: 'My bloody opera stinks, & that's all there is to it' (Letter 52). Moments of self-criticism draw attention to the inconsistency of Britten's mood during the writing process; in this case, uncertainty is followed by an attempt at reassurance as he plans to 'de-odourise' his work in due course. As a rule, Britten was reticent when it came to talking about his work but the letters show that he felt able to share his concerns with Pears who was often directly involved in choosing or editing the texts. Pears's replies frequently ease his partner's self-doubt, reminding Britten of previous successes such as *Rejoice in the Lamb*: 'that is still your best yet you know' (Letter 61), a remark that was intended to shore up confidence but also challenged the composer to live up to and surpass his earlier achievement. Pears acted as a sounding-board and, just as importantly, received progress reports, both satisfactory and unsatisfactory. Several of the letters record the frame of mind Britten was in when composing a piece, as is the case in January 1951 when we learn of his excitement about his beginning Act III of *Billy Budd*, and his consequent relief at being 'rid' of Act II (Letter 143).

Pears's correspondence indicates that he could also be self-critical. Britten composed nine song cycles and eleven major stage roles for Pears and accompanied him in innumerable recitals, but the singer still had times when he doubted his ability to give the music all the composer asked. Britten's response (in Letter 142) was to encourage, describing Pears as 'a lovely artist & I'm not prejudiced – madly critical'. The composer's critical ear was not confined to Pears's performance of his own music. After hearing him in a Bach broadcast in December 1956, he writes that the singer's interpretation was 'intelligent, gifted, simple, loving & noble, and with the lightest touch too', acknowledging immediately thereafter his 'luck to be alive with you around – & "how" around!' (Letter 206). This encouragement was invaluable, but Pears also drew support from Britten's music itself, writing, after work on the Michelangelo Sonnets, 'that's really only what makes me go on singing – you. and your music' (Letter 246).

Pears continued to be fascinated by what drove a composer to write music for specific performers. The shelves of the Britten–Pears Library contain the editions they owned of the correspondence of Mozart, Mahler, Tchaikovsky, Verdi and Fauré. The volume *Franz Schubert's Letters and other Writings*[16] was given to Pears after Britten's death, and contains annotations beside passages that recount the inspiration behind some of Schubert's songs. Like Britten, the composer was inspired by a particular singer, the baritone Johann Vogl. Given his own experience as a muse, Pears would have read Schubert's letters with keen insight.

✠✠✠

The locations shown on the letterheads – The Old Mill, Snape; 4 Crabbe Street, Aldeburgh, Suffolk; The Red House, Aldeburgh-on-Sea; or the handwritten Chapel House, Horham – give a strong indication of a sustained wish, mostly of the composer's, for remoteness. A disused windmill, converted by his sister's father-in-law in 1937, was Britten's initial base. In 1947 he and Pears moved to the nearby coastal town of Aldeburgh. The upper floors in their new residence Crag House, 4 Crabbe Street, afforded Britten an inspiring view, which he sometimes describes to Pears ('A terrific sea to-day, most wonderfully beautiful' in Letter 95). Born only thirty miles north in Lowestoft, where he grew up in a house on the seafront, Britten regarded living near the sea as essential, an important source of motivation for work. 'The view as I sit at my desk writing is beyond description' he enthused to Elizabeth Mayer in November 1948. 'Not a striking breath-taking view which distracts, but part of one's life, like eating & sleeping!'[17] His direct proximity to the North Sea in a town that welcomed an influx of seasonal visitors came at a cost. Britten was suspicious of fame and he noted as early as September 1947 the danger of becoming too recognisable: 'Everyone is all of a titter to have us here – & I think it's going to be fairly sick-making if we don't take a strong line about not seeing chaps & going out' (Letter 79). Although their professional lives were dedicated to performance on stage, they often felt uncomfortable to have their private lives under the public gaze. A decade after the move to Crag House, Britten sacrificed his sea-view partly in a bid to escape what he would describe to Edith Sitwell as 'the gaping faces, & irritating publicity of that sea-front'.[18]

In November 1957 they relocated to The Red House, an ancient farmhouse (whose exterior dates from the late seventeenth/early eighteenth centuries) one mile inland, exchanging residences with their friend, the artist Mary Potter. Britten purchased another retreat in 1970, Chapel House in Horham near the Norfolk border, mainly to escape the intrusive sound of aircraft that flew over Aldeburgh from an airbase at Bentwaters near Woodbridge. It offered a peaceful space where Britten would work on later pieces such as *Owen Wingrave* (1971) and *Death in Venice* (1973). Chapel House was also ideal for preserving a degree of privacy and both men let it be known to local residents that they wanted to maintain as unobtrusive a presence as possible within the community. The Red House, however, remained their principal home for the rest of their lives.

As is clear from the business appointments and engagements discussed throughout their letters, a London base was also a necessity. Recordings, meetings with publishers and fellow musicians and the impracticality of travelling back to the coast after concerts meant that over the years they kept a succession of residences for convenience. But Britten often resents the need to journey away from home, and much of his correspondence is written from East Anglia. The Earl of Harewood noted that 'concert giving', 'visits to the dentist', 'being rung up on the telephone' and 'auditions' were all part of Britten's anti-London bias, but he pinpointed the main reason: he associates the city 'with anything [...] except composing. And that which he does at Aldeburgh is, after all, his life'.[19] Britten enjoyed holidays abroad, and in distant parts of the UK, but tellingly his favourite destinations were Wolfsgarten and Venice, two places beyond Suffolk in which he also felt able to write music.

On receiving the first Aspen Award, in 1964, Britten declared that his music was nurtured by the 'small corner of East Anglia' near where he was born. There he was able to follow a daily pattern that helped him to compose. The 'cold baths & long walks' he mentions as a cure for a cold (Letter 290) had been a regular part of his routine since the 1940s. He would try to deal with correspondence before spending the morning in his studio, breaking to eat lunch in the early afternoon. This would be followed with a walk perhaps through the marshes of North Warren, Slaughden or along the beach, during which he would usually contemplate the work. Upon his return he would work from five until eight. The rest of the evening was occupied with activities such as reading or playing board games. 'The night is for sleeping,' he insisted, 'I go to bed early and get up early. When I am in a rush and have to get something off to the copyists, I may work into the small hours but that is on scoring, not composition.'[20] Rosamund Strode, Britten's music assistant, recalled that he generally planned composition projects to fit in with periods when he could remain at home.[21]

Pears's life, of course, followed a different pattern. His letters and office diaries attest to the frenetic schedule of travelling and recital work, and the correspondence chronicles the demanding schedule of a professional singer. He worked a good deal on the continent and was in regular demand as a soloist, particularly in performances of Bach and Schütz. He became a regular performer at the Ansbach Bachwoche, recording his 1959 appearance in a travel diary.[22] He could be harsh in his reports back to Britten when he thought a musician was performing inadequately, and generous when he thought he or she sang or played well. His views on the merits of conductors such as Eduard van Beinum or Karl Richter, criticisms of fellow singers or appraisals of instrumentalists are documented. His opinions were not just given as anecdotes, but would no doubt be recalled when he and Britten planned their own early music performances at the Aldeburgh Festival or in the series of 'Bach at Long Melford' weekends in the 1960s. Radio broadcasts in which Pears was singing could act as a link when he was absent from Aldeburgh, and he and Britten would often discuss them in the letters. Although, as the composer notes, poor radio reception of the BBC Third Programme, in East Anglia especially, was often a problem (mentioned, for example, in Letter 89). At the beginning of June 1954 Pears writes 'I wish I were with you instead of Europe-trotting, although with Grimes & Lucretia round my neck I can't feel very far away from you' (Letter 191).

Britten was at his most comfortable in Aldeburgh where work was interspersed with the mundane routine of the household. The homes were fitted out with modern furniture and the walls were adorned with an ever-increasing collection of fine art, most of which was acquired by Pears. Britten mentions his delight, for example, about newly acquired paintings by William Blake and John Sell Cotman after hosting a party in March 1950: 'everyone asked tenderly after & sent their love to you, & congratulated you on your taste!' (Letter 134). Pears often took the lead on practical matters to do with building and decorating, a responsibility that Britten was grateful to relinquish. 'The wallpaper is arrived, & looks awfully nice!' he writes in January 1951. 'I'm very pleased with it – it's nice & nursery for me! Thank you so very much for coping with it all' (Letter 143). The Red House offered slightly more seclusion than they had experienced on the seafront, but one of its greatest assets, as far as Britten was concerned, was the peaceful environment of a purpose-built studio in which he was able to compose. Workspaces were important to Britten. Early in 1972, for example, as he attempted to write *Death in Venice*, he reported to Pears 'I'm going to cheer myself up by working in your study: the library is a bit cold, & I'm going to get some inspiration from sitting on your chair –' (Letter 326). Despite his need for quiet, members of his family often came to stay: his sisters Barbara and Beth and Beth's children, Sebastian, Sally and Roguey, as well as his brother Robert, nephews John and Alan, are all mentioned, as are friends and colleagues E.M. Forster and John and Myfanwy Piper. Pears's letters contain few family references, his niece Susan Pears Phipps who later became their agent and his sister Cecily Smithwick being the only exceptions to this.

In November 1965 a valuation for insurance[23] of the 'joint property' of both men was undertaken and it included inventories of what was discreetly described as 'Mr Pears's Bedroom' and 'Mr Britten's Bedroom' respectively. Separate rooms were maintained for the sake of appearance, but in nearly all other aspects The Red House was their shared home and their correspondence gives a sense of its domestic atmosphere. They write about guests they have invited, discussions of work projects with colleagues, their dogs and the hosting of dinner parties. It was, as many visitors attest, a typical home environment. Following an afternoon in their company in 1971, the novelist Susan Hill noted that the 'obvious, domestic affection' she witnessed might have been that between a husband and wife: 'I remember thinking that this was a perfectly ordinary relationship which just happened to be between two men.'[24] The ordinariness is what they relished, but they recognised they were unlikely to be accepted as a domestic couple. Britten even briefly contemplates what he has missed in not experiencing parenthood (Letter 289), a comment that arises from friendships made with children.

Christopher Palmer stated that 'the childhood vision, once clouded over, can never be recaptured in its pristine purity; a fact of life that Britten was never able to come to terms with'.[25] This is true, but he strove to maintain a link with the 'vision' nevertheless. Recollection and intuition kept him in touch with what he remembered as an idyllic period in his life and it also influenced his music. He had been a very happy child, precociously talented and successful at school, despite bouts of ill health. He explained, at the age of thirty-nine, for example, that the reason why he was able to write such exuberant quaver-filled lines for the rabble boys' chorus in the coronation opera *Gloriana* was because he was 'still thirteen'.[26] Britten's fascination with childhood was also manifested in another form, in friendships made with a number of adolescent boys, many of whose names pass through his letters to Pears. Sons of friends, budding pianists and composers, young singers working on his operas, all received his loving concern, and the attention he gave them inevitably gave rise to speculation. He was undoubtedly attracted to what W.H. Auden described in a letter of 1942 to the composer as 'thin-as-a-board juveniles',[27] but he kept any sexual impulses he may have had under strict control.

As John Bridcut has pointed out, former colleagues such as Eric Crozier suggested that in these friendships Britten was attempting to embark on 'almost a return to his own youth'.[28] Pears showed more awareness of how easily such friendships might be misinterpreted and work against the composer in the form of gossip. Although there is no evidence in their letters, we know that the subject sometimes caused friction between them, mainly because Britten resented the need to feel shielded from wrongful suspicion. The occasional nature of the allusions in the letters shows how few of these friendships lasted. Usually, once the need for befriending had passed, Britten withdrew from the relationship. This does not appear to have altered the boys' later estimation of him as a man or musician.[29] As Bridcut explains, Pears understood that this connection with childhood was an aspect of Britten's personality which remained 'beyond their own enduring relationship'.[30]

✠✠✠

The body of correspondence still in existence derives from a number of factors. Keeping Britten's letters proved important to Pears for two main reasons: they had obvious sentimental value, but they also presented a relatively full and accurate record of their relationship, which was central to his intention of publishing them. A more prosaic reason was the age in which they lived, where writing letters, of putting pen to paper, was a far more common form of contact than it is today. As Britten and the poet W.H. Auden had helped to demonstrate in the General Post Office (GPO) film *Night Mail* (1936), 'the speed and reliability of steam trains [that carried mail] matched the geography of the country' ensuring the promise of next-day delivery,[31] and in the 1930s at least there were many deliveries during the day. The cost of inland mail (Britten and Pears kept stamped envelopes as well as the letters they contained) was not prohibitive. Between 1940 and 1965 the average rate rose from only 2 ½ d. to 4 ½ d. for a letter of up to 2 oz.[32] Frequent collection and delivery assisted Britten to 'catch the post' as he writes from Crag House in 1951 (Letter 160). Receiving written communication on a regular basis was, as Britten stated early in their relationship, 'life & breath' (Letter 27). Remaining in contact was not difficult and other correspondence, as Britten and Pears suggest usually in the opening lines of their letters, was often forwarded along with their private mail.

In addition to the 365 letters that comprise this volume, there must have been others that are not held at The Red House. There are noticeable gaps in the sequence that at times extend to several months, nearly two years in one case. Given their usually constant contact with one another it is unlikely that writing between the two simply ceased. There is no known suggestion of destruction and there exists the possibility that letters currently unknown may surface. Retaining their correspondence was of distinct importance to Britten and Pears, but interruptions in the story nevertheless occur.

Periods of absence were unavoidable and reluctantly accepted by both men. Biographers have drawn attention to Pears being away from Britten, particularly in the months when it was becoming evident that the composer's health was deteriorating, and the subsequent guilt he later felt.[33] Pears's apparent distance from Britten during these final years has also invited conjecture that he sought out other relationships, particularly with a number of younger men.[34] While he maintained good friendships with those he already knew, he also formed new ones at this time, evidence of which can be found in in his correspondence archive and in the letters he wrote to Britten. There is nothing to suggest, or deny, for that matter, sexual relationships with other men. His letters indicate that some friendships were built on his advisory role as a mentor to young singers, developed through his work for the Britten–Pears School, showing encouragement as it was warranted. Britten's illness may well have left a void, but Pears implied in his correspondence and in later comment that there was no substitute for his life with the composer. Following Britten's death he described on several occasions what their partnership had meant to him, speaking more candidly in public than he might have done a decade earlier.

In early 1977 in the BBC Radio 4 programme *A Sympathy with Sounds* he asserted that Britten's music was now more important to him than ever, still linking them together. He spoke of a performance of *Saint Nicolas* in which he participated immediately after Britten's funeral, acknowledging the composer's presence. 'I'm still entirely with him and he remains the centre of my life.'[35] He elaborated on the nature of this closeness three years later, during the London Weekend Television film *A Time There Was … A Profile of Benjamin Britten*, talking openly about their homosexuality. He was cautious of using the word 'gay', a description that Britten had not favoured because he had felt it was inappropriate to describe a lifestyle often plagued with 'difficulties and tensions and troubles', a reference to the shadow cast by illegality and suspicion which their own relationship withstood:

> It was established very early that we were passionately devoted and close, and that was it. Of course there were one or two little moments when things didn't go – it wasn't a superhuman sort of relationship, no; but there was very, very little that disturbed our relationship. And I was terribly conscious of his faith in me. I like to think that I returned that as warmly as he gave it. But I can't feel that I could reach his particularly extraordinary quality of trust, and faith, and love.[36]

Pears's disclosure is borne out in the correspondence: Britten's on-going dependence on his partner for emotional support, reassurance about his work and Pears's ability to 'live', as he termed it, in his music (Letter 351). Although he implies his uncertainty over whether he had been able to replicate this degree of trust, Pears was assured of the strength of their relationship regardless. It was for that reason he wanted his and Britten's letters to be read widely, believing the story they told could alleviate some of the 'tensions' felt by others who had experienced a similar inability to live as openly gay, even in the context of the nearly two decades that had followed decriminalisation. Their letters present the clearest and most accurate form of self-portrait and although they could not be entirely open about their partnership in public, they had no need to be anything other than entirely honest in their writings to one another.

Pears's final public comment on his relationship with Britten was made at the conclusion of *The Tenor Man's Story*, another television film that screened less than a year before his death, at the age of seventy-five. Showing signs of illness, a stroke he had suffered five years earlier, although still alert and articulate, he spoke to Donald Mitchell in the wintry setting of The Red House about his eventful life. When asked what had been his greatest happiness, he replied:

> Unquestionably of course my life with Ben. I mean Ben was for the best part of forty years my nearest and dearest. And […] I can't be thankful enough for that […] it was just a gift from God, something I didn't deserve. It was a gift.[37]

Appropriately, the film's title refers again to the work of Thomas Hardy.[38] Pears had made a special note in December 1956 of what Hardy conceived as the driving force behind his art, citing a Notebook entry in which the author recorded that his purpose was to show that 'the heart & inner meaning is made vividly visible' (Letter 207). Pears here points out to Britten that the same ethos applied to his and Britten's art, the writing and interpretation of music. It is self-evident in the works written for and dedicated to Pears such as the *Holy Sonnets of John Donne* (1945) or their most declamatory statement of love, the Michelangelo Sonnets, a song cycle they performed over one hundred times together. But the quotation is also an apt description of the relationship revealed in their correspondence, a series of letters that provide in every sense a 'personal and consistent view' of a shared life.

---

1   Peter Pears, 'Hardy and his Poetry'.
2   Stephen Greco, *The Advocate*, p. 39.
3   *Letters* Vol. I, p. 58.
4   *Letters* Vol. I, p. 56.
5   Stephen Greco, *The Advocate*, p. 39.
6   John Evans (ed.), *Journeying Boy*, p. 504.
7   Britten to Ralph Hawkes, 7 October 1940, *Letters* Vol. II, p. 868.
8   Britten's Statement (4 May 1942) and his Appeal to the Appellate Tribunal (June 1942) are reproduced in Paul Kildea (ed.) *Britten on Music*, pp. 40–1.
9   'In 1945 [CEMA] was combined with ENSA [Entertainments National Service Association], the Forces' Entertainment organisation, and was restructured as the Arts Council of Great Britain', Humphrey Carpenter, *The Envy of the World*, p. 6.
10   Britten to Bobby Rothman, 24 June 1942, *Letters* Vol. II, p. 1068.
11   Britten to Elizabeth Mayer, 30 September 1942, *Letters* Vol. II, p. 1089.

[12] Britten to Elizabeth Mayer, 19 July 1944, *Letters* Vol. II, p. 1211.

[13] Jeffrey Weeks, *Coming Out*, pp. 156–67. See also Derek McGhee, *Homosexuality, Law and Resistance*, pp. 117–18.

[14] James Lees-Milne, Sunday 5 December 1976, *Diaries 1971–1983*, pp. 219–20.

[15] For a discussion of another use of this 'language' see John Bridcut, *Britten's Children*, p. 21.

[16] Otto Erich Deutsch (ed.), *Franz Schubert's Letters and Other Writings*.

[17] Britten to Elizabeth Mayer, 5 November 1948, *Letters* Vol. III, p. 455.

[18] Britten to Edith Sitwell, 3 March 1959, *Letters* Vol. V, p. 124.

[19] The Earl of Harewood (George Lascelles) in Donald Mitchell and Hans Keller (eds), *Benjamin Britten: A Commentary*, p. 8.

[20] Interview with Murray Schafer in Paul Kildea (ed.), *Britten on Music*, p. 231.

[21] Rosamund Strode, interview with Nicholas Clark, Britten–Pears Foundation, Aldeburgh, 11 December 2008.

[22] See Philip Reed (ed.), *The Travel Diaries of Peter Pears 1936–1978*, pp. 73–84.

[23] The Joint Property of Benjamin Britten and Peter Pears, The Red House, Aldeburgh Suffolk, pp. 85–6, 91–2.

[24] Quoted in Humphrey Carpenter, *Benjamin Britten: A Biography*, p. 517.

[25] Christopher Palmer, 'The Ceremony of Innocence', *The Britten Companion*, p. 68.

[26] John Bridcut, *Britten's Children*, p. 8.

[27] W.H. Auden to Benjamin Britten, 31 January 1942, *Letters* Vol. II, p. 1015.

[28] John Bridcut, *Britten's Children*, pp. 6–7.

[29] John Bridcut, *Britten's Children*, pp. 286–7.

[30] John Bridcut, *Britten's Children*, p. 6.

[31] Duncan Campbell-Smith, *Masters of the Post*, p. 391.

[32] See M.J. Daunton, *Royal Mail: The Post Office since 1840*, p. 340.

[33] See, for example, Humphrey Carpenter, *Benjamin Britten: A Biography*, p. 582; Christopher Headington, *Peter Pears: A Biography*, pp. 272–3; Paul Kildea, *Benjamin Britten: A Life in the Twentieth Century*, p. 562.

[34] See Humphrey Carpenter, *Benjamin Britten: A Biography*, pp. 570, 586.

[35] Christopher Headington, *Peter Pears: A Biography*, p. 275.

[36] Peter Pears, *A Time There Was …* transcript of soundtrack, pp. 53–4.

[37] Peter Pears, *Contrasts: The Tenor Man's Story*.

[38] From *Winter Words*, No. 5 *The Choirmaster's Burial*.

I

'When I am not with you'

AUGUST 1937 TO JANUARY 1941

'He's one of the nicest people I know, but frightfully reticent,' Britten wrote in his diary after a night of playing and singing his songs with Pears in October 1937. Already acquainted, they got to know each other properly following the death in April of mutual friend Peter Burra, who had been killed in a plane crash. On 6 May they had travelled together to Burra's cottage in Berkshire to help sort through some of his possessions. Although they were each involved with their own social circles at this point, they gradually built a friendship through shared interests: going to concerts and films, dinner and weekend parties, playing tennis and impromptu late-night song recitals. Their earliest letters show that music was central to the growing connection between them. In August 1937 Pears reports on the first concert performance at Salzburg of the *Variations on a Theme of Frank Bridge*, which Britten had completed the previous month. He offers his impression of the Boyd Neel Orchestra's interpretation and suggests how the performance might be strengthened. These first letters also demonstrate how each encourages the other in their respective professions, with Pears reassuring Britten that his work is the best in the programme and Britten promising to compose more songs for Pears to sing.

In March 1938 they rented a flat together in London at 43 Nevern Square, SW5, after the marriage in January of Britten's sister Beth, with whom he had shared lodgings since the early 1930s. Britten was now also the owner of the Old Mill, in Snape, near the Suffolk coast, which from April he shared with fellow composer Lennox Berkeley. Although he and Pears had clearly become close and enjoyed one another's company, their lives remained separate, as did their careers. Between late 1937 and March 1939, Britten supported himself by composing incidental music for the BBC and for the stage. He worked for the Group Theatre who produced plays by young, left-leaning writers like W.H. Auden and Christopher Isherwood, with whom Britten found much common ground, personally and politically. He also worked with Auden at the General Post Office (GPO) Film Unit, but continued to compose major works such as his Piano Concerto (which he premiered in August 1938 at the Queen's Hall Proms), and began work on the song cycle *Les Illuminations* (initially written for Sophie Wyss, though later frequently sung by

Pears, for whom it became signature repertoire). Meanwhile Pears was making a career with groups such as the BBC Singers (1934–37), with whom he sang a solo in Britten's *Company of Heaven*, the New English Singers (from 1936 to 1938), as well as in the chorus of Glyndebourne Opera in the summer of 1938 (see Letter 4). He toured the United States with the New English Singers in 1936 and again in late 1937, and it was during these trips that he formed a close friendship with German-Jewish immigrants Elizabeth Mayer and her husband William, who was a psychiatrist in Amityville on Long Island, New York.

The worsening political situation throughout Europe in the late 1930s is only briefly mentioned in the correspondence, but the gradual descent into war is clearly a contributing factor in their decision to leave for North America. As early as October 1937, however, Britten had held hopes of going to America, professing envy at Pears's opportunity to visit and work abroad. When, in January 1939, their friends Auden and Isherwood left England for the prospect of a better future in the US, Britten and Pears followed them a couple of months later, leaving at the end of April on the *Ausonia* of the Cunard Line. Their reasons for leaving were complex, and no single one seems to have been the true catalyst. Certainly impending war spurred their decision, as both were confirmed pacifists; Britten also had hopes of a Hollywood job that seemed to him to be on the point of materialising (it never did). Also, he felt that the contemporary music scene in the UK was untenable for him as critics had not been as supportive as he had hoped. A further more personal motivation for Britten may have been his intense and at times fraught relationship with Wulff Scherchen, the son of conductor Hermann Scherchen, whom he had met in 1934. Britten was clearly emotionally involved with the eighteen-year-old Wulff, dedicating a song from *Les Illuminations* to him, but during the period that led to his departure for America, he became gradually more detached and eventually wanted to distance himself. Scherchen remained in his thoughts, and Britten continued to write to him for some time after leaving, although his letters establish the important place that Pears now held in his life. There were evidently also complications in his relationship with Lennox Berkeley – as a consequence, Britten states in Letter 7 that he is 'only too thankful to be going away', again suggesting that absence will ease a difficult situation. Pears's reasons for leaving have never been entirely clear, as he intended to return after only a few months' visit, whereas Britten seemed to have had a more permanent residency in mind, hence his emotion at the thought of saying goodbye to friends and family. During the crossing, lasting just over two weeks, they grew ever closer, and by the time they arrived in Toronto in June 1939, they had fallen in love. They consummated their relationship in Grand Rapids, Michigan, sometime between the 12 and 17 June, thus beginning what they themselves came to regard as their 37-year marriage.

Only five letters from their American period remain and all are from Pears to Britten. These first romantic letters are in fact mostly playful and silly – showing their shared sense of humour – rather than serious and passionate. Despite the levity, Pears professes his longing in ways that suggest dependence and incompleteness. 'When I am not with you,' he insists, 'I am like a pelican in the wilderness (always thirsty) or an owl (without its pussy-cat) in the desert' (Letter 12).

The comparatively small number of letters in this first period indicate how much they were together in these early years. Although their time in America was relatively short (they left for home in March 1942), it was formative for both of them, despite Pears's unfavourable descriptions of the country's cultural standards. It allowed them to firmly establish the foundations of their new relationship away from the restrictions of home, first within the supportive, surrogate family environment of the Mayers in New York, where they lived together for over a year (also often residing at the home of one of Mayer's fellow doctors, Mildred Squire and her husband Bill Titley). Between late 1940 and early 1941, they moved into the house on Middagh Street that Auden shared with a number of eccentric characters, including the burlesque artist Gypsy Rose Lee; here their relationship would have been scarcely noticed, and the situation reinforced their well-established shared sense of being 'outsiders together', frequently evident in their letters. The atmosphere of the house was deliberately bohemian and chaotic – as one party ended another began.[1] Britten especially found working in such conditions very trying, and they soon returned to the Mayers. The two men made good use of their adventure however: Pears embraced the musical richness offered by New York and took singing lessons, first with Therese Behr-Schnabel and then Clytie Mundy, with whom he remained in touch and studied further when the opportunity arose (see Chapter 3). Britten completed some of his most important early works, including his Violin Concerto, the song cycle *Les Illuminations* and *Sinfonia da Requiem*. He also completed an operetta, *Paul Bunyan*, with Auden as his librettist, an experience that gave him insight into the process of writing and producing a dramatic work. A further major composition from this period was the song cycle *Seven Sonnets of Michelangelo* which Britten wrote in 1940, dedicated 'To Peter'. They sang through and recorded the work privately several times while in the US, but didn't in fact perform it in public until their return to the UK. Britten did, however, enjoy a number of public performances of his other works – including his Piano Concerto (again playing the solo part himself) – touring such disparate places as Chicago, Champaign (Illinois) and Oklahoma City. Pears also found opportunities to perform through people he had met during his 1937 tour (such as Harold Einecke and his Bach Festival in Grand Rapids), and through a madrigal group (The Elizabethan Singers) he founded in New York. He also gave the American premiere of *Les Illuminations* in May 1941; the work received good notices, but Pears's singing was not to the tastes of American critics.[2]

During a trip to California over the summer of 1941, which was taken after the premiere of *Paul Bunyan*, Britten and Pears both began to feel more deeply their outsider status as Englishmen in America. Writing to his sister Barbara, Britten described their encounter with the Midwest: 'our hearts broke to see everyone looking so English, & all the names sounded Anglo-Saxon'.[3] The trip offered them the opportunity to think about their future in the US, as their homesickness was already well established, and was compounded by an article[4] by E.M. Forster about Suffolk poet George Crabbe. This led Pears to an edition of Crabbe's Collected Poems, which included the lengthy narrative poem *The Borough*. The poet's vivid descriptions of the Suffolk coast where Britten had grown up drew their attention even more towards home, and upon their return to New York in September, they made arrangements to travel back to the UK. After much difficulty given the treacherousness of any wartime Atlantic crossing, they booked passage on the freighter MS *Axel Johnson* and left New York on 16 March 1942, finally arriving in England on 17 April – taking twice as long as their outward journey. During the voyage, Britten and Pears began to sketch the plot, based on one of the characters from Crabbe's *The Borough*, for what would become the opera *Peter Grimes*.

---

[1] For further information about the residents of the Brooklyn House, see Sherrill Tippins, *February House*.

[2] Fellow composer-turned-critic Virgil Thomson was particularly acidic, stating, 'Mr. Pears, who sang it, has neither correct French diction nor a properly trained voice.' In 'Music: Hand Work and Hand-Me-Downs', *New York Herald Tribune* (23 December 1941).

[3] Britten to Barbara Britten, 17 June 1941, *Letters* Vol. II, no. 319.

[4] E.M. Forster, 'George Crabbe: The Poet and the Man', *The Listener* 25 (29 May 1941), pp. 769–70.

1 Pears to Britten

Salzburg

[27 Aug] '37
Friday 10.30pm.

Well, Benjie, I have dashed back to the hotel so that I can write down at once something about the concert. I think there can be no doubt about it that the Variations were a great success, as indeed the orchestra was and Boyd Neel – and I got a <u>very</u> strong impression that the Variations were the most <u>interesting</u> work in the programme – One yawned a good deal through the [Rutland] Boughton (I only got in towards the end of the Purcell) but the B. B. really kept one's interest the whole time – and more, of course. I was surprised how superbly the Romance & the Aria came off – the Romance was really <u>most</u> lovely. Curiously enough the one that didn't seem to come off altogether was the Moto Perpetuo – it didn't seem to make it's effect, perhaps the performance wasn't so good –

The Funeral March is very good Benjie – I thought it needed more strings (get it done by the BBC!) and Boyd Neel didn't quite allow enough room in it – e.g. the triplets – I think that's one of his troubles. But I think everyone was very moved by it – The Chant seemed a bit slight after it (I still rather hanker after the March repeated) – The Fugue got home allright – and I thought the Finale sounded v. impressive.

The Funeral March was the climax (as it should be, shouldn't it?) although one didn't feel completely settled till the March. (the Adagio sounded a bit uncertain) The Bourree and Waltz sounded just as they should have done. In some of the Variations more Bass tone was needed, but he only had 2 D. B's –

That's all I can think of at the moment – but it really was a grand show – I'll write some more in the morning, & see if I can get any press cuttings, & then I'll air mail it to you –

<u>SAT. A.M.</u>

The Boughton, Bax, Delius and Elgar sounded all really very much alike in essence – I suppose in being English – but there wasn't enough variety – The "esspresivo" of one was all too like the "esspresivo" of another – There was not enough <u>life</u> – and that, the Almighty be praised, is what you have, Benjie –

––––––

This is the only press as yet – The Viennese papers haven't noticed it yet, but I will collect what I can for you – I have been trying to get hold of Boyd Neel but lost him after tracking him half across Salzburg –

Much Love to you –

Peter

2 Britten to Pears

Peasenhall Hall,
Nr Saxmundham,
Suffolk

Oct. 24th 1937

Well Peter,

Have a good time in America.[1] Sing nicely, & come back with lots of money in your pocket. Don't get up too late & miss trains – it makes life difficult, & and, as you know, life's difficult enough any-how. I envy you alot going all over America – it would be good fun to go – Infact I must go myself before long – One of the thousand & one things I'm going to do before long.

How's Michael?[2] He'll be sad at your leaving. Come back with lots of courage, ready to seize any bull by the horns – & they are fond of it, I'm sure.

Meanwhile I'll go on here. I'll have written about four more vols. of music by the time you come back. More songs, & with luck a piano concerto. I'm feeling on first-rate terms with the Muse at the moment. I shall go up & down to London, & drift around the country: to Christopher next week; Wystan soon after; with Lennox down to Gloucester, & of course to the Bridges. I shall probably run away to the continent for Xmas, because I can't face the prospect of that in England this year.

yes – you're lucky, my boy.
Next year must be the beginning
of proud things. Singing – life
in general. No more of this
messing about with Morning Services
(either actually or morally !!) – but
la vie – grande in every sense (or
perhaps its masculine...).

Yes – you're lucky, my boy. Next year must be the beginning of grand things. Singing & life in general. No more of this messing about with Morning Services (either actually or morally!!) – but la vie-grande in every sense (or perhaps its masculine …).

Excuse this – only I'm horribly sleepy after a grand Sunday lunch of Sirloin & home-brew cyder.

> All my love & Bon Voyage
> <u>Benjie.</u>

---

[1] Pears went on tour with the New English Singers from 27 October 1937 to early January 1938.
[2] Michael Patton-Bethune (1918–40) had been a pupil at The Grange School, Crowborough, where Pears was the music teacher from 1929 to 1933.

3 Pears to Britten

I tried to ring you up but the Enquiries couldn't find your number anyhow, & I couldn't remember it – So I am wiring you. Lots of love Peter.

[*Letterhead:* 1 Queen Anne Row, Walmer, Kent. Deal 952]

[?1938]

Dear sweet B.

I saw Iris on Saturday and told her I couldn't do France on Monday (especially as the BBC rang me up & asked me to do a series of chorus jobs starting on Tues. & Wed. of this week.) May I come to you on Wed after the show which finishes at 5 – I don't know whether I come to Saxm'.h'm,[1] do I? There seems to be a 5.16 arr. S. 7.57 or 7.42 arr. S. 10.8.

I doubt whether I would catch the first one.

I leave here Monday & probably go to the flat or Charlotte St. for 2 nights. I couldn't refuse the BBC as it's 2 guineas for this Tues & Wed, & then lots more 2 guineas later – & I had to say Yes or No to them all.

---

[1] Saxmundham, Suffolk, the closest railway station to Snape.

4 Pears to Britten

I hope to get up on June 20th. Can you get me a ticket?[1] Shall I see you?

> The Old Cottage
> Laughton
> Lewes.

[30 May–5 June 1938]

Benjie my dear –

I was so very sorry not to find you in on Wednesday. I feared that I wouldn't but hoped to – I had the heaviest cold in history and so I fled back here as soon as I could, although I had thought of creeping into a Toscanini rehearsal. How are you, my dear? The flat looked as though you might have been entertaining someone – perhaps Francis?[2] or not yet? Tell me about it –

Things here go on just the same or thereabouts – We started Figaro performances last week and The Don starts on Friday – (I enclose the Pasquale dress rehearsal tickets –) I am enjoying enormously really getting to know my Mozart operas. Figaro really is the most sublime work. The scoring of Susanna's aria "Venite inginocchiatevi" is magical. I miss you very much, Benjie – and although a nice person called Denis Mulgan[3] has come to live with us, I am bored by everyone in the house and long for congenial company. Basil [Douglas] was down for a weekend which was nice, but it would be lovely to see you –

I'm hoping to go motoring with Mike [Patton-Bethune] in July abroad – Will it come off? I pray it will.

Write to me again.

> Lots of love
> Peter

Just as I had finished licking the envelope of this, your letter came – Francis sounds quite fascinating and just the sort of person I should hopelessly lose my heart to. My racket came very quickly and I am playing a little 3rd rate tennis – But my bloody cold won't go – We have a lot of running about and changing to do in Macbeth and one is always in drafts (or draughts?), so colds stick.

I hope you enjoyed Toscanini.[4] I listened to some, but our set went bad on us – The soloists sounded rather a mixed lot. Roswaenge too Wagnerian? Thorborg a bit flat? Soprano shrill and bass not heavy enough?

Exciting about Osbert, Make him do a Tenor Cantata!![5]

I'm running mildly after a sweet tough Stage Hand but as usual I can't come to the point!! I miss you v.v. much. Everyone's opinions here are so very reactionary and capitalist!

Much Love, Benjie darling. Give some to Lennox & Dorothy W.[6] but keep most of it for yourself. Has On this Island Vol 1 appeared yet? Do send me a copy when it does –

I'm doing a little playing for Heddle Nash[7] which is rather funny – I will listen at Whitsun.

---

[1] Probably for an evening of chamber orchestral works for the 1938 International Society of Contemporary Music (ISCM) Festival, or an English song recital at the Wigmore Hall.

[2] Barton (1916–2001), a friend of Britten from South Lodge School (1923–28).

[3] Oboist and pianist on the Glyndebourne music staff.

[4] Britten saw Verdi's *Requiem* on 30 May at Queen's Hall, including soloists Helge Rosvaenge (1897–1972), Danish tenor, and Kerstin Thorborg (1896–1970), Swedish contralto.

[5] Osbert Sitwell (1892–1969), who was to have written a ballet synopsis for Wassily de Basil (1888–1951), founder of the Ballet Russe de Monte Carlo. The project never materialised.

[6] Dorothy Wadham (1895–1990), Secretary of the ISCM.

[7] (1894–1961), tenor.

5 Britten to Pears

[*Postcard:* image of Snape]

The Old Mill

[6 Sep 1938]

Piers & I are coming up to-morrow (Tuesday) evening by car – arriving lateish (maybe 11 or 12). Will it be all right if we use your room just for the night? We are off for Worcester after the Prom: on Wednesday. Hope you had good weekend.

Love. B.

6 Britten to Pears

[*Postcard:* image of the Brussels Broodhuis]

Hope audition was success.

Brussels

[5 Jan 1939]

Having a v. good time as you could imagine with Wys & Chrys (& Jackie!)[1] about the place. F. André[2] was very good at the rehearsal this morning – hope ditto to-night. Shall be back <u>mid-day</u> SATURDAY at flat. If away – please Leave telephone number. Love B

---

[1] Auden, Isherwood and Jackie Hewit (1917–97), a friend of Isherwood.
[2] Franz André (1893–1975), Belgian conductor. Britten was in Brussels to play the Piano Concerto.

7 Britten to Pears

[*Letterhead:* The Old Mill, Snape, Saxmundham, Suffolk.]

March. 16th 1939

My dear Pete,[1]

Isn't everything bloody – just as one was allowing oneself to get too hopeful too – however, I don't think <u>anyone</u> can really trust Hitler anymore – although N.C. [Neville Chamberlain] (I wish his initials were W.C.) will have a good shot at it before he's turned out of power.

However – we're going away. Tho' still no news from Hollywood. I'll let you know as soon as ever I hear, of course.

Well, the car is a wonder, & I've become suddenly fearfully car-minded. Spent most of yesterday pulling her (or him!) to pieces at the garage. I managed her like a school-boy on Saturday – & even you wouldn't have been frightened.

I let L.B. [Lennox Berkeley] drive for a bit & it wasn't <u>too</u> bad. However, re. him we've had a bit of a crisis & I'm only too thankful to be going away. I had the most fearful feeling of revulsion the other day – conscience and all that – just like the old days. He's been very upset, poor dear – but that makes it worse! I wish you were here, old dear, because I want terribly to talk to someone. However, I'll see you soon I hope. Ian[2] comes on Saturday – & I go to Cambridge on Wednesday – & to town for one night on Thursday (<u>if</u> the Grillers[3] can rehearse with me, i.e.). Will you be round about?

Thanks for the Edinboro' rock;[4] it has been <u>much</u> appreciated. I found it here when I got back – & it <u>is</u> good stuff. And for the letter too. I'm longing to see you again – & scandal away!

Just written a terrific Rimbaud song – with string orchestra[5] – my best bit so far I think. Actually for Sophie [Wyss] at Birmingham – but eventually also for P.P. everywhere – !

Just had proofs of [Piano] Concerto.

Anynews of Iris – poor dear it'll be hell for her.

> Much love,
> <u>Benjie</u>

Excuse smudges – just emotion!!

---

1   The first and only known incidence of Britten referring to Pears as 'Pete'. This is the last letter before they leave for North America.
2   Scott-Kilvert (1918–89), editor and translator.
3   Griller String Quartet, led by violinist Sidney Griller (1911–93).
4   Confectionery.
5   *Les Illuminations.*

8 Pears to Britten

[*Letterhead:* Boosey Hawkes Belwin, 43–45–47 West 23rd Street, New York, N.Y.]

<u>Tuesday</u> [9 Jan 1940]

My darling Ben – It was marvellous to get your letters. The first from Champaign and then from Chicago – I don't suppose you'll get my last letter for a bit, as I sent it care of Goldberg[1] at Chicago – I only hope he doesn't open it, as my letter was compromising to say the least of it! You poor little Cat, frozen to death in 12° belowzero weather – I do hope it's not quite so cold now – It's 5° above here & that's summery compared to you. I got your night letter by post yesterday morning, and it was quite a bit different from the way I got it over the phone on Sunday – It was so sad that you were so depressed and cold – I wanted to hop into a plane and come and comfort you at once. I would have kissed you all over & then blown you all over & then —— & —— & then you'd have been as warm as toast!

I'm writing this, sitting in a large chair in Mildred's[2] office, balancing it on my knee – (not the chair) – I came up with her & Bill this morning & gave old McNamee her lesson – and I rang Heinsheimer[3] to see if he knew anything of Ralph. The Rex [ship] isn't due according to the papers till Saturday, that may mean she won't come till Sunday, but H. imagines he'll fly straight to you (grr!) you little much too attractive so-and-so – in order to hear the Concerto (so he says – Personally I don't think he gives a damn for the concerto) – Mildred has been terribly low lately – not on edge but just sort of worn out, so while Bill goes to his bloody lectures tonight, I thought I'd give her dinner & take her to a movie somewhere. I'm finding it pretty difficult to face sitting with them in the evenings now, it's easier when you're there – Dr. Mayer misses you very much. Everyone does – except me, and of course I don't care a brass farthing how long you stay away, because if you stay away a day longer than Wednesday I'm going to come & fetch you, wherever you may be, & as long as I'm with you, you can stay away till the moon turns blue.[4]

I wrote the enclosed[5] to you last night, intending to write my whole letter in the same way, but I really couldn't find a suitable quotation for Ralph & the Rex anywhere!

Beate's gone & that leaves a large gap. I had a huge talk with Elisabeth yesterday afternoon which she adored – she's very sweet and I love her –

I may perhaps go to Stewart[6] over next weekend & come back & meet you on Wednesday – I don't know yet. or will you come Tuesday? anyway I'll let you know –

I'm reading Of Human Bondage of Somerset Maugham & it's terribly good – Some wonderful school stuff, & of course the whole thing, in his subtle way, is quite <u>itching</u> with queerness. Perhaps I'll send you a copy to Chicago to read in bed –

Please give Harold & Mary[7] a whole lot of my love – I feel foul at not having written to them before, but I have every intention of writing to them in the next day or two – I shall never forget a certain night in Grand Rapids – Ich liebe dich, io t'amo, jeg elske dyg(?), je t'aime, in fact, my little white-thighed beauty, I'm terribly in love with you –

P.

1   Albert Goldberg (1898–1990), director of the Illinois division of the Federal Music Project.
2   Pears was staying at the home of friends of the Mayers, psychiatrist Mildred Squire and her husband, Bill Titley, superintendent of the Long Island Home.
3   Hans Heinsheimer of Boosey & Hawkes, USA.
4   Reference to *Paul Bunyan*.
5   Unfortunately the enclosure does not survive.
6   Steuart Wilson (1889–1966), tenor, distant relative of Pears.
7   Harold Einecke, director of the Bach Festival at Grand Rapids, and his wife, Mary.

9 Pears to Britten

Amityville.

[?10 Jan 1940]

```
This is just a note to tell my pussy-cat that the
sentiments which he has inspired in the breast of
a certain person who shall be nameless, persist;
that unless the aforesaid my pussy-cat returns to
Amityville, L.I., N.Y.,etc. at the time agreed upon
with that same certain person, that certain person
reserves to himself complete freedom of action, i.e.
to go forthwith to the vilest and least clean haunt
in Harlem village, and there to spend his days in
putting any young men he may meet to any uses, proper
or improper he may be pleased to choose.
     (signed) N. Chamberpot, Adolf Piddler, B.Gazzolini.

  imeanitppsocomeonwednesdayortherellbehelltopay
  ="+%&()_$/?
```

I had a little note from 🐱 today – which was nice.
I do hope that " is happy with Harold and Mary.
How did "'s rehearsal go?
Is "'s tummy warm?
" , dje tay mur.
" , esker twomaym?
" , dontget too bored with margot—! I've just
had another Xmas card from her. That makes 4.

[*Typed*]
This is just a note to tell my pussy-cat that the sentiments which he has inspired in the breast of a certain person who shall be nameless, persist; that unless the aforesaid my pussy-cat returns to Amityville, L.I., N.Y., etc. at the time agreed upon with that same certain person, that certain person reserves to himself complete freedom

of action, i.e. to go forthwith to the vilest and least clean haunt in Harlem village, and there to spend his days in putting any young man he may meet to any uses, proper or improper he may be pleased to choose.

(signed) N. Chamberpot, Adolf Piddler, B. Gazzolini

imeanitppsocomeonwednesdayortherellbehelltopay

=”+%&()_§/∶

[Handwritten]

I had a little note from [cat] today – which was nice.

I do hope that   "   is happy with Harold and Mary.

How did   "   's rehearsal go?

Is   "   's tummy warm?

  "   , dje tay mur.

  "   , esker twomaym?[1]

  "   don't get too bored with Margot! I've just had <u>another</u> Xmas card from her. That makes 4

I had dinner with Mildred at a <u>very</u> nice cheap little Italian place on E.58 st, well worth knowing – It was marvellous to have European food again. We didn't go to a show – but I just listened for 2 hours and then we drove back with Bill – Today it has been quite marvellous all day, and we went for a scarefying drive (in top most of the time at 8 m.p.h.) with der liebe Herr Doctor [William Mayer] to Bethpage Park which was very attractive. I have done lots of good work singing French very loudly through my nose – it gives me a very strange sensation in my larynx, but I think it's probably good for me. This perpetual change between hot indoors & very cold out is not too kind to the poor chords – Tonight we're going to see la Dietrich in her new film at Huntington.[2]

I spent ½ hour with the Dentist this afternoon – He didn't hurt me atall (I don't think he's that sort!) – He took my picture twice! (only molars) but unfortunately I have seven (7) teeth to be dealt with, so I expect I shall see lots more of him. But you need feel no pangs of jealousy – because there is only one person that I feel like that about, and he is unfortunately now staying in the largest furniture-manufacturing town in the world, and after that will be playing the zither in some silly symphony of his at the world's largest cattle-slaughtering-yard city.

Oh [cat] I love you P.

I wonder if you realise how much I
miss you – I am worth nothing atall without you.
Your dinner with all the Projectors sounds
ghastly, but I bet you were the Top.

---

1   Phonetic misspellings of bad French, 'I love you' and 'do you love me?'
2   The Marlene Dietrich film was possibly *Destry Rides Again*, released in December 1939.

10 Pears to Britten

<u>Amityville</u>

<u>Friday</u> [12 Jan 1940]

My darling Ben –
   How are you after your Grand Rapids visit and rehearsals? Not too tired, hoffentlich [hopefully], and the steissbein [coccyx]? Was it terribly hard sitting on it for
so many hours?
   We've suddenly had a ~~drop~~ rise in the temperature of a great many degrees, and
it's hot and muggy and raining and slushy and depressing and Bill's got "grippe"
and went to bed yesterday evening and is only up in his pyjamas in front of a fire
to-day, and although I worked v. well yesterday, today is not so easy – I miss Beate
very much – I seem to have done nothing but <u>listen</u> all day – & I'm sick of it – and
my heart —— well, I'm beginning to know what all these afflictions that one reads
about are like – talk of aching! It's creaking with pain – But it's not so long to wait
now, and I know it'll be so marvellous to see you again, I can wait.
   I'm not going away, as I have been working so well, and getting down to and I
think solving some vocal problems – If only Bill will get well and clear out so that I
can practise without worrying about him.

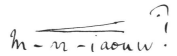

Mow! Mow! M – m – iaouw! [*crescendo, pause*]
         Much love –
              P.

11 Pears to Britten

[*Letterhead:* Park Congregational Chancel Choir, Grand Rapids, Michigan]

[before 18 Jan 1941]

My boy –

Thank you v.v. much for your letter which I got this morning – and which now lies close to my heart! You mew you, it was very sweet of you to write. Did you get a scrawl from me at Brooklyn? I missed yesterday I'm afraid – You know, it was full of the usual sort of runnings around, shaking hands, endless names entirely unmemorable. Saw Nita[1] quite a lot, she's a nice crazy girl & of course mad about you, you little Casanova you! Rehearsals going very well, excellent players & it really sounds e<u>x</u> tsellent – Harold not so hot at the organ but adequate – The choir has really bitten off too much to chew – The Mass is difficult enough but "Jesu meine freude"[2] is worse – They sing rather efficiently but so entirely without real imagination (H's fault). My choir hasn't nearly such good singers, but is much more interesting to listen to.

Nita's mother is playing the piano in the Cantata – very nicely, & we have no solo cello – which perhaps is a good thing –

Everyone asking after you – as if I would know anything about that! I have been giving them all intimate descriptions of various parts of your body – The usual comments are "Oh how inter<u>est</u>ing" or "De<u>lic</u>ious!" Num! num!

It's not terribly cold here – just rather beastly – I'll stay till Tuesday & arrive Grand Central 12.35 on Wed.

      Much much love
        Peter

---

[1] Unidentified.
[2] Bach's Mass in B minor and the funeral motet *Jesu, meine Freude*.

12 Pears to Britten

[18 Jan 1941]

My most beautiful of all little blue-grey, mouse-catching, pearly-bottomed, creamy-thighed, soft-waisted, mewing rat-pursuers! How are you? my beauty! If you aren't well and blooming, I shall have something to say to you when I come back, but of course I know you will bloom while I'm away, so relieved are you by the absence of my tiring presence! Odd as it may seem, I react differently; when I am not with you, I am like a pelican in the wilderness (always thirsty) or an owl (without its pussy-cat) in the desert – Mew, everyone is being very kind and Mrs Whitfield's an absolute darling and the children nice, but It's much too long to be here, & I only want to be with you – I rehearsed again with the organ this afternoon, & he's really terribly bad, but I suppose it'll be allright tomorrow – There's a reception after the show here for me, which I expect will be awful – I shall take 6 ½ benzhedines.[1]

I am always impressed when I come to these places, large prosperous cities, by the very high (really) standard of living, and at the same time extraordinarily low standard of culture – Really how Harold's choir can be so good & so – nothing – beats me. It seems Americans have either absurd & blind enthusiasm or else absolutely dry critical cynicism – In New York is the latter; here is the enthusiasm, very sweet but exhausting & a bit boring –

Mary is a very sweet person – I like her a lot – Plenty of talk of Margot of course – She is rapidly becoming, like W.H Auden, an American myth!

I have written out "Sheep"[2] for piano & voice – It's allright I think –

Just this minute had your telegram – You mew, you darling, you little white pearl you – I kiss you on both bottoms, & in front – I put my head between your legs & I look at you & look at you & kiss you – I kiss your navel & your tummy & your groin & you —— your lips your heart & you ——

My boy, my Ben – I love you, darling – P.

---

[1] Benzedrine, a stimulant.
[2] 'Sheep may safely graze' from Bach's 'Hunt' Cantata no. 208.

II

'My life is inextricably bound up in yours'

MAY 1942 TO NOVEMBER 1944

The freighter MS *Axel Johnson* reached the port of Liverpool on 17 April 1942. Its five-week journey across the Atlantic had, for its passengers Pears and Britten, been a frightening and uncomfortable experience. The ship had made its way by crawling up the coast of New England to Halifax, Nova Scotia, before a perilous twelve-day crossing of an ocean filled with submarines. Somewhere along the way, one of the vessel's funnels caught fire, apparently causing their protective escort to move on and leave the *Axel Johnson* to complete its voyage alone and unguarded, but fortunately without further incident. To make matters worse, the company on board the ship was, in Pears's estimation, 'rather desolate'.[1] He was unable to sing during the journey, but Britten, despite competition from people whistling in the corridors, and the ship's refrigeration unit right next to their cabin, was actually quite productive. His music manuscripts had been confiscated at the customs screening in New York, so on board he finished the *Hymn to St Cecilia* (text by Auden) and wrote out the portions of his Clarinet Concerto that he had completed prior to the voyage (eventually left unfinished). During the ocean crossing, Britten also composed *A Ceremony of Carols* for treble chorus and harp, inspired by finding a book of early English poems during the stopover in Halifax.

Upon disembarking at Liverpool, the two made their way to London together, but until they could find a flat to share they now had to separate. Pears made his home base with his parents in Barnes while Britten stayed with his sister Barbara in Chelsea. By September they found lodging with Ursula Nettleship at 104A Cheyne Walk, a situation less than ideal for privacy, so five months later they moved to a maisonette in St John's Wood High Street, keeping this as their London base. They would later share this with Britten's publisher Erwin Stein, his wife Sophie and daughter Marion. In December 1943, Britten returned to his pre-war composition retreat, the Old Mill in Snape, Suffolk, joining his sister Beth and her family (husband Kit Welford and children Sebastian and Sally). There, despite the sound of military aircraft (the 'bloody, bloody' aeroplanes – see Letter 48) he was able to complete *Peter Grimes*.

Pears was now gaining experience and recognition in London and on tour as a member of the Sadler's Wells Opera Company, working to bring music and colour to raise the spirits of a war-weary nation. Air raids interrupted sleep and made travel hazardous with trains delayed or rerouted without notice. Telephone calls were strictly monitored, three minutes being the usual allocation for a long-distance call, even when the line was available. Food, fuel and clothing were all rationed. Compared to the relative ease of life in America, the British public lived under a perpetual threat of bombing, and learned to live with the necessary restrictions on freedom of movement and communication that were imposed as a result. There was by now an embedded culture of support for the war effort, of 'Courage, Cheerfulness and Resolution', as encouraged by the Ministry of Information posters, despite the lingering national memory of the hollow truce of 1918, and the ever-present fear of air raids. Britten and Pears were no strangers to sacrifice, danger and loss, as their letters show, but they also expressed horror at the devastation on both sides (see Letter 33). Rarely uttered between the two, however, was the possibility that either of them could be killed in a bombing raid, a threat that cast its shadow whenever one or the other fell silent. They knew, however, that they were particularly fortunate, as Britten conceded in March 1943 (Letter 35), 'Still, it's not too bad; think of all the other married couples who are separated for everso much longer!!' The letters from this period clearly demonstrate how much each had come to rely on the other for support. Britten often discusses his work on *Peter Grimes* with Pears, including choice of librettist (Letter 33), while Pears offers a singer's insight into the nature of the role (see Letter 45).

Britten and Pears's most pressing problem was the expectation of military service. Both men were pacifists and thus immediately took steps to register as conscientious objectors, but with patriotic sentiment running high, establishing one's status as a CO on the grounds of pacifism was no easy matter. It involved writing a statement of belief and pleading one's case (complete with statements from supporters) to a potentially hostile tribunal. Even if the status were granted, some sort of service to the war effort as a non-combatant was generally ordered, with no guarantee that one would not be sent to the front lines. Imprisonment for refusal to co-operate – as friend and fellow composer Michael Tippett found – was a real possibility.[2] To their relief, the tribunal board ruled that Britten and Pears should serve by using their music to shore up public morale through recitals with CEMA and radio programmes for the BBC. Although their positive reception from audiences made recital work rewarding, often the more utilitarian performance spaces, such as factory canteens, were challenging. In truth, such recitals helped to hone their musical partnership as they explored new repertoire. They also provided the opportunity to put Britten's songs out to public scrutiny. As their reputation as a recital duo grew, they made new musical friendships as others faded. Former close friend Sophie Wyss, for example, the soprano for whom Britten had written a number of his early works, and whom he had often accompanied, was gradually excluded. In May 1944 Wyss made enquiries about recording *Les Illuminations*, but Britten had moved on, from both her friendship and her interpretation of his songs, and the record was never made.

Their time in America had created another problem. To leave the UK for 'refuge' in the US was denounced as the act of cowards and traitors and there were calls in parliament and the press for the UK citizenship of those who did so to be revoked. In October 1940, Ralph Hawkes informed Britten that he was having difficulties finding performance venues for his music because of his 'desertion'.[3] By September 1941, the composer had become the subject of public debate in *The Musical Times*,[4] and his and Pears's new status as conscientious objectors added fuel to this fire. Work for CEMA was considered a luxury – the coward's escape from the rigours of service in the armed forces. It was essential that they somehow heal this damage to their reputations and justify themselves through their music; for Britten, this meant accepting every BBC commission, as well as completing his opera. The future success of *Peter Grimes* became a key focus, and his anxiety about this is evident in the letters. For Pears, whose career had scarcely begun before their time in the US, it meant taking advantage of his much improved voice by seizing all opportunities to appear on stage or in recital. Furthermore, with homosexuality a crime and their public image already tarnished, it was essential that their relationship as a couple should remain hidden, known only to a few trusted friends.

After Britten's return to Snape, wartime travel restrictions made being together difficult if no CEMA joint recital was scheduled, or the composer had no London appointment to make the three-hour train journey a necessity. Although, late in 1943, they managed Pears's engagements so they could holiday together at the Lake District home of Clifford Curzon and his wife Lucille Wallace, the enforced separation told on their relationship. The strain of sleepless nights, interrupted postal service and missed telephone calls challenged everyone, and for two who had so recently lived together in peaceful America the tensions of this separation often seemed unbearable. Both men suffered feelings of alienation and anger at no longer truly knowing each other's lives. Insecurities boiled to the surface when seemingly well-made plans went awry that could not be instantly put right because of the communications restrictions, as related, for example, in Letter 15, where interestingly a frustrated Britten wields the spectre of Wulff Scherchen perhaps only half-jokingly at Pears in retaliation for his missing a phone call. Arguments also inevitably arose when they did meet, perhaps because it was easier to take one's leave when angry; but no sooner had one departed than they were writing to apologise and say what they truly felt, with each taking responsibility for the latest 'tiff'. Britten seems especially affected by their separation, often admitting to feelings of depression (see Letter 64) in Pears's absence. Pears, too, often fell into despair, but he deals with this in his letters with a characteristic lightness and wit, as he wrote to Britten in Letter 29 after having seen *Casablanca*: 'promise me that you won't leave me just as the Nazis enter London because you hear your husband isn't dead after all, and then turn up with him at the speakeasy I'm running in Newfoundland, trying to forget you'. Above all, they desired a life they could share, and both had plans for their future together, which needed only, as Pears outlined in Letter 23, 'getting the right place and relaxing and working together'. In a touching letter that foreshadows the remainder of their days, Britten wrote in April 1943 (Letter 38), 'my life is inextricably bound up in yours'.

At the centre of their daily lives during this period, however, was music-making, and their letters are filled with reports on their work and plans for joint recitals. Although they had already been performing together, their recital partnership found new heights with the first public performance of Britten's *Seven Sonnets of Michelangelo* on 23 September 1942. The work made an impression on both critics and audience, though apparently neither were aware of the true nature of the Britten–Pears relationship, despite the explicitness of the Italian texts. The cycle became a regular part of the recitals they gave in fulfilment of their war duties, alongside songs of Franz Schubert and Britten's folk-song arrangements. Meanwhile, under the auspices of the Sadler's Wells company, Pears made his debut both in London and on tour in a number of illustrious tenor roles, all of which paved the way for his success in the title role of *Peter Grimes*. His letters to Britten often mention these roles, from Tamino in Mozart's *Magic Flute*, to Vašek in Smetana's *Bartered Bride*, and the Duke in Verdi's *Rigoletto*, as well as Mozart's *Così fan tutte*, Verdi's *La traviata* and Rossini's *Barber of Seville*. For his part, Britten was writing new works (such as the *Serenade* in 1943), securing new commissions (*Rejoice in the Lamb*, for example) and beginning work on *Peter Grimes*. With its themes of the outsider ostracised by a hostile and unforgiving society, the opera made a profound statement of the sense of alienation he and Pears shared, not least as pacifists in a country at war.

---

[1] Pears to Elizabeth Mayer, 19 April 1942, *Letters* Vol. II, no. 372.

[2] Tippett was sentenced to three months' imprisonment in Wormwood Scrubs in June 1943 for refusal to accept non-combatant duties; he served two months.

[3] See Britten's letter to Ralph Hawkes, 7 October 1940, *Letters* Vol. II, pp. 867–9.

[4] A war of words between Pilot-Officer E.R. Lewis, composer Gerald Cockshott, *Musical Times* editor Harvey Grace, a Mr Eric Halfpenny, and ultimately Britten's friend, composer E.J. Moeran.

13 Pears to Britten

<u>New Theatre, Hull.</u>

Wednesday 1.0 P.M. [?20 May 1942]

My own darling –

Just a note to tell you that I love you – & that I haven't yet had an answer to my reply paid telegram tho' there may be one at the Theatre (I haven't been there yet). Anyway I can't do anything about it, 'cos we have a matinée tomorrow as luck would have it & I <u>have</u> to do one or the other show. I'm writing to the Clerk to the Tribunal to explain my absence <u>if</u> they decide to have it tomorrow. What more can I do?

The broadcast was a success I think & Basil [Douglas] wants me to do a "Songs for Everybody"[1] in August. Most of the Hoffmann Company listened & enjoyed it.

The music you sent to Liverpool hasn't <u>yet</u> arrived. I don't know what's happened to it.

Apparently Geoffrey Dunn[2] got Exemption at his appeal to go on with his work, teaching & singing etc. Frank Howes[3] appeared for him & was very eloquent. Couldn't you get Ralph Hawkes to appear & speak for you? Have you heard any more?

<u>7.0 pm</u>

Just heard, my honey bee, my Tribunal is postponed – They don't say till when.

I love you, I love you, I love you – always.

P.

Iris has just been turned out of her flat by the Thatchers. & suggested taking a lovely one in Manchester Square, of which we could have bottom half at £2 a week, sharing bath & kitchen. Quite separate. What do you think? Might be useful but complications could arise. Love Love

---

[1] BBC Radio programme.
[2] (1903–81), tenor and translator.
[3] (1891–1974), music critic and historian.

14 Pears to Britten

Glasgow.

<u>Sunday evening</u> [24 May 1942]

My darling, my beloved darling, I just don't know how I'm going to face not having you for five weeks – In fact, I know I'm not going to try, because I shall steal away for a weekend at all costs, before I die of desperation – If this is anything like what I am to expect, I may as well give up now – & I'm sure this is not bad really – a dreary journey, a frightful city, a bleak room, a landlady like the Ugly Duchess, no hot water, fire which won't burn, nothing but sausages till Tuesday, & then coping with emergency rations – the list is endless. & above all no you – I don't think you really know how much I need you and want you always.

<u>Wednesday</u>
I'm sorry this letter's hasn't gone on before, but you know as a matter of fact there's no news and all I want to say to you isn't news but as old as the hills!

It was heavenly to speak to you last night and the night before – The difficulty of getting anyone by telephone at any time is acute here – Incompetent & unbelievably slow – I got on to Basil [Douglas] last night after endless efforts & talked to him about my singing for him. I think I may try Carmen, Manon & Lalo[1] in English. It should be allright.

Thank you ever so much for your telegram today about my tribunal. It's a relief – The complication would have been too intense – I <u>do</u> hope you've found a solicitor. I shall be with you all the time my darling tomorrow at 10 on – I pray it won't be too unpleasant. By the time you get this it will be all finished – How I hope you will be happy – If you would like me to come down for Sunday & Monday, I might easily manage it – (leave Glasgow 9.0pm Sat, arrive Euston 7.0am Sunday etc) I should love to come, or would you rather that I put it off till the following weekend?

Any how my honey bee I love you, love you, love you & I expect your call tomorrow evening at 9.30!

Bless your sweet heart
always your loving
P

---

[1]   Arias from Bizet's *Carmen*, Massenet's *Manon* and *Le roi d'Ys* by Lalo.

15 Britten to Pears

When do you arrive this week-end? Come soon, please.

11 Tryon House
Mallord St, SW3.

June 1st [1942]

God – you blighter.

Here am I – wasted a bob on wiring you, & then cut short a pleasant evening with Stephan Spender[1] to be back at 9.30 intime for your call – to find you'd rung at 9.10 (if I'd taken a taxi I should have been in in time for that call – so that much for good resolutions). I then cajolled the exchange into giving me a call by 10.15 (there being over an hour's delay), which the sweet things did by 10.10 – &, if you please, 'Mr Pears has just gone out.' No wonder I'm cross. Why the hell can't you organise your time abit – Why the hell don't you do what you say, be in till 10.15 – why the hell – well, & so on. And all because I wanted to speak to you so badly. Boohoo. Boohoo.

Mostly because I've had such an awful time with Wulff.[2] Poor dear he's had such a hell of a time – but it's accentuated the old hard, vindictive side of him; the old conventional communist, materialist, side; the boasting, garrulous side too – so that he's completely unbearable. Although, I must admit it, he was looking very pretty – & in retrospect, well – perhaps he is … but that's only because I'm so cross with you, you old so & so. Boohoo.

Seriously – poor old KHWS. he's the first real bad shock I've had since I got back – I've just grown completely away from him. He rather wanted to come back to-night, I think, but I choqued (choaked?) him off – but, damn it all, perhaps he'd be better than … here I go again – blast you, why can't you be in when I want you – Sorry. But I miss you so much – & it's Thursday since I spoke to you.

Friday's do with Pierrot Lunaire & Façade[3] was pretty awful really. Horrible audience, snobby – and stupid. The pieces very faded – & Constant Lambert completely inaudible. Hedli did remarkably well – & since I'm feeling peevish with you tonight – I think you might have sent that wire to her. And did you write to the Tribunal & thank them??? Nag, nag. I know – but it's darned good for you. Afterwards there was a horrible party at the Savoy – where I was dragged away from a nice table with Hedli, Louis, Willie, Constant & all,[4] to sit with two godawful whores, whom Ralph was lugging around. & (of all people) Sidney Beer!!![5] I was livid. They all got (Hedli etc) so beootifully tight & I remained desparately sober. Boohoo – why don't you stick around instead of dashing up to Scotland – God, if you prefer the Scotch to me, I'd better pack up shop & go – but, perhaps, it's the Bally-Boys – How are they?

Then I went down to Sophy [Wyss] & Arnold (senior) & Humphrey for the weekend – & I thought that was going to be disastrous – Sophy was feeling ill &

Arnold (home on leave) was military and very tired, & I was terrified of arguments. However everyone cheered up on Sunday – Humphrey is a sweet & engaging kid (5 ½), & had a long walk with Arnold, & we all motored over to Bradfield where Sophy sang with an amateur (and how) orchestra under Finzi[6] ("I prefer this to those horrible professionals" sort of thing – ugh!), quite prettily, & there were some sweet things around (who are filling my mind now, because of course if one can't rely on … one must have something … etc. you old she-deville). I'm too sleepy to go on with this diary – but I came back this morning & saw Wulff, then 'How Green was my Vally' (easier than talking to him – but a <u>lousy</u> picture) then Spenders & then waiting for you … but we <u>Won't</u> go into that again. Because anyhow I love you very much, & I wish to God (reverently, this time) you were here in bed with me. The enclosed sweet note came from William [Mayer], whom you MUST write to AT ONCE – SEE?!!   All my love, you old so & so.   B.

---

1   Stephen Spender (1909–95), poet, associated with Auden's circle in 1930s.
2   Wulff Scherchen (b. 1920), 'KHWS'. Dedicatee of the 'Antique' from *Les Illuminations*.
3   Works by Schoenberg and Walton.
4   Singer Hedli Anderson (1907–90) with her husband, the poet Louis MacNeice (1907–63) and composers William Walton (1902–83) and Constant Lambert (1905–51).
5   (1899–1971), conductor and founder of the National Symphony Orchestra.
6   Gerald Finzi (1901–56), composer.

16 Pears to Britten

Lyceum Theatre

<u>Edinburgh</u>

[?3–4 June 1942]

Dear Sir –

Luckily for you, in our conversation over the telephone of yesterday evening, you took care to warn me that I was to pay no attention to a letter in your handwriting addressed to me here. I say luckily – because if I had not been warned, I should very probably have taken it to have been written by my angelic sweet-tempered & imperturbable pussy-cat – & frankly I shouldn't have known what to make of it. But, of course I know, the artistic temperament will peep out occasionally, stifle it how you will – you old tree-shrew you! However, I gave such a good performance last night[1] that all your Billingsgate is powerless to disturb me! So there.

I'm sorry about Wulff. It's a great pity, but I imagine he needs very strong & beneficent influences all the time – Good old Hedli! Glad she did well – Her teacher is joining our cast doing Esmé Percy's[2] part. I'm writing to William at once – I had a letter from Elizabeth, enclosing a picture of you that David took at Amityville – It was only half the original, the other half being Bobby,[3] which she tactfully cut off – I will show it to you at the weekend. I'm enclosing a letter for someone, is it the Tribunal or the Labour Exchange? I didn't gather from Margot's letter who was the kind person involved – We'll stay at Barnes for the weekend, nicht, Margot seems rather lonely –

I have to go – I have a matinée – Much love –

P.

---

[1] Pears sang Hoffmann in Offenbach's *Tales of Hoffmann*.
[2] (1887–1957), actor who played the part of Pitichinaccio in *Tales of Hoffmann*; Percy appeared in a number of films, including *Pygmalion* (1938).
[3] American friend David Rothman and his son, Bobby. Britten developed an attachment to Bobby Rothman during their time in the States. See *Letters* Vol. II, pp. 998–9.

17 Britten to Pears

11 Tryon House, Mallord St, SW3

June 12th 1942

My darling – It was so heavenly to hear your voice, a few minutes ago. But don't those blasted minutes shoot by? One never has time to say what one wants, but anyhow over that cold instrument one never could say what one wants. It'll just have to wait until Saturday week. How grand that'll be. I do need you so desparately – I'm afraid I get such fits of depression when you're not around. I have been feeling all this beastly business so heavily on me recently, and the horrible loneliness – but I mustn't get sentimental, even if the radio is playing the Vltava![1] Dear Elizabeth, & dear William & Beate. What lovely people to know – & above all, my darling, what a lovely person you are to know – I don't know what I have done to deserve you! I talked about you to Margot the other night for hours – I don't know what she thought of it! But I don't care neither – I don't care who knows.

I am just going to write off to Basil [Douglas] to tell him I've done the songs for you.[2] I talked the matter of the arrangements[3] & the new translations with Leslie Boosey this afternoon & he was very interested. I must get copies of them from Iris.

The opera [*Peter Grimes*] is going well – I am delighted with Montagu's attitude to it, & he's steaming ahead. I'm afraid he may get called up as the M.I.5. (a sort of FBI) ~~have~~ are putting obstacles in his way of getting the MOI job, because he's a party member – a nice paradox with the new 'alliance'!! I do hope he won't have to go.

I had dinner with Barbara & Helen – & of course they both ask tenderly after you – you've made quite a hit, my dear, but that's nothing extraordinary is it!! I must write some letters now,

All my love. I'll expect a ~~cabl~~ wire on Monday to <u>Snape</u>
                    B.

<u>Don't</u> please give the score away – they're <u>scarce</u>.

---

¹ Symphonic poem by Smetana.
² *The Seven Sonnets of Michelangelo.*
³ Probably Britten's orchestrations of Schubert's *Die Forelle* and Schumann's *Frülingsnacht.*

18 Britten to Pears

<u>as from</u>   11 Tryon House,
Mallord Street,
<u>S.W.3</u>

June 24th 1942

My darling,

This is just to say I hope you got the music O.K., (that Margot remembered to post it), & to say thank you for one of the most heavenly week-ends of my life – no, <u>the</u> most heavenly. I couldn't have believed that one could have felt so completely at ease, & at one with a person, as I feel with you. Please come back again soon – it is very lonely without you.

I spent a long time with Arnold[1] – Margot took me there on the way to her sister – & then came down to Princes R.[2] He is a dear person – we must see alot of him when you get back.

I have had a busy day here – first of all arranging about the possible 'let' of the Mill – which will come off I think. I go down there to see the people on Saturday – & then Montagu & Enid are going to spend next week there – to help me incidently arrange the linen & inventories etc. etc. But I'm going to keep the Mill part for us if we want it later. I've spoken to Beth about it, & she thinks it a good idea. I see Ethel Bridge tomorrow.

Good luck on Monday – I hope to goodness I can get a Radio to listen on down there – I must find one. Surely Hart[3] will have one. I'm seeing Basil [Douglas] tomorrow evening, which'll be nice. Excuse haste my dear, but I just wanted to thank you for being you & for coming into my life when you did – but why didn't you come ten years earlier – that's my only complaint!   All my love.   B.

[1]   Possibly Arnold Gyde (1894–1959), husband of singer Sophie Wyss.
[2]   Princes Risborough in Buckinghamshire, home of Montagu and Enid Slater.
[3]   Caretaker at the Old Mill, Snape.

19 Britten to Pears

The enclosure is for obvious reasons! I am cabling to-day.

104A. Sept 25th 1942

Darling – Here are the shirts, & I have put a hank & a sock in too in case you need them. I miss you just dreadfully – in fact it is difficult to take much interest in what one's doing without you around. How are things with you? I hope you weren't too tired to sing well last night, & the next few days won't be too bad. Relax as much as possible – stay in bed late in the mornings, & above all wrap yourself up & don't go around without a coat. – This weather is so awful. There – that's what you get if you attach unto yourself a …! I was at the Wigstein playing the Celesta last night. Quite nicely, but it's a peskey little instrument – I nearly pushed it over trying to make a noise on it! I found counting the bars a trial tho' – Dennis Brain helped me, & we got on alright, except one spot when I had (in the Durey)[1] to do the same thing for about 12 bars & forgot to count them. However, when Reginald Goodall[2] started looking angry, I decided to stop! Everyone is crazy over you, old thing – infact I'm getting quite jealous! John Davenport[3] was rhapsodic (maybe a little to Lennox's disappointment??) – strange people at the Wigstein last night said, where had you been all this time. Above all, the little stage shifter there, who'd been at it then 40 years, said you were remarkable (he didn't know we had any particular (hm) friendship) & that you could & would make for yourself the greatest possible career, & 'I've heard Caruso, & Morel,[4] too!' quite lyrical; & to get praise from that kind of person is sumpin! – all the while Sophie [Wyss] was screaming away, & not a word from him about her. I was nice to her, & it was quite easy. The folk song idea is dropped (thank goodness) (probably – thro' Decca), & she wants me to play Fauré for her – I said, well maybe I was signed or going to be for HMV & she seemed contented to leave it at that. I'm too fond of her to be rude, & not interested enough to be critical. In other words, just weak, weak, weak. I know, you old so & so. All my love, my heart. Saw Wulff yesterday, & he was impossible – but Barbara's going to take him on now – says I shouldn't see him much, with which opinion I am in complete agreement. Much love, you old success you. Ring or write.

Love to Esther: B.

1   Britten was playing in *Images à Crusoe* by Louis Durey and *Image* by Germaine Tailleferre
    at the Wigmore Hall.
2   (1901–90), conductor.
3   (1908–66), writer and critic.
4   Enrico Caruso (1873–1921), Italian tenor and Victor Maurel (1848–1923), French baritone.

20 Pears to Britten

In the train

[?23 Nov 1942]

My beloved darling –

I've just left you & we haven't started yet – I <u>have</u> to write down again just what you mean to me – You are so sweet taking all the blame for our miserable tiffs, our awful nagging heart-aches – but I know as well as I know anything that it is really <u>my</u> fault. I don't love you enough, I don't try to understand you enough, I'm not Christian enough – You are <u>part of me</u>, and I get cross with you and treat you horribly and then feel as if I could die of hurt, and then I realise why I feel so hurt and aching – It's because you are part of me and when I hurt and wound you, I lacerate my very self – O my darling do forgive me – I do love you so dearly and I want you so dreadfully – I am so ambitious for you, as I am for myself. I want us both to be <u>whole</u> persons. This division is deadly. One sees one's faults, decides what to do, & doesn't do it. We have got to have more control over ourselves, to <u>know where we're going</u> –

I don't know how I shall bear not having you again – and even next week no better –

And I do love you so, my darling – Even these quarrels & agonies have their uses – They make me love you all the more –

Goodnight, my darling boy –

I kiss you.

P.

21 Britten to Pears

104A. Cheyne Walk
<u>SW10.</u>

Nov 23rd 1942

My darling,

My hand is falling off, my eyes are falling out, my bottom is aching with so much sitting on, & I'm so sleepy that I can't think, but I must write a note to tell you one or two things, & to say that you are in my thoughts all the time, & that I make myself a bore by talking about you all the time. Sir John W.[1] (who is about 60, & proud of it, tough & very very, o so, Scottish) finds nothing organically wrong with me (luckily he didn't ask me about my morals, which might make the decision not unanimous). but finds that I have practically no resistance to germs whatever – he suspects as a result of the Sulpha Nylamide[2] in 1940 – it has that effect occasionally – & must have a long cure – I don't exactly know what he wants yet, but is going to write to me details, send me stuff & says I must give up coffee!! Boohoo. I was with him nearly 1½ hours, & was pretty well exhausted by the inquisition. However I had a nice lunch with Louis & Hedly, who was sweet (& I have quite changed my mind <u>again</u>!), & then a mad afternoon, with Stein, printers, copyists, & harpists, & then back here by 7.0 to have a cheerful evening with the telephone & a few letters. And you my darling? Hedli tells me that last night wasn't much fun to sing. Too bad. I'm sorry they didn't realise what they weren't appreciating. I hope the week won't be too strenuous & that Mabel will be simple & easy. Do you know your stuff yet? Try & come back on Friday if you can, but if it's too tiring just don't bother. I can stick another week.

I am still a little disturbed by our Saturday night tiff – Worrying as to whether I am not good for you – not caring enough for your health & work. But, in all humbleness I say it, give me a chance to reform, my dear. I swear in the future I will look after you. Only I just can't bear the thought of separation. I just don't live in times like these.

Take care of yourself.
And need I say it – I love you.
   <u>B</u>
Wire me if you want your ration book – I leave for Snape midday Wednesday.

---

1 John Weir (1879–1971), at the time Physician Royal to King George VI.
2 Sulphanilamide – a precursor to modern antibiotics, used to reduce infection rates during the war years.

22 Pears to Britten

Worcester

[24–6 Nov 1942]

My bunch of blue ribbons!

Just a line to show I haven't forgotten you! & to say that I had a vile journey & a horrid factory but am just getting over it –

Also, I return on Friday arriving at 5.10 unless you hear au contraire. But probably I shall have to leave late Sunday night for Birmingham!

Much love to you my pretty one

Ever your loving hubbie   P.

23 Pears to Britten

Worcester

[late Nov 1942]

My darling –

It was lovely to have your letter[1] this morning and to feel you with me again – I hate being away from you so terribly – I have such plans of our life together – Do let us start as soon as possible, getting the right place and relaxing and working together – I do so love you my darling and this maddening life of perpetual motion is no good – Enjoy Snape – how I wish I were with you, and give my love to it.

Mabel is being awfully sweet – She is a very sensitive good artist – Sometimes as a person that funny Christian Science streak appears, a sort of solemn obstinacy – but she is very serious and understanding –

Another factory today – Much nicer, small audience but nice people.

O my pussy cat –
O a matterofat
I love you my darling –
     P.

---

[1]   Letter 21.

24 Pears to Britten

Midland Hotel.

B'ham.

Monday P.M. [?30 Nov 1942]

My only darling –

I suppose I must have some excuse to write to you other than say just that I miss you terribly and love you so very very much – And so I will also tell you a piece of good news – I have <u>no</u> mid night factory on Friday! I can catch a 2.0 train or so, & be with you by 6. Won't that be Heaven! An extra night together.

A Bad canteen today – lousy snooty audience.
> Much much love my sweet bee
> > P.

25 Britten to Pears

You arn't free to sing the [Michelangelo] Sonnets to Glock[1] on Monday evening next, are you? Can you let me have a card about this?

> > > > > 104A.

> > > > [?late Nov–early Dec 1942]

My darling,

So sorry that our conversation was so uncommunicative – But Ursula was in the room & I couldn't say much. We have patched up our little scrap, but I find living here very difficult. She has been in bed all day & had to be waited on abit.[2]

Anyhow, it was heaven to hear your voice, & to know you'd written. Now I look forward to the letters. So sorry you had such a vile journey, & are working so hard. But we'll have a quiet time this Friday & Saturday – what heaven; I can scarcely wait for it, my darling. I go tomorrow to Mrs. [Ethel] Bridge – Friston Field, East Dean 316. It'll be heavenly to be there, all away from this ghastly rush. But I'll have my time cut out to do all this work.

By-the-way the Bank has sent on my pass-book, so there's no need to worry about that. So sorry to have bothered you my darling – in fact I never seem to do anything but bother you do I? But I promise that when we're living alone together that I really will behave outside as I feel inside about you – & need I say ~~that~~ how that is? Never never have I or could I love anyone as I love my darling.

Be careful,
> B.

---

[1] William Glock (1908–2000), then music critic of *The Observer*.
[2] Britten and Pears were at this time living in Ursula Nettleship's flat, but moved out in February 1943.

26 Pears to Britten

Birmingham

[before 7 Dec 1942]

My darling –

Just a line to say Good Morning and how are you? I should like to wake you up with a kiss but I guess I shall have to postpone that for a couple of days more. Many thanks for your letter & the forwardings – Sweet letter from Michael [Mayer]. I've answered Joan Cross saying Yes with pleasure. I'm afraid next Monday night is no good for Glock – I have a Christmas Oratorio at Hitchin though I shall be back that night late. I've been seeing various people here, all rather nice. But factory concerts are real agony – the getting up and imposing one's music through a mike past clattering plates is only just compensated for by the pleasure it seems to give some of the people. But it is bitter agony.

Much much love my only b.

Your loving

P.

Lot of love to Eth.

27 Britten to Pears

Friston Field

East Dean   Nr Eastbourne,

316   Sussex.

[?Dec 1942]

My darling man,

Eth is just going off to the post; I hadn't realised that it went so early, – so this ~~has~~ can only be a scribble, to say how your letters have been life & breath to me. My darling – to think I have been so selfish as to make you unhappy, when you have so much strain, & such hard work to bear. But I too have come out of this week-end a better person. I seem to be getting things into order abit. Again it seems to be a matter of 'O man, know thyself' – & of knowing what I really want – & living that knowledge. I promise, my darling ......

It is lovely being here. You must come soon & consummate it. Eth is an angel, & I think I make her very happy coming. We talk always about you.

I don't think the maisonette that I saw yesterday will do – too far away & too many rooms & abit gloomy. But we can go & look again on Saturday. I called you last night, but you were already out, I'm afraid. I'll try again to-morrow night.

Meantime – I live for Friday, & you. My man – my beloved man.

B.

28 Pears to Britten

Midland Hotel

[early Dec 1942]

My boy – It was such heaven hearing your voice – I woke up again at once – I'd been wiling away the time re-reading Mr Norris of which I've found a Penguin.[1]

You know, I've been thinking an awful lot about you and me – I love you with my whole being, solemnly and seriously – These last times have made me realise how serious love is, what a great responsibility and what a sharing of personalities – It's not just a pleasure & a self indulgence. Our love must be complete and a creation in itself, a gift which we must be fully conscious of & responsible for.

O my precious darling, parting from you is such agony – Just hearing your voice is joy –

Goodnight, my Ben –
Sleep well. I shall think of you all the time –
Your loving man
P.

Lots of love to Eth.

---

[1] Isherwood's novel, *Mr Norris Changes Trains*, in a Penguin paperback edition.

29 Pears to Britten

[*Letterhead:* Midland Hotel, Birmingham]

[*after Nov 1942*]

My beloved darling, my little pussy-cat –

This is really only to tell you (probably all in vain because you won't get it – and you'll leave just as the post arrives!) that I love you and miss you terribly – Every loving couple I see I envy – I go to the movies & weep buckets because every situation I translate to our personal one. Oh! I do hope we'll never be in quite such a dilemma as Humphrey Bogart & Ingrid Bergman get themselves into in "Casablanca"; promise me that you won't leave me just as the Nazis enter London because you hear your husband isn't dead after all, and then turn up with him at the speakeasy I'm running in Newfoundland, trying to forget you – promise me, you won't, will you? For one thing, I'm sure I should never behave as nobly as Bogart does! Bee!

Look, I've got to rehearse a little while here on Friday Morning 10.30–11.30 or so, so I shan't be back intown until the afternoon – See you then –

Love! Love! Love.
P. xxxooo etc.

✠✠✠

Britten and Pears moved in February 1943 from the flat they shared with Ursula Nettleship to 45A St John's Wood High Street. Pears was still performing predominantly outside London both in CEMA concerts and touring with Sadler's Wells. At the beginning of March while in the middle of working on the libretto for *Peter Grimes* with Montagu Slater, Britten was hospitalised with measles.

✠✠✠

30 Pears to Britten

Somewhere in Suffolk.

Wednesday night. [3 Mar 1943]

My darling beloved heart –

It's just twenty four hours since you went, since your poor pathetic little face last looked at me out of the ambulance, and it seems that it was years ago and that I shall never see you again. Thank God that's only what it seems like; as Barbara told me tonight when I rang her that it was measles not s-fever [scarlet fever]! That <u>does</u> mean only 3 weeks instead of a lot more. I am loving you so terribly every moment and I shall love you every moment when we are together again. Life doesn't matter without you. it's just half-time. My B – My darling little B.

I left miserably this morning, the telephone still not working, the plumber still not come etc. and came down to Ipswich with Arnold, and Ursula met us with Florence[1] and drove us over to here (Bedingfield) a <u>most</u> lovely Elizabethan house, host & hostess professionally charming retired diplomats, & fundamentally rather hopeless & awful – son killed in war etc. Two concerts in Eye, singing rather tiredly –

<u>Thursday night</u>

I've been having a sort of gastric attack – frightful diarrhoea and pains. At first I thought I was going to sicken for measles & would join you, my pussy cat, but I seem to be better tonight – so I guess it's nothing but worry and/or bad food. We had one concert this evening at Diss. Quite nice, but how terribly I miss you! I only do half the job without you! Mrs. Nielsen[2] rang up this morning to say the telephone was OK & the plumbers had been & your room (– sorry! our room –) had been fumigated, and the clothes removed & would be returned on Friday! So things are moving – I'm going to make that place really lovely for you by the time you come back, my only pussy B.

I do hope you weren't too worried in the raid last night! Was the noise frightful? & did you get a decent night's sleep? or were you taken down to a shelter? Oh my beloved boy I thought of you all the time – We could just hear noises here, & I could only pray that you were allright. It was a great relief when Barbara told me it was in Willesden way –

I'm not going to write any more now – but I'll write again & leave it at the hospital.

Much much love my darling. Be careful of yourself & be good. Always yr. loving P.

---

1   Hooton (1912–88), cellist.
2   Mrs Neilson was the housekeeper at their London home.

31 Pears to Britten

[*Letterhead:* Post Office Telegram]

1.15 London [postmark 9 Mar 1943]

Benjamin Britton Ward 14 Grove Hospital Tooting SW17

= TERRIBLY SORRY BEN CANNOT GET DOWN THIS AFTERNOON BUT WILL DEFINITELY COME TOMORROW 2 OCLOCK LOVE = PETER +

32 Pears to Britten

[St John's Wood, London]

[postmark 9 Mar 1943]

My darling, I've just sent you a telegram to say I shan't be down today – I'm terribly sorry about it, my sweet boy, but it's such a long way to fit in between these hectic rehearsals & everything – But I promise to come tomorrow, as soon as ever I can after lunch and I'll stay till 5.

Much much love my adorable B; it was heaven seeing you on Sunday looking so much better, & your little face no longer feverish – Be good & take care of yourself.

I kiss you all over – behind the ears & between the legs!

immer dein [always your]

P.

Guti[1] is back, & I am bellowing!

---

1   Julius Guttman, Pears's teacher in 1943.

33 Britten to Pears

Grove Hospital,
<u>Tooting Grove SW17</u>

March 11th 1943

My darling –

One stamp left, so whom to use it for …? As if there could be any question —— !!! My dearest, I am thinking about you all to-day, rehearsing Tamino[1] &, I hope, practising abit, & to-night you'll look so beautiful & sound so wonderful, I know. How I wish I could see you – I really think I <u>must</u> come up to Blackpool for the Rigoletto.[2] Do you mind? – if I'm well enough? Then I should get a Flute as well and I want to see it so badly.

I am going to do lots of work on P. Grimes to day, to see what really is wrong with it. And then I shall write a long letter to Montagu & hope he can fix it abit. I am sure it isn't <u>fundamently</u> hopeless; there are too many things I like about it. For one thing it goes <u>naturally</u> into operatic form – it doesn't embarrass me to think of those people singing, & singing English. And another, I see so clearly what kind of music I want to write for it, & I <u>am</u> interested in the people & the situations, & interested in a musical way.

It isn't often that one can get an opera scheme that comes so near what one wants. I'm beginning to feel that Montagu may not be the ideal librettist; but who? Wystan, well – there are the old objections, & besides he's not to hand. Louis – more or less the same objections, & I don't know how I could work with him. Eddy – well, perhaps; let's see how the Rescue[3] turns out – I doubt whether he again is a good enough poet, whether he isn't too pretentious, again. It'll be interesting to see what Tony Guthrie has done. Yes, I think I must come to Blackpool!

I've just had a sweet letter, with no complications!, from Eddy. He makes quite a promising suggestion about the Scot. Ballad. I think we malign him, you know; I know he's a neurotic but at least he can control himself!

A long letter from Robert [Britten] – he's persuaded Marjorie [Robert's wife] to see a doctor – wonder of wonders! – I wonder if it'll do any good, but it's an effort in the right direction. If she's ordered away for a rest, it might solve matters abit.

I love the Swift, my dear – it was sweet of you to bring it for me. The Graham Greene[4] that Enid sent is a very good tale, with a strong atmosphere. But awfully disturbing! I had to be comforted by the Mahler[5] after reading it last night – what a miracle that work is – I think I have almost more <u>affection</u> for that piece than for any I know.

No news, my darling. I go on. Didn't sleep so well last night, because the tooth was abit restless, & it got so awfully hot in here – with the fire & no windows open (because of black-out). But thank god no alerts – but I mustn't be a fool about them; think of what the Germans are going through now – poor devils. How I wish to God it would all stop. I feel every day that it goes on longer makes things worse – takes us all further into the mire of hate & hopelessness.

It was heaven to see you for that nice long time – sorry if I was very quiet – but it was nicest just to lie quietly & to watch you, & to know you were there. If it is difficult for you to come on Sunday – don't bother, it's more important for you to rest. (But if you do come – it would be lovely!) Good luck in everything – in Sevenoaks & with learning & practising. I'm with you in thoughts every moment, my own darling. Take care of yourself. Don't get cold.

Immer dein [always your]

B.

---

1   Main tenor role in Mozart's *The Magic Flute*.
2   Pears was to make his debut as The Duke in Verdi's opera.
3   The radio drama for which Edward Sackville-West wrote the text and Britten the music was to premiere on 25 November.
4   Possibly the novel *Brighton Rock* (1938).
5   Symphony no. 4.

34 Pears to Britten

[St John's Wood, London]

[?12 Mar 1943]

My own bunch of beauty –

Got your letter when I arrived back today – Flute went well, & have just been fitted for Clothes for Rig – Scrumptious!

Re enclosed, I'll ring Mabel & will send Sophie [Wyss] a card. See you Sunday
Much love, fudge.

P.

35 Britten to Pears

Old Mill, Snape,
Suffolk.

March 21st 1943

My darling –

It is such heaven to hear your voice, even if only over the telephone. But doesn't it seem ages since last Sunday? – and now we still have to wait until Friday. Still, it's not too bad; think of all the other married couples who are separated for everso much longer!!

I am so relieved you will have one free day. By-jove, you do deserve it. I have been thinking of you all the time, working like a nigger, & hoping you've not been getting too tired. Iris said you sang simply beautifully yesterday. What a curse it is that I haven't been able to do these concerts with you – but at least I've been able to write things for you, – better than nothing.[1]

It is lovely that you are enjoying Rigoletto – I bet it'll be good. I have been studying the score carefully, & have lots of ideas about it! I wonder if they agree with yours.

I was <u>very</u> impressed with Joan Cross on Monday, you know. She has the most lovely <u>warm</u> quality in her voice – really the only English Soprano who does something to ones middle like Lehmann does. Her top doesn't seem terribly free tho' – but probably thats lack of practice. One thing I noticed at that broadcast – you know when the two voices are singing high in octaves, the soprano (owing to the higher frequencies) nearly always drowns the tenor – but it was <u>not</u> so this time. You were finely audible all the time. The voice sounded <u>good</u> you know. I can see why Guty was pleased.

I called Iris & she comes on Tuesday. I think she'll enjoy it here. It is very quiet – Beth is occupied with the kids all the time (Sebastian grows more ravishing every day!) & I shall still be spending alot of time lazing in bed (like now). But I don't think she'll mind, will she? Beth's trying to fix with Christine & Mrs Burrows[2] so that she hasn't anything to do.

I hope Margaret [Neilson] <u>hasn't</u> got measles. Poor Mrs. Neilson will be worried if she has.

Much love, my only darling. Take <u>great</u> care of yourself – & you'll have a lovely rest next weekend.

Here's Elizabeth's letter – what a pity she didn't get yours.

All my love – my P.

B.

---

[1] Pears was singing in a number of Friends War Relief Service and CEMA concerts while between March and April Britten was composing the *Serenade*.
[2] Two local residents who provided domestic help at the Old Mill, Christina Podd and Theresa Burrows.

36 Pears to Britten

Opera House
<u>Blackpool.</u>

Tuesday [30 Mar 1943] –

My darling –

I'm just writing this before I go to bed, just to tell you how much I love and miss you – and that last weekend was pure heaven but not long enough – The journey up and all was fairly hectic although Blackpool is half empty and I found a room at a very expensive but comfortable hotel where I still am – There is a waitress looking after me who adores opera (she will have been 4 times in these two weeks) and she gives me everything I shouldn't have – lots of extras, etc.! So I'm not doing so bad. Though there is noone to take your place curiously enough!

I'm afraid if you want to see me in Rigoletto you'll have to come here on Saturday or Southport on Wednesday, as I shan't be doing any in London – I'm doing Traviata instead so I shall have learn that fairly quick too. The Rig. Costumes have arrived and are quite stupendous! The rehearsals are going very well too & I'm falling into the part easily.

Will you please buy a bottle of Complevite[1] in Sax & take it? It's the same as Pregnavite only doesn't sound so rude! and please do take it with pleasure & not grumpily! <u>please</u> to please me. Promise to obey!

How are the songs?[2] I do hope I didn't damp your poor old enthusiasm too much about them – Don't be discouraged – Don't forget, my darling, that I am only as critical as I am because I have high standards for you –

All my love, my honey –

always your

P.

Use your sweet ration before the end of the week!

----

[1] Vitamin supplements taken to support the immune system.
[2] Britten was continuing work on the *Serenade*.

37 Britten to Pears

Old Mill,
Snape, Suffolk

~~March 31ˢᵗ 1943~~
April 1ˢᵗ 1943

My darling,

These telephone conversations are so damnably unsatisfactory, when there is someone in the room, & one cannot say what one feels. I am sorry about it, but at anyrate it was glorious to hear your voice, & to know that you had found rooms. You old blighter, you promised me <u>faithfully</u> that you'd ring on Monday – I was so worried about you arriving there with no where to go – & I sat up till mid-night waiting! You beast! Still you are forgiven, as usual.

Things go on the same here – I work alot (don't worry, the Nocturnes [*Serenade*] will be worthy of you by the time I've finished!) correct proofs, write letters (mostly to Ralph or Decca), go long walks with Iris, & have rather beastly alerts – Monday night was nasty, & closer than Sunday – Still it might be much worse, & on the whole I am enjoying myself alot. If only you were here – you <u>must</u> start giving up jobs so you can work & do things you <u>want</u> to do. It is infuriating about no Rig. in London. Are you sure that's final? Can't you give up some little job to do it – I am sure it will be so good. But anyhow Traviata will be, too, and there will obviously be a chance to show Londoners a good Duca later. But what a sweat to learn it so quickly – lucky we chose a programme for Cambridge that doesn't need much work.[1] I'm looking for winners for you in the Schubert albums – I think I've found some, too.

It was so heavenly to have last week-end with you. I do love you so, you know, & loathe being without you. Next week is too far off still, & you have so much to do before it. Nevermind, I'm sure it'll all be grand, & relax as much as you possibly can.

Iris is well, & I think liking being here. Beth is fond of her, & they get on very easily. Sally is sweeter than ever, & Sebastian, if possible, naughtier than ever. But I like him all the same, & he is very attractive & strong-willed. What a hand-full for uncle later!

The Goehr situation has clarified abit.[2] His turning the cheek has conquered Ralph who now agrees to letting him conduct the Nocturnes at the BH concert later – the best arrangement since there's now no hurry, for me or for you to learn them.

The post – as usual. Much love & all luck in the world for all your shows – a good Duca, a good St. Matthew, Alfred & all.[3]

My darling man.

Dein

<u>Ben</u>

Love from Iris, Beth, Seb, & Sal.

1   A recital with pianist Clifford Curzon at the Cambridge Arts Theatre on 25 April 1943. They were performing the Michelangelo Sonnets with a selection of Schubert songs and Britten folk-song arrangements, and the UK premiere of Britten's *Mazurka Elegiaca* for two pianos.

2   Britten asked German conductor Walter Goehr (1903–60) to conduct the *Serenade* (here, 'Nocturnes') in his concert series, but Ralph Hawkes was reluctant as it competed with the Boosey & Hawkes premiere.

3   Pears was continuing as The Duke in *Rigoletto*, and was also to sing in Bach's *St Matthew Passion* at the Royal Albert Hall on 11 April; his debut as Alfredo in Verdi's *La traviata* took place at Sadler's Wells on 29 April.

38 Britten to Pears

<u>Old Mill</u>. Snape,

[6 Apr 1943]

My darling,

This is not a real letter – you know what little news there is – but only a Coda to our inevitably emotionally-restricted telephone talks. I love you, my only one, & think of you every moment – my life is inextricably bound up in yours, & so I wonder every moment exactly what you are doing – how Rigoletto is going how you are managing to get to Hull & back, whether you are too exhausted to sing at all – & all, etc. etc. I can't wait till I see you – don't think because I demured a little at coming on Thursday, be a that I am not every bit as excited as you are, but I'd got it into my silly head that you were only back on Friday, & had made arrangements accordingly (Iris is coming up with me) – but, it is all settled, & I'll tell you details on the telephone. You poor dear, when <u>are</u> you going to get a little time to rest & relax?

I had a sweet letter from William explaining the resigning this morning (I sent the cable) & one from Michael [Mayer], more hopeful about his future.[1]

Until Thursday, all my love.

<u>B.</u>

1   Mayer had resigned his position at the hospital in Amityville, NY, citing an intolerable work situation.

39 Britten to Pears

Old Mill,
Snape, Suffolk.

May 22nd 1943

My darling,

I <u>hope</u> by the time you get this you'll have rung up as you promised you'd do – if so all the questions will be answered – but that's no reason not to write me a note, saying other things! How is everything with you? The weather here is heavenly, & so far things have been wonderfully quiet (touch wood). Mrs. Neilson is managing alright, but inclined to quarrel with the villagers.[1] The less I see (or hear) of Margaret [Neilson] the better. I'm working hard, & not too badly I think. And how's the voice? I'm afraid this continued heat won't be so good for it. Good luck for everything. I'm longing to hear how the Seasons[2] went. Did you learn it in time?

About Wednesday – what are we singing? If you let me have a note (in town on Tuesday) I'll meet you from your train & we'll go straight down together, if you'll have changed. And you <u>are</u> busy on Thursday evening, arn't you? My poor old darling, how I yearn for the 5th for you, when you can relax. I'm thinking Dartington may be a good idea for you. (No news from Esther, by-the-way) – it'll mean so much less to do. How I long to see you again – it's years since that rather terrifying time in town, but it's heaven to have you near me. Lovely letters from William & Elizabeth <u>and</u> photos. All my love, my heart; come back soon.

B.

---

[1] Mrs Neilson and her daughter, who took care of the flat in St John's Wood, had come to Suffolk to help at the Old Mill.

[2] Oratorio by Haydn.

✠✠✠

In the months between May and November, Pears continued touring the provinces with Sadler's Wells, performing in *The Magic Flute* and *Rigoletto*, among others, returning to London with Smetana's *The Bartered Bride* in November. The combination of travelling and performing with the opera company as well as fitting in many recitals and oratorio concerts was gruelling and both he and Britten were concerned it was beginning to wear him out, but the experience was clearly beneficial for his development as a singer. Meanwhile after recovering from the measles, Britten completed a number of works including the *Serenade* and *Rejoice in the Lamb*, and arranged folk songs to perform with Pears. In January 1944 Britten began composing *Peter Grimes* in earnest. In the letters that follow we get a glimpse of Britten's compositional process, and Pears's involvement in how the opera develops.

✠✠✠

40 Britten to Pears

[Swansea]

[18 Nov 1943]

My darling – This is only a scribble just to tell you who I can remember to have been asked for next Monday – 3 Steins, 2 Slaters, 1 Martin,[1] 1 [Holland] Rogers, 1 Cross, 1 Johnson?[2] 1 Britten (Barb.), 1 Hurst, 1 Curzon, your darling self, & me. Any more? I can't remember. (Berkeley?)

It was heaven to hear your voice, & to know you're feeling better. Practise hard & get the golden box back in its proper working order again. Something goes wrong with my life when that's not functioning properly.

It's been nice here, only Erwin had one hell of a cold, which I've picked up of course. The little boys are abit of a worry, but I think will be fine in the end. They sing so well, that one gets cross with Simms that it's not perfect.[3]

I go to Dartington tomorrow, & then back to home & thou on Monday – early train. Sing nicely in Wales – I'll be thinking of you.

I find Theocritus, even in these ghastly translations; very moving. Au revoir my Hercules, – I nearly signed myself Hylas, but at nearly 30 that's alittle exaggerated![4] But any how, all my love my heart —— B.

---

[1] Christopher Martin (1902–44), the Administrator of the Arts Department at Dartington Hall School.

[2] Elizabeth Johnson (1903–76) was a friend and devoted fan of Pears.

[3] Britten was in Wales to rehearse the Morriston Boys Choir for a performance and recording of *A Ceremony of Carols*. Ivor Simms was their choirmaster.

[4] Possibly *The Idylls of Theocritus*, translated by Banks and Chapman (G. Bell and Sons, 1911), part of the original collection at The Red House. Theocritus wrote that Hercules (Heracles) loved Hylas because of his youthful beauty.

41 Britten to Pears

[*Letterhead:* Yarner Farm, Dartington, Totnes, Devon.]

Nov 24ᵗʰ 1943

My darling –

This is only to say what absolute heaven it was to see you; and how sweet it was of you to come all these weary miles to cheer me up – which it did, with a vengeance. I only hope you don't feel too weary after it, & were able to charm all their old hearts with Vasek[1] as usual! I'm afraid it was selfish of me, but I can't be unselfish where you're concerned – I just want you so terribly that all my usual control evaporates. I am feeling loads better – still a bit wobbly, & the beastly old boil is a nuisance still, so it looks like Monday, not Saturday as I'd hoped for, but I am much more cheerful, & not such gloomy company as I was when you were here. But thank you so much for bringing all those heavenly presents with you. I love the Bali pictures – quite crazy over them – & the Michelangelo too – tho' I haven't got down to the texts yet. I had some more nice letters this morning, so I've really had a pretty good birthday, inspite of germs & things.[2] Take care of your self my heart, sing nicely at Melksham, & have some good Guties & sing better & better. Hedli [Anderson] says the ~~show~~ Rescue[3] is going pretty rockily with not enough rehearsal & that no one believes I'm really ill! – sick making that. Maybe I'll listen abit & gloat to-night. Cecily sends love & says I'm <u>still</u> a good patient which no one seems to believe!

Much love, heart – I love you so, every day more. Be nice to me even at 30!

Your own   Ben.

I stupidly wrote on 2 sheets instead of one, & I haven't got time to fill up this middle bit as I have got to have a rest, & the post goes before I wake up & I want you to have this tommow ~~by~~ to let you know I love you – which you never guessed, did you?

---

[1] The tenor role in Smetana's *The Bartered Bride*.

[2] Britten came down with the flu, necessitating he stay longer with Christopher Martin and his wife Cicely at Dartington.

[3] *The Rescue*, BBC radio play with incidental music by Britten.

42 Pears to Britten

In the train on the
<u>way to London from York</u>.

[7 Jan 1944]

My own heart's darling –

I should have written to you directly I left you on Tuesday – I had been so very horrid to you I'm afraid all day Tuesday – very irritable and snappy, & it was a wretched parting to take of you, and I was very contrite all the way up – I <u>do</u> love you so, and hate it so when the devil is in me. Don't judge me too hard. Kenneth[1] said that we were as different types as could be, so perhaps we mustn't be too surprised if sometimes we differ – but it isn't very often really is it?

We had a good quiet journey up arriving at 2 o'clock a.m., only two others in the carriage & they slept all the while – The Barber [*of Seville*] went fairly allright – very ragged in spots. Joan is really quite "poorly" (to use one's Aunts' word) & apt to be on & off temper – & I think maybe my future relations with her will have some difficult moments. Long talks with Herbert,[2] rather depressing. Curious how everyone tends to find Laurence[3] as the evil genius – The whole company gets very tense on tour – & one is conscious of many currents –

York is a lovely place – The Minster is absolutely superb. the <u>biggest</u> of all the cathedrals. Went to Evensong yesterday – <u>wretched</u> singing – boys were hopeless little hooters & no sound at all & no ensemble – The whole service dead – not even a humble routine – nothing. I shall go to Aberdare tomorrow (Sat.) morning & back to London Sunday & on to Leeds same day – Better than Cardiff Leeds direct which takes 14 hours –

X X X X X

Much love my honey bee. I love you darling

P.

---

[1] Kenneth Green (1905–86), who painted a double portrait of Pears and Britten for Mary Behrend in 1943; the portrait is held in the National Portrait Gallery, London.

[2] Probably conductor Herbert Menges (1902–72).

[3] Lawrance Collingwood (1887–1982), conductor.

43 Britten to Pears

<u>Snape</u>
Jan. 10th 1944

My own darling P.,

You can't imagine how my thoughts have been with you thro' all your travels & concerts this week – I don't believe you have really been out of my mind for ten seconds all together! I can't wait to hear how Samson[1] went, & whether you were pleased with yourself, & if they liked you – not that there could be much doubt of that! I hope the travelling wasn't too impossible, & that you managed to get food, & comfortable seats & all. Where do you stay this week? I trust you have remembered to get yourself a hotel! I ought really to have got this off so that you could have it on arrival, but I have been so busy all the days, & so lazy all the evenings, I am afraid, and anyhow I have been waiting to get yours (which I hope'll arrive in the morning), to see if there ~~has been~~ is any thing particular to answer. Well, at last I have broken the spell and got down to work on P.G. I have been at it for two days solidly, and got the greater part of the Prologue done. It is <u>very</u> difficult to keep that amount of recitative moving, without going round & round in circles, I find – but I think I've managed it. It is also difficult to keep it going fast & yet paint moods & characters abit. I can't wait to show it to you. Actually in this scene there isn't much for you to do (I haven't got to the love duet yet); it is mostly for Swallow, who is turning out quite an amusing, pompous old thing! I don't know whether I shall ever be a good opera composer, but it's wonderful fun to try once in a way! Otherwise I do nothing at all, except a little reading, and one or two letters (after my great burst of correspondance on Friday). The kids seem well, & are terribly sweet – don't forget Sally's 1st birthday on 13th, by the way. Sebastian's a real~~ly~~ honey and gets more charming everyday – in ten year's time he'll be a real menace, I'm afraid! Beth is well, rather worried & over-worked because Christina's ill & away, & Joyce[2] may get called up; but nothing definite yet, luckily, & it may not happen.

And you – you old so- & so – I miss you most dreadfully. I suppose we'll have to get used to this separation, but it's hellish hard. I wouldn't have dreamed that I could miss someone so much. I suppose you're so busy that you seldom give me a thought – but just now & then, think of me thinking of you! Take care of yourself – look both ways in crossing roads, wrap up well, & don't get your feet wet – because you belong to me! Ring up from time to time because it gives me strength to go on.

Love to Joan, & tell her, that inspite of her P.G.'s going to be a knock-out!

All my love,

my darling,

B.

PS.

Your letter (& sweet card, with the lovely touching story on it – could we ever attain that pitch of discipline? – not likely I'm afraid) has just come. I am just as guilty about the day of tensions as you are, in fact I thought I was a great deal worse – but please don't reproach yourself, my darling. Kenneth's drawing of me[3] showed me all too clearly what you have to put up with! I am sorry that the opera squabbles get you down – but try to ignore them as much as possible – you can't do anything about it, & I'm afraid you'll have to stick it for a bit longer. Anyhow remember that it has been, & is a great experience for you.

Sing well, old dear – & better & better …!

       Lots of love

          B

---

[1]   Oratorio by Handel.
[2]   Joyce Burrows, another of the local people to provide domestic help at the Old Mill.
[3]   Possibly a study for Green's portrait of Britten (1943).

44 Britten to Pears

<u>Snape</u>

[before 11 Feb 1944]

My darling – This is only a scribble to say a few things that one can't say over the bloody telephone. I love you, I love you I love you. I am hopelessly homesick without you, & I only live every day because it brings the day, when we shall be together, nearer. Take care of yourself – <u>don't</u> sing too soon, & rest as much as you can. I shall listen ~~for~~ to you on Friday – I do hope it goes well, & Sunday too.

After a slow start P.G. is now swimming ahead again – I've nearly finished the scene! Montagu & I have made some good improvements I think, & I'm writing some lovely things for you to sing – I write every note with your heavenly voice in my head. Darling – I love you more than you could imagine. I'm just incomplete because half of me is in Manchester!

       All my everything

          B

45 Pears to Britten

[Incomplete – only the second half survives in the archive.]

[?1/2 Mar 1944]

& after waiting till 12.30 am at the Central Hotel, was very kindly allowed to share a room with another man – And so here I am on my way back to Liverpool, having spent £5 & 36 hours on an entirely useless journey, & having had two breakfasts & a railway station lunch between Tuesday & Thursday nights (I expect!). What Ibbs[1] will say I don't know – I shall just have to invent a late train into Liverpool. Oh bunch! & it was all really because I was too tired on Tuesday night to check up on the train – If only I thought I should learn from this sort of mistake! But I know only too well that I don't profit by my mistakes – I'm such a hardened old sinner. I don't suppose I shall ever be asked to Greenock again. They took good care to tell me that they specialised in asking new artists. Heddle Nash & Isobel Baillie[2] had both made their Scottish première there, & had been back 3 or 4 times!!

Oh dear, oh dear! & it was 23 guineas too!

Are you warm at the Mill? I do hope so & that there's plenty of coke – There's deep snow up here – I longed to get off & see Lucille[3] as I passed through Cumberland! Oh for a holiday! I expect it's Freudian my missing trains – I just can't cope with the work – & I couldn't have wanted to do any thing <u>less</u> than <u>sing</u> at <u>Greenock</u>! Ben my darling, Peter Grimes was quite madly exciting! Really tremendously thrilling. The only thing you must remember is to consider that the average singer hasn't much gift for intensity off his own bat, so make sure that the tempi etc make a tense delivery inevitable – Actually I feel very much that you have already done this, only you know what most singers are; the bit I was thinking of was Swallow in the Prologue – Can it sound pompous at that pace? Aggressive yes – & perhaps that's enough. The more I hear of it, the more I feel that the queerness is unimportant & doesn't really exist in the music (or at any rate obtrude) so it mustn't do so in the words – P.G. is an introspective, an artist, a neurotic, his real problem is expression, self-expression. Nicht wahr? [Is it not so?] What a part! Wow! All my love my B. yr devoted P.

---

[1] Ibbs and Tillett, the London concert agency who acted for both Britten and Pears.
[2] (1895–1983), Scottish soprano.
[3] Wallace (1898–1977), harpsichordist, married to Clifford Curzon.

46 Pears to Britten

<u>Saturday</u> [8 Apr 1944]

My darling, this is just a scribble in a train waiting in Pontypool Rd Station on our way from Abergavenny to Newport, & it wishes you a very happy Easter, my bee, although it won't reach you till after Easter – I do hope you are all having a happy time together and are eating lots of eggs and thin mints – I have had rather a pleasant 48 hours surprisingly – I got a seat on my 5.55 train on Thursday which a million other people didn't! and reached Abergavenny at 11. o'clock & found a charming market town & an excellent & comfy hotel, and slept well & had a good breakfast & Good Friday lunch off turbot, & took a 1.15 bus to Brecon which is a most lovely little city in heavenly country – Everything was full of frühling [spring], bächlein [streams] galore, and all very Schöne Müllerin[1] 1st half! There's a Brecon Cathedral & birds in the high hall garden, <u>all</u> calling Maud Maud Mawd Mored! We were put up above a Cafe & given many eggs & buns, & this morning we have caught a 7.30 bus to Abergavenny whence we now pursue our journey by a steaming juggernaut of steel & iron – Altogether the best sort of Welsh excursion! & of course Elijah,[2] with plenty of time for me to think about Schubert, between glucose "If …" & sugary "Then …".[3]

The Americans are in occupation hereabouts & I must say that I don't blame any Welsh girl who might have yielded to such charming & persistent advances as were made by a blonde Virginian to a little Newport lass in the train on Thursday – He was very gay & drunk, but luckily for everyone, fell asleep after teasing her for 20 minutes. But how alcoholic they all are – A bit too much!

I gave old Mary J.[4] your love which pleased her hugely – She's really a sweet old dear. and my! what a Jezebel.!

Well my sweety pie, I shall see you on Friday, shan't I & much much love till then ever your loving P.

My love to Beth & Barbara & Sebastian & Sally

---

[1] Song cycle by Schubert.
[2] Oratorio by Mendelssohn.
[3] 'If with all your hearts' and 'Then shall the righteous shine forth', tenor arias from *Elijah*.
[4] Mary Jarred (1889–1993), contralto.

47 Britten to Pears

<u>Old Mill</u>

[before 9 Apr 1944]

My darling,

This is just to wish you a very, very happy Easter, & to tell you how I wish I were with you. Have a nice rest, if you can, go to Michael,[1] and relax as much as possible. I wish you were here; when I think of the old days when you could just hop in to the car & arrive at anytime day or night, I g̶o̶ want to cry. But perhaps they'll come again, one day, & one will be able to put all one's mind on one's work – I think that's one reason why Grimes is being such a brute at the moment. Still, I am over the worst now, and I can at least see ahead.

Working i̶s̶ at the Schöne Müllerin with you is going to be heaven. I think we ought to do a wonderful show of it. But I think I shall have to transport this awful old piano to the Wigmore – I am making such nice noises on it!

I'm waiting for your call tomorrow night – I do hope Wales wasn't too awful, but I would give alot to have been there to hear your voice – lucky Welsh!

Ursula was here yesterday – & Barbara has got here now safely for Easter & is enjoying herself. Isn't it tragic about Michael Halliday[2] being missing. I feel very odd about it now – poor silly old dear that he was.

All my love my dearest darling
      B.

Had a note from Cecily – nothing definite about TB.[3] Yet

---

[1]   Possibly Michael Tippett.
[2]   Friend of Britten at South Lodge School in the 1920s; one of the dedicatees of Britten's *War Requiem*.
[3]   Christopher Martin was diagnosed with tuberculosis, and would die in hospital on 6 August.

48 Britten to Pears

<u>Snape</u>

May 9th [1944]

My honey,

I don't know when I'm going to have the joy of hearing your voice on the telephone again – tonight you're being eaten by lions (lucky things); tomorrow, you're fire-watching (lucky fire) – so I thought I'd write a scribble to say I love you & miss you terribly, & long for Monday. It was heaven – the week-end, quietly alone with you; the B's [Behrends] are such sweet hosts, and it couldn't have been lovely, could it? I've written them a note – & said you probably won't have time to write.

It is nice here (as nice as it can be ohne dich [without you]) Sebastian is sweet; as is Sally, & Beth seems in good form. The opera is going ahead at last, & the garden looks nice. Only the aeroplanes are bloody, bloody all the time. Ursula is around – but mostly with the local hostlery.

I gather you didn't have time to see Erwin – but no matter. Little Sir W.???[1]

Take care of yourself, my darling – nurse that heavenly voice of yours – We must do a superb Serenade. See you Saturday at 12.30 for lunch. The Rothmans have sent a lovely parcel of cookies & candies – I'll bring some up for you!

All my love, my dearest,
     Ben.

Of course the real reason for writing
is that you must be running out
of a certain commodity for railway trains ——

---

[1]   The meaning of Britten's comment is unclear, beyond a reference to his arrangement of the folk song *Little Sir William*.

49 Pears to Britten

[10 May 1944]

Honey-bunch, it was heavenly to have your sweet letter & to hear your sweet voice just now – You know, I do <u>mind</u> being away from you, although I'm not sure it isn't an entirely bad thing in small doses, though I doubt whether absence <u>could</u> make this old heart grow fonder! I'm filled with terrors from time to time as to what may be happening to you (I had a fearful panic in the Severn Tunnel yesterday!) & I do beg you to look after your sweet self most carefully – I began thinking how v. important reality, as we imagine it, is – & although I really don't mind not existing if you don't exist too, I hate having to rely on my memories, even of a day or two ago – Do you agree, Bee? ~~But~~ So by all means let us die together, but also let us live together too, hein [no]?

Here are two letters just come for you – one too awful, the other very sweet – only the title is lacking on the card! Baron is it or Earl? Have you written to Pamela Elliot (?) the fiancée of the prisoner of war?

Just been rung up by Arthur Servent[1] – He's ill-ish & wants me to stand by tonight for Bohème[2] – Apparently the Queen is coming! Oh Lud!

So I must go & flap!

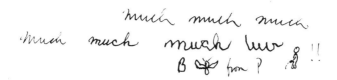

Much much much much much much luv
B ['Bee'] from P ['Pee'] !!

---

[1]   (1902–90), tenor.
[2]   Pears sang Rodolfo in Puccini's opera at Sadler's Wells in April and May 1944.

50 Pears to Britten

[10–11 May 1944]

My own beloved heart darling, this is only just a line to tell you that I think of you all the time, even when I'm being eaten by lions or thrown to the Lady of Shalott, or, as now, just waiting at some station on the way to Stoke on Trent. You are with me all the time and I plan absurdly, and day-dream stupidly with you all the time. (We have just passed a station apparently called Earl's Cement! v. odd!) Perhaps I'm even more conscious of you when I'm away from you than when you're with me – Am I rather horrid to you actually sometimes? Because I couldn't be nicer to you when you aren't here! Does that help at all? My honey. I think also a lot about reality & time & space & such trifles, as a result of your not being here & yet being here. I do love you quite terribly –

I <u>had</u> to sing Bohème last night to the Queen & the Princesses (their first opera – most unsuitable I should have thought!) & we were informed that we gave pleasure! My father & mother were madly excited about it! It was Vic. Sladen[1] as Mimi – not bad at all & no bad mistakes – but [Lawrance] Collingwood really stinks. Phew!

It's dirty music! However it's all probably a good training for Peter Grimes, which is after all what I was born for, nicht wahr? I shall be glad when this week's over, & Monday night comes round! Mrs. Nielson is looking after me frightfully well & has very sweetly been taking food to my mother – She's allright really when she has time to be –

FRIDAY noon.

Last night went very well – They liked me, I think, & of course saved your, as encore, "Wonder – Wander";[2] as indeed, they did at Llanelly. I have to keep you with me as much as possible! And I have now got through 2/3rds of my 5th rate music for the week! Wow! Shalott is as odoriferous as her vegetable namesake! & what a pome! Tennyson being very un-queer & boring.

Maurice J.[3] is quite an efficient accompanist, & Kathleen Ferrier a nice singer! By the way, I've got to do Barber on Monday! !

Much much love.

     ['Bee'] from ['Pee']

---

1   Victoria Sladen (1910–99), soprano.

2   Britten's arrangement of Niles's song *I wonder as I wander*.

3   Maurice Jacobson (1896–1976), composer of the cantata, *The Lady of Shalott*.

51 Pears to Britten

The Bells of Peover.
Knutsford. Cheshire.

[?17–18 May 1944]

My darling bee –

I'm writing in the train on my way in to M'chester after a lovely walk through the most hayfeverish country – So forgive scrawls!

I just feel that perhaps I was rather cross the other night over the phone about the recordings of Les Illuminations. But I do mind so terribly about them – It's grand that Sophie [Wyss] should do them so often (the train has stopped) but not permanently on wax! I couldn't bear to think that people will imagine that's the right way to sing them – Besides a performance like that surely can't wear so well – I mean when you've heard it twice, you've heard it all. which is wrong.

Of course, I didn't only write this to say that (if you understand me) but also to tell you that I love you, love you, love you (in spite of the wild movement of this train)

I want you & miss you terribly! my honey my little mouse catcher –

    Love Darling

      P.

52　Britten to Pears

<table>
<tr><td>I asked Erwin for the Grieg
<u>myself, so don't worry (ha, ha,).</u></td><td>I've done my C.O. thing have you?</td></tr>
</table>

Old Mill,
<u>Snape</u>

June 12th 1944

Honiest, bunchiest.

It was lovely to hear your voice over that unspeakable machine last night & Saturday. Sorry I was so involved on Sat. & so depressed on Sun. – but the latter is a thing which usually happens when I'm away from you; so we'd better not be apart too long. or I may shrivell altogether up in my depression. My bloody opera stinks, & that's all there is to̶o̶ it. But I dare say that I shall be able to de-odourise it before too long – or I'm hoping so. The week-end was abit hectic – helping organise the concert, the artists, & the village after. It's much easier to play than organise, I find – especially difficult is showing people into their seats – I couldn't find the numbers, & o – the confusion when people sat down in the wrong ones! However it went well – Korchinska[1] played well, Winnie Roberts[2] so-so, but Michael Head's[3] abit dim – but then most singers (save one – who … who?) are to me. Ursula's still around, which is un peu disturbing I find. All that coupled with news doesn't exactly help P.G. but I hope to be clearer in the old head from now onwards.

Kalmus[4] wants us on Sept. 28th to do Boyhoods End, Berg & Mahler at Wigstein for BH.[5] Is that too soon do you think, & did we <u>definitely</u> promise Johnny Amis for his club? I'd <u>like</u> to do it then, because it comes in my "off" week; but we can discuss all this when we meet.

Abelard[6] is a knock-out; I read it in about 2 days (<u>really</u> read it, too!), & it kept me a̶w̶a̶y̶ awake nearly all one night. It is agonising, but one reaches the end feeling better for it. What torments those two suffered – poor angels – do take care of yourself my dearest – lock your door at night – unless of course you do really want to sing the top F in I Puritani![7] I'm now reading Emma[8] to sooth myself.

The kids are well, if a bit over excited – Sebastian got wild with joy at so many visitors to flirt with & enchant, & we are rather feeling the consequences! But he's a honey, & so is your god-child too, you know. She [Sally] walks now, & says hallo (in a cockney accent – <u>most</u> s̶u̶r̶p̶r̶i̶s̶i̶n̶g̶ startling!).

Excuse scribble, my darling – but I want you to get this. Don't feel too bad about the Sadlers W. Op. Co. See Joan; talk her round – you've got lots of influence over her, & you must <u>use</u> it. Ralph Hawkes won't be any better, you know.

I love you, I love you, I love you. Take care of yourself – & practise the Grieg.

　　　All my love.
　　　　　Ben.

1   Maria Korchinska (1895–1979), harpist.
2   Winifred Roberts (1923–2012), Australian violinist; wife of conductor Geraint Jones.
3   (1900–76), singer and composer.
4   Alfred Kalmus (1889–1972), music publisher.
5   Song cycle by Tippett, written for Pears and Britten, and a selection of songs by Berg and Mahler, for a Boosey & Hawkes recital at the Wigmore Hall.
6   *Peter Abelard*, a novel by Irish writer Helen Waddell.
7   Opera by Bellini.
8   Novel by Jane Austen.

53 Pears to Britten

Hippodrome Theatre
<u>Coventry.</u>

[?15–17 June 1944]

My bee –

It was lovely having your letter this morning and I am sitting down right away to send one back to you with my love, my love and my love.

I had a fearful time on Monday when I arrived here trying to find digs and it wasn't until 8.30 that evening that I got somewhere, and pretty averagely boring it is – Tiny bed-room, & general living – dining room with a dog that persists, and flowers that make me sneeze! So I spend most of my day out and about! But what a life touring must be for the poor unfortunate chorus & orchestra – Everything must depend on their digs – If they are alright, then life is tolerable; if not, then life is unspeakable! I shall certainly stay in Hotels whenever I can – There's at least room to move about in! But there's no studio to practice in or anything!

I don't believe your opera stinks – I just don't believe it; anyway if it does, by all means be-Jeyes it, and have it as sweet as its writer for me when I see it. I shall definitely try to catch the 5.26 from here which is due at Euston at 7.50 on Saturday, so I may quite possibly hear you, & shall eat with you, & sleep with you!

I'm sorry you had such a hectic week end – I should like to have been there to have been shewn to my seat by you! Give Ursula my love & tell her to go away! I won't have you being badgered by people. In my digs of course I wake up to loud wireless at 8.0 & then news at 9.0, and I come home to news at 9.0 – though I must say noone really seems to be interested in the war as such – I think they would all like it ended at once. It must be too appalling across there just now & every town destroyed.

I will write to Johnny Amis about September 28th – I'm inclined to say yes to Kalmus, for Michael's [Tippett] sake apart from other things, as I couldn't really do another date till December & by then we shall probably be in the middle of our Band concerts, won't we? & we can always polish off a date for Johnny some other time say in December – I mean, for Johnny, we can do what we like & know, whereas we shall have to work at Berg & Mahler, nicht wahr?

Much much love to you.

I simply cannot make up my mind about the Gallery – We won't have too much time to work it, enough for a certain amount of newish –

Will this do:

Il mio tesoro (Don Giovanni)
Concert aria: Misero! o sogno o son desto (K. ?)   Mozart   ← Yes please!
                                                                          such a good one to
                                                                          begin with & you
                                                                          play it so well!

Am See
Ach! neige
Dass sie hier gewesen   Schubert.
Vom Mitleiden Mariä
Auflösung.

To the Motherland
Bright Night   Dweller   When you are old & grey   F.B.
W[ind] & Wave   Grieg   or   Goldenhair   [Frank
By the Stream   Adoration Go not happy day   Bridge]
A bird's cry   ? So perverse
The Hunter

54 Pears to Britten

[28 June 1944]

My own heart –

I miss you very very much – & it was heavenly to talk to you this morning – though it's just as well that you aren't here – Just before lunch a thing came to ground in the houses below St. J. W. Station in Finchley Rd opposite Wellington Court that big block of flats, & some of our windows went & there are some slight crackings in plaster etc – but nothing else – All the windows out in the High St.

But don't worry – I shall see you Saturday shan't I, & we'll have a lovely weekend together –

All my love, honey

P.

55 Britten to Pears

Old Mill, Snape.

June 29th 1944

Honey, my darling,

I am nearly crazy with worry about you – praying that you can get some sleep & arn't too worried. It is the bloodiest business and I can't wait to get you out of it all. What a curse about the windows: I do hope the damage isn't too great, & can be easily put right.

Things are nice here, but I've been having rather a difficult time. Work won't go well, & the news about Piers,[1] & worry about you & Barbara & all, is adding up to quite a depression. But it will all be dispelled on Saturday – & won't we enjoy yo ourselves!

I hope you called Sarton[2] about the records, & that Erwin has sent the Carol[3] ones on to St. Johns Wood as I asked him. It'll be nice to take them to Ludlow.

No more now, my darling: I love you more & more everyday, & long to see you. Hope the voice is as golden as ever!

All my love, & life,

Ben.

---

[1] Dunkerley, an old friend of Britten, was reported as missing in action.

[2] Harry Sarton (1906–51), Decca Records executive.

[3] *A Ceremony of Carols.*

56 Britten to Pears

<u>Old Mill</u>

July 12th. [1944]

My darling,

Not a sound, or a tinkle, from you so I thought I would scribble a hallo to you before I dash down to the post – having been writing over-due letters since lunch. How are you – my beautiful? I hope the journey was OK. & that you found rooms all right. Let me know <u>soon</u> where you are, because I loathe not knowing. I had a hectic day in London – those things around <u>all</u> day, with bumps & sirens galore – had lots to arrange, saw Ralph & fixed about P.G. at the Wells (I've written to Joan) – had to arrange about letters with Post office (Kay[1] is gone away); they're all being sent to Barbara (since we're going away from here soon, there didn't seem any other central address), & she's being posted with your address (<u>when</u> I know it!).

I've had a letter (crossing mine) from Ronnie O.kaying 22nd. Beth says she'll take Mrs. Neilson if the Wells don't open in London – as I shouldn't think they will.[2] But do let me know soon – & ring up, or write – because I <u>do</u> love you & want to hear from you, because I <u>miss</u> you – See – honey?

All my love.
B

---

[1]   Unidentified.
[2]   The Sadler's Wells Opera Company was in a quandary about returning to London due to aerial bombing.

57 Pears to Britten

[*Letterhead:* From PETER PEARS, ~~67 Hallam St. W. 1.~~   ~~Welbeck 9549~~]

Sunday [16 Jul 1944]
"   derland

My little sweet & honey bun –

Thank you very much for your letter – It was lovely to hear from you, & it was nice to talk to you & it will be nice too again in a little while, 'cos I'm going to ring you –

This place is dreary past all description; one wastes one's time in the biggest possible way – One rehearses 10–1 & 2.30–5.30 & is then tired & hasn't energy even to read – or else one does a show – But above all it shows me my own weakness in that when I have some hours to spare (a thing I have been longing for) I am too bored to think of anything! It's impossible to work, no piano, no room – &

it's impossible to do anything else without you, my boy & so you see I miss you – terribly – Never shall I tour again in this way! An occasional guest performance or tour – yes – but never weeks at a time.

How goes the opera? Well? I want to start work soon on P.G. I'm afraid it looks as if London season is on – only thing is Joan has written to Chris [Martin] that <u>if</u> we give up, can we evacuate to Dartington & rehearse there! – Nice idea!

Much love, my pigeon

P

Just been over to Durham – wonderful cathedral!

58 Britten to Pears

<u>Old Mill</u>

July 16th 1944

Honey darling,

I hope all is well with you. It was lovely to hear your voice yesterday – altho' we had so much beastly business to talk over. Don't worry about mail – it is turning up regularly at Barbara's already, & she only hasn't sent yours on because it was only printed matter, & any how she hadn't your exact address until yesterday. So don't be cross no more!

Well, your scene with the apprentice is going on well. It is difficult to do, & I get terribly upset ~~but~~ by what I'm creating, but it is nearly done, & I think will be good & effective. There's alot of stuff for you to get your teeth in to!

I can't write much to-day – it is the first warm day we've had, & Beth & the kids are going to take tea out & have a bathe at Iken; & if I can get enough of P.G. written I'm going with them.

Sorry that Sunderland is such a stinking hole. Never mind – not much longer, & we'll be together in Devon! Let me know as soon as you know your August plans, as I have to make various arrangements.

Be good, my honey – I miss you & long for you terribly.

All my love.

B.

59 Britten to Pears

Old Mill, Snape,
<u>Suffolk.</u>

Aug. 20th 1944

Honey darling,

Take care of yourself. Even if you feel fit, go slow. Don't rely on Sadlers Wells to look after you – after all they are most interested in their production. But rest all you can – don't count expence – eat well, & taxi often. I hope & pray you'll have a quiet time. I send you the Contract,[1] & a sweet note from Elizabeth – but I don't bother to enclose your mother's card as it isn't really any more than a hullo. Ring her sometime. Give her my love. This is only a scribble to send my love; I'll write later on in the week, & do ring up often because I'm on tenterhooks about you – <u>really</u>! All my love, my honey; I love you really & ~~truely~~ truly.

     B.

---

[1] To appear in *Peter Grimes*.

60 Britten to Pears

[?before 12 Oct 1944]

Honey darling,

So sorry to miss you on the 'phone this morning. I rang at about 10.30 thinking that you were going to be there all the morning to rehearse with Norman.[1] But Mrs. N. [Neilson] said you'd gone, so I didn't have the comfort of hearing your voice as I'd hoped – But I hope you'll be phoning one evening before too long. I'm writing this as I shan't be able to phone <u>you</u>, not knowing where you are.

I've phoned Ralph & written Joan saying that she will get her contract at once (she wrote me). Also about orchestra – I hope there's not going to be any hitch in <u>that</u> direction. The scoring's going quite fast – done about ⅔ prologue in a day & a half. Enid [&] Carol[2] here to-night. Montagu tomorrow morning. Hope it'll be quiet for them – we had an exciting evening, but I must say it's more bearable when you can see things happening – quite a fine firework display! I've started the Evening Hymn – what a piece that is! I've also fallen flat for Fairy Queen.[3] It's a marvel. But tell me, where can one find out the plot & dialogue? What's it all about – whence the Chin a man? Sadlers Wells <u>must</u> do it before long. I'll fix rehearsal with the Zorians[4] – preferably on Wed. aft. with me & Thursday morning at Northampton. Couldn't you possibly get there the evening or night before – or if you're coming on a sleeper – get off at Peterboro' & avoid the double journey? <u>Please</u> phone about this.

    Lots of love, my beloved one. Do rest & take it easy. Refuse all dates!   Your   B.

---

1   Accompanist Norman Franklin, with whom Pears gave a number of recitals for CEMA and the Friends War Relief Service.

2   Montagu and Enid Slater brought their daughter, Carol.

3   Britten completed realizations of both of these Purcell works.

4   Zorian String Quartet, led by violinst Olive Zorian (1916–65).

61 Pears to Britten

Newcastle

[16–18 Oct 1944]

My honey –

    These two letters for you. + a lot of love from me – Bless you!

    Staying at Durham – Heavenly place. Superb place – spent this morning on my knees in the Cathedral almost in tears – Somehow I find beauty nowadays almost too much. It's like Rejoice in the Lamb.

    That is still your best yet you know.

    Much much love   P

PTO

    Met Cyril Smith & Phyllis Sellick[1] here. Badly wanted copies of Scottish Ballad to play in Portugal in December – Can't get any satisfaction from Boosey & Hawkes – Couldn't you get 2 proof copies to them? Nice people!

    Love

        P.P.

---

1   Cyril Smith (1909–74) and Phyllis Sellick (1911–2007), husband and wife piano duo.

62 Britten to Pears

[after 19 Oct 1944]

Honey my darling,

    It was an oasis in a desert of loneliness to see you last week – yes I know one meets lots of people, & the house here couldn't be much fuller, but I only come alive when you're around, and things mean much more when we're together. However I've got so much to do (& so have you too, I know, yo wicked old thing careering around like this) that I hope the next fortnight will fly like the wind, & we'll be together in Shropshire anyhow for a night, & then the week in Bristol won't be so far off.

I had a valuable day in London – saw lots of people, worked with Montagu, Eric, Clifford (after his broadcast & dinner with him & Eddy, I went up to Highgate), Basil Wright[1] about the film,[2] & altogether got lots of things 'off'. Now I'm here, working at pressure with Arthur Oldham (he is very quick, & a great help) before Erwin comes tomorrow to chase me.

Take care of yourself, my honey darling, rest & don't work too hard. Everyone (even Ursula) seems to have liked the broadcast,[3] so forget that bloody man. All my love, for ever & ever.

Ring or write or something – please, soon.

        Love, love, xxxx

          Ben.

---

[1] (1907–87), documentary filmmaker. Produced and scripted *Night Mail* at the GPO Film Unit, for which Britten wrote the music.

[2] *Instruments of the Orchestra*. Britten's music from the film was published as *The Young Person's Guide to the Orchestra*.

[3] A CEMA recital given by Pears and Britten at St Matthew's in Northampton was broadcast on 19 October on the BBC Home Service.

63 Pears to Britten

[Incomplete – only the second half survives in the archive.]

& alive loveliness – I cannot tell you what the whole day was like – It was a most thrilling & moving day – We saw a seal close to, & a brief hail storm with gigantic lumps of hail smote us & the sun shone & the East wind blew & the Cheviot hills on the mainland looked too romantic – I wanted you to be there terribly – We must go there some day – Over everything, the feeling of tremendous historical events – Christianity in England practically started there – Northumberland is altogether a very remarkable part of the world. It has been such a joy having real exercise & getting away from towns I feel [*indecipherable*].

Will be ringing you tomorrow night & shall probably come down Wednesday night to London. See you Saturday next.

    Much much love – my bee, my heart

        Your P

64 Pears to Britten

[?late Oct 1944]

My own Putto –

It was heaven to see you & touch & taste. Without you I tend to the lowest depths of depression – another fortnight! – I'm going to try & see if I can't come back with you to Lancing, but it may not work – We'll see –

Here are some figures for you – On Sunday (i.e. tomorrow I will add one or two more about household expenses – Have we ever thought of asking Periton to get us off something for Mrs. N's [Neilson] keep & lodging – i.e. food & rent?

Much much love.

P

There's a tiny query about one commission. I <u>can't</u> make out whether it was charged or not – In any case, it would only be a question of ½ of 1£.9..3 or so.

65 Britten to Pears

Old Mill,
<u>Snape</u>

[28 Oct–2 Nov 1944]

My heart –

before I go further – please sit down <u>at once</u> and ~~right~~ write me a card to Yarner Farm, Dartington, nr. Totnes, saying where & when we are performing at Shrewsbury on Thursday – & also one to Esther too. <u>Please</u>, my dear, otherwise I'll have palpitations not knowing where or what to do.

Now – how are you? Not to dreadfully tired, I pray, & able to get abit of rest occasionally. How was Hiawatha?[1] How did 'he'd seen he said a …' whatever it was, go? (a good sentance that). I suppose you didn't get to Lucille [Wallace]. Maybe you'll go later.

Things are so-so here – Snape is rather licking its wounds after it's 'incident',[2] which has complicated people's lives abit. We've had the house full of Sievekings'[3] little relations – their house being uninhabitable. Poor Arthur Oldham's nice old lady (who'd fed him up with eggs & butter etc.) has all her windows in, and her ceilings down, & so he can't go <u>there</u> any more. Poor Beth, she has been worked terribly hard, helping people clear up too, & has had Erwin here ~~too~~ as well, is putting him up here. But I think it's probably a good thing I am away next week to give her some rest, & a chance for Jemima-James[4] to develop nicely. The kids of course are having a whale of a time, but my work has suffered abit – especially as Lennox's stuff had to go off in the middle of it all. I've sent off an arm chair to 45a as well, which we can spare from here.

Aunt Effie[5] died on ~~Tuesday~~ Wednesday – poor old thing, it was abit of a miserable end for her. But Barbara's been sweet, and comforting. It's a moral for one – a life entirely selfish ending up with only an unwilling family to care.

I had a tough evening ~~last night~~ yesterday – Arthur came by the 8.9 – no taxis could meet, & so I took out the Morris & the battery (again) conked, & I had to cycle in – wait for 40 mins at the station & walk out with him, arriving 10 pm! I slept like a log all night as a result.

Sophie's [Wyss] at it again – another long letter – including a nice lot of copies of press cuttings, showing how good she & I are together – the woman's a moron. How can a person be so daft? I must say my tolerance is wearing abit thin. My darling – only till Thursday now – it's getting near, isn't it. All my love. I'm writing a nice back-ground for you to sing against.

Be careful.

Your B.

¹   Samuel Coleridge-Taylor's cantata trilogy, *The Song of Hiawatha* (1900).
²   A 'doodle-bug' bomb had narrowly missed the Old Mill. (See *Letters* Vol. II, p. 1229.)
³   Lance Sieveking (1896–1972), BBC producer.
⁴   Beth was at this point several months pregnant with her third child, Rosemary (known affectionately as 'Roguey').
⁵   Euphemia Hockey (1876–1944), sister of Britten's mother, Edith.

66 Britten to Pears

Old Mill

Nov 8ᵗʰ 1944

My honey darling,

I hope you got the parcel. I sent it off on Monday – or rather I got the Neilson to do it, after having coped with Val Drewry.[1] I got back here on Tuesday, & on your advice, there's no one here this week, & I'm getting ahead with the Te Deum & Motet.[2] The former is going well, nothing very important, but slightly honey.

I hope things aren't going too badly with you – that you are able to cope with everything in your old inimitable way. I think of you every moment, & hate not to know what's happening exactly to you.

Is there a chance of you being able to get to London next week? It looks as if I shall be there from Wed. to Sat. (15–18) – since Charles Münch[3] of Paris Orch. is over here and doing the Variations [*on a Theme of Frank Bridge*] all over the place, & the only place I can catch it is at Wembley on Friday. But don't tire yourself, honeyest, because we'll be together in Bristol for quite abit. I had a nice ~~further~~

week-end at Lancing; had a long go at Jasper re Charles, & Charles re Jasper.[4] The boy is really a nice thing, & has an astounding really genuine musical mind. But whether he'll be a composer, the Lord knows.

I went to see Emmie Bass about the Dartington Festival, & she is writing to Joan re dates & things. As far as I can see, & she agreed, you & Joan are the only snags – all the rest can do it. So if you can work it – for Christopher [Martin]'s sake – or even one week of it – do please try. I'm writing to her direct about it.

I had a long 'go' with Eric on the opera – as far as I can see, you were quite wrong in your hunch, it was only Joan's nerves – because things are advancing rapidly from Eric's end – if only they can find a theatre. Eric is standing out against Princes for it – & rightly too.

Excuse scribble, my darling – but I only wanted to send my love, & wish you luck with the 'Child'.[5] Give Michael my love, & say how much I wish I was there for it. Sing nicely, as ever – & write or ring if you can possibly. I don't see why everyone else should hear your voice & me never———

Wystan has sent his book; the Tempest is <u>very difficult</u>, but got lovely bits. The Oratorio is as long and grand as ever.[6]

All my love how I wish I was with you.

B.

---

1   A friend of Lennox Berkeley. Berkeley was in the process of moving from the Old Mill, Snape.
2   The *Festival Te Deum* and 'motet' (chorale) for the radio programme *Poet's Christmas* (see Letter 69).
3   (1891–1968), French conductor.
4   Jasper Rooper (1898–1981), then Director of Music at Lancing College; Charles Dakin, a pupil.
5   Pears was performing in Michael Tippett's oratorio *A Child of our Time*.
6   Auden's *For the Time Being: A Christmas Oratorio* (1944), which also contained 'The Sea and the Mirror: A Commentary on Shakespeare's *The Tempest*'. Auden had intended that Britten should set the oratorio.

67 Pears to Britten

Theatre Royal
Glasgow.

[8–9 Nov 1944]

My own B –

It was completely heavenly seeing you & working with you – Work with you is totally different in kind from any other sort – It becomes related to life immediately, which is more than any of the other stuff I do, does (including "Così")[1] – And being with you was being alive instead of half dead – Thank you so much, honey.

Now have I got to wait until Bristol? I wonder if I can slip back for the 15ᵗʰ – Don't rely on it, but among other things, we ought to do some work at the Debussy[2] for Dec. 10ᵗʰ. I have written to Felix[3] retracting the Lutenists. I don't really think they fit in, & besides we must concentrate on Debussy & Folk Songs –

Much much love

Take care of yourself

P.

The enclosed may please you.

---

[1] Pears sang Ferrando in Mozart's *Così fan tutte* with Sadler's Wells in the 1944–45 season.
[2] They were to perform *Trois Poèmes de Stéphane Mallarmé* and *Trois Ballades de François Villon* at the Wigmore Hall in a concert with the Zorian String Quartet.
[3] Aprahamian (1914–2005), concert promoter and music critic.

68 Britten to Pears

[*Postcard:* images of Aldeburgh]

<u>Old Mill.</u>

[?7 Nov 1944]

I forgot to say in my other letter that I've heard the new Serenade 'takes' – & they are terrific. The Dirge especially is a really super bit of singing, & Orch: & Dennis are also fine. I'm abit worried about the matching tho'. Erwin's flat has been drenched as the house caught fire, but luckily the P.G. score is safe. Thanks for your letter – I'm glad about A.K.H.![1]

Sing nicely

Love Ben.

---

[1] A.K. Holland, music critic of the *Liverpool Daily Post*.

69 Britten to Pears

[11 Nov 1944]

Honey darling – it was heaven hearing you last night after all this long time – much too long. I ache for you.

I am just this moment off to town – to make this ruddy speech which is giving me the creeps! However – no one really expects me to be able to speak so I suppose it doesn't really matter! I wonder what you'll think of the Te Deum. the Eddy bits – I've done 2 as they were so tiny. The last will, I believe, make you smile.[1]

So glad about everything. Sing better & better – & my God there'll be a part for you in the Oratorio! It's a superb piece.

The enclosed letter came this morning – can you ~~answer her~~ find time to scribble a note to her.

All my love – my darling
                                          B.

---

[1]   Britten composed two motets on texts from Auden's *For the Time Being: A Christmas Oratorio*: 'Chorale (after an Old French Carol)' and 'A Shepherd's Carol (Oh lift your little pinkie)' for the BBC radio programme *Poet's Christmas* produced by Edward Sackville-West, which was broadcast on 24 December 1944.

70 Britten to Pears

Old Mill,
Snape,
Suffolk.

Nov 20ᵗʰ 1944

Honey darling,

Such ages since I heard from you or of you. Where are you; how's everything going; and above all, <u>are</u> you going to be able to get to London next Friday, as I am planning to be there too, & longing, longing for it?

Lots has happened since we spoke – I've been in London, had a mad rushed time, did 200 things in 3 days, got back here mid-day Saturday, with Eddy – had a nice week-end, & now I'm back at the score again. As I told you I got the Te Deum & 2 Motets done, & they're now in the hands of printers & copyists etc.

My speech went quite well – I spoke about 10 minutes, without notes, about necessary of travel for young artists – not as well as I'd hoped, but better than I feared. What I found was that I could think when I was standing on my hind-legs which I'd always doubted. It was a pretty putrid show otherwise – the bright spot being of all people Stephen Spender, who was surprisingly nice & sympathetic.

I stayed those 3 days with Barbara – killing 2 birds – giving the Steins room, and letting them get their furniture in place (it looks very nice now), & also being with poor old Barbara who's not at all well – running a permanent temperature, & D&V.[1] Nerves alone I think.

Then there was a dinner given by the French Ambassador for Charles Munch[2] which I had to go to – very posh, (he sent <u>his car</u> for me as I had to be late!! – I'd forgotten what it felt like to glide through the London streets in a thing that size! Rather dull people there, but Mlle Nicole Henriot[3] was nice, & he's a real charmer – <u>and</u> a damn good conductor, as I found the next night at Wembley. The L.P.O. isn't so hot an orch. but he made them play wonderfully, & had a very good idea of the piece. I believe the piece was wonderful when played by the BBC under him – did you hear it? It seems to have made quite a sensation around the place – & I must say I thought bits of it had worn well. I've been asked to conduct the LP.O in the Sinfonia [*da Requiem*] on Jan 6th – on the strength of this, I think. Russell[4] was all over me.

I also saw Clifford, Peter Cox & had a long meeting with Eric. I gather things are moving towards Covent Garden abit – but the betting's on P.G. at Sadlers Wells, I think now. The reproduced vocal score is <u>lovely</u>! Most beautifully written & reproduced.

Kit was here too for the week-end – & most surprisingly Eddy clicked well with him & Beth – & we had a pleasant week-end altogether. He has got nice things about him – & with me is very simple and intelligent. We <u>walked</u> over to Iken Rectory – burgled the house, & inspected it thoroughly – & it has such <u>immense</u> possibilities that I've found out the agent & written to him. It is the most divine spot, & the house isn't half bad. So there – my honey – see what love can do.

Please excuse hurry, but I've got to get on with score. Michael's sick that you can't do Dec. 24th with Liverpool Phil. when he conducts the Child.[5] I s'pose you can't get out of the Messiah?

I can scarcely wait till Friday. I'm seeing about hotel for Bristol – possibly Wed. Thursday – 1 train.

All my love.   Ben
            Love you, darling.

---

[1]   Gastrointestinal upsets.
[2]   Munch conducted the BBC Symphony Orchestra in a performance of the *Variations on a Theme of Frank Bridge* on 15 November.
[3]   Henriot-Schweitzer (1925–2001), French pianist who performed Liszt's Piano Concerto no. 1 in the same programme.
[4]   Thomas Russell (1902–84), violist and secretary of the London Philharmonic Orchestra.
[5]   Michael Tippett wanted Pears to sing in a performance of his oratorio *A Child of our Time* (he had sung in the premiere in March), but Pears was already booked for Handel's *Messiah*.

III

'I don't know why we should be so lucky, in all this misery'

JULY 1945 TO APRIL 1949

Although the war officially ended in Europe in 1945 on 8 May, its effects nonetheless persisted. The Allied victory brought rejoicing and an end to the nightly blackouts, the constant whine of sirens and the threat of air raids, but the return to 'normal' life was tempered by the scale of devastation and a profound sense of loss. Britten and Pears were among the fortunate, having come through the war unharmed. Moreover, they were able to carry on with their music-making. Britten had time to compose, largely uninterrupted, giving him the space needed to work on *Peter Grimes*.

He completed the opera, still under the shadow of war, in February 1945. Rehearsals began almost immediately and despite some tensions that arose around the work's suitability for the reopening of Sadler's Wells, there was in the press a sense of excitement about the prospect of an English opera by an English composer. *Grimes* was premiered on 7 June and propelled Britten and Pears to new heights, solidifying their reputations both at home and abroad. In July 1945 the composer embarked on a tour with violinist Yehudi Menuhin to play for the survivors at Bergen-Belsen and other German concentration camps. Upon witnessing the most appalling consequences of the war, he acknowledged his and Pears's good fortune, mixed with a sense of guilt and disbelief: 'I don't know why we should be so lucky, in all this misery' (Letter 72).

Ultimately, their efforts to produce *Grimes* and the operas that followed led to the founding of their own opera company in December 1946, the English Opera Group (EOG) and the Aldeburgh Festival of Music and the Arts (1948), in which their musical partnership was a central focus. The Festival was Pears's idea, the fruit of discussions following a financially disastrous July 1947 tour by the EOG to Holland and Switzerland, in which the group lost around £3,000. In response, Pears brought up the idea of a homegrown festival: 'Why not make our own festival? A modest Festival with a few concerts given by friends? Why not have an Aldeburgh Festival?'[1] The questions were timely, for the EOG was in need of a home base. Furthermore, a

Festival of their own gave them the means to showcase Britten's music, Pears's voice and the work of friends who could match their own high standards.

As the shroud of war lifted, the two began to establish an international fame as recital partners, even as Pears was furthering his reputation as an interpreter of the Evangelist in Bach's Passions (particularly the *St Matthew Passion*) as well as Bach's cantatas, and of the tenor arias in Handel's *Messiah*. Their success, both individually and jointly, opened up further opportunities for performing. Britten's compositions during this productive period included chamber operas *The Rape of Lucretia* and *Albert Herring*, song cycle *The Holy Sonnets of John Donne*, large-scale concert works *Saint Nicolas* and the *Spring Symphony*, as well as folk-song arrangements and realizations of Henry Purcell – 'our Purcell' as Britten writes in Letter 82. Many of the new works were written for Pears, but the composer was also inspired by other performers and friends such as Kathleen Ferrier and Nancy Evans. Pears came under increasing demand as a soloist, having been engaged on a semi-permanent basis by groups in Amsterdam, Edinburgh and Liverpool.

Many of the letters from this period, which date from 1945 until April 1949 as they leave on a recital tour of Italy and Belgium, are noteworthy for the critiques that Pears makes of other performers. Comments on other musicians frequently appear, some of whom evidently fall short of his own exacting standards. Pears is critical in his evaluations of the Bach *St Matthew Passion* performances in which he took part in Holland. Britten, too, could be particularly harsh about other tenors (he reserves his worst for a tenor also known for the role of Bach's Evangelist in Letter 85), but always in the service of elevating and reassuring Pears. At one point, he goes so far as to compare him to the great tenors of the previous generation (Gigli and Schipa), noting, 'there's nothing they've got you haven't', even as he prods him to continue to improve (Letter 120).

Pears obviously still harboured doubts about his singing, despite his success. Britten recognised his uncertainties and made continued efforts to encourage him. The singer travelled to New York in mid-October for a series of lessons with Clytie Mundy, who convinced him to rethink certain aspects of his technique, making suggestions that were both physically and mentally taxing (see Letter 96). Pears expresses how much he misses Britten during his time in New York, yet we begin to see glimpses of a mature artist, as when he writes in Letter 88 'Performances are really the only sure way of getting to know a work, even though it may take many years to get it quite right.' Despite the success of *Grimes*, Britten also faced difficulties. Uncertain he would be able to reach such heights again, he confessed he often found it hard to make a start or even to find the right notes as work progressed. He described these problems to Pears as he began composing *The Rape of Lucretia*, the first of his chamber operas: 'It is loathesome starting pieces – I always regret that I'm not a coal heaver or bus-driver and not have to depend on things you can't control' (Letter 77).

As their reputations grew, so too did the demands on their talents. Pears often worried that Britten was working himself to exhaustion, and his fears were realised in December 1948. They were scheduled to undertake a tour in Holland but Britten became ill with a suspected stomach ulcer and had to cancel after only a couple of performances. He was thrown into a panic over feelings that he had let Pears down, and eventually suffered a bout of depression, revealing in several letters that he was 'at the bottom of the well' and that only a letter from the absent Pears had temporarily bolstered his mood. He was ordered to rest for three months, and so in January 1949 Pears took him to Italy in hopes that the depression would lift, but unfortunately it soon came back. Upon their return Pears urged him to change his work habits to allow for what he described as more 'breathing spaces', writing, 'One should see lovely things unworried – I insist that this is the last year that you are worried outside your work – Your work must got [sic] slower – we are getting older, my B.' (Letter 119). Finally in March Britten's depression began to abate; he returned to composing, and a notable sense of relief becomes apparent as he informs Pears 'my happiest & most treasured memory is of the wonderful peace & contentment of your love & friendship' (Letter 121) and reveals that he is happily working again: 'I had a good mornings work – tra-la, trala' (Letter 123).

In late August 1947, Britten and Pears moved to 4 Crabbe Street in Aldeburgh, an expansive semi-detached house with numerous windows overlooking the North Sea. Here they took on Barbara Parker, a local resident, as housekeeper for the first few years. Also for a time, Britten's friend Eric Crozier (who collaborated with the composer on a number of works as librettist) occupied the attic room. The Festival was already in the planning stages when the move took place. As Letter 79 indicates, Britten and Pears had achieved the status of local celebrities, and they felt the need to guard their privacy. The views from the house, particularly Britten's study, were stunning and the garden gate offered easy access to the seafront, Crag Path, and sea bathing, an essential activity for the composer. Captivated by the seascape, he shares his enthusiasm in his letters to Pears. For example, he responds to Pears's description of New York as 'the ugliest place in the world' (Letter 90) where there is a 'metallic taste in the mouth on the streets all the time' (Letter 94) with an effusive account of his view from Crag Path: 'big racing clouds, lots of bright sun, & the gigantic waves all white' (Letter 95). Aldeburgh, it would seem, was the idyllic setting, a place of inspiration as well as escape from the busy metropolis and with the advent of the Festival it provided an ideal opportunity for Britten and Pears to work together for a concentrated period of time. Both felt that their partnership was the most important thing – Britten writes in December 1948, 'I do adore working with you, & think we really achieve something together' (Letter 107).

---

1   Eric Crozier, 'The Origin of the Aldeburgh Festival', p. 6.

71 Britten to Pears

45A

[?22 Jul 1945]

My darling,

This's only a scribbled note because I'm very sleepy, haven't practiced the old Kreutzer[1] at all, & want to go to bed soon.

I hope the journey wasnt too bad, & also that you arn't too lonely. It was bloody that you had to go off – we all felt miserable at leaving you, but none so miserable as I! But Joan will be arriving to-morrow, & that won't be so bad. See alot of her – she loves you dearly & needs you.

I slept till 10.30 (after drugs!) this morning, & spent most of the morning in bed. This afternoon at the British Council working out the records & casting.[2] Eric is going to be engaged by them as producer to manage everything. So things are under control. He's seeing Peter Cox to-morrow too. We plan opening May or June, with the New Op. Co.

Well, honey darling, I go off to-morrow 3.0. Pray for me. I only hope Yehudi [Menuhin][3] remains nice. How I wish it were you! However – it isn't for long, & it can't be as bad as I imagine!

Take great care of yourself, my darling. You know how I love you, & believe in you.

Bless you.

All my love,

B.

---

1   Violin sonata by Beethoven.
2   A proposed recording of *Peter Grimes* which never came to fruition.
3   Britten was travelling to Germany with the violinist for a series of performances in concentration camps. Despite having been liberated, the inmates of the camps were held effectively in quarantine until they could be released safely.

72 Britten to Pears

Old Mill,
Snape,
Suffolk

August 1st 1945

My own darling,

It was heaven to hear your voice after this mad week. I was terribly disappointed that you didn't call last night, & had given up hope until your wire at 8.0 this morning, & you at 8.45! I do so hope this lousy tour isn't being too hellish for you – don't take any notice of those ludicrous fools – they couldn't matter less. Just sing as well as you can, & spend the time with Joan & Laurence & Reggie[1] – & think alot about next week when you'll be here! It seems ages since you left on that hideous train – & what a gloomy crowd of us meandered across Regents Park home! I can't tell you all about the trip now as we are going off to Aldeburgh in a moment & I want to post this before I go. (I've been lazy this morning & corrected proofs in bed – & only just got up!). Yehudi was nice, & under the circumstances the music was as good as it could be – with all that travelling all over the country & two, & sometimes three concerts a day. We travelled in a small car over bad roads, & got hopelessly lost often. But we saw heavenly little German villages, with sweetest people in them (I swear that the Teutons are the most beautiful (& cleanest) race on earth), & we saw completely destroyed towns (like Münster) which haven't been cleared up & yet have over 20,000 people (looking just as clean as ever) living, God knows where, in them. And then on the other side there were the millions of D.P's (displaced persons) in, some of them, appalling states, who could scarcely sit still & listen, & yet were thrilled to be played to. We stayed the night in Belsen, & saw over the hospital – & I d̶ needn't describe that to you. On the whole, the Military Government seems to be doing a good job, & not as brutal or callous as one might fear – but o – what insoluble problems. It was good to be able to do even this minute bit – & I'm determined to do it again, & to organise other things too. Unnra[2] (under whom we were), British Council, & Emmie are all going to help.

Honey darling — I want to see yo so badly. And to tell yo all. But it isn't too bad, to wait till next week, when some of these people han to wait for ever for their beloveds. I don't know why we should be so lucky, in all this misery.

Honey darling – I want to see you so badly. And to tell you all. But it isn't too bad, to wait till next week, when some of these people have to wait for ever for their beloveds. I don't know why we should be so lucky, in all this misery.

Plans are going ahead for the Opera Company – Dartington is fixed, Tennants[3] are extremely interested, & Ronnie has a man with money. Rosemary[4] is in Hospital already (thanks to old Barbara). Ronnie is coming here this week-end, & I expect most week-ends too.

Take all the care in the world of yourself darling. I hope to have something to show you when you get here.

And all, all, my love.

      B.

---

[1] Joan Cross and conductors Lawrance Collingwood (1887–1992) and Reginald Goodall (1901–90).

[2] United Nations Relief and Rehabilitation Agency.

[3] H.M. Tennent, theatrical agency.

[4] Rose-Marie, wife of Ronald Duncan, who contracted tuberculosis.

73 Pears to Britten

Royal Hotel
Bangor

Saturday [4 Aug 1945]

My own honey bee

I got your darling letter yesterday afternoon – It was so heavenly to have it and I read it over and over again – The days are going very quickly really and I shall soon be with you – How I wish it was tomorrow – My whole being longs to be with you, my darling – to feel you and hear you and look at you – I want to hear all about Germany – Your letter makes one hope, in spite of all the horror.

We went down to Dublin on Tuesday morning (you were already back, thank God, – I had your wire on Monday) until Wednesday evening, and I must say it was like a breath of heaven – no war – no bombs – smart brightly painted house, young people in tweeds and summer frocks instead of uniforms, and any amount of good food – We all built ourselves up like mad, & even Ulster food which is better than English, seems very dull. The Free State are being very good about Europe too, they were sending over 300 milch cows & many tons of sugar to Belgium while we were there (though they are short of sugar in Eire too).

It's very Catholic of course, and there are beggars & extreme poverty, but they are comparatively free – The worst are the English landed gentry with hard voices like my sister! (Honey! love you!) We are coming to Belfast on March 2nd you & I, & Dublin is open-armed to us – They have done the Serenade & Les Illuminations (though there's only a tiny Group of lively music lovers) & I suggested that we should go down & do Les Ill. & you conduct it?! However let's wait & see. (Bee! love you!)

We see very little of the rest of the Company – Anna Pollak[1] came to Dublin with us, she's very sweet & her Dorabella is a lot better – She could be very useful to us in small ways She would do anything & is mad keen & adores us – I told her a little & she would come at the drop of a hat. There are one or two other good singers in the Chorus, intelligent sweet & mad keen; I think we could get pretty well anyone we wanted. All very exciting. Roderick Jones[2] spoke to me last night again saying how sick he was at not being able to record Grimes, genuinely sick, I think, but Legge[3] wouldn't let him go, & these people are like Edmund[4] – they daren't cut off from a sure job yet. (Bunch! bee!)

I could go on writing and writing and don't really know or care what I'm writing about (Honey!) because you're back and I'm going to see you in a week (my boy!) it's a week a whole bloody week seven days 168 hours 10080 minutes God knows how many seconds (my beloved) & then my own darling I shall be with you close to you my lovely boy & you will have all of me your lover

your self

P

---

1   (1912–96), mezzo-soprano; would later sing Bianca in the first production of *The Rape of Lucretia*. Dorabella is a role in Mozart's *Così fan tutte*.
2   (1910–92), baritone who sang Balstrode in the first production of *Peter Grimes*.
3   Walter Legge (1906–79), at the time administrator with Sadler's Wells Opera Company.
4   Donlevy, baritone, sang Ned Keene in *Peter Grimes*.

74 Pears to Britten

Bangor

[?4–5 Aug 1945]

My honey fudge,

This is only a little note written late at night in bed to tell you that I love you in spite of the rather surly way you answered the telephone this morning, and that you are a sweety pie, and I suppose you expect me to write you letters all the time – but what about I should like to know – The weather? It is fine but windy – The food?

It is plentiful and good – The people? They are young and beautiful –

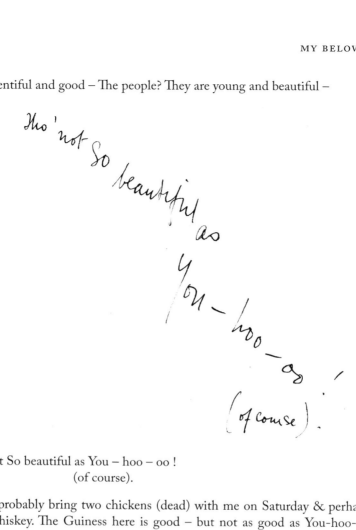

Tho' not So beautiful as You – hoo – oo !
　　　　　　　(of course).

I shall probably bring two chickens (dead) with me on Saturday & perhaps some Irish whiskey. The Guiness here is good – but not as good as You-hoo-oo! Bee! Love!
　　　　P.

75 Pears to Britten

Royal Hotel
<u>Bangor</u>

Sunday [5 Aug 1945]

My own beloved darling –
　　This is only the fragment of a note to welcome you back and tell you that I have missed you and wanted you terribly all the time – I do so hope you have taken care of yourself and haven't had too ghastly experiences – Life is awful here without you

and I can't bear the thought of another fortnight of it – Joan is very sweet but very much a woman – and I'm not interested in women – only one man & I rather think you know who that is – !

I'll ring you up on Tuesday morning early in hope of getting you – Monday night I am on in "B.B."[1] so won't have much chance to get you except perhaps at 6.30 or so.

I shall come back over Friday night August 10th via Stranraer.

Much much love to you

     My own B.

       P.

---

[1] Pears was performing in Smetana's *The Bartered Bride*.

76 Britten to Pears

Old Mill.

Bank Sunday [6 Aug 1945]

My darling –

Thank you for your sweet note – it was heavenly to get it & to have it. It has made these three dreary weeks more bearable. But we are now into the last week – thank God. I can't wait till you're here. It's looking so beautiful and the weather's so perfect. I hope all this horrible vaccination will be over when you arrive – not that it's bad now, but I can't bathe, & I want so badly to bathe with you –

Your voice has just come over the telephone. I feel sick that you're alone this week-end, but it won't be too long –

Ronnie, Kit, Barbara & Helen are all here. It's quite smooth. I am very fond & impressed by Ronnie – & we are discussing the opera hard. I think we can make Lucretia into a lovely piece – with you & Joan as such commentators! My other work is slowly going ahead – but I'm abit weary, & can't get down to much yet. But it's heaven to deal with Donne[1] instead of Montagu!

Excuse the shortness of this, but we're just off for a picnic, & the other's are shouting. I've found a wonderful Bach fugue (independant) for key-board (A minor, very fast).

All my love, darling.   B.

---

[1] Britten was composing his *Holy Sonnets of John Donne* and was ill from vaccinations he had before touring the concentration camps.

77 Britten to Pears

Please don't forget my sleeping pills – necessary companions at this moment!

Old Mill
<u>Snape</u>

Jan. 26th 1946

My honey darling,

Well – I've taken the plunge and old Lucretia is now on the way. I started last night and I've now written most of the first recitative before the drinking song. I think it'll be alright but I always have cold feet at this point. It is loathesome starting pieces – I always regret that I'm not a coal heaver or bus-driver and not have to depend on things you can't control. Perhaps it's as well you won't be coming here this week-end, when I should badger you for encouragement that perhaps you wouldn't feel up to giving! Now I shall have to rely on my self – always a risky business. Esther was here last night – & was very sweet & helped Beth with her W.I.[1] problems a great deal. She is a really sympathetic & intelligent person, & I'm devoted to her. She got on well with Beth, who thoroughly approved of her! Of course we talked alot about you (my favourite pastime), & she, like me, is nicely prejudiced which makes it so easy.

I'm afraid I talked to her abit about Park Crescent (knowing that you'd once talked to her about a similar problem), & she confirmed my feeling that, ideal as the place may be, we must be very cautious – unless we want yet another move in six months time after a quarrel which would be a thousand pities. Couldn't Joan have that maisonette, & we go across the road? But I'll trust you absolutely, old thing, do what you feel – but do it with your eyes open.

I miss you just enormously, & get crashingly bored with myself. Still it's got to be, & I've got to get on with the piece. How goes Grimes? <u>Do</u> take care, & if you have a vestige of temperature – go straight to bed. All my love, my darling, I love you

B.

---

[1] Women's Institute.

78 Britten to Pears

Old Mill,
Snape.

[?Spring 1946]

Honey darling,

Here is the lame-duck letter [unknown enclosure]. If you have a moment write & say hallo to him – he needs cheering I think, & seems to have fastened himself on you!

Everyone is thrilled with the concert. I miss you more than I can say. I am abit frizzled up with Lucretia – but am ploughing away at the score.

We've ordered 15 fruit trees for your orchard. I've told Tony Meyer yes to the good wishes. Are you coping with the Magazine & Davenport?

Nicholas,[1] the mutt, rang up for the programme for Lugano today!!

Hope you arn't too cold. It's bitter here. But I've just had ersatz sun in Sax. to make up for it.

Love you, darling love you.

B

What are we going to do about Aldenham School?[2] Do you feel like going for 25 Guineas? What'll Emmie say?

---

[1] Choveaux – occasional secretary to Britten and employed by Boosey & Hawkes.
[2] In Hertfordshire.

✠✠✠

Surprisingly, only two letters from 1946 have survived, possibly because Britten and Pears were working closely together for productions of *Peter Grimes* at Sadler's Wells, in Sweden and in Switzerland, where they also took time for a month's holiday in May to early June. Britten's new opera, *The Rape of Lucretia*, completed in early May, was premiered at Glyndebourne in July and then toured abroad. After a further recital tour of the UK and the Netherlands, Britten began work on his next opera, *Albert Herring*, in December, which also marked the official founding of the English Opera Group (EOG). He and Pears toured extensively in the first half of 1947: to Switzerland, Belgium, the Netherlands, Sweden, Denmark and Italy. They also worked together on productions of *Peter Grimes* in Germany in March, and *The Rape of Lucretia* in Basel in June, as well as the premiere of *Albert Herring* in June. They then went with the EOG to Holland (for the Festival) and Lucerne, Switzerland with *Lucretia* and *Herring* in July and August. Upon their return, they moved into Crag House on the Aldeburgh seafront, and Britten revels in describing its delights.

✠✠✠

79 Britten to Pears

[*Letterhead:* ~~The Old Mill, Snape~~]

Crag House,
Aldeburgh.

Sept 4th 1947

My darling,

It is a heavenly day – the wind has gone round to the West, & the sea is as still as a mill-pond. I'm sitting in the study (?) – upstairs, right in the window in the hot sun. I have to go round to the bank with Barbara [Parker] to arrange about accounts, & to the electricians to see about the removal of all those pimples all over the ceiling in the big room, in a few moments – but I wanted to get a note off to you by the week-end to remind you of the things you already know so well.

Little David[1] went off yesterday morning – rather sadly, poor little thing. His home life is hell, but I think his existance has been made a little brighter by being treated properly for a few days. Barbara was sweet to him, & he poured his heart out to me – rather self consciously, but the old feelings were genuine, I'm sure. Eric came last night, & its lovely having him here. We've already bathed twice – cold sea, but wonderfully clean & refreshing after those stuffy Swiss lakes. I've also got Lionel,[2] & his mother & three pathetic sisters installed in boarding-houses all over the town – but eating at that nice Crabbe house where we had that party last year.

I saw Marjorie[3] yesterday afternoon – she isn't well, bad lumbago – but I think the "Festival Idea" has cheered her – she thinks it the idea of the century, & is full of plans & schemes. We haven't yet been over the Jubilee Hall, but I'm full of hopes. Do you know she got 390 in for our concert last year? Even if we have to cut it to 300, that isn't quite so hopeless economically as we feared.

Beth comes over to-day for lunch with kids. I'm afraid this sounds horribly like just a holiday – but it isn't so really, because I'm getting down to the Quarles[4] & planning the [Spring] Symphony, talking over St. Nicholas & Herring with Eric etc. etc., quite like work – but everything in this place is pleasurable. It must sound beastly to you – but I hope Edinburgh isn't being too nasty for you, & that there aren't too many functions which you have to attend which are boring or embarrassing.

I suppose Illuminations is to-day – & then just the Mahler & then – Aldeburgh![5] I can't wait to get you here! Lots of decisions on curtains paints, furniture to be made. I'm afraid this weather can't last – but it probably had better not, if we're to get any food at all next winter.

If you see the Mauds – give them my love – we can probably arrange to see Humphrey before he goes to school on 18th or 19th. Poor kid – I'm sorry for him, what a nightmare new places are.

I've already been to see the nice friendly town-clerk about making our address Crabbe Street – I think it can be managed! Everyone is all of a titter to have us here – & I think it's going to be fairly sick-making if we don't take a strong line about not seeing chaps & going out. Barbara is being pestered with invitations to bring Mr. Britten to tea to meet dear Mrs. so-&-so who's <u>so</u> musical. But she's being very firm.

All my love, my dearest. Sing nicely – don't let Walter[6] worry you by his slop. My love to Kathleen. <u>Don't</u> try & sing too loudly.

Come here quick, because I <u>think</u> you'll like it.

      Your devoted B

<hr>

1   Spenser, sang Harry in *Albert Herring*.
2   Billows (1909–2004), of the British Council.
3   Margaret Spring-Rice (1887–1970), a neighbour of Britten from Snape, was active in the development of the Festival.
4   Britten's *Canticle I: My Beloved is Mine*, with a text by Francis Quarles.
5   Pears was at the 1st Edinburgh Festival, singing *Les Illuminations* and Mahler's *Das Lied von der Erde* with Kathleen Ferrier.
6   Bruno Walter (1876–1962), German-born conductor.

80 Britten to Pears

[*Letterhead:* ~~The Old Mill, Snape~~]

                                        Crag House,
                                       <u>Aldeburgh.</u>

                                    [?4–12 Sep 1947]

My darling,

    It was heavenly, and a great relief after these long days of silence, to hear your voice last night. I am very glad you are enjoying yourself quite abit, more at any rate than you thought. I am glad also that the festival is being such a success – congratulate Rudi[1] from me. Next year he must engage us properly, & the Group too! Don't worry about the Mahler – I hope you'll get lots of rehearsal & get used to the excitement of singing with the orchestra, because if you <u>do</u> relax I'm sure you can get it over perfectly. I'll listen, all ears, to it. I hope to goodness it comes over well.

I've been working all the morning all though the sea's looking tantalising –
there's quite a stiff breeze, & the waves look grand in the sun, & the swimmers
very pretty! But as I'm going to Lesley's to-morrow I have to get some work on the
Quarles done. I wonder how it will turn out.

Eric has started S. Nicholas & it looks good – I think he's developing well as
a poet – & very settable. I've given him the Creation[2] as a model – a good one, I
think.

I'm writing this scribble because it is so difficult to phone at that house – small
room, smell of cooking, & people over-hearing. But all the same I'll telephone
when I get back from the Broads to see how you are & tell you about it all!

Barbara P. says that we can use almost any size or shape or colour of curtain, if
you're buying 2nd hand complete curtains. But if you're buying <u>new</u> stuff to go in
the big room (the most urgent need!) – she'll put in some measurements to guide
you at the end of this. The colour of the carpet at the moment in there (a new one
B. bought) is a lightish blue. The walls will be white with an offness of pink. The
greatest need otherwise is lamp shades, table lamps & above all standard lamps as
the lighting system now is dotty.

Much love, my darling – longing to hear you, but above all to see you next week
& to be with you … I miss you, most dreadfully.

Your devoted
<u>B.</u>

---

1   Rudolf Bing (1902–97), organiser of the Edinburgh Festival.
2   Oratorio by Haydn.

81 Britten to Pears

Buswell's Hotel,
<u>Dublin.</u>

[Dec 1947]

My darling –

I hope this will catch you in between journeys, or at any rate before the
week-end. But I'm not sure, because I'm certain that Irish Posts are as dotty &
casual as everything else here – & letters may take ages.

I've been thinking lots about you – considering now you are getting on – how
the Messiah feels after all this time, & whether you stayed in York, or Lincoln,
& if you got a decent hotel to stay in. We have found this simple, pleasant place
thro' Reggie Ross Williamson – friend of John P. & Lionel – who is attached to
the Ministry, Legation, or whatever, here – it is immediately opposite to the <u>Dail</u>

– you'll probably remember. We had a pretty stinking journey over – no heating in train to Holyhead – when we arrived hours late (at 3.45) & a fearsomely rough crossing, when I was not sick, but sleep was impossible because one was so knocked about. But it was worth it, & we're spending quiet days, walking around, looking at book shops, gossiping & oh – how we eat! Jammet's is on top if it's form, tho' expensive – & the Dolphin (where we eat once when we were here before – do you remember) gave us a terrific lunch. We stay here till Saturday & then we go down to near Arcklow, Shelton Abbey Hotel, which is a converted private house owned by one Lord Wicklow, friend of John P. & John Betchiman.[1] It seems to be a nice spot, & Reggie R.-W. is going to drive us down on Saturday morning.

Life here seems much the same as it was – shops <u>filled</u> with things, & prices lower than in England. Poverty seems enormous; I'd forgotten what <u>real</u> rags on people look like, & find it heart-bleeding. The infinite number of dirty & charming small boys is moving – do you remember? – selling papers, violets, or God-knows-what. If we can buy things to bring back, we don't yet know, but I believe the customs are strict to a degree. Dismal as life is in England now, I find this terrific difference between rich & poor (& the rich are now very rich, because of the boom in visitors) even more dismal – very old fashioned.

My dearest old thing – I hope all goes well with you, that the voice is functioning as it should, & that you don't find sitting thro' Messiahs, or coping with lousy conductors too tiring. Give my love to Dr. John I.,[2] & sing his indulgences lusciously for him – you'll be giving him the thrill of his life, I know. Let him talk to you after, it'll give him fun, & be amusing besides ......!

Don't be depressed about the Schöne Müllerin.[3] It <u>wasn't</u> bad, & I'm sorry I was so stinking to you. Let it be a lesson to us, <u>not</u> to work in these conditions again. One programme – wider spaced-out. Let's think again about the Holland & other programmes; let's be firm about them. But please, just because I'm a nervy, & upsetting bed fellow, don't give me up & take to J.I. or H.S.;[4] I think in my wasp manner I'm good for you in some ways, & if conditions are better we can do <u>really</u> good performances, not just serious & tasteful ones. By-the-way, Eric suggests we get Meili[5] in for one of our Wigmore recitals. What do you think? Did you see, lying around, the dicerning note from George Barnes about our programme with him?

All my love, my darling – sing nicely. Give my love to Humph & Jean if you see them. And to Boyd [Neel] too.

We should get back fairly early on Tuesday morning, so don't lock up the front-door. Lovely as this holiday is, I yearn to get back to you again – & miss you most dreadfully. We scarcely have a meal without saying – "what a pity Nancy & Peter arn't here!"

All my love & my self,   B.

1   Betjeman (1906–84), poet.
2   John Ireland (1879–1962), composer and Britten's composition teacher at the Royal
     College of Music.
3   Song cycle by Schubert.
4   Ireland and Humphrey Searle (1915–82), whose songs Pears was singing in recital.
5   Max Meili (1899–1970), Swiss tenor.

82   Britten to Pears

[*Letterhead:* English Opera Group, 295 Regent Street, London]

Dec. 18th 1947

My darling,

Well – all my chores are done – the BBC. have got their score, & yesterday we
posted off to Nancy a "Charm of lullabies" (??) all nicely washed & brushed, & quite
charming & successful I think now – five of them. And Yesterday Eric & I went
over to Ipswich & talked in the middle of Mabel's Rural Music Concert – I for
about 3 minutes (quite accomplished, my dear, with even a little humour ("laughter"
according to the E.A.D. Times)) & Eric for about 10 about the Festival, so that's
off my chest. And now, I am beginning St. Nicholas, & enjoying it hugely. It'll be
difficult to write, because that mixture of subtlety & simplicity is most extending,
but very interesting. I have just got the details of the choirs from Jasper [Rooper],
& it looks quite hopeful. I think St. Michael's will have be relegated to the galleries
(where anyhow all girls should be in Church), because they are obviously the most
efficient, & their breathy voices are obviously most suited to the wind noises & so
forth. Yes, writing's all most exciting & interesting, but it doesn't get any easier.

How are you, my dear? I hope the Messiah's are going nicely. I wish you were
broadcasting it because I'd love to hear you do it again. I wonder what you're doing
about next Monday – let me have a card to say, will you? But then I suppose as
usual the Third Programme will be quite impossible. I shouldn't feel over-inclined
to be nice to Columbia after the Interlude Record scandal, but if you're committed
– I suppose that's that. If you want me to ring you any time Saturday or Sunday
wire me.

The enclosed note from Schouwenberg[1] is peeving – but I don't feel inclined to
go over P. Diamand's head, although I'm feeling peeved with him at the moment
(it seems the cancelling of Theo's[2] date was his fault, & I've had a most creepy-
crawling letter from him about it). What do you think? Drop me a line (a long one,
too) & I'll answer whatever you want. I must write too to Schowenberg about this
Concertgebow Jubilee piece muddle[3] – he's not an attractive character.

Mable sang most beautifully last night – her performance of the Shepherd on
the Rock[4] with Steve Waters[5] was really remarkable. And yet she doesn't seem to

get the audience; it's a mystery. She also sang some of our Purcell most finely – If Music (3ʳᵈ) & B.V.'s Exp.[6] – which she must record. I don't know a more accomplished singer to-day (altho' I know a greater).

The house is lovely – really quite warm, beginning to look more furnished with pictures an' all. Looking forward immensely to your coming, which will complete the furnishing –

Talking of Mable – she's <u>quite</u> alot thinner, & looked lovely last night. But, alas, Tony G's reaction to her as Polly[7] was fatal, also to Kath – but still I don't feel hopeless about persuading him.

I must go now – poppetty – darling – love you lots & lots – & come home quickly. Take care of yourself.

All my love & self,
    B.

---

[1] J.W. de Jong Schouwenburg of the Concertgebouw Orchestra.
[2] Olof (1924–2012), Dutch violinist.
[3] Schouwenburg assumed that Britten had agreed to a commission, but Britten insisted he had not.
[4] Schubert song.
[5] (1914–89), clarinettist with the EOG orchestra.
[6] Purcell realizations.
[7] Role of Polly Peachum in *The Beggar's Opera*.

83 Pears to Britten

[*Letterhead:* Hotel des Pays-Bas, Amsterdam]

[?16 Mar 1948]

My dearest of honey-buns

Here I am – arriven – back again in Omsterdom – but a different hotel – first impression is faintly disappointing – Small (and alas! Single) room ohne bad [without bath], but quiet and no trams atall going round the corner quickly at all hours – However I'm not going to judge it too harshly until I've had a meal which I expect to be super terrestrial – There is no superabundance of youthful charm – not to compare with Willy and the rest,[1] but also there is no middle-Indonesian-Emma period hall with gamelan-type chandeliers, and that's a blessing – The crossing was very quiet – no excitements and hardly a movement. Peter D. came to see me as soon as I arrived (one hour ago) & we've just had coffee – He's not going to Paris – Paul C.[2] has been & come back very depressed by it – Apparently Paris is very jittery and uncertain – expecting strikes all the time, & since the 5000 franc affair no one has any money to go to theatres & the Nederlansche Opera is postponing their visit – Hirsch & Malherbe[3] are quarrelling & M. has been sacked – It sounds as though we're well out of that.

Miss you – Bee – wish you were here – will write again soon.

Much much love –

P.

---

[1]   Staff at the American Hotel, Amsterdam.
[2]   Cronheim of the Dutch National Opera.
[3]   Georges Hirsch (1895–1974), Réunion des Théâtres-Lyriques Nationaux administrator; Henri Malherbe, director of the Opéra-comique.

84 Pears to Britten

They tell me the St M[1] <u>is</u> to be broadcast on Sunday – 11–30 & 2

[*Letterhead:* Hotel des Pays-Bas, Amsterdam]

<u>Wednesday midnight</u> [17/18 Mar 1948]

This is really only just to say Goodnight to you, my honey, & to tell you that my first concert has just finished – The Bach cantatas – I think I sang quite well – the Meine Seele[2] particularly – The other is odd & rather difficult – tempi specially – The Musica Antiqua has really only one 1ˢᵗ class performer – the flautist – Johann Feldkamp – amazing – Stotijn too was good – Nicholas Roth tries hard & isn't bad – Boomkamp is quite a good technician but no feeling for rhythm atall – & the cembalist H. Brandt Buys[3] is awful – real old pedant musicologist – banging away on a terrible modern German harpsichord, sounding like tintacks dropping onto corregated iron – & always either forte or forte according to which manual he plays – He's writing to you by the way asking for a piece for his students at Utrecht – unless you want to meet the Utrecht students (you remember Utrecht?) I should on no account do it for him. They finished the concert tonight with some of "Musicalische Opfer".[4] What an extraordinary piece!

I had a rehearsal with van Beinum this morning – very nice & slightly boring – Ernest Häfliger[5] (Swiss tenor) was there, singing tomorrow instead of Vroons[6] – not very impressive but nice –

Vroons very nervous in Bach!

This hotel is not really as nice as the American – Good food but that's really all – although the waiters as you get to know them have a certain fun – But there is music every evening in the Restaurant!!

Much, much love to you My B from
                    your P

Good morning to you – B – (Thursday.)

---

1   Bach *St Matthew Passion*.
2   Bach Cantata no. 189.
3   Pears's fellow performers were: Johann Feltkamp (1896–1962); Haakon Stotijn (1915–64), oboist; Nicholas Roth, violinist; Carel van Leeuwen Boomkamp, viola da gamba; Hans Brandts Buys (1905–59).
4   Bach *The Musical Offering*.
5   (1919–2007).
6   Frans Vroons (1911–83), Dutch tenor.

85 Britten to Pears

[*Letterhead:* ~~The Old Mill, Snape~~] 4 Crabbe Street
                                        Aldeburgh

                                                March 17ᵗʰ 1948

My darling old thing,

Only a note to tell you that (as you probably have guessed) I'm thinking about you all the time, & being with you in spirit through all the big things you must do this week. I'll listen all over the continent on Sunday in case it's to be broadcast.

Things are going quite well here. The booking started on Monday for the Festival, & by mid-day to-day about ¼ – ⅕ of the tickets were all sold, which is a good beginning I think. Elizabeth [Sweeting] is up to her eyes, but little Miss Parker[1] is doing well, & Mrs Galsworthy is standing by all the time, with Margery [Spring-Rice] near![2] We had a committee yesterday which was rather wild – too many people, & Fidelity not too skillful at controlling them. She & Margery stayed to dinner afterwards & we talked "Pfaff" till a late hour, which is quite a business. Barbara [Parker] wasn't too pleased, as it turned out (too late to change plans) that it was her birthday, & would have liked a ceremony, I think. Still, I'm taking her & Elizabeth out to dinner to-night, which ought to put things right! Beth & Sally were here for the night. Sally – <u>very</u> sweet, & considerably better away from her difficult brother & charming sister. It was nice having them, & Beth was very dear.

The work[3] goes well, & pretty fast. I'm enjoying this bit, & allowing myself a bit of space to develop the music. But I must stop myself too much "canonizing" of the music, which is probably more entertaining to write than to listen to!

I look forward to hearing your "Evangelist" again – if only to get Eric Green[4] out of my head! I was really disgusted at the sloppiness of his actual singing – it was really 'faked' singing I felt, – at the hopeless word distortion (the Je-sers all the time). And the embarrassing "big moment" of Peter's going out – I admired the way at Rotterdam that you gave this moment its importance, but yet kept it in the <u>style</u> of the whole. I <u>loathe</u> the long pauses there, as if the "<u>going-out</u>" of Peter were the climax of the whole terrible story of the crucifixion – You're a very great artist, honey.

I've written a note to Basil [Douglas], & am doing so to Jasper. Any more to do? Did you tell Emmie we don't need hospitality at Tiverton?

I hope the Hotel is nice – but go & have a drink at the American & give the small things my love – esp. Willi!! Your room's beginning to look nice without the awful black paint.

Lots of love my dear – take care of yourself. Sing nicely.

Love to all the friends . . .   Ben.

---

1   Britten's secretary.
2   Members of the Aldeburgh Festival Council.
3   Britten was at this time working on his version of John Gay's *The Beggar's Opera* as well as *Saint Nicolas*. He is probably referring to the latter.
4   Eric Greene (1903–66), tenor.

86 Pears to Britten

Pä Bah

<u>Friday</u> [?19 Mar 1948]

My darling –

Just got your letter, which was lovely to have – Thank you very much for it – I'm so glad things go well – Surely ¼ sold in the first three days is rather good – Peter was very impressed by the brochure – thought it looked extremely nice – comparing very favourably with Edinburgh – he hopes to come over for the last weekend of the Festival – he's being very nice to me – After the Cantatas I went back to 20 P-delt Street & saw them all – they (Goldbergs too) were apparently impressed by me, though not so much by the players. Last night I had the public rehearsal of the Matthäus, and it was allright but a bit dull and a bit depressing! I don't know. Van Beinum really doesn't know it & has no idea of 18th century music nor have the players, I believe – I don't think Bach is really supposed to sound quite like that – but never mind. Had a snack-je after at the Italian restaurant, which is really the best food in Amsterdam, & Peter was very intelligent & nice – sehr sympatique [very sympathetic] – As I am a grass-widower here (alas!) I'm going abit social – Today: 1.0 lunch with the Frank Martins.[1] 5.30 (!) dinner with the Dora Lindemanns.[2] Sunday:

Lunch with Mrs Goldbeck: evening chez Diamants. Monday: Lunch Henrietta Bosman, evening my two Dutch queer admirers. Tuesday evening: Nicholas Roths, So you see! Some duty, some pleasure. Some mixture. I ought to try and fit in a visit to Ré Koster too I suppose, Oh dear!

The Christus is better this year (Bogtman)[3] I think – Lindeman is a bit disappointing the other much the same – Häfliger was good but not a knock-out. Voice rather similar to mine I should think – The performance _is_ being broadcast, that nice blond radio man was there yesterday testing it. (though you'll probably get this letter on Monday!)

I wonder – wouldn't it be nice if I came from Harwich to Aldeburgh on Thursday & spent the day there (night too[)] if you could possibly get me to the Albert Hall by 10 (!) –

Forgot to tell Emmie about Tiverton! Have you decided that we definitely go on that night or not? or what? Oh dear! you decide.

Much much love to you –

miss you very much & will see you soon –

P.

Please give much love to Barbara [Parker]. If I came on Thursday I might spend a hour shopping in Ipswich – felt for my room and so on.

---

[1] Frank Martin (1890–1974), Swiss composer.
[2] Dora van Doorn-Lindeman (1918–2008), Dutch soprano.
[3] Laurens Bogtman (1900–69), Dutch baritone.

87 Britten to Pears

[*Letterhead:* ~~The Old Mill, Snape~~] 4 Crabbe Street
Aldeburgh
[20–21 Mar 1948]

My darling –

You finished the Passion about ten minutes ago – it came over beautifully (altho' I missed ½ hr of it because you said 11.30!), & your voice sounded full & beautiful. It was a most thoughtful & moving performance from you, it gets better & better, altho' I can imagine alot of it irritated & bored you as much as it did me. Of course much of it "came off" very well because of really remarkable wind playing, & the choir sounded good too. But my feelings about the soloists hasn't changed (over the radio Dora van D.L. sounded unbearable above E, hard & cold & no vowels apart from 'ah'). I wasn't enamoured of the Christus neither who was very sentimental.

They all <u>emote</u> so terribly, & pull the music around. Of course it all comes finally from lack of technique – they want to express something, but all they can do is to slur up or down or sing louder. That's what you needn't do, & thank God you don't – & so the extraordinary dignity of the work, & it's heartbreaking controlled pathos came over inspite of all the blemishes. I <u>like</u> Annie Hermes' (?)[1] voice; it has real edge to it – but I wish she wasn't so insecure & sloppy. Poor Vrons – but it might have been worse – he sounded as scared as a rabbit! The Peter bit came over wonderfully – it is an <u>extraordinary</u> conception, & you do it incredibly. How were the other performances? The thing that struck me so particularly to-day (the orch. being so good) was the three different levels of approach to the "scourging". 1ˢᵗ – the direct narration of it – then the translation of it into agonised protest – then in the aria the same ♩♪ sublimated into the highest blessing (the aria wasn't so well done – too fast for poor Annie). It reminded me strongly of the agonised marked body in the Colmar altar, & then the serene head above it.[2]

Thank you for your sweet letters. I hope you'll get this before you leave. A pity that the Pays Bas is a disappointment – mind we go back to the American next time! Have you seen Mrs. Goldbeck? I had a sweet letter from her full of your praises. Love to Peter & Maria & all the Cronheimery. Dashing to post now.

All my love, & congratulations.

Your devoted

B

----

1   (1906–95), Dutch contralto.
2   The Isenheim altarpiece by Matthias Grünewald (c 1475–1528).

88 Pears to Britten

Pays bas Hotel

<u>Monday noon.</u> [?22 Mar 1948]

Well – my honey – now it's Monday morning and the worst & most difficult is over – and I've been re-reading your letter and wish I were with you – It must be heavenly at Aldeburgh these days – It's nice enough here but —— but –.

I wonder if you heard yesterday – It <u>was</u> broadcast, & I hope you got my letter telling you so in time – Saturday had been allright bei mir [by me] vocally until towards the end when I began to feel old – I had caught a cold behind the nose on Friday – After the performance on Sat., I went round to Peters for tea & sandwiches etc & though the speaking voice was allright, the whole box felt a bit aged – And yesterday morning it really felt 100, so I went (you'll never guess) to

Dr. de Vivere! & he dropped onto my cords, & that was a bit better – & actually I think it went rather well didn't it honey? Just one or two A's I would have "dared" a little more open & loud, if I'd felt quite certain. It has been terribly useful doing it – Performances are really the only sure way of getting to know a work, even though it may take many years to get it quite right. Van B. isn't really <u>any</u> good at Bach – The whole performance was depressing – None of the voices were <u>too</u> good. Tempi were dotty, the whole solo arias not enough rehearsed, ensemble terrible often, & the sweet harpsichordist at one time apparently fell into her keyboard. Organ too loud – and oh! The Alderman & the Minister of Fine Arts & Mr & Mrs de Jong Schouwenburg & all the stiff audience in black – trying to hope it was better than that old Nazi Mengelberg,[1] & yet missing him & longing for him. I made one or two tidyings up in the long recitatives which I think improves it & keeps it going – "Peter Weinete" [weeping] not too good I'm afraid – coldy & nervy. Van Beinum plans doing it in London next spring! His wife (!) hoped I would do it with him – He's a funny one. Had lunch with Mrs. Goldbeck in the interval – She's getting awfully deaf, & is inclined to shout her opinions on the bad performance all over the artist's room & the restaurants!

After the performance, we went for tea to Peter's, & then Maria & Peter & I had dinner up near this hotel & afterwards to Simon & Maria Goldbergs, which was all a bit tiring, & I was pretty dead.

However I had breakfast in bed this morning & shall have tea with Henriette Bosman & dinner with my two Dutch queer friends, Zegel Koelwijn and Fritz van der Selde! Wonderful names!

Everyone always asks after you & sends lots of love always – and I miss you very much indeed – Shall I come to you on Thursday? Much much love to you honey
　　　　P.

I've got Barbara [Parker] a nice birthday book.

---

[1] Willem Mengelberg (1871–1951), Dutch conductor, Concertgebouw Orchestra and Nazi sympathiser, banned from conducting in the Netherlands from 1947.

✠✠✠

In late March, Britten and Pears launched a frenetic schedule with a recital tour of south-west England through early April. Their main concerns during the spring and summer were the success of the first Aldeburgh Festival, held 5–13 June, and subsequent tours by the EOG. They allowed themselves a break to play tennis, sail, and bathe in the North Sea during August. After further EOG performances, Pears travelled to the US to study with Clytie Mundy in October, and the letters show how difficult they found it to be apart, particularly after months of working and living together.

Owing to the vagaries of the postal service between Aldeburgh and New York, the order of Letters 90–106 is somewhat confused with Pears's letters sometimes arriving in Aldeburgh two at a time. Where possible, we have tried to pair replies with the letters they answered using a note.

✠✠✠

89 Britten to Pears

4 Crabbe Street
<u>Aldeburgh</u>

Oct. 18th 1948

My darling Peter,

Your sweet & comprehensive wire has just arrived, & I am put out of my agony! Judging by the fact that it arrived about 7.p.m. (<u>our</u> time), you can't have been very late in arriving, which is immensely relieving, because my worry was more that you would be detained & bored to desparation than have an accident (which I was sure you wouldn't have). You must be now happily with Elizabeth [Mayer], & talking, talking …! I long to get a note about the journey; how it was, whether boring and/or frightening & uncomfortable. I loathed, more than any moment of my silly life, leaving you. Thank God I was with Lesley, because I made a fool of myself in the car. I caught the 4.50 easily, but walked to it across Liverpool Street in a dream, only being aroused by a man's shout that I had dropped a packet of £5 notes on the ground – I hadn't bothered to put them in my pocket properly!

Beth met me, & was infinitely sweet & understanding! I loved being with her & Sally & Roguey. Sally's now very sweet, but Roguey not well – very pale & thin. Kit was quite human too. Beth took me to Ipswich this morning – I tried on my new suit, which will be quite becoming I think, tho' the Tailor is a bit pompous. My visit was spoiled by seeing half a head-line on an Evening Paper "… believed lost" – & immediately feared the worst. My heart only got back to normal beating when we arrived back at Hasketon! She brought me over here for tea-time, plus Annie the new temporary Swiss girl who seems nice. We had tea – Barbara [Parker] very cheerful, because they seem to have had a whale of a time in Amsterdam. She & Beth got <u>very</u> fond of each other, which is immensely satisfactory – altho' Aimy[1] Nichol seemed to have been rather scared & damping. <u>Then</u> your wire arrived, Beth went back (slightly Bols-tiddly), we had supper, & now I am waiting to hear Nancy do the lullabies.[2] I'll finish this in the morning to tell you how they were, & then I'll send it off quick, with my love. Good night – my darling.

Tuesday morning … The 3rd programme was up to its tricks, & we heard the lullabies thro' a mixture of Latvian Brass-bands, & Viennese Commentary – so there wasn't much atmosphere! But the tempi seemed O.K.

It is a heavenly morning – sunny, cold & incredibly beautiful. I shall write letters, go & pay in some cheques, see gas company about radiation here, &then walk – think of the Spring piece,[3] which I hope to start to-morrow. I'll send you a packet of selected correspondance when there are enough to bother with; so far only cheques & a sweet note from Ursula. I had one from Jetty B this morning – she is broadcasting the piano concerto to-morrow from Hilversum & adores it (see how love is blind!). She says why do you go to U.S.A. You couldn't sing better!

Lots of love to Elizabeth, William, Beate & all – & Clytie, John, Meg & young John too and Ralph & Clare – do hope the money business isn't embarrassing – Blast the silly treasury.

All my love, dear heart – take care of yourself – come back soon and safe.

Till then,

　　　Your B

Lots of love from Barbara (P) & from Beth.

---

[1]　Unidentified – first name very indistinct.
[2]　Britten was attempting to listen to a broadcast of Nancy Evans singing *A Charm of Lullabies*.
[3]　The *Spring Symphony*.

90 Pears to Britten

Tuesday morning. 19th Oct [1948]. 240 E.49.
N.Y.C.

Well, my darling old honey bunch, here I am – and there you are – in the loveliest place in the world in the nicest house in the world listening to the sea and getting ready to work – and I'm getting ready to work in the ugliest place in the world listening to the traffic + hoping not to be run over by it.

The aeroplane is a great modern invention, of great use in dragging one rapidly from latitude to latitude – It is not wholly uncomfortable and Flight No. 151 of A.O.A. was entirely safe and ever so hospitable. The hostess was graciousness itself, the sherry was fair, the steak at Shannon was enormous, the nightcap soothed (the seconals helped) – Bright shone the moon over the Atlantic, even Gander[1] was faintly glamorized – but best of all, I had sitting by me in the plane an American who didn't open his mouth for 19 hours – ! Perhaps this was the main reason for thinking that the trip was really very easy and I wasn't frightened at all – not at all.

It's lovely to be with Elizabeth, who is exactly the same, and we talk – all yesterday & all this morning we have talked – I went to see Clytie last night – She is not too well – very tired & low (or high) blood pressure. I start work with her tomorrow morning. Meg was there & Marc – Meg very sweet but I shan't see her act as she's left her play – I'm having dinner with Ralph & Cardelli[2] tomorrow night. I must go off now up to William's office to take him his glasses – !

Much much love to you from me & Elizabeth.

There's only one place I want to be in – one person I want to be with – you know who & where –

P.

---

1   Town in Newfoundland, Canada.
2   Giovanni Cardelli, financial backer and producer for the Broadway production of *The Rape of Lucretia*.

91 Pears to Britten

Thursday evening [21 Oct 1948]

Not [*Letterhead:* In Flight A A AMERICAN AIRLINES]

Bunchy darling – two more days gone – still wish I were with you in Aldeburgh. I've really had enough of this tiring boring place – I'm working hard – v. hard – for Clytie, who isn't awfully well – but I'm improving a bit I think – I had my first lesson yesterday & another today, each time in the morning & then I return in the afternoon and practise there by myself.

Last night I was at Ralph's & Clare's flat to meet Mr Cardelli – quite a nice young man who adores Lucretia – but their plans for Broadway production make it sound like – to me – a certain flop – But any way why on Broadway? Because the Met's dead any way. etc.

Betty Bean was there – not too bad + very keen and helpful – I had a long session with Ralph about our tour – & Alfred Wallenstein[1] came in while we talked & wants us for two dates in Los Angeles – There will be no difficulty in booking us.

Poor Aksel[2] had his first concert last night & I gather that it was all rather distressing and tragic –

I went down to see Beate in Brooklyn this tea-time – It was nice to see her again, very much the same, with a sweet baby[3] – Elizabeth is just as always, & it's lovely to be with her (but a little exhausting too – she has so much to say & talk about!)

But I want to come home! I've booked my seat for November 15th arr. London 16th morning – Please write to me, my B. I miss you very very much –

All my love xxx p

1   (1898–1983), American cellist.
2   Aksel Schiøtz (1906–75), Danish tenor, who had suffered partial paralysis after surgery for a brain tumour in 1946 and was struggling to return to singing (which he eventually did, as a baritone, surviving a further tumour in 1950). Before his illness he had alternated as the Male Chorus with Pears in the first production of *The Rape of Lucretia* at Glyndebourne in 1946.
3   Muki Wachstein (now Fairchild).

92 Britten to Pears

4 Crabbe Street,
<u>Aldeburgh.</u>

October 22nd (? Friday) [1948]

My darling Peter,

I am longing to have a note from you saying how you are, & how the journey was, & if & when the lessons are started … etc. etc. With luck there may be a note to-morrow; I've counted out the days on my fingers to see when it is possible to get a letter by Air-mail …?! It all goes peacefully here. Weather a bit over-cast, & a beastly depressing West wind which I hope will turn into a healthy Easter soon. I work all day, except in the afternoon when little Miss Parker comes and we wade thro' letters together, <u>gradually</u> catching up on the dreary pile! Then I walk, & ~~wal~~ work after tea till a lateish dinner & then listen to the Radio (which is intolerably interfeared with now) or correct proofs till a lonely bed … The work started abysmally slowly & badly, & I got in a real state. But I think it's better now. I'm half way thro' the sketch of the 1st movement, deliberately not hurrying it, fighting every inch of the way. It is terribly hard to do, but I think shows signs of being a piece at last. It is such cold music that it is depressing to write, & I yearn for the Spring to begin, & to get on to the 3 Trumpets & Tenor solo!

I listened to Jetty Bosmans playing the piano concerto – some of it not bad, but pretty heavy & clumsy the 1st two movements. She hasn't got much sense of rhythm, & obviously minds too much about what she's playing! The reception as usual was awful – Hilversum.

To-night, Arthur is here & we are going to try to get Wozzeck from Hamburg,[1] but I'm not hopeful. He is getting on with Norah[2] like a house on fire – she says he's the model guest, which I'm sure he is. He is working madly, has finished ~~two~~

one & half done two sonnets for you already. I'm looking forward to seeing them. Barbara [Parker] is well, happy I think, ~~the~~ & the Swiss girl is splendid – but there may be some legal snag about keeping her; It would be a bore if she had to go, as she's intelligent & charming.

And you..? I wonder how it is all seeming. I hope the Russian Bogey doesn't obscure everything. Here it seems more dormant, tho' the Times & all agitate it pretty frequently. There is no mail to speak of for you, except some bills, the urgent ones of which I've paid, & some ~~the~~ receipts. The enclosed nice one from Ursula may please you! There has been a bite for the house [3 Oxford Square], & Caplan is dealing with it, Erwin says – let's hope it comes off. The telephone is half-in, has been for the week. When it succeeds I may give myself the pleasure of a transatlantic call, if the gnaw gets worse. Still a month is not for ever, & there's alot to be done in the month!

<u>Saturday morning</u>. As usual, the reception last night was hopeless, & Arthur got a very strange impression of the work. Actually the performance was very poor, only Wozzeck having any idea of character <u>or</u> pitch. We were lucky if Marie was within a fourth of her notes! You must get us to imitate the small boy singing "hop-hop" at the end. Arthur was quite bewildered, even with the score (perhaps <u>because</u> of it, because really it makes the simplest passages look like Chinese). I alternated between mad irritation at the ridiculous excesses of it, with the ludicrous, hideous, & impossible vocal writing, and being moved to tears by the incredible haunting beauty of lots of bits of it. If <u>only</u> he could relax in the relaxed bits!

Your sweet note[3] has come this morning – my morale, sagging all the week, has soared again! I am relieved the journey was easy & good, & I am praying the return one will be similar. So sorry about Clytie; give her lots of love from me. It is lovely to think of you with Elizabeth, William, Meg & all; if only the traffic were normal I wouldn't worry abit! Please, darling, remember to look <u>left</u> when stepping off pavements (is that correct ————— … yes, I think so).

Don't feel you've got to do too much Ralphing, & Cardelli-ing. Have a rest from business matters, & <u>don't</u> try & sell you or us too much. It doesn't matter really whether we go to Indiana University or Sascatchewan, <u>really</u>!

My very best, & only love to you. Take the greatest care of yourself, my darling.

Lots of greetings to friends, & write <u>often</u> please – You mustn't practise <u>all</u> day!

       Thine own,

         B

---

[1] A radio broadcast of the opera by Berg.

[2] Norah Nichols, widow of the poet Robert Nichols, and neighbour.

[3] Letter 90.

93 Pears to Britten

Lots of love to Barbara.

c/o [*Letterhead:* Dr William Mayer, 240 East 49 Street, New York]

Sunday A.M. [?24 Oct 1948]

My own darling honey –

Your letter[1] arrived yesterday morning – <u>most</u> gratefully received – it was heavenly to hear from you – oh! How I wish I was with you in Aldeburgh – I am full of nostalgia here, and only Clytie's lessons keep me – They are very useful and exciting and I think I progress greatly – If only she lived in London!

New York has been looking itself – sometimes lovely in bright clear sunshine and sometimes drizzly and dreary – I had dinner on Friday evening with the Mundies – very simple and nice – and now Clytie is resting at the weekend & I had no lesson yesterday or today – Yesterday morning Ralph & Clare & Betty Bean & I went to a young persons' concert at Hunter College, where they played the Y.P.G.[2] Too small an orchestra, and a dreary commentator through a loud speaker, and a dim conductor called Thomas Scherman. Then we all drove in Ralph's handsome Buick up to Aaron's[3] house about 15 miles up the Hudson. It was terribly nice to see Aaron again – I'm really very fond of him – Victor[4] was there too – a bit of a tubby celestial coal-heaver! and a new girl hanging around. Lots of love to you from Aaron & he is coming to Europe next spring & will be in England for the Aldeburgh Festival so I've insisted he comes down! Isn't that exciting? Couldn't he lecture? on American music?!!

After lunch Harold Shapero[5] came over & played his piano sonata to Ralph who is interested (He was the boy who played his trumpet sonata at Tanglewood in '40 d'you remember?) – A dreary piece just like Beethoven! My! What next! Then Aaron played a bit on records of his new Clarinet Concerto for Benny Goodman. just Aaron – competent & a bit dull. Then I sang 2 or 3 of the Michelangelo with Aaron! Very funny! & then we all drove back – & spent a quiet evening here! William getting up & turning the radio on and off every 8 ½ minutes! He's just the same, fidgetty as ever – rather a worry to them all because of dizzy & fainting spells he had a year ago, & he won't relax and take it easy –

Ralph is beginning to get busy on our tour! madly keen of course! I am trying slowly & diplomatically to soft pedal it all & to keep it on a small scale, but it takes time! 1<u>st</u>: he wants to know your reaction to this:– Wallenstein offers us the Los Angeles Orchestra for three concerts, same programme at each; it would mean you taking over the whole programme: Purcell-Britten perhaps. What d'you think? The fee is very good $3000 – It would mean a week there rehearsing & doing these 3 concerts. I myself am rather <u>for</u> it – as it would mean a whole week in one place on one programme trying to improve it. But of course it <u>entirely</u> depends on you being willing & able to cope with a whole evening's conducting: eg. Chaconne, Orpheus

Brit,[6] Sinfonia da Requiem, Serenade, Grimes' Interludes. And if you can't face it, then you have only to say so! really my darling! Ralph of course is trying to edge more days in each end – he wants us to catch Q. Eliz. on Oct 15th. I try to push it off to Q. Mary on Oct 22nd. He wants us to stay till December 3rd; I try to keep it November 30th. Well, we may have to give in at one end but not both! I'm trying to keep it to New York & East as much as possible, with just Chicago on the way to the West Coast perhaps – I've no doubt that we can do whatever jobs we like. By the way, N.C.A.C. definitely do not want us again which is all to the good. But everyone is very keen. You've no idea the prestige P.G. at the Met. has given you! They are doing it again this season!

Very very much love my B. Write often to me. Longing to come back.

ever your own Peter P

---

1   Letter 89.
2   Britten's *The Young Person's Guide to the Orchestra*.
3   Copland (1900–90), American composer.
4   Kraft (1915–76), Copland's partner.
5   (1920–2013), American composer.
6   Britten's Purcell realizations.

94 Pears to Britten

<u>LETTER NO. 4.</u>   240 E 49
                                                                        NYC

<u>Tuesday evening 26th</u> [Oct 1948]

My own honey bee – It was lovely to have your second letter[1] this evening when I got back – Elizabeth had put it on my bed to wait for me! I'm so happy to hear that you are starting & that it isn't going too badly (the Spring do, I mean.) I wish – I wish – I wish I were with you – Dreary old New York – bloody old windy old smelly old Broadway – d'you remember the metallic taste in the mouth on the streets all the time? and the witchs' Kitchen steam on the pavements?

On Sunday evening William drove me all round Manhattan on a typical William drive – The only notable thing being the really gigantic blocks of new municipal flats holding 30000 families! going up very quickly! This country is incredibly rich. Then Monday I went to Clytie's and worked hard by myself in the next room while she taught some one else, though she still kept an ear on me, and then I had my lesson – That is the routine each day now – It's quite hard work, but I improve! only just the top notes are still not sure! but they will be!

After 3 hours singing, I went to a movie Cocteau's Ruy Blas (fair) and then met Peter & Maria and had dinner with them in that little Italian restaurant behind Carnegie Hall, d'you remember? Pictures of musicians on the walls etc – quite Good food – Peter & Maria a bit dazed by New York – She's enjoying her work with Schnabel[2] very much. <u>Clifford</u> is here playing next week & I have been asked to meet him! Oh dear what shall I do?

I had another work today at Clytie's (no lesson today) & met some of her pupils – She <u>is</u> a good teacher. Arthur Kent[3] may come next spring to England in John's musical. He would be a wonderful Macheath?![4]

Ralph is off to Canada for two days today; before he left, he rang me & asked me if I would advise Brian Sullivan the Met. Grimes (Jagel[5] is not going to do it again) & also coach Mr. Cooper the conductor.[6] Really!

Yesterday morning I spent a little time listening to the old recordings of Paul Bunyan – They had suddenly been sent from Columbia University & he (Ralph) had heard some & thought the Ballads were so wonderful, and wants to take them out and use them separately – It made me cry & shudder to hear P.B. again. The performance was appalling! and some of it is faintly embarrassing, though I believe by <u>drastic</u> cutting one could make a pleasant thing of it still. The ballads <u>are</u> quite sweeties! They really are – So I've copied down the tunes & Elizabeth has the words & I'll bring them back to you to fix slightly!

~~Me~~ I should have had dinner tonight with Meg & Marc – but she put it off as she's terribly busy rehearsing her new part, which is opposite Robert Morley in "Edward, my Son".[7] She's quite a big star & has been offered a movie contract.

So – instead of going out Elizabeth & I have been nostalgically sorting out all sorts of Britteniana – tearing up some things & not tearing up others! All sorts of names are unburied again – like Tony Synakowski! And Natalie Boshko Brown! They are both flourishing you will be pleased to hear! But the memories of that time are all so confusing and confused – what a time and what fools (<u>really</u>) we were to stay in America – I don't mind the idea now of coming to this country for a month once a year, but if we go anywhere, let's go to Australia, South Africa, anywhere but here. Not but what the food is good and does make one feel better! I sent off some parcels today & will send off some more soon – I'm spending incredibly little money so far –

Please give my love to Barbara & Arthur – I'm so glad he's getting on with my piece.

And please give a very great deal of love – in fact <u>all</u> my love (including Barbara's & Arthur's) to someone I love very much & miss quite terribly –

      P.

---

[1] Letter 92.

[2]   Artur Schnabel (1882–1951), piano teacher and editor of Beethoven.
[3]   (d. 1992), American bass-baritone.
[4]   Leading role in *The Beggar's Opera*.
[5]   Frederick Jagel (1897–1982), American tenor.
[6]   Emil Cooper (1877–1960).
[7]   Robert Morley (1908–92), theatre and screen actor; co-wrote and starred in the play *Edward, My Son*.

95 Britten to Pears

4 Crabbe Street
Aldeburgh

[28 Oct 1948]

My darling Peter,

This is only a scribbled note to tell you we're now on the telephone Aldeburgh 323. It is in Barbara's [Parker] room – they haven't yet put in the extension to the dining room, but that'll be along soon. So, if you feel <u>particularly</u> lonely ring, of an evening – but it's safer to wire before, just <u>in case</u> I should be out! I won't ring you unless there is something terrifically important, or I get similarly lonely. But while your sweet letters continue to arrive so regularly I think I prefer them to a hectic 3 minutes with fading, & not daring to say what I really feel ......

The work is at last progressing, & is on the whole very good I think. I've done, roughly, three movements including the Nashe[1] – lots of things not right yet but coming along slowly. I hope you'll be pleased, but you're so very severe a critic that I darn't hope!

A terrific sea to-day, most wonderfully beautiful; big racing clouds, lots of bright sun, & the gigantic waves all white. Don't be jealous, because you'll be home soon, & anyhow I expect by now you'll have settled down & feeling easier, & are adoring the work with Clytie. Of course I do see how tired you must feel, & I expect you're irritated by the provincialism of so many of the people you meet. I hope by now you have restored contact with ~~see~~ sweet Elizabeth & the family. Nice to see Aaron! It sounds a wild party. I wrote to R.H. [Ralph Hawkes] yesterday, & incidentally said I would agree to the Los Angeles Show – after all I shan't have been conducting all the Summer – I hope!

No particular news – nor letters. We go on evenly from day to day. Barbara & Helen come for next week-end & we all go over to Lowestoft on Saturday – Arthur & John[2] (coming to Norah's for week-end) & Norah will probably come too. Doris Brown came in. Elizabeth [Sweeting] was here for last week-end, & young Jim[3] for a lesson (very depressed by R.A.F.).

But how I miss you, my darling. I'm planning to come up to London on 15ᵗʰ (most <u>urgent</u> business!). Be careful, keep safe & well – your devoted
                                                    B.
(Love to all).

---

1   'Spring, the sweet spring' by Thomas Nashe (1567–c 1601), included in the *Spring Symphony*.
2   Lindsay (b. 1926), pianist.
3   James Butt (1929–2003), composer.

96 Pears to Britten

Letter No 5!

c/o [**Letterhead:** Dr William Mayer, 240 East 49 Street, New York]

Friday morning [29 Oct 1948]

My darling – I've just got your little note[1] with the Dutch enclosure – It <u>is</u> rather nice to have letters from you! The day is made on which one appears and I feel contact with you and the time doesn't seem quite so long before I see you again – I suppose the days aren't really quite as long as they seem and while I am working with Clytie I am convinced that it is all very well worth while – She is being most awfully helpful settling several bogies for good, I hope – We have worked at the Magic Flute aria together, at Comfort ye & Every Valley,[2] and Grimes bits particularly end of Act I Scene II, (what har-. etc)[3] – It's seems a question of two things primarily, post-nasal resonance and just hard work in the TUM – i.e. support – I <u>must</u> just work harder for my top-notes, but not in the throat – only in the diaphragm! Oh honey, wish I were with you –

When did I last write to you? Tuesday evening I think – well, Wednesday was much like other days – lesson & work at Clyties, with walk about New York for exercise – In the evening Wystan came here for dinner, and after dinner Louise Bogan[4] and Jimmie & Tanya Stern[5] – All quite nice but I didn't feel very wonderful, I don't know why – I'm inclined to feel tired in the evening – It's an exhausting place this city – The weather has been really rather wonderful – The first 2 or 3 days were wet, but now it's bright and sunny and warm too.

I sent off yesterday to Barbara P. a large tin of wonderful Bourbon Biscuits (d'you remember them? Chocolate sandwich – very good) – It's really rather an enormous tin and I thought perhaps you could share them with the Haskerton household. I'm sending something to pretty well every body – I have no other expenses –

I'm <u>furious</u> to discover that Decca have <u>issued</u> "Sweet Polly" "Ash Grove" "Bonny Earl" and "Hey ho!" – quite without our permission! They have recently been sold here & have had wonderful reviews (for what's that worth) But I played "Ash" & "Polly" & they won't do (although the recordings themselves are good) – What can we do about it? I'll bring a copy back perhaps. Ralph of course doesn't mind, as the reviews are good & presumably people will buy them, and that's all he wants. I must stop and write to Lesley & then go off to my lesson.

Much much love my honey – always
                            P

It's 12 days since I saw you, and there are still 18 days to go – Oh dear.

---

1   This note has not survived in the archive.
2   Arias from Handel's *Messiah*.
3   'What harbour shelters peace?'
4   (1897–1970), American poet and Poet Laureate from 1945 to 1946.
5   James Stern (1904–93), writer, and his wife.

97 Pears to Britten

<u>240 E 49.</u>

<u>Saturday afternoon</u> [30 Oct 1948]

My own honey – you mustn't get bored at my writing so often to you but I do love you very much and I am loathing New York and feeling neurotic and hypocondriac and only want to be with you at home instead of in this dreary city.

Last night after my usual day of work and lesson (all very admirable) I met Peter & Maria for an evening meal and afterwards went to Simon Goldrey's apartment for a cup of tea and a talk – Maria G. was there too, all very friendly and nice but oh! Why wasn't it in Aldeburgh –

Today I should have had lunch with Wystan but I've pulled a little muscle in my back and made an excuse of that to call it off and have stayed indoors. Tonight I go to Clytie's for a meal to meet young John & Charlotte.[1] Tomorrow William & I go for a drive and for lunch out to the Ocean or somewhere taking Peter & Maria with us.

Ralph rang up today again – very keen about our tour – He seems to have arranged a week in Toronto & Montreal, and also some Colleges are after us – All very satisfactory and boring –

I seem to have given in on us coming on Queen Eliz on October 15th with Town Hall concert on 23rd or 24th – but I've insisted we leave by November 30th – Is this fairly allright?

Oh dear!

Wish you were here!

And me

With thee!

Bunch.

P.

---

[1]   Mundy's son (1917–2004), a medieval historian at Columbia University, and his wife.

98 Britten to Pears

Long letter from Humps, who sends loads of love to you. (a wonderful letter.. he says "his classic beak is a stinking good man"!!)

Aldeburgh

[Late Oct 1948]

My darling –

This is only a scribbled note – Miss Parker has been here taking horrible official notes, & I am just off on a "thinking walk", but I want just to send you my love & thanks for your sweet note (no. 2)[1] arrived this morning. I do hope by now you will have got at least one of mine – this post is terribly slow; I think the hold-up is between here & London. Also, I hope you're feeling happier. I think most of the cause of your depression was physical – its that damned journey – much more exhausting than it seems, even if it goes smoothley! Don't work too hard, or see too many people. I hate to think of you wasting your time on the Betty Beans of this world – or the R.H's & Cardellis, for that matter! I must say the Lucretia project sounds dotty, but I presume they have got their eyes open. Is Novotna[2] having a gusset let in to enable her to sing the part? What a dreadful pity about Aksel – whatever happened? Or are the New Yorkers insensitive to that kind of singing – for all his weaknesses, he is a cultured & sensitive person, & artist.

Are you still looking both ways crossing the street? Lesley has had her op. successfully & without complications. Send her a p.c. if you've time – to the Westminster hospital. There is a large photostat of a J.C. Bach aria from Brit. Mus. – d'you want it sent? Much love, my darling – I'm living for Nov. 16th!! xxxxxx   Ben

¹   Letter 91.
²   Jarmila Novotná (1907–94), Czech soprano.

99 Britten to Pears

4 Crabbe Street

Aldeburgh

Sunday [?31 Oct 1948]

My darling Peter,

I am so sorry that I haven't written for a day or two, but I have been awfully busy with other drearier sorts of letters, mostly dictating to little Miss Parker – she is quite good, but alas getting deaf, & we have difficulty in agreeing on the number of s's. Life has been ticking over, each day nearer to your return, thank God.

Barbara & Helen have been here this week-end, sweet people, & nice to have them. We went over to Lowestoft for the day yesterday, with Norah Nicholls, Arthur & John. It was a grey, misty kind of day, perfect for the Herrings & that mysterious kind of drab beauty of the Markets. We saw them unloading, & Scotch girls gutting, & some remarkably fine looking fishermen & boys, terrifically tanned & strong, in their curiously attractive clothes. You'd have loved it! The day also had it's depressing side, of the cemetary & meeting sad older friends. I had a nice little reception at the library, a deputation to meet me, & I made a little speech presenting them with some priceless (you know in which sense I use the word!) manuscripts. It is quite touching & slightly exaggerated!¹

I went for a nice long, marsh walk with Barbara this morning – she is a sweet creature, devoted & sympathetic. It is nice that she & Helen now are considering retiring to a home in this part of the world. I wonder if it will come off. This afternoon, Beth & the three kids have ~~taken~~ come over to see them, & are now banging at the piano downstairs.

My work has been truculent; it is just the difficulty of finding the right notes (and of knowing what one wants!) 3 pieces are more or less satisfactory; the rest are bothersome. But I refuse to hurry them.

I had a long talk with Lesley on the phone to-day – she is out of hospital, & at home with Leslie & all the boys around her! Scarcely peaceful – but she seems fine. As soon as she is ready to travel Leslie will drive her down here for some days to recuperate. Morgan may come next week too, which will be nice. Eric has rented a house in Southwold! He seems to be coping alright, but I somehow feel guilty that he's so close & yet not actually here. But I had to be quiet for this work, & having him means Group planning, & Festival discussions.

And you, my darling? Wie gehts? [How are you?] Better – I hope. I hope there'll be a letter tomorrow, saying that you're well, enjoying yourself, working well, resting a lot, & longing to come home …!

I must post this now & entertain the family. I wanted to send you my Sunday love, & you know you have every other day's love too.

I hope Clytie's better – my love to her & Elizabeth too & all the family.

> Your devoted
>
> B

---

[1]   The Lowestoft public library (now the Suffolk County Record Office) established a 'Benjamin Britten Collection', to which Britten donated several early manuscripts.

100 Pears to Britten

<u>240 E 49</u>

<u>Monday evening</u> Nov. 1. [1948]

My honey – Only an evening scribble to answer yours[1] which came this morning – so glad you're working well – wish I could hear it – I'm working well too – got a top E♭ today – glad you didn't hear it – Clytie's doing me a power of good – she really is – and I only hope I can cling on to all she's teaching me – she's certainly developing the voice very much – bottom as well as top. I'm getting a bit fat on American food, B. – v. sorry! So glad you have important business in London on November 15th, 'cos I fancy I shall have important business in Aldeburgh on 16th (unless the plane's late) – Longing to get back – It's election day tomorrow here – usual nonsense less than before – Dewey[2] forgone conclusion – Peter & Maria & I drove out with William yesterday to Jones Beach – It was a most lovely day – very American fall colours – William's driving as ever – I should be hearing Clifford tonight, but I've torn a muscle in my back, & although it's better, I pleaded that! Who should I meet on 57th St on Friday but Francelia from Grand Rapids, d'you remember? My! how she talked –

much much love to you – P.

PS: Please remember to lick up yr letters! The last one flew the Atlantic wide open!

---

[1]   Letter 95.
[2]   Republican presidential candidate, Thomas E. Dewey, was unexpectedly defeated by Harry S Truman.

101 Britten to Pears

love to all Mayers – of course & the friends you see

<u>Aldeburgh</u>

<u>Nov 2nd 1948</u>

My darling
    Your two letters[1] have arrived to-day, one by each post so I feel <u>very</u> spoiled. It is sweet that you write so often, but I am really depressed that you are feeling homesick, & hating New York so. Is it just tiredness, or <u>is</u> the place as hopeless as I feel it is! Your letters reflect so clearly what I remember of it that I get depressed by it, too. Still – it is not so long now – when you get this there'll be not much more than a week left – ! I am planning a little excursion for that week-end. Esther has written to Beth suggesting that she should go & see the school & I propose to drive her (either direct to Lancing, or leave the car in London, all depending on the petrol situaggers) spend Sunday night at the school, & then meet you on Tuesday morning! I will find the time of the plane from the London office. That is something to live for …
    I was <u>horrified</u> to hear your news about the Decca records. That is maddening of them, and quite against agreements & law. I rang up Erwin & Roth[2] about it, & they are consulting together now – they may even get in touch with Ralph. I feel it rather lets us out of doing Illuminations, if we want to.. It <u>is</u> a bore, because I remember how poor those records were.
    The enclosed note came from Basil [Douglas] – would you write to him if you think it ought to be changed? I've written him a note saying I'm not happy about the plan of it, but not suggesting anything, till my Lord & Master gives <u>his</u> opinion. (My darling – I <u>hate</u> you being unhappy – it makes me wretched too).
    All the other letters for you are from business, & dull people & can easily wait. No news yet about Oxford Square, alas. The Steins move next week, I think. I may ring Caplan to see, the next day or so –
    My work goes slowly on – I'm fairly sure of the first 3 movements, but not happy about the next two yet. The formal problem is a corker. But I like the plan of the work, & its atmosphere, anyhow. I've got some sweet poems. I can't wait to show it to you – and it <u>isn't</u> so long now, really it isn't – when you get this letter it won't be. I hope you can get your stuff in London done in time to get down here by Wednesday evening – then you'll have a clear week, I hope. We've got a lot to do – of every kind of thing!! Have you had time to work at the Amsterdam programme – memorising, etc? I've looked at the Mozart[3] abit.
    This isn't a nice tidy letter like yours, my darling, but as usual I'm rushing to post it. Miss P. comes after lunch for letters, & it usually takes most of the afternoon till I'm done, & then I have to rush for the post.

Barbara [Parker] is well, & is writing herself, I think. I go to Fidelity to-night for dinner. Marjory [Spring-Rice] comes back to-day, too, so I'm not too cut off.

But I miss you, most dreadfully. Come home quick, & safe & sound.

Your devoted B

---

[1] Letters 94 and 96.
[2] Ernst Roth (1896–1971), also of Boosey & Hawkes.
[3] Songs for a recital at the Concertgebouw they were to give on 7 December 1948.

102 Pears to Britten

[?3 Nov 1948]

[*Typed*]

"%0   sorry
24o west 49
n.y.c.

dear sir,

i the undersigned would like to know why i have not received any communication written or otherwise for eighty two hpurs. I would respectfully suggest that denotes total lack of interest in the undersigned, and that it is not a particularly amiable way of bee-having-bee, d'you see? i have half a mind to stop this letter at once. There is no particular news. Peter and Maria came here after supper last, night and we had a very pleasant talky evening. William and Elizabeth got on very well with them and liked them very much. The weather has been hellish – hot muggy wet rainy dirty smuts in the eye and pain in the head. Prima donna crises in the Lucretia do. Both the Lucretias, no longer being or never having been great singers, are particularly anxious to have the DRAMATIC critics and not the musical. Novotna is now doubtful and Tourel[1] is mentionedas a possible! She at least has a pretty good mezzo, while the others are just old tired sops. I'm off in a few minutes to hear Yvonne Lefebvre(?)[2] play at French Culture House. She makes her Début here Sunday week, but I shan't hear her, coz – I don't suppose ti'll interest you – I've decided to fly back two days earlier,i.e. Nov.13,Saturday. arriving Sun. same time (leave here 13.30). I say it's because Clytie Doesn't work at Week-ends, but really I cant bear to go on writing letters to you. you wouldn't be in London then would you? Why should you? Oh my bee. only ten more days!   much much love

---

[1] Jennie Tourel (1900–73), American mezzo-soprano.
[2] Yvonne Lefébure (1898–1986), French pianist.

103 Britten to Pears

(Lots of love from Elizabeth who's just rung up)

> 4 Crabbe Street
> <u>Aldeburgh.</u>

> <u>Friday</u> [5 Nov 1948]

My darling Peter,

   This is only a rushed note because I want to get one off before the week-end
– I have to go to Ipswich with Marjorie this afternoon, & there won't be time for
letters to-morrow. Your sweet note[1] came this morning. I am glad it seemed abit
more cheerful than the others – I hope it means you're relaxing a bit more. It is
certainly exciting about the voice … keep it up my dear! I promise you not to write
any E♭'s in the Spring Symphony, but don't let it get about, because Webster'll be
wanting you for I Puritani,[2] & <u>then</u> won't the Shaw-failures[3] love you!

   It is really heavenly here, & I can't wait for you to enjoy it with me. The weather
is perfect to-day – sea looking like a pond, & really warm sun. I sit here at my
desk, watching the fishing boats go out, do their stuff, and come back all full up
with sprats & herring. We've had some big seas too, which were most thrilling
to watch, & to feel the spray. The windows got thick with salt. My work is going
better, but I'm up against quite a snorter of a formal problem now. I've sketched out
six already – the Winter one (Orch. & Chorus), the Spenser (3 trumpets & you!),
the Nashe (everyone), the Clare driving-boy (with soprano solo), a Herrick Violet
(for Kathleen), and a lovely Vaughan one about a shower for you.[4] And now …
well, we'll see – lots of possibilities; I'd got it all neatly planned, but it's coming out
different, bigger (& I hope better!).

   I had a nice dinner with Jock[5] & Fidelity the other night – quiet, relaxed & gay.
I'm very fond of those two, especially in that mood. I go off to a wretched R. Music
School do in Ipswich with Marjory after lunch – a bore, but I must help the poor
dear in a rather measly situation.

   The enclosed note will amuse you – a typical family reaction[6] – only writing to
complain about things, seldom to praise – &what a complaint (not even <u>daring</u> to
mention the title, or perhaps he'd forgotten. I suppose it's the F-F-D (sh-sh-sh!))
Dirty old man. Which is he?

   I'm taking up the matter about Decca with them here – they <u>mustn't</u> do that
kind of thing. I'm quite ashamed to let those records be heard.

   Could Jennifer[7] do Lucy? For Belgium in March (that is all fixed now)? It
doesn't seem likely that Rose[8] can manage it. Eric is pressing for Mabel to do the
Holst[9] – it'll probably make you cross, but I can't see an alternative at the moment.
The Holst & new piece[10] (Easdale & Guthrie are getting to gether) must be cast
out of Herring crowd.

My dear – it'll only be a week when you get this – unbelievable, but <u>quite</u> long enough. Beth & I will probably motor up to the Airport from Lancing that morning, if there's time. Come back safe & sound, & we'll have a blissful week together in this sweet home. Much, much love,

Your devoted B.

---

[1] Letter 100.

[2] Opera by Bellini.

[3] A pun on Desmond Shawe-Taylor, critic.

[4] For Parts I & II of the *Spring Symphony*; poets Edmund Spenser (1552/53–99); Thomas Nashe (1567–c 1601); John Clare (1793–1864); Robert Herrick (1591–1674); and Henry Vaughan (1621–95).

[5] John Gathorne-Hardy, Earl of Cranbrook (1900–78).

[6] A relative of Pears had written of his disapproval of their recording the folk song 'The Foggy, Foggy Dew', considering the song's (for the time) bawdy subject matter offensive. He had suggested in his letter that the recording should be destroyed.

[7] Jennifer Vyvyan (1925–74), soprano.

[8] Rose Hill (1914–2003) sang Lucy Lockit in the premiere of Britten's version of *The Beggar's Opera*.

[9] *The Wandering Scholar*, chamber opera.

[10] Brian Easdale (1909–95), *The Sleeping Children*.

104 Pears to Britten

<u>Monday</u> [8 Nov 1948]

My honey – Thank you so very much for <u>two</u> letters[1] which have now arrived I last wrote my scruffy typewritten screed. In the meantime you'll have had my change of plan – two days earlier – I <u>do</u> hope this won't upset your plans with Lancing too much – Don't bother to meet me – & I'll come down too to Lancing! I'm longing to see you again – New York has definitely seemed a great deal more tolerable now that the end is in sight – ! We had a quiet weekend with William and Elizabeth – drove up to the Wallings for lunch – nice to see them again – & I went last night to Poulenc & Bernac's[2] first recital here & after to Doda Conrad's[3] for a party – They were well received & have very good notices but there was a fatal lack of warmth and color in the performances – Schubert! Nacht & Traüme! Uh uh! – Met several old friends & acquaintances – Eva Gauthier, David Diamond, Marc Blitzstein, Eugene List, Sam. Barber, Freda Rothe;[4] Clare & Ralph were there. Lots of love to you all the time – I was received with open arms in the Music Library – ! quite a reunion – Please thank Barbara P. v. much for her letter & say, thanks to her information, I won't bring a pressure cooker back as they cost just about the same as the ones she quotes – so I shan't bother.

> V.v. much love to you   xxxx   Peter
>   oh! oh!

---

1   Letters 101 and 103.
2   Francis Poulenc (1899–1963), French composer and pianist; Pierre Bernac (1899–1979), baritone.
3   (1905–97), German bass.
4   Eva Gauthier (1885–1958), Canadian mezzo-soprano; David Diamond (1915–2005), American composer; Marc Blitzstein (1905–64), American composer; Eugene List (1918–85), American pianist; Samuel Barber (1910–81), American composer; Friede Rothe (1914–2003), musicians' agent.

105 Britten to Pears

> 4 Crabbe Street,
> <u>Aldeburgh.</u>
>
> Nov. 9th 1948

My darling Peter,

This may or may not reach you before you leave – I am rushing it off to post just in case I'm lucky & the posts work as they should. It is <u>thrilling</u> that you're coming a day or so early. I hope very much to be at the Airport to meet you, but if there are terrific delays, or eccentriccities of arrival, I <u>may</u> miss you, in which case, you'll find me at Oxford Square.

I'm not sure whether the Lancing thing will work or not as a result this week-end – Beth may go alone, or if you felt inclined we might all drive down. But I think you'll probably not want to go, especially if the journey is delayed or difficult. Don't ~~wh~~ worry, we'll leave this till you arrive. I can't <u>wait</u> for the arrival of the plane, my darling – you'll here a great rattle as you land, & it will be my heart beating.

Much, much, love.

> Your B

106 Britten to Pears

4 Crabbe Street,
Aldeburgh

Nov. 28th 1948

My darling –

How I wish this fog would lift – not only from the land, but from your whereabouts! It is horrible not to know where you are. Actually I have just been talking to Lesley & I gather that the plane actually <u>did</u> leave at 10.31 this morning. It would be too cruel if you had already left the field & gone to Victoria [train station], & were at this moment in the middle of the channel with the prospect of a night of discomfort in the train in front of you.[1] But I daresay I shall soon know. You may not even get this letter; we may be together[2] before it reaches you. I'll send it off in case to bring you my love – all of it, every scrap. Do take care of yourself – nurse, not only your throat but every bit of you. If you have stood up to the discomfort of these last two days – you could take anything!

Morgan is here – nice to have him, but I'm afraid I'm not a gay companion! I suppose I'll cheer up when I get your wire!

Lots of love, my darling.

In haste, your devoted B.

---

[1] Pears was on his way to Geneva to perform Britten's *Serenade*.
[2] For their planned recital tour of Holland beginning early December.

107 Britten to Pears

Aldeburgh.

[mid-Dec 1948]

My darling,

I am so very sorry that I was beastly on the 'phone last night – selfish & unsympathetic. Only excuse is – it's a bit of a shock all this business, & I get <u>madly</u> depressed.[1] It is one thing thinking gaily about a possible free time, & another being ordered to rest for 3 months, & to have to forgo all the things with you, my darling, to have to be separated too, for so long from you at times when I thought we'd be travelling & working together – & I <u>do</u> adore working with you, & think we really achieve something together.

My only way of coming sane thro' this miserable time is to think that this will make it possible for us to continue working together in the future, & if I <u>didn't</u> rest we might have had to cut it out altogether – because I was physiologically unsuited for it. which I know I'm not!

Here are the few letters – I'll send on any others that arrive. Take care of yourself, my darling – you are so precious, not only to me, but to ~~som~~ so many, many people. I wish you were broadcasting on an audible wavelength – because then I'd be able to enjoy you – but at anyrate I shall be able to hear that you are well.

All my love, my angel. You are very sweet – too sweet to me.

B

P.S: I'll let you know definitely when I hear about length of time from Dr Acheson. Only we'd better say now – nothing till end of Jan. Could you tell Peter D.? Give them my love, if you see them.

(ALCI??)²

---

[1] Britten was forced to cancel their tour of Holland due to severe stomach problems.
[2] Agenzia Lirica Conartistica Internazionale, their Italian agents for planned tour in April.

108 Britten to Pears

Aldeburgh.

[Dec 1948]

My darling,

The enclosed exciting photos of the American Landscape arrived to-day from William. They made me laugh abit – as I hope they will you!

My X-ray is on Thursday & we should have decision by Saturday. But I've talked again with Dr Acheson & he strongly advises the 3-months break even if there is no ulcer there – which he thinks there isn't. He also suggests a second ~~oppin~~ opinion, which I don't feel inclined to, but feel that Peter Diamand & Emmie might feel inclined – in view of the cancellations. What dost thou think?

The other note from (I think) Suzanne Lilar[1] – could you give to Peter D. to cope with, in view of the money proposals & fact we couldn't do it anyhow?

I hope to speak to you for a moment to-night – I hope I can catch a glimpse of your sweet voice over the air, but I don't really think I shall be able to. There is the first <u>Council</u> meeting of the Festival to-night at the Wentworth [Hotel]. To pass the programmes.

All my love, my darling. Lots of luck in the concerts & a pleasant journey to Holland. Practise abit so that you can DASH or HASH them convincingly!

Your ever devoted

B

The other note (rather nasty, I felt) can go in the New York file!

---

[1] (1901–92), Belgian writer.

109 Britten to Pears

4 Crabbe Street
Aldeburgh

Dec. 27th 1948

My honey,

The enclosed letters have just arrived, & I hasten to send them on to you. Nothing of wild importance – do try & subdue Jetty's generosity if you can – but it is a forlorn hope, I fear! Also lots more Christmas cards – some joint ones – Fello Atkinson, Betty Bean, Catherine (Lawson?), Reggie Goodall; Anne (W.).[1] I won't bother to send these on – let them be an extra inducement to you to come down again QUICK. I miss you dreadfully, Poppetty, can't think why I have to have this dreary thing to stop me being with you. I am jealous of Boris Ord[2] playing the Purcell for you, & furious at the same time that I shan't be able to hear you at all. However Pye[3] do now write that they are going to lend me another, & better, set – so maybe the Third Programme will be able to stand up better to Paris & Latvia.

I'm sure the wisest thing is to move the furniture & stuff to Melbury Road – there's no point any more in you suffering discomfort in the hope of a few pounds in Rental Premium. Anyhow, try & get to see Caplan & talk the matter over with him. I can't bear to think of you living this dot & carry-one kind of existence – so you'd better do something about it to stop me worrying! – So there.

I did a little bitli of workli this morning – with a singular lack of achievement. I suppose it is good to have made a start, but I can't say I feel up to it yet.[4] I must have patiensce, I suppose.

Please give lots of love to the Steins, & ~~the~~ tell them I'll be writing about the nice present.

Take care of yourself, my dearest one – & come back safe & well to your faithful,

loving & rather dreary,

Ben.

1   Fello Atkinson, London architect; Betty Bean from Boosey & Hawkes in New York;
    Catherine Lawson, mezzo-soprano who sang in *The Beggar's Opera*, and was married to
    EOG clarinettist Stephen Waters; conductor Reginald Goodall; the singer Anne Wood.
2   (1897–1961), organist and choirmaster at King's College, Cambridge.
3   Pye Ltd, Cambridge, radio manufacturers.
4   The *Spring Symphony*.

110 Pears to Britten

22^A Melbury Road
<u>W. 14</u>

<u>Thursday</u> [30 Dec 1948]

My own honey bee –

Just a note scribbled to you while waiting for breakfast to send you all my love
& thoughts – I shall probably ring you later but I know you like letters.! A lot of
people thought about you last night & wished you were there – Olive & Norina &
Marjorie – Joan, George & Boris too, who did as well as could be expected – i.e.
much better than most of the dreary hacks but not like you, my bee! I must say I
<u>adore</u> that music – I have an absolute passion for it I must do it better and better.
We spent most of yesterday on it – & I shall spend most of today & tomorrow on
Monteverdi, which may not be very easy either.

How are you my honey? <u>Do do do</u> not worry about things – <u>Don't</u> hurry yourself
into work. It doesn't matter if you have a month or two off – much better that you
relax & get better slowly & surely – So <u>dont</u> worry!

The Spring Symphony can wait – Put off even the Dutch performance if you
want to – It couldn't matter less.

I'm enclosing Otto's letter, but I beg you don't get too het up about it – It was
bound to be a shambles anyway, & Otto himself doesn't seem to be too depressed
about it[1] – The Abraham letter is amusing[2] – Kubelik[3] was here when I got home
last night – quite interesting about Prague etc.

I've sent you two books as a token of my esteem which I hope you will enjoy
– Just dip into them –

All my love, B-li
Your devoted
P.

1   Otakar Kraus (1909–80), Czech-born baritone who had played Tarquinius in the premiere
    of *The Rape of Lucretia*, wrote with news of the Broadway production, which in his view
    was a travesty. He had been cut from the cast.

[2]   The musicologist Gerald Abraham (1904–88) had written to tell Britten that some Russian composers he had met in Prague had described the composer as 'a decadent bourgeois formalist'. Abraham thought he had convinced them otherwise. (Abraham to Britten, unpublished letter, 24 December 1948).

[3]   Rafael Kubelík (1914–96), Czech conductor.

111 Pears to Britten

Adelphi Hotel
<u>Liverpool</u>

[?2 Jan 1949]

My darling old Bee,

It's Sunday morning & rather gloomy & I lay in bed late this morning & now it's 11.45 & I'm having a beer in the Louijnge – I've just written a long letter to Ralph, all about your stomach – which is let's face it a depressing subject though it be yours & very beautiful. Still who wants to write about it? Paint it perhaps – shall I get Denis Wirth-Miller[1] to paint your tum? It might be interesting.

I had a lovely lunch with Esther on Friday. She <u>is</u> a darling – & if you don't want to go abroad, & if her Swissli maid (new) is O.K. we could go to her for 3 weeks. Would you like that? It'd be warmer & you'd be spoiled – Think about it –

Sargent is hell – heller – hellest. no – dunkel.[2] God how I hate it – no rhythm no phrasing no style no taste. Isobel Baillie[3] was better for having gone round the world. Norman Walker[4] had certain spring-like tones in his winter voice – The shortest day is over.

Marjorie Thomas[5] had a lovely voice – & did it nicely – She's quite a nice girl – without imagination & essentially bourgeois but fresh still. like a <u>young</u> mouse.

You always say that the middle of the day is the time to drink – I must say a beer, after no breakfast, at noon is heaven. I think I shall have another!

Bee darling do get well soon – I hate you being depressed & ill, & you know I just can't be with you all the time. Except in spirit!

So <u>don't worry</u> and remember there are lovely things in the world still – children, boys, sunshine, the sea, Mozart, you and me – I love you my honey – my honey Bee – My pie – Love you.

P.

[1]   (1915–2010), artist.

[2]   Malcolm Sargent (1895–1967), conductor; *dunkel* here probably means 'conceited'. Pears was to perform Handel's *Messiah* in Blackpool with the Liverpool Philharmonic conducted by Sargent that evening.

³ (1895–1983), soprano.
⁴ (1907–63), bass.
⁵ (1923–2008), contralto.

112 Britten to Pears

4 Crabbe Street
<u>Aldeburgh.</u>

Jan. 2nd 1949

My darling,

This is only to confirm what you <u>may</u> not have heard over that dreary wire last night – I go to-night to Beths, & probably Wednesday or Tuesday to Glemham – all depending on if I can face my brother or not – & back here on Thursday. I don't really want to go, but owing to the general situation here it's better to let poor old Barbara [Parker] have a bit of a time to steady & think straight.

I go rather alarmingly up & down. Some days, when there is an effort to be made (or someone I love around ……!) I feel fine, & then the next day flat as a yesterday's pan-cake. Still, it's getting better & I can't wait to go away with you, my poppetchen. I hate the idea of you doing these dreary Messiahs – do let's try & do a decent one of our own next year. Surely <u>after</u> Christmas would be a possibility; we'd get the people we want.

I hope everything next week goes well & that the voice keeps up the extraordinary quality it's got now. It is so exciting. I hope to have a talk with you the next day or so, so I won't go rambling on longer now. Anne is expected over to tea in a moment & I want to post this.

Take great care of yourself my darling – relax a lot, & don't worry (nice – me saying this). It is disappointing to a degree that I shan't be able to hear properly any of the programmes.

I love my books – I have found lots of lovely things in them both, & they are very tender collections, & extraordinaryly sympathetic. Of course the de la Mare[1] is a wider & finer one, but the narrowness of the Ransome[2] collection gives it a most moving quality.

Much love, my darling,

   see you … not so long,

     B

¹ The anthology *Love* (1943).
² Unknown volume by Arthur Ransome (1884–1967).

113 Britten to Pears

as from: 4 Crabbe Street,
Aldeburgh.

Jan. 4th 1949

My darling,

I am writing this from Beth's – seated in the nursery before a nice fire watching Sebastian make obscure looking "Slag Dump Catchers" or what not, with his Meccano. Beth has gone in the Morris & pouring rain to Ipswich to meet Robert & John[1] to come to stay to-day, & this afternoon I beat a (not too) hasty retreat when Jock fetches me & I go to Glemham till Thursday; then back to Aldeburgh. Rather contrairily Barbara P hasn't gone away as planned – not till to-morrow & won't be back till Monday when Eric & Nancy & Barbara B. will be leaving – but I feel it's all actually best that way. Don't worry about that situation, my dear, it has got on to quite a discussable (I won't exaggerate & say "unemotional" quite!) level, & will be solved amicably I am sure, for us all.

I was relieved to see that you were spared Sargent on Sunday[2] – probably only a negative advantage, but anyhow an advantage, I expect. I hope the rehearsals go well in London now, & that Ivan[3] comes up to scratch. He's got quite a mouthful to chew, especially as regards the Orchestral side. I hope they play well & co-operate with him. I'll listen, but I have no hopes of hearing anything recognisable. Perhaps the Cranbrook wireless will be better. One or two things about Old [Saint] Nic. Try & bully Woodgate[4] into the right tempi, please (& Ursula – especially don't let her take the Gallery Girls in the Pickled Boy section too quick). I've been thinking about the difficulty you have in number III. I feel it all will be better if done with a more nasal coloured tone – 'specially the Heartsick phrases – don't try & do them too big, but accentuate the two notes $\left(\widehat{\overset{\bar{v}}{\underset{\text{Heart}}{}}}\right)$ & I think that will give you the agonising quality. Don't worry about the crescendo on the G at ⑪ on "Still"; leave it to the orchestra, even taking the note off earlier if you want. I've marked it thus in the score. Above all don't worry about it! In the last number – don't let Leslie get too slow in the middle section – drag him on. If the chorus don't make enough noise in the crescendo, let the tenors go up an octave at "Glory be" as we did in Holland. Sorry, dear heart, that this letter is all instructions, but I feel abit worried about not being there. Ring up if there are any queries – Rendham 24.

I hope you are well, & not getting wet in this filthy weather. How was the party? – I expect Sophy [Stein] was in a state of nice excitement, especially as Harewood was there!

I'm getting better my dear, but don't think work will really be possible until later after we've been away, perhaps. I can't wait till that moment. Have you any suggestions where we can go?

– Darling, you have just rung so most of this letter has become superfluous. But I'll send it because so little love can come over the telephone wire! – especially when people are listening. Please give my love to all the chaps in the shows, orchestra & singers <u>&</u> to Grace Williams[5] if she's there – and a kiss!

> Lots of love,
>> Your devoted
>>> B.

---

1   Britten's brother and nephew.
2   Owing to a severe chill, Malcolm Sargent had not been able to conduct the *Messiah* in Blackpool, but the concert had gone ahead with the Liverpool Philharmonic's chorus master, J.E. Wallace, in his place.
3   Clayton (1913–66), conductor.
4   Leslie Woodgate (1902–61), conductor, BBC Choral Society.
5   (1906–77), Welsh composer and long-time friend of Britten's.

114 Britten to Pears

> 4 Crabbe Street
> <u>Aldeburgh.</u>
>
> Jan. 9th 1949

My darling,

Eventually your sweet letter arrived – almost one whole week after you wrote it – but it couldn't have arrived more opportune-like, because I was at the bottom of the well, & it was the best bucket & strongest rope to lift me out of it! It was a darling letter, quite a vintage one, & I won't tell you exactly where-abouts on me I carry it, incase it'ld make you blush.

Eric, Nancy & Barbara are here – it is nice having them, & Annie is coping splendidly. She is a grand cook, & I can't think what Barbara P. was making all that fuss about. We help all abit of course. Peter Diamand came down for the night, but he's staying at the Wentworth. It is nice to hear all his news, very amusing & hair-raising about U.S.A. – but dear, o dear, <u>how</u> I hate the thought of it all ...... You cannot imagine the inanity of all these Lucretia notices; they still arrive, almost by every post – what an ass Ralph is to send them![1]

I'm feeling <u>heaps</u> better, my dear – & the rum did no harm, honestly it didn't. If I hadn't had it, probably much greater & chronic harm might have been done – at least to the furniture & wireless, if not to me! So in future, I don't think I shall try to listen to wireless at all – try & forget that it is all happening. After all I know old Nic (& Leslie [Woodgate]!), & I've heard the Holst & can't anyhow hear P.G.

How's that going? – I at least hope that Rankl gets your tempi right. I'm so glad that you bullied Leslie about the Nic one, now you can do the same with Karl! Isn't it strange how one's sympathies have all gone over to Webster & Rankl in this silly Beecham business?[2] Nancy suggested that we should club together & send a muzzle to the silly doddering old fool!

Beth & Robert & John are coming over to tea this afternoon – it'll be nice for the latter two to see the house & sea & all, but I can't pretend I look forward to it.

I gather, you secretive old thing, that you <u>have</u> had the furniture moved from Oxford Square! I am so glad, because now at least you'll have a quasi home to go to with all your things. It's so nice that it has turned out better than I at least feared.

I must <u>really</u> get up now & entertain my guests. So goodbye for the moment, my darling. I can't bear to think that it is still a week longer – but I suppose I must.

Next week has sorted it self out neatly – the Mauds on their own initiative have suggested coming on Friday (which leaves us free for the following one!), & Morgan is coming on Monday week.

By-the-way, if you want a cheque just let me know how much – I hope to get Egypt news from Fidelity soon.

<u>Enormous</u> & glorious parcel from Elizabeth – loads of food – very sweetly done up. Nice letter from Clytie – <u>if</u> you had a moment do write to her; she wants to hear from you, darling.

Alls my love, my everything, my darling.

Take care of yourself.

Your devoted

B

---

[1] The Broadway production of *The Rape of Lucretia* was not a success.

[2] Thomas Beecham (1879–1961), conductor, had earlier that week made derogatory and typically inflammatory public remarks about the Royal Opera House, specifically the appointment of Karl Rankl.

115 Pears to Britten

W.14

?49–50 [dated by Pears]

My own darling honey bunch –

It was heavenly talking to you yesterday evening and finding you so much happier – only <u>do</u> take care & don't overdo it – I'm afraid you'll have a reaction now & go to the bottom again – Be sensible, b., please.

Life goes on as usual here – Joan had a cold yesterday & couldn't rehearse but I shall be meeting her and Karl [Rankl] this afternoon at Covent Garden for a rehearsal.

<u>Later.</u>

Joan <u>still</u> had a cold, so I didn't rehearse. Saw Mr. Perriton this morning – a very useful session – He would like to see you if you could face it, but quite understands if not! but could you send him all figgiwiggies[1] for year ending April '48 – Mr. Newman says you have them –

Longing to see you, bunch – Not long now – Saturday.

> Much much love.
> P.

---

[1]   Figures for completion of their tax return.

116 Pears to Britten

22A Melbury Road. W.14

[before 15 Jan 1949]

My own honey –

I didn't mean to be cold last night, but it seemed to end up like that – v.v. sorry, my darling – I love you really & am longing to see you again on Saturday –

Could you please fill up & <u>sign</u> the enclosed form & return with <u>passport</u> to Erwin at B&H. presto.

I do hope you aren't bored with the idea of Venice An Italian agency told me today that the weather will be allright. Oh dear!

> Much much love
> my honey bee
> P.

117 Britten to Pears

4 Crabbe Street,
Aldeburgh.

Jan 11th 1949

My darling,

Here is the cheque. I made it 200 just to show my affection.

Settle what you want, where you want for us to go to. I'll fall in with anything. If you want travellers cheques get B&H to arrange it for you (Mr. Newman, forinstance).

If you have a chance to see Barbara this week – if you've got an evening free & want a meal, or lunch (she's often at Yarners) ring her, & suggest it – her number is Flax. 6202. She'd love to see you.

Excuse the tiny note, but I've been writing lots of other madly over-due letters all the morning – Elizabeth, Clytie, Jetty etc.

All my love – can't wait till Saturday – Good luck for rehearsals

love & good luck to Joan – &

love, everso much, buckets full,

to you,

Dein

B.

118 Britten to Pears

Aldeburgh.

[19 Feb 1949]

My darling,

Here are the scores. Is that all? I am sorry I was so gloomy yesterday, but it was the bottom of the well for me. Work was impossible, & I felt absolutely desparate. I think it was the reaction after Italy, & especially coming back to the hopeless realities of the E.O.G. financial crisis! However I spent the afternoon at Glemham, & went to bed early with lots of pills, & now to-day it is heavenly weather & I'm feeling better.

I'm thinking of you alot during these days of rehearsal & chasing around. I hope you don't get too tired. I miss you most dreadfully – but I must learn to stand on my own two legs, & realise that Italys can't go on for ever!

I tried to hear the Haffner & Exsultate[1] last night, but gave it up as it was too interrupted.

How was it? And Berger?
>Tons of love,
>>Ben

---

[1] BBC broadcast of a Mozart concert featuring Erna Berger (1900–90), German coloratura soprano, and the Philharmonic Orchestra conducted by Paul Sacher (1906–99), 18 February 1949.

119 Pears to Britten

<u>Kensington</u>

[?mid–late Feb 1949]

My own darling poppet.

The parcels arrived yesterday, and with them your dear letter – My darling, our heavenly three weeks together was a sample merely of what our life ought to be, and indeed of what it quite often could be. We have got to try to get more of these breathing spaces because that is what they are – in between them one is far beneath the surface swimming busily about – Let's come to the surface more often! One should see lovely things unworried – I insist that this is the last year that you are worried outside your work – Your work must got slower – we are getting older, my B., and it is no longer seemly that we run around like children – in our work or in our play – !

I must go and rehearse – My first lesson[1] was most interesting – I go again this afternoon –

>All my love to you, my honey –
>I love you –
>>P.

---

[1] With singing teacher Eva de Reusz, who also taught Nancy Evans.

120 Britten to Pears

Kensington

[?Feb 1949]

Darling P –

Perhaps after all we'd better NOT telephone, because we always get cross – !

But somehow even getting cross, or feeling you're cross with me is better than silence, so perhaps after all we'd better keep it up! Anyhow, thank you very much for ringing.

This is only to send on two little notes. I must say I think your "Coz" is very attractive, and gay. And also intelligent. Could you at least, <u>think</u>, about the Vellani one – she was the nice secretary, wasn't she? And answer it when we think about programmes in general?

Dr Acheson has just been – he's a nice kind man. He says my depression is natural, & I musn't worry about it! By-the-way in the bottom of the well last night, I started putting on records – Ponselle,[1] a very good singer, not perfect musically, but lovely voice & extraordinary technique, Gigli & Schipa,[2] – & feeling very disatisficed with the latter two, I put on your record of Nacht & Traume[3] & do you know, poppetty, that there's nothing they've got you haven't – the quality of your voice (& it's a bad record too) is much lovelier than theirs. What they've got, which isn't the fashion today, is this extraordinary worked-out quality, even with all the exaggerations that it means: A pause really is a pause, louds are loud, & crescendos & dims are immensely strong & long. Of course the latter two (G. & S.) nearly always do it in the wrong places, & are shockingly unmusical. I think what you have got to work to is this immense "effect-ness", & with the musician-ship you've got, & all the technique & voice advantages – you can lead them by miles. It was an interesting (& gratifying!) contrast.

All my love, darling,
take care of yourself,
B.

---

[1] Rosa Ponselle (1897–1981), American soprano.
[2] Beniamino Gigli (1890–1957) and Tito Schipa (1888–1965), both Italian tenors.
[3] Schubert song.

121 Britten to Pears

4 Crabbe Street
<u>Aldeburgh</u>

[2 Mar 1949]

My darling,

Here is the first batch. Hope they all arrive O.K. I had a look at Seraglio[1] before I packed it – what a <u>lovely</u>, <u>lovely</u> piece! I wish I could here you do Belmonte some time – how nice if you could do it at Salzburg next year! Or Geneva.

It's a heavenly day, rather oppressed by bad Group financial news, but it can't spoil the wonderful light on the sea – rather like the Chioggia trip, but perhaps not quite so blue. My memories of the three weeks grow lovelier & lovelier – but unlike most memories they don't make me unhappy or nostalgic, only contented & looking forward. Lovely as Venice, Bellini, the little Carpaccio boys,[2] Mimosa and the wine-dark sea off Portofino were, my happiest & most treasured memory is of the wonderful ~~pie~~ peace & contentment of your love & friendship. Love, such as I felt we had in those 3 weeks, is a rare thing – as beautiful and luminous as this sea outside, & with endless depths too. Thank you, my dearest.

I saw Mr. Robinson, the footman this morning & liked him immensely. But I must talk some things over with Beth, & then talk over the 'phone with you. But I think he'll do.

My love to everyone; hope Erwin is better. When you've seen Morgan, if you can, ~~pe~~ & we know his plans, I'll ask him down here, perhaps?

All my love, my dearest,

    Ben

---

[1] Mozart's opera. Belmonte is the tenor hero.
[2] Paintings by Vittore Carpaccio (c 1465–1525/26).

122 Britten to Pears

[?before 18 Mar 1949]

My darling

This is only to say good morning & to say I love you, & miss you, & long for you to come back on Friday, & how I hope that you've had a lesson to-day, & that it was a nice one & pleased you & Madam [de Reusz] too, & that the opera libretto[1] is pounding ahead with Morgan still at full steam & irrepressible, and that I like the Spring Symphony, apart from one still beastly bit that I can't, <u>can't</u>, <u>can't</u> get right, but I suppose I shall one day, and how are you, and are you taking your blood-pressure pills, & if not, why, & hadn't you better go & see the Doctor again,

& tell him what's the matter with them, and to ask you what train you think you'll be on on Friday, & that it doesn't seem likely that ~~Eric~~ we will be able to come to Ipswich because Eric's got to be in London for a Director's meeting, (did you see or talk with Anne – a bit important) & to send you my love, & my love, & my love, & kisses & my love ——

    Your B.

---

[1] *Billy Budd.*

123 Britten to Pears

[?after 7 Mar 1949]

My darling –

    Two letters, both a little unpleasant – so sorry!

    We had a nice day with Cecily & Walter[1] & they were really charming to us. You must really manage to pay them a visit – Cecily is devoted to you – & you'd like to see all the chaps & the lovely house & position. We then went back to Ipswich & heard 37 children for the opera![2] Some, happily very promising, & one poppet of a tough small boy!

    Hope you are well & working – writing any letters … ??!!

    I had a good mornings work – tra-la, trala.

        All my love, my darling,
            B

---

[1] Smithwick, Pears's sister and brother-in-law.
[2] Auditions for *Let's Make an Opera.*

124 Britten to Pears

Elizabeth sent a cheque for the Ass: which
<u>I'm keeping for your endorsement. Love, B</u>

4 Crabbe Street,
<u>Aldeburgh</u>

April 8th 1949

My darling,

    I hope soon to have news of you, how the journey was, & how you're feeling. I'm thinking of you all the time, wishing I were with you & enjoying you (in every way!). At least I shall be able to hear you on Sunday, or as much of you as my work will allow me. I am pushing on terrifically with the children's opera, not stopping to think what I'm doing or how it is – because I have to deliver some of the score on Thursday to Erwin! I think anyhow that it's gay enough, altho' possibly not very distinguished – and also it's easy, which is something! It's funny writing an opera without you in it – don't really like it much, I confess, but I'll admit that it makes my vocal demands less extravagant!

I enclose Elizabeth's sweet note, because I thought you'd like to see it – the rest I'll keep till you're back. There's nothing much. Sweet letters from all at Dartington – really thrilled with what we gave them. We have really a very loyal & warm lot of friends.

All goes smoothly here, although Olive & Robinson don't seem over friendly. I hope that doesn't boil up. On the other hand Miss Hudson's cooking virtuosity seems as terrific as ever.

We have to take the early morning plane on Wednesday week to Italy – which is a bore, but it is a very long way & as we don't arrive till 4.0 pm, I think we must do it. The Austrian visa matter seems simple.

Give my love to all the friends – Bertus as well. I hope Nancy sings well & makes an impression. Love to all the Diamands, Mrs D. esp.

And as much as the world holds to you – my darling – my love & complete confidence in all you do.

Your devoted Ben.

125 Pears to Britten

<u>American Hotel.</u>

Monday A.M. in bed [11 Apr 1949]

The Bach arrived incredibly quickly! On Thursday evening! v. many thanks. P.

My own honey darling –

Your adorable letter has just arrived, brought up by the scruffy little pageboy, & so I'm writing straight off to you waiting for my breakfast to come – I was terribly happy to have your wire last evening – I got it when I came back from the Diamands where I had tea after the Passion – Jetty, Pam H.J., Hazel[1] & one or two others very sweet – I've been rather a neurotic voice-conscious old tenor this week – Wolverhampton & Birmingham were pretty dreary – the weather was awful – pouring showers & B'ham with the shops shut – the only relief was that I found a copy of "Curious Relations"[2] & yelled with laughter for 2 days. What a funny book. Then the car-journey to London was no fun & the flight was allright

except for last 10 minutes which were bumpy – & then it was <u>boiling</u> <u>sweaty</u> hot
in the Concertgebouw for Thursday's general probe [dress rehearsal] – & I thought
my voice had gone – I really did – So I stayed in bed all Friday & inhaled & fussed
& saw no-one – & same on Saturday – & I thought "I can probably make tonight
but what about Sunday?" & then I made Saturday allright & went straight back to
bed & inhaled etc. oh dear! & then Sunday <u>was</u> allright after all! What a fool I am!
but thank goodness you weren't here all the same – I couldn't have borne to see your
nervous little look in the eyes – ! Honey – bee!

So now it's Bertus & his do – I hope that'll be allright.

It'll be lovely to see Nancy – She's staying at Rotterdam.

I'm glad you liked the [St Matthew] Passion & that it came over well – I am
getting to know it better (with, I hope, certain advantages) but so is van Beinum
– & I'm afraid that has its disadvantages – All those choruses that <u>will</u> accelereate
in the last 2 bars – & the ensemble & tempi in the arias – & "Wahrlich dies war
Gottes Sohn!" – terrible. They get wilder with the years–

Häfliger's voice is really excellent, though he's not a <u>sensitive</u> musician. What
did you think of Jo?[3] First of all, she's a darling! Then, though she sang flat in the
"Aus Liebe", I thought she sang the G major 6/8 Aria nicely – & I <u>do</u> think all
things considered she <u>is</u> the right person for Spring – Her voice is cool – but has
character & I find charm – She would sing the Driving boy nicely I think & also
our Duet, which is not heavily scored – Apparently above A according to Jetty she
has difficulty – but what is there above A? I can't remember.

<u>So</u> glad the Children's Opera is going so well.

You are an old poppet & I do love you very very dearly – & am longing for next
week-end!

By the way, a dozen bottles of assorted sherries should be arriving from Harvey's
of Bristol, also a lot of nice dishes for oven & table combined – from W'hampton.

All all my love –

  honey –

    bee –

      my boy –

       P.

John Nicholson[4] is looking thin – I'm worried about him – The sweet pageboy
asked tenderly after you. They are sorry for me being alone!

---

[1] Jetty Bosmans with two unidentified companions.
[2] Novel by Anthony Butts and William Plomer.
[3] Vincent (1898–1989), Dutch soprano.
[4] Prep school friend of Britten; he was also the son of the Britten family solicitor.

IV

'You are potentially the greatest singer alive'

LATE 1949 TO JANUARY 1954

The early 1950s found Pears and Britten both flourishing with success, bolstered by an increase in commissions for new works from Britten and demand for Pears as a soloist, both in the UK and abroad. In addition to the hard work of composing and performing, they continued to oversee the English Opera Group, which experienced numerous financial and administrative difficulties, and to develop and expand the Aldeburgh Festival in keeping with their own standards and philosophical outlook. However, there came expectations of even greater achievement from audiences, critics, fellow musicians and, most significantly, from themselves.

By this time, Pears was in demand as both a concert artist and on the operatic stage, but with increasing pressures to perform he began to suffer from throat problems. Not surprisingly, he felt insecure about being unable to sing at his best before an audience. Thus, Britten's letters during this period are filled with reassurance; for example, after listening to a broadcast of Bach's *St Matthew Passion*, he writes 'The voice sounds so full & so rich, & with so much variety, & this glorious musical phrasing […] There can never have been an Evangelist like you – it's wonderful to be born in your lifetime to hear you do it' (Letter 158). With the weight of such high standards, it is no wonder that both men became so critical of their individual abilities and relied upon their appraisal of one another to ease their doubts. Britten acknowledges this in a letter of March 1951: 'It was lovely to play [*Billy Budd*] to you, & you gave me back my confidence which had been slowly ebbing away. In a work of this size & tension that is one of one's greatest problems. I believe that is yours too – if one aims high (& you achieve your aims so often) one is so desparately ashamed when one knows one is missing them' (Letter 157).

In truth, both men were working themselves to the point of exhaustion. Britten's physical ailments, coupled with the time constraints from working on two complex and significant operas – *Billy Budd* for the 1951 Festival of Britain and *Gloriana*, composed in honour of Queen Elizabeth II's coronation in 1953 – resulted in his being unable to give recitals with Pears as frequently as in the past. By necessity, then, Pears had to work with other accompanists – including Gerald Moore, who stood in for Britten in October 1950 at the Leeds Festival, and later more often with Noel Mewton-Wood in 1952 and 1953. This situation was surely difficult for both: for Britten, there may have been the thought that Mewton-Wood, an exceptional pianist, might technically be preferable and replace him as an accompanist, while Pears, still nervous about the security of his voice in performance, was having to develop a whole new musical relationship, and needed reassurance. After a letter (now lost) in which Pears must have confided his concerns, Britten wrote back: 'Don't worry about the concerts, I am sure they are fine – anything you do will always be that. But however good Noel is, I am certain that you & I together have something very special, & it won't be long before that happens again!' (Letter 181). Pears sang with other pianists and conductors, after all, many times throughout his career – it would have been impossible to do otherwise. But Britten would never accompany or compose for another tenor in the same way as he wrote for Pears – that would have been unthinkable.

The pattern of their life together was changing in other ways too, as the more durable friendships and working relationships began to form into a circle which, for practical as well as personal reasons, centred on the household in Aldeburgh. Britten needed help with the more arduous and time-consuming aspects of preparing scores for performance and publication, particularly for the larger operatic works. He had made use of assistants in the past, for example Arthur Oldham, Jim Bernard and Martin Penny, but this period saw the introduction of Jeremy Cullum, as secretary, and Imogen Holst, who became Britten's first long-term music assistant. Holst's involvement came about after Pears attended a residential music course in February 1951 at Dartington, where she was Director of Music. 'Imo', the daughter of the composer Gustav Holst, shared Pears's love of early music, particularly Schütz and Monteverdi. His letters are full of praise for her abilities and enthusiasm, and Britten admits to being envious of Pears enjoying music for its own sake again: 'I really do envy you this quiet minstrelsy tucked away from the hideous commercial world. Try & persuade Imo to go back there occasionally in the future, & ask me to come to – with my viola even!' (Letter 153). Holst assisted Britten with the score for *Gloriana*, moving to Aldeburgh in September 1952, where she became a central figure in the musical life of the town. Britten found her knowledge of early music and her formal dance training extremely useful when composing the Courtly Dances for *Gloriana*; ever resourceful, Holst sought out experts to teach her the Elizabethan dances Britten was attempting to emulate in his music. She would also advise on programming for the Festival and EOG, and worked with Britten on several publications including a realization of Purcell's *Dido and Aeneas* (1951, revised 1958–59), a jointly edited series of recorder music for Boosey & Hawkes, and later a book for children, *The Story of Music* (1958).

Thanks to the financial security Britten's success had granted, he and Pears enjoyed travelling with a variety of companions – in September 1951 they took a boat trip across the North Sea to Rotterdam then up the Rhine with friends including Basil Coleman and the Aldeburgh fisherman Billy Burrell and his brother John, then in March 1952 they went on a recital tour in Vienna and Salzburg, followed by skiing with Marion Stein and her husband, George Lascelles, Earl of Harewood, in Gargellen, Austria. The Harewoods were, as the letters indicate, essentially an extended part of Britten and Pears's family. It was also during this period that Britten and Pears first met Prince Ludwig and Princess Margaret of Hesse and the Rhine, staying with them at their estate, Schloss Wolfsgarten, in March 1952. The Hesses opened their home to the couple, offering Britten another retreat for composing and, often, to convalesce. They developed a close friendship with 'Lu' and especially 'Peg', despite their obvious differences; the Hesses were clearly from an elevated social sphere, and there are occasional references in the letters to difficult patches in their friendship. But they shared a love of music, art and travel and often holidayed together.

Another interest, for Pears especially, was collecting fine art. Although he had acquired a number of works in the 1940s, it was in the early 1950s that he began in earnest. A significant purchase in March 1950 of William Blake's *St Paul Shaking Off the Viper* is mentioned in Letter 133. References to paintings and sculpture begin to appear in their letters more regularly, alongside the inevitable glimpses of domestic details – renovations, wallpaper, curtains, new housekeeper Miss Hudson, muslin, teacups and other 'nesting' peripherals. The regular pattern suggested by the letters is of Britten at home, trying to compose, writing to Pears that the house is overflowing with guests such as librettists E.M. Forster and Eric Crozier to work on *Billy Budd*, and William Plomer for *Gloriana*. With the administration of the Aldeburgh Festival and EOG practically running from the house as well, it is unsurprising that Britten writes in 1950 after a recent flying visit by Pears: 'I didn't seem to see enough of you, my dearest. It's no good – we <u>must</u> have the house to ourselves!' (Letter 141).

The letters from this period begin just after Britten and Pears toured North America from mid-October to December 1949. The tour was important as it was their first joint tour of the US, and although they had come to dislike the States, as comments in their letters show, they were bound by their desire for the success of the Aldeburgh Festival to maintain professional ties in the region. They gave over twenty recitals across America and in Canada, taking the opportunity to recruit artists for the 1950 Festival along the way.

126 Britten to Pears

[*Letterhead:* English Opera Group]

[?late 1949]

My darling P.,

These two little notelets – hope the insurance one isn't too violent – you must do something about it – so must I, incidentally, but I have changed my card! Hope the throat's better, & that Silbiger can & will help. <u>If</u>, only if, you have time, have a look at the Constable,[1] but don't bother. I know you've got lots to do. I'm here all the time, so ring if you want to chat – I love it! Everything's very comfy: I expect to get down to work, now. Miss Hudson's good & kind.

Hope, against hope, you can manage the week-end. It's awfully good for me to see you.

Love you.

B

Poor Mary B. does run off the rails in her musical judgments sometimes. doesn't she? But she's an enthusiastic dear.

---

[1]   Pears purchased Constable's portrait of his son, Charles Golding Constable, in 1950.

127 Pears to Britten

Les Hirondelles
<u>Leysin</u>

Saturday 21st [Jan 1950]

Honey-Kin –

Here I am[1] or rather me-voici parcequ' il faut toujours parler Français ici (pardonnez mois cette Bironette sacrée!) – Le voyage était très convenable. L'avion etait arrivée sur l'heure et j'ai gagnee ma train sans difficulté – Hier il y a̶ avait du brouillard ici et ~~était~~ il faisait froid aussi, mai aujourd'hui le soleil rayonne et brûle.[2]

This is really a sweet place, the village is typical Swiss, not as nice as Zermatt, but very pretty with lots of snow about – This clinic seems after 16 hours to be very well run and pleasant – All rooms face South & one has a balcony in which one gets just all the sun – The rooms are very simple and institutional but quite adequate – Food, good average not de-Luxe Swiss-li – View very fine with a fierce mountain just opposite called Les Dents du Midi – very appropriately.

One has breakfast at 7.15(!) though I am not washed before (others are) I am allowed to make my toilet at my leisure – Lunch is at 12 – one rests from 1–3 and sleeps – That is all I know so far. Otherwise one is left blissfully alone – In bad weather it could be hideously dull, I imagine – but I seem to have brought the Sun with me – It snowed for two days just before I came – Even now it's not going to be exciting, but then I'm not here to be excited – ! There's a movie which has performances on Saturday and Sunday – At the moment, I feel as if 10 days here will fill the bill – till Monday week 30th – and then a little wandering – One can't get into Geneva for the day from here, it's too far & too expensive – I might try Montreux or Lausanne one day, but these railways up & down the mountain are so expensive! I think everything seems dearer – one good Swissli ham roll at the railway station cost 1 fr 20 c. which seems an awful lot.

I do hope you're having a happy time, my bee – I do miss you, you know – I'm doing my best to relax and be convalescent but I'm really feeling immensely fit and full of ideas – Please don't overwork and get tired, yourself – I expect you'll profit by not having me with you – Give everyone my love – but keep the major part of it for yourself, my old fudge – Je t'aime

   P.

---

1 Pears had gone to Switzerland to recover from an attack of the shingles.
2 'here I am, because here one must always speak French (excuse this cursed little ballpoint pen!) The trip was quite decent. The plane arrived on time and I got my train without difficulty. Yesterday there was some fog here and it was also cold, but today the sun is shining and hot.'

128 Britten to Pears

P.S. If you can get me a kids' Diary – Pestalozzi,   <u>Saturday</u> [21 Jan 1950]
without difficulty, I'd be obliged! Love.

[*Letterhead:* Grey House, Burghclere, Newbury]

My dearest,

The weather to-day here is ideal mountain weather – you really needn't have gone away! Sun & cold, with snow just round the corner. I hope you've got the same. I thought about you all yesterday – rather to the detriment to my behaviour at the various functions – & pictured you arriving at the clinic & the quick eye roving round for the blonds! I so wonder what it is like – but don't bother to write & say, just remember to tell when you get back.

The day with me was to schedule. I packed. Met Mr Henry Foy,[1] was not enthusiastic about his personality, but feel he may be right for the Group. He's a flowery cove, moustache & curly hair (how I <u>hate</u> curls). But musical, & a good business man. The Directors' meeting was abortive (not enough directors for a quorum!) but we discussed well; Elizabeth [Sweeting] was maddeningly vague, & Eric maddeningly precise as usual. But James Lawrie & Erwin good. I think we'll get Foy. No Arts Council news yet.

I seized a sandwich & then caught 2.35 at Paddington with sister Barbara. Rather a distracting journey with train full of young Pangbournians.[2] Saw a heavenly meeting between two flowers on Reading Station – such pleasure at re-uniting after the holidays was heart warming – the Greek Anthology level.

It is lovely here – quiet, comfortable & interesting talk as always with Mary & Bow. Barbara a little piano [quiet], & rather nervous, but I hope she'll settle down to-day. It is pathetic the thought of them leaving here – they were built for this house, & it for them. Perhaps it's superstition, but I can't picture them lasting long in the new cottage. Tomorrow Pipers, & Tuesday Dartington.

All my love, get better & better.

Dein B.

---

[1]   General Manager of the EOG from March 1950.
[2]   Pupils from Pangbourne College in Berkshire.

129 Pears to Britten

Hirondelles

Leysin

Tuesday [24 Jan 1950]

My darling honey –

Your letter arrived today – It was heavenly to have it – I was frightfully pleased – Letters only seem to take 2 days getting here – I hope they don't take any longer from here to you – because I've decided, Fudgie, that I don't want to stay on here – I'm perfectly well again, and am really only miserable not to be with you – and I want to get back to some gentle work too. If you were here, it would be different, 'cos you would be getting a holiday, which might be good for you – But now I just don't want any more of Switzerland, or of anywhere else much but England – So I hope to fly back on Saturday 28th and come down to Lancing for the weekend![1] So there! I want to be with you – (There aren't any blonds here either but that wouldn't matter anyway!)

I shall leave here (which is all very nice but frightfully boring – & the sun hasn't appeared for two days – & the food is v. dull & it's essentially for sick people & I'm <u>not</u> sick any more) on Friday – Shall go to Berne for the night, & then fly back from Geneva on Saturday – I don't know when you will get this letter, but I shall send a wire on Thursday evening, I expect.

I have been for long walks here in the snow, which is really v. nice. I've also had a few French lessons with a sweet old Professor from Strasbourg. I went into Lausanne yesterday as it was so dismal here; that was quite interesting – but everything is much more expensive than it was – And I don't know somehow the Swiss way of life seems a bit stale, & I want to get back to dear old England! and my sweet old Britten! So don't be too cross with me, will you B? Lancing + you and Esther is much much better for me than Laysin – you and Esther –

I can't tell you how I'm looking forward to coming back!!!

Much much love

P.

---

1   Britten was scheduled to go to Lancing on 28 January.

130 Pears to Britten

[?early 1950]

My darling old Honey –

It was lovely to have your letter this morning – & thank you very much for the varied passions which I think will suffice – I have my English Matthew[1] uphere I think –

I miss you very much indeed and tend all the while to be neurotic & depressed, but am allright really & am resting etc. not getting up till noon –

Had a rehearsal last night with the Weolian 4tet[2] & Robin Orr[3] came too – What a nice chap he is! but not alas! a very wonderful composer.

Emmie told me yesterday that she has had a confirmatory telegram from Salzburg, that they have definitely engaged someone else – for Joan's part![4] It's unspeakable & we must make a fuss – First, I think you should write to Franckenstein resigning from the S. Society[5] – so I think should George – Perhaps a telegram to Puthon at Salzburg I'm not sure, & quite a bit later I can be a nuisance – I should prefer not to do anything until they have all the printing out – always provided that I have not had a contract signed by Taubmann for me!

I've written to George about it –

Much much love, honey bee

ever yr. P.

I called in at the National Gal. of Brit. Sports & Pastimes (Strafford House off Oxford St.) & saw the most gorgeous Constable – "Boys fishing near Stratford Mill" Wow!

[1] Copy of Bach's *St Matthew Passion*.
[2] Aeolian String Quartet.
[3] (1909–2006), Scottish composer.
[4] For four performances of the *The Rape of Lucretia* at the Salzburg Festival in August 1950.
[5] Salzburg Festival Society.

131 Pears to Britten

22A Melbury Rd

[early 1950]

My honey –

This is just after our phone talk – (I do enjoy talking to you!)

Arthur Benjamin's [Viola] Sonata is 18 min. (Elegy – Waltz – Toccata).

I have asked Marguérite D'Alvarez to judge costumes at the Ball & she has accepted![1]

Isn't there a – (yes there is I have just rung Walter Bergmann[2] at Schotts!) Suite in A minor for Fl. Str 4tet & Continuo (quite possible for Harp according to W. B.) by Telemann. about 15–20 min. John Francis[3] has played it.

There is also a much shorter Vivaldi Concerto for Flute & 4tet.

& Schotts have a Flute & Strings piece by <u>Seiber</u> called Pastorale & Burleque.

much love.   P.

[1] The contralto (1883–1953) was to judge a fancy dress ball, held to raise funds for the Aldeburgh Festival.
[2] (1902–88), editor at Schott's Music Publishers.
[3] (1908–92), flautist, member of the EOG orchestra.

132 Britten to Pears

4 Crabbe Street

<u>Aldeburgh.</u>

March 17th 1950

My darling,

La Travy[1] has just arrived – & I am terribly thrilled with it! What a lovely present – you could have hardly (Gainsborough[2] perhaps excepted!) have given me something which pleased me more. I have already wasted far too long in browsing over it, but it didn't matter because I'm in a bit of a muddle over Billy [Budd] & not ready to start on him again yet. Anyhow one learns so much from Verdi so B.B. will be a better opera for your present, I've no doubt!

I'm going over to Braintree to-morrow morning to fetch back the car – running on 3 breaks (don't worry, I'll drive carefully!) – & then Wards here will take it to pieces & see what's wrong. They can't get the hub off because they've not got the right tools, yet.

Morgan is going on well – a bit of a leaky problem still, but cheerful & keen to work. May[3] is sweet person who is nice to have around.

I hope all the work goes well this week. I hope at least the new wavelengths will improve the 3rd prog. reception. It was maddening last night. Are you working with Madame? But rest, as much as possible, dearest, even tho' it's boring!

This is only a scribble, to send my love, & warmest thanks for the Verdi. A great thrill!

> Love, lots of it,
> Your devoted old
> <u>Ben</u>

---

[1] A score to Verdi's opera, *La traviata*.
[2] Thomas Gainsborough (1727–88), painter.
[3] Buckingham, a nurse and the wife of Forster's long-time friend, Bob Buckingham. Forster was recovering from a prostate operation.

133 Britten to Pears

I'm still stunned
by the Blake.[1] Can
you manage to bring it down?

<u>Aldeburgh</u>

[?22–4 Mar 1950]

My darling –

This is only to send you my love, & to hope Liverpool isn't too trying & Malcolm[2] neither. Relax and just sing as beautifully as you can, a flower growing on a dung heap!

I don't think I've ever felt quite so close to you as in these last few days; it was pure Heaven, & I thank God for you, my darling. I don't think you ever realise how much you help me (much more than Mr Perriton's £200 per year!). You give me a loving critical confidence – in every way. I wish I could do a 100th part for you. The love is there, there's no doubt (I think you realise!) of that – but the rest is inadequate, like me generally. Please forgive & go on loving!

The journey down, long and boring. But Francis[3] met us, & we whizzed back in Ward's car. May goes to-day, but Morgan will be all right, I'm praying. Erwin & Sofie will tell you about the party – rather charmless except for Marionli's oration!

Lots of love, & all myself,

Ben.

---

1   William Blake's *St Paul Shaking Off the Viper*, which Pears had purchased.
2   Pears was singing the *St Matthew Passion* with the Liverpool Philharmonic Society, conducted by Sargent.
3   Francis was evidently employed by the local Ward's Garage as a driver.

134 Britten to Pears

Aldeburgh

March. 30th 1950

Love, of course, to Peter & Jetty etc. etc.

My darling,

Only to send my love – nothing more. I hope all is well with you – that the journey up & the flight were good – that you are now happily established in the American Hotel, flirting with all our blond young friends, drinking sociable Bols', seeing nice people & singing as only you, my dearest, <u>can</u> sing![1]

We go on here. Morgan seems better. He's dry to-day, thank goodness, & therefore more cheerful. He came to the Boyd Neel[2] last night, & like me enjoyed some of it. They played most of a dull programme with really great brilliance & verve. It is nice to hear people play as if they minded. The Suk Serenade (drab piece if ever there was one) was delivered with great conviction & obviously impressed. Alas, the Byrd & Mozart were as you'd expect – with-out any knowledge or authority, & so the ravishing & moving pieces made no effect, that is, comparable to the others. It was a great success, & every one who came (about 100–120) enjoyed themselves. But probably as a result there'll be no 2nd concert – there being no funds. I had a tiny party after – about 15 people – including all the usual, and as well the Smiths (sister & bro. in law of Christopher Wood)[3] who seemed nice. The Blake & Cotman[4] made sensations – as well they should. The former looks terrific over the fireplace. And everyone asked tenderly after & sent their love to you, & congratulated you on your taste!

It's heavenly that you'll be here next Saturday week – I hope the interval isn't too hard – but, I know you'll sing well, & give loads of people real pleasure.

My love to – you, my dearest. It was ~~hea~~ an interlude of heaven to have you with me. Billy Budd progresses.

All of me

to you

B.

---

1   Pears was in Amsterdam to sing at a British Council house concert and Bach's *St Matthew Passion*.
2   Boyd Neel Orchestra in concert at the Aldeburgh Parish Church.
3   (1911–90), harpsichordist and teacher at Trinity College of Music.
4   Cotman's *Draining Mills at Crowland*, since reattributed to the School of Cotman.

135 Pears to Britten

[*Letterhead:* American Hotel N.V., Amsterdam]

[3 Apr 1950]

My old honey-bun –

It seems already a long time since I spoke to you on the telephone – was it Friday? and today's Monday – I'm longing to be back with you, I can't tell you how much –

Things go allright here – The Songs at the British Council on Friday were well appreciated, and Jetty's song[1] had really quite a success. She is feeling happy now, because some songs she wrote for Noemie Perugia[2] had a great success 10 days ago, it appears. Anyway on Friday all was happy – only the Roth Trio's participation was tinged with gloom – They played a very silly piece by Leighton Lucas,[3] and also Beethoven's Geister-Trio![4] Kennen Sie das? [Do you know it?] Frighteningly awful –

Saturday was the first Concertgebouw Mat. Pas., and it wasn't too wonderful – E. van B. [Beinum] has really no understanding of Bach at all, and, what was surprising, no feeling for the stimmung [mood] of it – I spoke to him about it, and yesterday's performance was noticeably better, but I am very bored by it – and I look forward to Rotterdam (rehearsal this evening) –

Peter is being very helpful and kind – driving me everywhere – and Maggie Schil[5] is a darling – Jo[6] seems to be in rather a nervy state – she made a passionate attack on Peter for using foreign singers in the Holland Festival, & it was all rather embarassing – Here singing is very tense, too – I wonder if you heard the broadcast

– We only had 40 minutes interval, which in many ways is better than a huge lunch break – but maybe not for Aldeburgh!

I've picked up a book by a Suffolk chap I wot not of. Arthur Young's Travels in France & Italy (1788) – a great agriculturist from nr. Lavenham – A really lovely lively account, & a breath of fresh Suffolk sweet air, which I need v. badly, my pussy-cat.

I'm flying back 11.50 on Thursday arr. Heathrow or is it Northolt at 12.35, very quick! Lesley will drive me down on Saturday morning, erster ding [first thing].

How I'm longing to see you! Very much love to Morgan – I do hope he's still dry – !

           All ofme to you –
               P.

---

1   *The Artist's Secret.*
2   (1903–92), French soprano.
3   Cassation in F.
4   'Ghost Trio'.
5   Maikie Schill, a musician's agent.
6   Vincent (1898–1989), Dutch soprano.

✠✠✠

The middle months of 1950 were extremely busy for Britten and Pears. After the Aldeburgh Festival and a number of other performing commitments, Britten also began work on *Billy Budd* with E.M. Forster and Eric Crozier, as well as a realization of Purcell's *Dido and Aeneas* with Imogen Holst. Apparently the composer's engagements were so numerous that Forster grew concerned Britten would not be able to finish *Budd* by their deadline, but as Britten urged Eric Crozier in a letter of 29 August 1950: 'Please tell [Morgan] if you get a chance that I <u>always</u> do twenty things at once, & that there'll be a good chance of the opera being done in time!' In early September Britten and Pears performed at the Edinburgh Festival, after which they spent several weeks on holiday in Italy, returning in time for a 25 September recital in London with Kathleen Ferrier. On 4 October they were to have performed at Leeds, and two days later Britten was to have conducted his *Spring Symphony*, but as Letter 136 (below) makes clear, he had fallen ill.

✠✠✠

136 Pears to Britten

[*Letterhead:* Harewood House, Leeds]

3 p.m. [4 Oct 1950]

My own darling honey-pot,

Only just a scribbled note (I can't find a pen in my bedroom & I daren't ring a bell!) to say that we had just lifted the receiver to call you when Marion's call came through (Don't be cross! I just couldn't ring before – The concert[1] lasted till 12.30 – There were the usual official drinks at the Museum & then when we arrived back here, we were madly late for lunch) –

I'm really v. relieved you aren't coming up – I'm sure it's right, but don't go down to Aldeburgh till I come back – at least, please don't, unless you can't bear not to.! I <u>do</u> hope you're not worse – are you? Be good & careful & <u>don't</u> <u>worry</u>. I'm spending the whole of tomorrow with Bardgett[2] on the score, & it will be <u>all</u> <u>right</u>.! (I love you!)

This morning was as good as could be hopefully expected – Certain things went quite well & he didn't spoil the whole thing – I was in good Madame! I don't <u>actually</u> think I shall do a Dominions tour with Gerald Moore this winter! not actually, B. but you get better see?

Much much love & from everyone here.

Your loving   P.

---

[1] Pears gave a recital with pianist Gerald Moore (1899–1987) as part of the Leeds Festival.
[2] Herbert Bardgett (1894–1962), chorus master of the Leeds Festival Chorus, who was to conduct Britten's *Spring Symphony* on 6 October in the composer's place.

137 Britten to Pears

Melbury Road

[5 Oct 1950]

My darling P,

Thanks everso for your nice comforting letter. Fearfully glad that Moore wasn't too Moorish, & that you Madam'd away – knew all the time you just have to be separated from your old boring accompanist! So now you're probably closeted with Bardgett – with Anne [Wood] too, I hope (do remind her, not too heavy glissandi in the Herrick (⟨musical notation⟩). It is sweet of you, & I'm sorry to be a bloody nuisance. But I'm afraid the old Doctor was right – I couldn't have done it. The temp. & throat are allright, but I feel absolutely done in, & depressed. It's these filthy pills & injections, I suppose. But they're stopping now, thank Heaven. I don't really think

I'll go to Aldeburgh yet – want to see you, & besides there's all this hopeless EOG muddle. Another bomblet from Elizabeth [Sweeting] about it this morning. He's a very silly little man.[1]

I hope all is nice & comfy with you, & that you don't have to see too much of those old Christies.[2] (Glad to miss them I must say!). Marion's been in alot, & is terribly sweet – gave me a bottle of St Emilion 1943, which the Doctor ordered – in a big way!! – got to drink & drink – shades of Southend Pier & all. Barbara's been in too & is very kind & chatty, & Lesley comes this morning – which is nice – Because I like being talked to, & can't read much.

Love, or whatever's suitable, to whoever's suitable. Did the fish arrive?

Must stop now – because I sweat so when I write! Longing to see you – lots of love. I'll write tomorrow.   Love you

B

---

1   Henry Foy, General Manager of the EOG; he was fired in October 1950 for financial corruption.
2   John Christie (1882–1962), founder of Glyndebourne Opera, and Audrey (Mildmay) Christie, soprano (1900–53).

138 Britten to Pears

[*Letterhead:* 4 Crabbe Street, Aldeburgh]

Oct 16th 1950

My darling,

Just found this, upstairs here on the big round table under everykind of junk! I wish that I'd had time to arrange it for you, but it is rather a job & I expect you want it quick.

It was a heavenly weekend – completed my cure. I am now as well as anything, & so pleased to be back at Billy again. The Act's started well I think.

Have a nice time in Holland & Germany. Forget all about E.O.G. problems, and only bother about Madamising, & ~~singing~~ enjoy the lovely music. Send lots of postcards! Lots of love to Peter & Maria, & of course to any particular little friends at the American!

Perhaps I'll have a word with you before you go. I am going, on the off chance, to Lowestoft after lunch to-morrow. What time do you fly on Wednesday?

It's heaven that you enjoyed being here – come again!!!

Your loving   B

139 Britten to Pears

Willie [Walton] & his wife come for next
weekend, but they'll be away on the
Monday morning

[*Letterhead:* 4 Crabbe Street, Aldeburgh]

October 21st 1950

My darling P.,

Just a scribble to send my love & to say all is going well here. I hope your journey was good & that you are now happily established among the beauties and uglinesses of Germany. Don't let the rubble of Cologne get you down; be cheered by the other sights around you!

How was the Messiah? Did Julianna[1] sit it out, or did the longeurs of the score defeat her? I hope you're madamising nicely, & were pleased with yourself. How is Van Wearing?[2] & her harpsichord. I hope that'll be a nice experience. Anyhow it's lovely music.

Well, we're very occupied here. ~~After~~ The work goes well, & I'm pleased so far. The E.O.G. situation remains sordid & confused. Elizabeth has unearthed more & nastier troubles, but I suppose it'll be cleared away one day. Basil [Douglas] has decided to come to us, but I'm worried about whether the situation is clear enough for him to resign from the BBC. for it. However he's in touch with Lawrie & Elizabeth, & should know the worst. I feel we'll go on, but with curtailed activities – which <u>may</u> suit him as it would only come out as a part-time.

Michael's [Tippett] here till Monday – & Johnny came last night for the week-end. We've dined with Pammy, Norah & Arthur.[3] Rosemary Hastings was here yesterday (very nice & cheerful, & we mutually enjoyed discussing a certain singer!), & the Kings-Köhler party went well – but I told you about that on the 'phone. It was heavenly to hear your voice. Thank you so much for ringing. By-the-way, if you could cable me some of the broadcasting times & dates from Cologne I'd love to try & get them?

The wind is round in the East, & it is cold & exciting, & I'm feeling exhilerated as I always do. The glorious Indian Summer's over, but I find working easier ~~to do~~ in this weather.

The Nicholsons[4] are just about to arrive for lunch so I must run & post this.

Heavenly to think you'll be here fairly soon. I can't wait to have you here.

Your devoted

B

---

[1] Queen Juliana of the Netherlands (1909–2004; r. 1948–80).
[2] Janny van Wering (1909–2005), Dutch harpsichordist.

[3]   Lady Pamela Cadogan, Suffolk friend; Norah Nichols, neighbour, and Arthur Oldham.
[4]   John Nicholson, friend of Britten at South Lodge School, and his wife, Pat, noted amateur musician from Lowestoft.

140 Pears to Britten

[*Letterhead:* Dom-Hotel-Köln]

Monday evening. [?23 Oct 1950]

My darling old honey-pot – It was wildly exciting to have your wire <u>and</u> letter when I arrived here this evening – So frightfully glad about Marionli[1] – What a thrill for everybody – Sofie must be wild. I suppose its in todays paper – I haven't seen it yet – I know it wasn't in the Observer yesterday –

How very sweet of you to write to me yet again, & I not having written once – I have been spending a good deal of time copying out basso continuo parts for the unknown cellist here. Work has been going quite well with Janny van Wering – She's sweet and amenable and efficient but not more – She was very much alarmed at your realizations at first, but I quietened her down & told her to modify it for the hpsich – & it does now –

I've seen a lot of Peter & Maria – Lunch there Thursday – drinks there (with Henk Keining) & supper on Saturday, tea again yesterday, & a farewell visit this morning – She's a <u>very</u> remarkable creature – <u>So</u> brave, so intelligent & so honest – A <u>great</u> believer in us & a pillar of support.

I went with Peter this morning to look over the "Kleine Comoedie" (?) – a quite <u>charming</u> little theatre near the Munt, which we might have for "Dido"[2] in the Festival – I think it's <u>wholly</u> suitable – 500 people, tiny stage (like Aldebrough) v. nicely equipped. I was very taken –

"Messiah" was pretty fair hell. A pretentious little pedantic monkey conducting[3] who wanted his own hard rigid tempi – I wouldn't have it. Jo [Vincent] sang charmingly, if a teensy bit flat at the top. What a gifted creature. The Freesian was Roes Boelsma[4] (or something) not very cowlike – un poco après Kath. [a little like Kathleen Ferrier] & the Bogtmans[5] "oberafineerde")[6] as one paper called him – Wonderful garglings in "raging" rah-oh-ay-oh-ay-ah-oh-yah-eh-yur." etc – The whole thing with no cuts. De arme Koningin [the poor Queen] – She was very sweet & shy & Dutch – & Surrounded by little Freesians.

Here everything looks as it did 6 months ago – No less rubble – no less beauty – the liftboy! – um – no less ugliness – bald heads & swollen necks. Horrid heavy Cathedral. But I can tell you more tomorrow – My latest news is that I finish recording on Friday it seems, & perhaps can fly home on Saturday, might come down on Sunday ? was glaubst du [what do you think] –

Very very much love –

deine P.   P.T.O

How terribly nice of Basil!
I have an idea!! Tell you next week![7]

---

1   The birth of David Lascelles (21 October), the Harewoods' first child.
2   Britten was working on a realization of Purcell's *Dido and Aeneas* with Imogen Holst.
3   Jack P. Loorij.
4   Roos Boelsma (1909–2006), Dutch contralto.
5   Laurens Bogtman (1900–69), Dutch baritone.
6   Probably 'ongeraffineerde', crude.
7   Unfortunately there is no indication of what the idea might have been.

141 Britten to Pears

[*Letterhead:* 4 Crabbe Street, Aldeburgh]

Nov. 20th 1950

My darling Peter,

I opened this letter to see if it were important – & it is rather! If you want to have it sent right away down here, let us know, & we'll cope with room & things. Do you want Beck[1] to do it for you, & keep it in condition for you? I think he's very good. Perhaps you'd like to talk to him about it when you're here next weekend.

I've got on quite well with BB. this morning – but feeling abit flat & exhausted after the week-end – & also abit unsatisfied that I didn't seem to see enough of you, my dearest. It's no good – we must have the house to ourselves! – nice as friends are. But I was pleased with our talks with Joan – she's a real dear, & if controlled, got very good ideas.

Just off for a thinking walk, & maybe a snoop at some birds on the way!

Looking forward to next weekend everso

Lots of all my love,

Ben

---

1   Probably Paul Beck (1895–1958), piano tuner.

142 Britten to Pears

[*Letterhead:* 4 Crabbe Street, Aldeburgh]

Dec 9th 1950

Poppetto mio,

Here is the revised sketch of the proposed changes: this is because of the possible shed in the garage which may materialise opposite. (If this does <u>not</u> materialise, Mr French[1] says we can get one in in this revised plan later without affecting the scheme fundamentally). If we have the green baize door which you want (& I agree – a lovely idea) then we can borrow some light by unblocking the big passage ~~with~~ window at the bottom with about 2 foot of window showing below the ceiling. Not difficult this. I will telephone you on Monday ~~after~~ about this all, so he can go ahead & estimate.

<u>Don't</u> be depressed about your singing my darling. You are potentially the greatest singer alive, & in this rather difficult stage, you remain a lovely artist & I'm <u>not</u> prejudiced – madly critical. Take Jomelli[2] as a singing exercise – but try & enjoy Pylades.[3]

In haste – lots of love
    Your devoted
        B

---

[1] Walter French, Aldeburgh builder, who completed a number of projects for Britten and Pears at both Crag House and The Red House.
[2] Singing exercises by Niccolò Jommelli (1714–74).
[3] Tenor role in Gluck's *Iphigénie en Tauride*; Pears sang Pylades's aria at a recital at the Friends House in London on 11 December.

143 Britten to Pears

[*Letterhead:* 4 Crabbe Street, Aldeburgh]

Jan 5th 1951

My darling,

Just a scribble to send my love & to tell you all my thoughts will be with you this evening (Sat.). How lovely that you are excited by it all, & even, in a way, looking forward to it. I'm so glad also that Kleiber[1] turns out to be so sympathetic & good. I hope this will be only the first of many shows you do together.[2]

Nancy & Eric are coming over for lunch & I shall do abit of work on the great Battle scene with him. It needs greatly tidying up. I've started Act III & am quite excited by it. It's nice to be rid (temporarily) of Act II about which I'd got quite a thing.

The wallpaper is arrived, & looks awfully nice! I'm very pleased with it – it's nice & nursery for me! Thank you so very much for coping with it all. I'm sorry to have been such a bore about it, only the men were rather marking time and I've got abit bored with having them around, nice as they are.

I'll meet you in Ipswich on Sunday – can't say how I'm looking forward to that. If you could get Erwin or Sofie to ring me on Sunday morning (you won't have time to bother about trains before) saying when you are arriving in Ipswich – please?

Well, sweetheart; enjoy yourself, think of Mozart, & that incredible music. It's so nice to think of you happy in a performance of this kind.

All my love, as ever,

B

---

1   Erich Kleiber (1890–1956), Austrian conductor.
2   Pears was singing Tamino in Mozart's *The Magic Flute* at Covent Garden.

144 Pears to Britten

[*Letterhead:* 4 Crabbe Street, Aldeburgh][1]

[26 Jan 1951]

Honeypot – darling –

Just heard from Miss Hudson that you couldn't get through – <u>Do</u> take care – drive <u>v.</u> carefully – hope it isn't too hellish –

Much much love

P.

Just off to C. G. for Flute.

<u>Heavy</u> <u>snow</u> here! Ugh!

---

1   Pears was writing from 22A Melbury Rd, London.

145 Britten to Pears

[*Letterhead:* 4 Crabbe Street, Aldeburgh]

Jan 28th 1951

My darling,

I don't suppose there'll be a chance to speak to you before you go up North to morrow so I thought I'd post you my love. I tried to get you twice on Friday &

Saturday but missed you just – sickening, but it was nice to know you were off to the Pipers. You'll have enjoyed that. I hope you behaved well as a godfather & said all the right things. I also home that Thos. Sebastian P.[1] won't follow the later development of his name-sake!

I brought back Morgan on Friday – no mishaps (only a puncture before we left!). He is very well & is in splendid form, helpful over Billy, agreeing to ~~postpt~~ postpone Claggart problems, & understanding the working situation. So I didn't have need to worry! Jim[2] is better, & hopes to get up abit to-day. Eric, Nancy & two rather grizzly friends staying with them (literary females) are over in Aldeburgh to-day & They are eating at the White Lion & Eric's coming in to work this afternoon (actually I hear his footsteps now, & so I must run!). Hope that goes smoothly.

I hear your M. Flute was better than ever on Friday. I'm so very glad. Certainly Nicolas[3] was the tops. Lots of love & every good bit of luck for Klebski.

My darling!

Ben

---

1   The christening of the Pipers' son, Thomas Sebastian (b. 14 August 1950).
2   James Bernard (1925–2001), composer, who was assisting Britten with the score of *Billy Budd*.
3   Pears sang in Britten's *Saint Nicolas* in Cambridge on the previous Thursday, 25 January 1951.

146 Pears to Britten

to [*Letterhead:* 4 Crabbe Street, Aldeburgh][1]

[?29–30 Jan 1951]

My own honey bunch –

I wish I were coming down to you today instead of going up North – London is v. gloomy fog & cold – & Manchester will be worse I fear. Oh dear!

My address will be c/o Mrs. Lindley Roselea, Planetree Rd, Hale, Cheshire. Tel: ~~Rin~~ (Manchester) Ringway 2839. That is until Friday when I go to Sheffield[2] & come down via London on Saturday – probably by the 3.20 train with Joan – I can't quite make out when Sophie F[itch3] will come, but the 2 Basils on Sunday I fancy –

Could you be an angel & send the Min. Score of Schütz "7 Last Words" which I think you have up in yr room to Miss Florence Burton, Arts Dep[t]., Dart[n]. H[ll]., Nr. Tot[n]. D[n]. [Dartington]

V. v. much love –

fudge –

t'amo –

P.

1   Pears was writing from 22A Melbury Rd.
2   Pears was to sing Britten's *Serenade* at the Sheffield City Hall on 2 February with the
    Hallé Orchestra, conducted by Paul Kletzi.
3   Sophie Fedorovitch (1893–1953), theatrical designer.

147 Britten to Pears

[*Letterhead:* 4 Crabbe Street, Aldeburgh]

Feb. 20th 1951

My darling,

Here are the two notes. So very happy that last night was so good; a lovely way
to end your first Cov. Garden season.[1] Did you see David [Webster] or any of the
other potentates there?

I'm having a wild week-end here – Tony Gishford has written to say, can he
come with Eddy (he knows him) & just now came a wire from Morgan wanting to
come too (very upset by Gide's[2] death – probably that's the reason) one only now
needs the threat of Menotti[3] to materialise, of coming down to Aldeburgh to see
me, for the week-end to be thoroughly gay! I think I shall retire upstairs & let them
fight it out themselves alone. God – hope this weather doesn't continue – violent
wind & rain to-day.

Hope you're feeling more cheerful, poppetchen – don't let depression depress
you! I don't mind your being quiet – just love having you with me whatever your
mood. I'm sure it's the aftermath of 'flu.

Lots of love to all at Dartington.[4] Don't let Peter Cox engage Clements[5] for too
long – I think the appointment is a bit risky.

Just rushing to post.

> All my love & all,
> <u>Ben</u>

P.T.O

– for a shock.

> P.S. I've FOUND Inge-lise's[6] cheque!
> Now you can buy another picture
> – ha – ha!

1   Pears's final performance in *The Magic Flute*.
2   André Gide (1869–1951), French writer, who had died the previous day.
3   Gian Carlo Menotti (1911–2007), Italian-born American composer; partner of Samuel
    Barber.
4   Pears was in residence at Dartington from 20 February to 2 March.

⁵ John Clements, chorus master of the BBC, who was to replace Imogen Holst as Music Director at Dartington.
⁶ Inge-lise Bock (1905–59), Danish concerts agent and director at Tivoli Gardens, Copenhagen. Britten and Pears had performed there on 27 July 1950.

148 Pears to Britten

[*Letterhead:* Arts Department, Dartington Hall, Totnes, Devon]

Wednesday – p.m. [21 Feb 1951]

Here I am, my honey, after nearly 24 hours here – We had a weird journey down with every sort of weather, beginning fine & then rain, thick sleet, fog, snow and cold! arrived here after midnight – am staying with Peter [Cox] in his new flat in one of those modern houses we saw, one that belonged to Joos.[1] Really very comfortable.

This morning I attended a harmony class of Imo's where we studied a Bach chorale – She is quite <u>brilliant</u> – revealing, exciting. Then she came to lunch here & talked all about India[2] – then this evening from 6–7, I played the <u>viola</u> (!!) in the orchestra rehearsing "St Paul's Suite"[3] – greatest fun. Tomorrow Schütz! How are you, Poppeti mio? I hope you had a good day's work, many thanks for letter – so hope that Eddy & Tony won't be too much – Carlos[4] got the Keene & a bunch of Cotman[5] etchings for £17 in all! v. exciting – more tomorrow. Good night.

¹ Kurt Jooss, German ballet dancer; taught at Dartington c 1934–49.
² During 1950 Imogen Holst studied with Rabindranath Tagore in West Bengal.
³ Work for string orchestra by Gustav Holst.
⁴ Carlos Peacock, art historian and curator at the Tate Gallery, London.
⁵ Charles Keene (1823–91), artist and illustrator; etchings by either John Sell Cotman, or his son, Miles Edmund Cotman (1816–58).

149 Britten to Pears

[*Letterhead:* 4 Crabbe Street, Aldeburgh]

[?21–4 Feb 1951]

My darling –

More nice fannery. I'd love to see you as Vogel[1] – Can't I be your Schubert?!

Elizabeth [Sweeting] & I are going over to Lowestoft this afternoon to see Glatcher (Dir. of Ed.) about possible boys & girls for Lets Make.[2] Miss Hudson's coming too to see about muslin.

Hope your drive down was nice, & that you're now enjoying Dartington, Imogen, Minstrelsty & Perotin.[3] Love to all.

No news. Billy [Budd] goes on allright, I hope. Nice evening with Arthur & Nora – worked abit with Arthur & then played 'Up Jenkyns' till – late hour.

All my love

B.

---

[1] Johann Michael Vogl (1768–1840), the baritone for whom Schubert wrote many songs.
[2] For performances of *Let's Make an Opera* in March and April in Cambridge.
[3] Pérotin (c 1160–1205 or 1225), composer at Notre Dame Cathedral, Paris.

150 Pears to Britten

[*Letterhead:* Arts Department, Dartington Hall, Totnes, Devon]

Friday – A.M. [23 Feb 1951]

My honey pot –

It was lovely to talk to you (which I have just finished doing!) & to hear your voice even though a long way off. Don't get too worn out this week–end – I'm terribly sorry everything isn't quite as set as it should be, curtains etc – but it takes a long time to get a house just right, and one can't spend all one's money at once – V. glad you found Inge-Lise's check and letter – Where <u>was</u> it?

Having a lovely time here, got up at 7 this morning & walked by the river, birds singing sun shining, this is far the most beautiful time I've ever been in Devon – & it's much more open up here than at Yarner.

Lots of rehearsals etc with Imo & the chaps. She's in tremendous form & quite brilliant at her job – I talked & sang Monteverdi last night – I hope it was allright, but I hadn't got very much to say – so I sang instead! We're working at the Schütz solo cantatas with sweet chaps – & v. keen. Lovely music –

Tomorrow & Sunday are free – shall probably go into Brixham on Sat., & walk on the moors on Sunday –

v. v. much love to you –

my pie –

ever yr loving

P.

151 Britten to Pears

[*Letterhead:* 4 Crabbe Street, Aldeburgh]

Feb 25th 1951

My darling,

Your two sweet notes[1] have given me lots & lots of pleasure. Sweet of you to write so fully & sweetly. I am hugely glad you are enjoying yourself so – it must be lovely. I'm afraid the good weather hasn't lasted – it rains alot here. But you will have lots to keep you amused indoors. Fancy you playing the viola! I wonder if you were as fine as I was at it – bet you can't compete with my vibrato ⌇⌇⌇⌇⌇ !

No time for a long letter. The week-end is going quite nicely. All getting on well. We went over to Pammy's yesterday for tea, & for drinks to the Cranbrooks. Thismorning Eddy went to mass, I worked with Morgan, & then played them Act. I. They sleep downstairs, & I'm just off to post before getting them tea. Eddy <u>loves</u> the house, & says <u>most comfortable</u> – so you needn't apoligise about not having got it more ready – but if <u>you</u> hadn't done so much I can't think what it would have been like under <u>my</u> direction! You've been an angel.

Covent Garden[2] descends on us to-morrow, and then, I hope, back to work!

All my love, & to Imo & Peter [Cox]

　　　Your devoted,

　　　　　B

P.T O.

Peggy Ashcroft[3] can't, alas, come & read. Any suggestions? Isaac Stern,[4] neither, so Manoug[5] will play – in some ways a good thing, I think, don't you?

Love to Dorothy & Leonard[6] if they are there.

---

[1] Letters 148 and 150.
[2] David Webster.
[3] (1907–91), actress invited to appear at the 1951 Aldeburgh Festival.
[4] (1920–2001), violinist.
[5] Manoug Parikian (1920–87).
[6] Elmhirst, founders of the Dartington College of Music and Art.

152 Pears to Britten

[*Letterhead:* Arts Department, Dartington Hall, Totnes, Devon]

Sunday. [25 Feb 1951]

My honey –

Everything goes on lovely here – lots of Schütz & Monteverdi – am teaching the young and adore it. Imo in tremendous form – very happy with Peter [Cox] – went over yesterday for a drive to Brixham, & have bought 2 chests of drawers for your bedroom & a mirror for mine! How are you my bee & all your distinguished guests – Hope you aren't quite worn out.

V. much love to you

P.

153 Britten to Pears

[*Letterhead:* 4 Crabbe Street, Aldeburgh]

[?26 Feb 1951]

Darling –

This notelet has just arrived & so I send it on.

Lovely to talk to you this morning, & so very happy you are enjoying yourself. I really do envy you this quiet minstrelsy tucked away from the hideous commercial world. Try & persuade Imo to go back there occasionally in the future, & ask me to come to – with my viola even!

Lots of love.

B.

154 Britten to Pears

[*Letterhead:* 4 Crabbe Street, Aldeburgh]

[27 Feb 1951]

Darling P –

In haste, I hope this reaches you before you leave. The enclosed notes have just come. I wasn't aware of having written a rather 'sad' letter to John [Piper], but maybe I was depressed unconsciously (not surprising considering my darling is so far away) when I wrote & it shone through.

Well, all my guests are departed & I hasten to add, thank God. It was a wild week-end, with a climactic luncheon to which Eddy & Tony stayed, tho' Morgan went. I played Billy thro', & all said nice things. I think Act.II Sc. I is excellent, but o how the rest worries me! Webster cried a little & embraced me (– !) & is generally nice about everything. I was dead when they all went, but fine to-day & back at work. No more now – just off to Lowestoft to audit 40 children !![1]

Hope you're still enjoying your dear self.

All my love & all

B.

---

[1]   For performances of *Let's Make an Opera*.

155 Pears to Britten

[*Letterhead:* Arts Department, Dartington Hall, Totnes, Devon]

<u>Thursday.</u> [1 Mar 1951]

My Sweetest old pot of honey –

I am slowly coming to the end of my stay here – We did the 7 Last words & a cantata by Schütz on Tuesday, yesterday 2 more solo cantatas, a Purcell song with violin, & [Gustav] Holst's Voice and Voilin Songs[1] – & today comes Tancredi[2] & other Monteverdi bits & a Buxtehude cantata – What wonderful music & really what a heavenly week it's been – Imo has been in tremendous form, & has adored it & she has had the sweetest lot of studants, madly keen – & one or 2 v. promising players, & all adoring the music – 17th century music – very exciting – It has also been very rewarding for me – & I am quite sure that somehow we have got to use Imo in the biggest way – as editor, as trainer, as teacher, etc – she is <u>most</u> impressive –

I go back to London, Schumann & Brahms[3] tomorrow – oh dear!

How are you, my honey? It has been heavenly having your letters – thank you so much for them all & for sending things on – So glad the weekend & Webster were a success –

I'm coming up to London tomorrow. Fri – may ring you before – anyway – v. much love my fudge –

P.

---

[1]   Four Songs for Voice and Violin.
[2]   Monteverdi's *Il combattimento di Tancredi e Clorinda*.
[3]   Schumann, *Spanisches Liederspiel*; Brahms, *Liebeslieder Waltzes*; rehearsal for an EOG performance in London on 6 March.

156 Britten to Pears

Wystan can't come, so we're trying Stephen [Spender]. Also, Thorndyke[1] instead of Ashcroft – it would be lovely to have her here, don't you think?

[*Letterhead:* 4 Crabbe Street, Aldeburgh]

March. 1st 1951

My darling,

One or two more documents which I send on. Again this is only a scribble, but life is wildly hectic & never a moment. Things have got terribly chock-a-block, this week, because, partly, of the auditions in Lowestoft (we go again this afternoon, with Norman)[2] and because of Charles Stuart[3] descending on me yesterday with a ghastly photographer – a maddening, sickening, wasted afternoon. However I played squash with Jim [Bernard] after & imagined the little ball was him & worked off some of my feelings <u>that</u> way!

So you're probably back in town – it'll be a little dismal after the pleasures of Dartington I'm afraid, but for me, at anyrate nicer to know that your nearer to me! Can't you slip down for a night or something, possibly? Any how we'll talk together on the 'phone one of these days & plan.

All my love, my darling. Thank you so much for your sweet notes.

B.

---

1 Sybil Thorndike (1882–1976), Shakespearean actress. She gave a poetry reading at the Aldeburgh Festival on 11 June 1951.
2 The auditions for *Let's Make an Opera*, conducted by Norman Del Mar (1919–94).
3 Music critic at *The Observer*.

157 Britten to Pears

[*Letterhead:* 4 Crabbe Street, Aldeburgh]

March 16th 1951

Darling Peter,

Just a scribble to send you the tendrest love, & good wishes for everything. It was lovely to hear your voice & an unspeakable relief to know you'd arrived safely, although you'd obviously had a beastly journey. I hope all is going as well as possible. The Passions, at least the Concertgebouw ones, can't be very good I'm afraid – most <u>irritating</u> of them to have this dreary conductor for you. I'll be listening on Sunday of course. I've had to put Piers off this week end as Dr Acheson has said I mustn't talk more than absolutely necessary. It is only laryngitis (whoever you spell it) & not serious, but unless I stop talking & stay in it'll go on and on. So I'll try &

arrange for Piers sometime next week-end. Basil [Douglas] & Martin[1] may come down with you on Sunday, but we'll be talking about all that.

Weather has gone back to bloody again – after a heavenly, nostalgic Spring day yesterday – so I don't feel so bad about not going out. Work is going on slowly but steadily towards the end of the Act, & I'm on the whole pleased. It was lovely to play it to you, & you gave me back my confidence which had been slowly ebbing away. In a work of this size & tension that is one of one's greatest problems. I believe that is yours too – if one aims high (& you achieve your aims so often) one is so desparately ashamed when one knows one is missing them.

My love of course to Peter [Diamand], Bertus, & all friends whom you see. And come home quick & safe, & we'll have a lovely week of you here.

All my love, my sweet. It was a heavenly oasis to have you here this week.

B

The enclosed cutting will come as a shock – poor, poor Toby![2]

---

[1] Martyn C. Webster, Basil Douglas's partner.
[2] Possibly a reference to George 'Toby' Wentworth-Fitzwilliam (1888–1955), whose claim to his father's earldom was discounted by a High Court ruling which saw him illegitimised in March 1951. A press cutting regarding the trial remains in the Britten–Pears Archive.

158 Britten to Pears

[**Letterhead:** 4 Crabbe Street, Aldeburgh]

March 18th 1951

My darling,

I've just come upstairs to my desk, having finished listening to Part II – only Part II I'm afraid since I stayed in bed all this morning (only just popping up to switch on Hilversum to hear your first sweet notes). Most unfortunately the stupid Radio Times gave the wrong time – damnable of it because it now costs 3d – of the start of Part II so I missed the Petrus episode – but I heard all the rest, & my darling yours is a <u>great</u> performance.[1] The voice sounds so full & so rich, & with so much variety, & this glorious musical phrasing. But above all there is this noble conception of the part, this dignity, this felt but sublimated emotion. There can never have been an Evangelist like you – it's wonderful to be born in your lifetime to hear you do it.

But what a curious performance? Why all the cuts? Surely there must have been a revolution among the old Dutchies at their yearly ceremony being so truncated.

Hard for you too, to go on sometimes with so little breaks. One sees too, how right Bach's form is – how one misses the musical, purely musical, comments. Some of Jordaens[2] I prefered to Van Beinum, – he seemed sometimes to know the work better, & some was more sensitively phrased. How I loathe the accelerandi at the end of the choruses though. And poor Jo [Vincent] – more in tune, but _how_ slow off the mark. The windows here rattled when she breathed. How is the old dear tho' – give her my bestest love. Hermes[3] as Frisian as ever, & o, what a Tenor! Bogtman less exaggerated (what I heard) but sounding to me 101, & I don't think of Jesus as an old man.

My throat is improving – I inhale, & paint, & drink cough mixtures, & from time to time Dr Acheson pokes little periscopes down my throat so far that they almost come out – you know where! I try to talk very little which helps. Piers I put off, but Paul's[4] here. He's quite sweet but a little one-track & dim – don't think he'll keep Jim [Bernard] long, nor would I honestly mind because I feel he doesn't bring out the best in him. Perhaps I'm wrong, one can so easily go wrong on first impressions.

Miss Hudson says – if you _can_ find some tea cups, very welcome. But I said you were very busy, & anyhow we could probably find some in Liberty's or somewhere.

Budd goes on – I've finished Act III (tho' not quite satisfied with the very end) & I'm well in to Act IV! And going rather nicely.

Must run to post – or get Miss H. to do so.

All my love – do come back quick & safe. I'll think of you. Love to Bertus & Kath – hope those go well, & judging by your voice to-day they will, as it sounded as fresh as a daisy.

My darling, love you.

    B.

---

1   Bach _St Matthew Passion_.
2   Hein Jordans (1914–2003), Dutch conductor.
3   Annie Hermes (1906–95), Dutch contralto.
4   Dehn (1912–76), critic and screenwriter; partner of James Bernard.

159 Pears to Britten

American Hotel

Sunday A.M. [18 Mar 1951]

My old Sweetie pie –

How are you honey-je? Working hard and well, but not too hard, I hope – I wish I were with you – It was a lovely two days together, my fudge, but in a week we shall have more than a week together, & that will be heavenly –

Here I am almost half way through my visit – I shall be off in an hour to the Concertgebouw for my 3rd & last Passion there, & then comes Bertus. Mr. Jordaens is is a competent dull little bourgeois conductor, slightly more Bach-like than Van Beinum perhaps but duller and the soloists drag & get very Dutch – I am sick of this performance – The chorus make a huge ugly noise, the orchestra doesn't know how to play Bach, & the overall effect is dismal – I look forward to Bertus. I have told Peter I won't do this Concertgebouw performance next year – Maybe I'll come for Bertus Let's see –

Joan is here, enjoying herself being a producer, & bossing people – I went to a rehearsal of Ballo[1] – It has <u>wonderful</u> music – & Brouwenstijn[2] will be most moving – Vroons[3] allright, & the baritone good but provincial. I saw Otto – I doubt if he can do the Aldeburgh Verdi, as he has Klingsor in Parsifal the next day at C.G., & presumably a dress rehearsal –[4]

Peter D. seems a bit distrait by the Holland Festival . politics and economics seem very tricky just now.

I saw Kath last night – very sweet & dear – She sings with Bertus –

Sorry about the writing! Am in my lonely bed. (only one of your young friends left now) I am sending parcels to you – chocolate & I hope butter etc –

Much much love to you my honey bee –

Yr devoted P.

---

[1] Verdi's opera *Un ballo in maschera*.
[2] Gré Brouwenstijn (1915–99), Dutch soprano.
[3] Frans Vroons (1911–83), Dutch tenor.
[4] Otakar Kraus (1909–80), Czech-born baritone, was already committed to sing in Wagner's opera *Parsifal* at Covent Garden, so was unable to perform in the Verdi operatic highlights concert (commemorating the fiftieth anniversary of Verdi's death) at the Aldeburgh Festival on 15 June 1951.

160 Britten to Pears

[*Letterhead:* 4 Crabbe Street, Aldeburgh]

[?1951]

Poppetty mio,

Here in great haste – to catch the post are the measurements:

	Length Height (of canvas)		Frame
Cotman:	19" x 24"	A-11	3 ½"
Constable (boy):	11 ½" x 14 ½"	A-6	2"
Piper (big):	28" x 24"	A-11	4 ½"
Spenser Gore:	23 ½" x 18 ½"	A-11 3c wat	4 ½"
Blake:	{ 11 ¾" x 15 ¼"	A-6 5 in one	2"
	{ ~~Blake~~ Black mount 3" – white 1 ¾"		

I've included the Gore because maybe it'll be a little lonely unlit, unless we can arrange the standard lamp so – what about the wee Constables & Turner?[1]

Here also is the sketch plan of the new room. Do you see what I mean about the small-ness of the outer hall. I'll talk to Mr French about an archway, as it is now & a curtain.

I'm <u>much</u> better. I'll be getting down to work to-morrow. Lots of love – hope you are really felling all right. <u>Don't</u> go about too much & get wet & tired – it's treacherous weather.

Dein wie immer [Yours always]

Ben

---

¹ References to artwork owned by Britten and Pears in 1951: Cotman, *Draining Mills at Crowland*; Constable, Portrait of Charles Golding Constable; Piper, *Loxford: Drop Curtain for Albert Herring*; Spencer Gore, *The Haystacks*; Blake, *St Paul Shaking Off the Viper*; Constable: *Cloud Study*; *Suffolk Landscape* and *Seascape* (neither now believed to be by Constable); Turner, *Coastal Scene* (now thought not to be by Turner).

161 Britten to Pears

[*Letterhead:* 4 Crabbe Street, Aldeburgh]

[early 1951]

Darling –

In haste, these notes have just come & I send them on prestissimo. I've sent off Roberto's opera¹ too. By the way, if you see him <u>do</u> ask him how his piece² is going, & when we can have it etc – also about Noel Mewton-W.³

Hope to-morrow will have gone well.

<u>Longing</u> for 8ᵗʰ

Your devoted

B

---

¹ Roberto Gerhard's *The Duenna*.
² Gerhard's Concerto for Piano and String Orchestra.
³ Noel Mewton-Wood (1922–53), Australian pianist; accompanist to Pears between 1952 and 1953.

✠✠✠

On 9 April Britten and Pears gave a recital in Vienna showcasing Purcell, Dowland and Thomas Arne alongside Britten's folk-song arrangements. In May they performed at the London Season of the Arts (part of the Festival of Britain), with

EOG performances of *Albert Herring*, *The Rape of Lucretia* and Britten's realization of Purcell's *Dido and Aeneas*. They also gave the premiere of Tippett's song cycle, *The Heart's Assurance*, written for Pears. Afterwards, they went on to Festivals in Holland and Cheltenham, then to a performance of the *Spring Symphony* at the Royal Festival Hall on 21 July. Britten worked on *Billy Budd*, finishing the opera on 10 August, but illness postponed completion of the scoring.

✠✠✠

162 Pears to Britten

[*Postcard:* image of shepherds from Chartres Cathedral]

[12 Sep 1951]

This is a very very beautiful place, we have found St. Nicolas tucked away in the corner of a window looking very beautiful & bright – Lots of pilgrims from everywhere London suburbs, Italy, & Berlin. Wish you were here. Love. P.

à Vendredi [see you on Friday]

[*additional note by Esther Neville-Smith*]

I couldn't have believed anything could be so wonderful – form and colour and Peter and the sweet French people. We think of you at every fresh sight of beauty and choose out what we think you would specially enjoy, like these enchanting shepherds.

Love, E.

163 Pears to Britten

[*Letterhead:* Dom-Hotel-Köln]

Saturday Evening [6 Oct 1951]

My own darling honey bunch – The bells are ringing away in a very big deep way outside my window and it hardly seems possible that we were chugging past this place only 10 days ago – (I can't make this biro work) –

Sunday afternoon

Sorry the pen defeated me, but here's a pencil. The cathedral is still fine but too heavy, and there's some fine glass – I went down & watched the great paddle tugs go by dragging their barges, & I thought of John, and me going down to shave – I

seemed to do nothing but shave or make beds! What a lovely time that was, honey!
I did enjoy it.[1]

Well now the old boy[2] has been at us, beating away – he couldn't be nicer to me,
though, I'm sure I'm no Oedipus.[3] he wants accents accents all the time, spitting
out words – We have just spent a nice Sunday recording ¾ of it, from 10.30–2.45 &
now we must finish it tonight at 8. Oh dear!

On the plane over I met Emil Wertheimer from Manchester – You wouldn't
remember him, & went to an operetta here on Friday night Die liebe Augustin[4]
– we came out after the first act! And now the nice thing is that Peter & Maria
have arrived for 3 days or so, & I shall drive back with them on Tuesday – they are
sweets. They are just going to take me out for a drive now. It's been lovely weather
here, fine but beginning to get a little colder now –

My Oedipus is not made easier by the fact that Le Berger [The Shepherd] is
sung by Helmut Krebs[5] (wonderful name) of the Berlin Städtische Oper who sang
the part of Oedipus for the 4th time this season in Berlin on Friday night! He's
really allright I suppose – He has sung all B.B. parts – he was Albert in Berlin – &
sings Serenade Sonnets etc – all very cosy! he has an efficient hard loud squeezed
voice – but much more efficient than me!

Wish I were back with you –
I don't enjoy doing these things alone. I have no self confidence –
      Much love much love
How was David [Webster] & Budd – wish I were at home
          all my love
            P.

---

[1] In September Britten and Pears had crossed the North Sea and continued the two-week
    boat trip up the Rhine with friends including Basil Coleman, Aldeburgh fisherman Billy
    Burrell and his brother John.

[2] Stravinsky.

[3] Pears was singing in a performance and recording (5 and 7 October) of Stravinsky's
    Oedipus Rex in Cologne, conducted by the composer.

[4] By Austrian composer Leo Fall.

[5] (1913–2007), German tenor.

164 Pears to Britten

American Hotel
<u>Amsterdam</u>

<u>Wednesday</u> [10 Oct 1951]

Honey bee –

Did you expect to see this address on the top of my paper? Peter & Maria drove me back here from Cologne yesterday evening & I'm staying till tomorrow evening when I'm off to Maastricht for "Les Illuminaggers" on Friday & Saturday – I don't really look forward to it – I caught rather a cold yesterday & today I'm staying in mostly, just going to see Maria for a little while this afternoon –

Oedipus seems to have gone fairly allright I think – Did you hear it, I wonder? I had a wire from the Wertheimers & Lindleys from Manchester saying it had come over very well and so on. It was nice in many ways to be working again after so long – At least I can face it now – I do hope Vere's[1] going to be tolerable – I've been looking at it a lot. It's a wonderful part, & I <u>ought</u> to be able to do it superbly but oh dear …

I'm longing to be back again with you – This is the last time I shall be abroad for 3 months – Isn't that wonderful? No doubt I shall be very glad to go to Switzerland at the end of January, but until then give me England –

I probably shan't have time to see anybody here – (I shall take a 6.45 AM train from Maastricht here on Sunday & then fly back on Sunday afternoon) but I hear that Jettie Bosmans is much better and back at home – Van Beinum is quite recovered, it seems, and conducting hard – He opens the season here tonight I think;– Peter is terribly fed up with the Holland Festival; at the moment it seems quite possible that there won't occur a festival next year – everybody fighting & being terribly provincial and nationalistic, personal attacks on him – etc.

All sorts of greetings to you from Heinz Rehfuss[2] & of course Mr. Helmut Krebs who only waits for your new Tenor roles in Berlin! Mr. Fineman doesn't inspire too much confidence – He says that several places want the group, but as a rule can't guarantee themselves more than 2000DM (90£), our performances cost 5000DM each, & he wants the British Council to guarantee 3000 DM per perf, for 2 weeks – At present they <u>think</u> they might do a week & he awaits their answer – In any case, he says it has been <u>very</u> difficult because he is <u>so</u> busy – I'm not over-mad about him – He wants us in November 1952 for a bit; shall we? and show those German sausages a thing or two!

How are you, my pie? Is scoring going all right? How was D. Webster etc? There's an American sitting on my right in the lounge, & I hope he won't be Billy Budd – I suppose there are <u>some</u> nice Americans –

By the way it's Marion's birthday soon, & also your godson's[3] – & Erwin's & Sofie (?) – couldn't we have a grand family party? By the way Erwin & I talked about the future of Melbury Rd. & ourselves; & the door is wide open for us to go when we want to – Very much love to you my old huggable honey bear – your devoted old mate – P

[1] The role of Captain Vere in *Billy Budd*.
[2] (1917–88), German bass-baritone.
[3] Britten was godfather to David Lascelles, eldest son of the Harewoods.

165 Pears to Britten

The White Swan Hotel
Halifax.

[20 Dec 1951]

My darling old Honey-Pot –

Time marches slowly on – from Leeds to West Hartlepool and from West Hartlepool to Halifax – from City Hall to Town Hall to Victoria Hall – from cloth to ship-building to wool – from sweet friendly hospitality to dull Grand Hotel to smelly old White Swan – from nice cold high tea to dehydrated LNER to starchy LMS[1] – from scratchy orchestra to unspeakable organist – from Kath to old Mary to Madame Edith Furmedge, & from Ada Alsop[2] to Ada Alsop to Ada Alsop to Ada A. … and away from my bee, from my bee, from my bee – O for the wings of a dove and O not for the wheels of our national railways —— rather O for the tyres of a bus. From conductors with good intentions & no technique, from organists with lofty ideas and no taste, from trumpeters who know they can play, from violas who know they can't, and from Ada Alsop —— Good Lord, deliver us. From basses with cork legs and wooden voices, from obsequious treasurers and enthusiastic secretaries, from audiences who clear their throats and from large unresonant concert halls, Good Lord, deliver us. From north-country towns where there's always Early Closing, from the rain in Leeds, the drizzle in Halifax & the sou' sou' easter in Hartlepool, from hospitality and hotels, Good Lord, deliver us. From the frog and the rheum & the quinsy,[3] Good Lord, deliver us –

We beseech Thee to hear us, Good Lord.

My literny's dun
    my honey bun –
Now wot about yew
    my honey dew?
Are you quite well
    my honey bell?

And if not, why
   not, my pie?
                    ――――――

It seems a v. long time since I saw you – & it's going to be a b. long time till I see
you again.

Ring me up late Saturday night.

My honey bee   P.

――――――――――

¹   London and North Eastern Railway and London Midland and Scottish Railway.
²   (1890–1956), contralto and (1915–68), soprano.
³   Laryngitis, mucus and tonsillitis.

166 Pears to Britten

[*Letterhead:* 4 Crabbe Street, Aldeburgh]

Monday ~~Tuesday~~ 10 pm [28 Jan 1952]

My honey –

Just got the permit – very many thanks – poppet.

Can you possibly say which of these dates you prefer? & tell the lady – I don't
mind a bit which.

Shall be arriving from Bale [Basel] at Kensington Air Ter.¹ at 6.50 on Friday
(Swissair). Don't forget next Saturday evening is Brains Trust² on Opera at 7.0. I
am (not now) writing a note to Kath to tell her we can't stay to supper – (I <u>think</u>
she asked us to –)? / Just finished talking to you! Honey bee!

Much love
        P.

V. stupidly forgot to ask you <u>please</u> to find ① a Schütz Eulenburg score of Seven
Last Words (there should be two – one, mine – & another with the title written
down the spine in ink – it's the <u>second</u> which I have to give back to its owner) ②
also – a BBC loan copy of the same piece in an English edition by the Faith Press
ed. C. Ked.y. Scott. I had them with me in Scotland & took them to Aldeburgh, &
like a fool left them there – they can't be buried very deep – in my room upstairs?
desk or table or revolving book case? downstairs? lying on music in shelves? <u>Please
bring them with you on Friday</u>

Dreadfully sorry –
>   B. dear –
>>   P.

Met Carlos P. in the street today – Your Constable[3] came from <u>him</u>!!

---

[1]   West London Air Terminal, Kensington.
[2]   BBC radio panel programme.
[3]   Carlos Peacock had given Britten a portrait of the artist's eldest son, John Charles Constable.

167 Britten to Pears

[*Letterhead:* 4 Crabbe Street, Aldeburgh]

>   May ?th 1952 [29 May 1952]

My darling P.,

Here is a gloomy document from Corder's – !! What do you think of it all? I <u>ought</u> to confirm the order for the grey carpet for my room, but it is so wildly expensive that I almost think perhaps not – or perhaps the cheaper one you thought of? Anyhow I think we can leave that ~~to you~~ till you come down next week-end.

>   { The work's going ahead, but the basin (blast it) is not
>   { here yet. It's on order, & being coped with.

I hope the next few hours won't be too terrible, ~~but~~ that you won't be too tired after Billy Budd for Love in a V.[1] I shall listen, all ears, to your darling performance – it is awfully good, you know.

Imo is here & it's lovely to have her. We're just out for a walk so I'm in a hurry to finish this.

It comes with all my love
>   Ben.

---

[1]   Arthur Oldham's opera, *Love in a Village*, in which Pears sang the part of Hawthorn.

✠✠✠

After the Aldeburgh Festival (14–22 June), which featured Arthur Oldham's *Love in a Village*, Britten and Pears gave a series of recitals in Copenhagen. Pears sang a recital with Noel Mewton-Wood in Dartington on 12 July, then he and Britten took a second holiday, a motoring tour of France with the Harewoods from 16 July to 21 August. They wrote to Mary Potter on 2 August, 'We're enjoying the holiday but rather resent having to give concerts occasionally!' Also during this trip, they read through the first draft of William Plomer's libretto for *Gloriana*, and Britten began composing the opera on their return. Pears continued singing without Britten, giving recitals in London, Oxford, Camberwell and various other places with Mewton-Wood, Norman Franklin and Gerald Moore throughout September and October.

✠✠✠

168 Britten to Pears

[*Letterhead:* 4 Crabbe Street, Aldeburgh]

November 17th 1952

My darling Peter,

You remember the glamourous German youth who visited us in the Summer – Lederhosen & all? – well, he's just written the sweetest letter, presents of sweets & a tie, & lots of love to you. He ends with a P.S. as follows: ——

"I was told to-day that there will be a performance of the Matthäus Passion by Bach in the Altenburg Cathedral near Cologne on March 22nd 1953. Our music teacher, Mr. Paul Nitsche is the conductor, of the performance, which will be arranged by the Westdeutsche Konzertdirecktion Köln. Would you be so kind as to ask Mr Pears if he would sing the part of the Evangelist ......"

Or have you already heard about it? Perhaps you could write to your agent direct? I am <u>very</u> keen they should hear you do it sometime in Germany?!

I heard via Erwin via George that there's no definite news of William[1] yet. Let me know when there is –

Lots of love, my darling – excuse haste, rushing to catch post

Love to M & G. & D. [Harewoods]

Ben

[*On reverse, note in Pears' hand:*]
V. difficult to adopt 2 foreign children not in this country.
Getting out of Germany – <u>into England</u>.
? Impossible to get Br. nationality before 21.

---

[1] Plomer was ill and possibly needed an operation.

169 Britten to Pears

[*Letterhead:* 4 Crabbe Street, Aldeburgh]

[?1952–53]

My darling,

Here is the invite – have a nice garden party – my love to George's Aunt[1] if you see her.

I hope I'll be O.K. soon – sure I shall. But I think the concerts this week end <u>are</u> rather unlikely – I'll telephone you anyhow.

Lots of love – longing to see you.

Dein [yours] –

B

---

[1] The Queen Mother.

170 Britten to Pears

[*Letterhead:* Harewood House, Leeds]

[early Jan 1953]

My darling –

One or two letters which I've opened for you – mostly nice, nothing urgent. Others I have forwarded to you direct. I hope Glasgow wasn't too dreary & that (inspite of the <u>silly</u> Ibbs T.[1] mistake!) you found a hotel. We all thought of you a great deal & wished you the happiest of New Years. I <u>do</u> hope it will be for you, my dearest – all the things you love, & none of those you hate. (I hope 'Essex'[2] will be in the first catagory!).

All goes well & easily here. I've started work – work quietly all the mornings & then walk & talk for rest of day. The Spenders came on New Years Eve which was surprisingly nice – Stephen very aimiable, but he's a poor confused, rather silly creature I'm afraid.

How nice about Morgan – we sent a wire to him & Kath[3] from us all, including you. I'm pleased about Kath too.

Well – my poppage – I must go on with Act III Sc. III – I put these in the post for you. I do hope you manage to get down to Aldeburgh for a night. Bon Voyage – enjoy Switzerland & come quick home; I'll be waiting for you!

All my love,

<u>B</u>

NB!!!

<u>Have you written to Yvonne Lefebure?</u>[4]

1   Ibbs and Tillett, the London concert agency who represented Pears and Britten.
2   Pears's role in *Gloriana*, on which Britten had now started work.
3   Forster was named Companion of Honour (CH), and Ferrier a CBE in the 1953 New Year's Honours List.
4   (1898–1986), French pianist.

171 Pears to Britten

Tuesday morning [6 Jan 1953]

My darling –

I'm just off to Der Schweiz [Switzerland] and it's snowing here – or only just stopped – so it's as well that I'm not flying like John & Jessie[1] are at this moment – I shall almost certainly come back on Saturday night to London, & must stay up here for some days I think – Flat business,[2] another treatment from Dr McCreedy[3] (had one very good one yesterday – he is nice) etc., so I will probably stay until the 15th up here.

How are you? Your ears must have burned a lot of yesterday – first of all Imo & Leonard Isaacs[4] & I seemed to talk a good deal about you, & arranged for you to conduct the Aldeburgh Variations[5] & Holst Concerto[6] in a Pre-view Programme of the Festival, in the Studio on June 16th or so (programme to include Bartok Sonata & Trumpet Sonata (Addison?)[7] & possibly songs by me – a mixed lot but designed as a pre-view of the Festival & helpful to rehearsals etc. Hope you agree to this –

Then last night I was up with Paul Hamburger[8] for supper – Keller[9] should have come but has 'flu or something, so Donald Mitchell came instead – very sweet, young, dotty & enthusiastic – you were of course the main topic of con. Why not? You're my main topic of thought – honey – bunch –

I do hope you're getting on allright & are happy – Please give lots of love to everyone – I look forward very much to seeing you again, my own Bee –

Much love

ever your P

1   Blackwell, Pears's sister and her husband.
2   Pears and Britten planned to move from 22A Melbury Road.
3   Dr Michael McCready.
4   (1909–97), BBC Third Programme music organiser.
5   *Variations on an Elizabethan Theme 'Sellinger's Round'* (1953).
6   *Fugal Concerto* for Flute, Oboe and Strings.
7   Possibly a new commission from John Addison (1920–88) that did not materialise.
8   (1920–2004), Austrian-born pianist.
9   Hans Keller (1919–85), Viennese-born writer and author of many articles about Britten.

172 Britten to Pears

[*Letterhead:* Harewood House, Leeds]

Jan. 9th 1953

My darling P.,

Your letters have made me very happy. Thank you so much for them. I have been thinking so very much about you, thanking God you haven't been flying in this weather, wondering how it is all going. I hope the horn player wasn't quite so panicky as the Birmingham one!

Here, all goes the same. I work hard – am getting on quite well, nearing the end of the last scene now – we walk (slowly!) & talk (a little!) but it is good to be quiet & relaxed! Tony Gishford was here last night, & dear William [Plomer] comes this afternoon which will be lovely. George went to London for the night, & is generally rather moody with Ma'am[1] – but otherwise sweet & intelligent. I shall go back on Monday or Tuesday, I think. And expect you on Thursday or so? I hope all goes well with the Flat arrangements. It'll be lovely to have something of our own – I look forward to that alot. I'll be able to come up, these next weeks, quite abit to help you I think – to give you my expert advice!

I was thrilled that you were asked to do 'Vere' [in *Billy Budd*] in Berlin. Please do it, if you can. It means so much to all of us if you will – it's so very valuable for the work to have you doing it. Please!!

Just out for a walk with Ma'am & David so I must stop this. It's only a Welcome Home to bring all my love, my dearest P.,

B.

---

[1] HRH Princess Mary (1897–1965), mother of Lord Harewood.

173 Pears to Britten

2 Orme Sq
[26 Jan 1953]

My own sweet darling honey-bee –

Only just a note to send you much much love & to hope that you are feeling better – I am so sorry you've had this dreary attack – You'd better not come up on Friday or if you do, get Jim to drive you,[1] but if you don't feel up to it, DON'T COME!

I hope you haven't felt too horrid – I wish I could help you – Take great care of yourself – It's probably the same as Marie Young had a week ago – everybody's getting it – Send a sample to Mrs. B!

Last night's concert[2] was quite fairly allright, spoilt by two mad women in the front row who whispered loudly at certain crucial quiet passages! Agony! Quite a good house – & Joan Hammond's[3] concert made £600 or so for the School![4]

Much love my old B.

> From yr much
>> older but loving   P

---

1 Jim Balls was owner of the local garage at Saxmundham.
2 Recital at the Victoria and Albert Museum by Pears, Dennis Brain and Noel Mewton-Wood.
3 (1912–96), New Zealand-born Australian soprano and champion golfer.
4 For an opera school attached to the Royal Festival Hall.

174 Britten to Pears

[*Letterhead:* 4 Crabbe Street, Aldeburgh]

Jan 27th 1953

My darling P –

Sweet of you to ring, & sweet of you to write. Thank you so much. I'm really feeling better – all that is wrong now is a flatness as a result of the fever.

Here are some notes that have arrived for you.

Looking forward to Friday & seeing you. Love to George & Marion & to David.

~~Lots of~~ All my love,

> B.

175 Pears to Britten

[?late Jan. 1953]

Darling honey-pot!

Just to say that it's good to know you're better – & to let you know that we've postponed Nelson[1] to Feb. 14th owing to Jean Watson's[2] illness & inability to find another mezzo. Also Arda[3] can't read a note, & Nancy is slow (as you know) & it is too tricky & difficult to do badly – So. —— Lennox says if you <u>do</u> come up on Friday will you go there for dinner?

I daresay I shall speak to you about all this later on the phone –

Could you be an angel and remember to bring for me to London:

1. Copies for Noel of Mahler 7 Last Songs, Knaben Wunderhorn (Rheinlegendchen) & Um schlimmer Kinder. They should be either on top shelf or
   2nd shelf under Piper Herring.[4]
2. Copy of Under the Greenwood Tree![5] Perhaps on top of ~~Barbara's~~ your old
   music cabinet.
3. Schubert volume with | Du bist die Ruh
                        | Allmacht
                        | An die Musik
4. Messiah, any edition.

   _____

V. v. sorry for trouble.
            & much love.
                    P.

_____

[1]   Concert performance of Lennox Berkeley's opera *Nelson* at the Wigmore Hall.
[2]   (1909–2003), Irish-born mezzo-soprano/contralto.
[3]   Mandikian (1924–2009), Greek-born soprano.
[4]   Piper's *Loxford: Drop Curtain for Albert Herring*.
[5]   Song by Thomas Arne.

176 Britten to Pears

                                                              [before 7 Feb 1953]

[*Letterhead:* 4 Crabbe Street, Aldeburgh]

My sweet P.,

Just one or two notes that have arrived –

We're getting on, the cellar is nearly clear, & so we expect to feel less damp
to-morrow.[1]

I think we're going to try sleeping here to-night.

Hope Bournemouth isn't too horrible. I'll try & listen on Sunday.[2] Love to
Szymon.[3]

It was heaven, a real ray of sun to have you here. Please come back soon & let the
sun shine again.

            All my love
                    Ben

_____

[1]   Damage caused by the devastating North Sea floods resulting from a storm on 31 January.

²   Pears's Bach recital at the Victoria and Albert Museum was broadcast live on 8 February.
³   Goldberg (1909–93), American violinist.

177 Britten to Pears

[7 Feb 1953]

[*Letterhead:* 4 Crabbe Street, Aldeburgh]

My darling,
    Lovely to hear your voice.
Do hope Bournemouth¹ goes well, & the V & A. to-morrow. I'll listen if I can.
    We're getting on here, & most of the mud's gone now, thank God!
    All my love,
        B

---

¹   Pears gave a recital that evening at St Peter's Hall with Noel Mewton-Wood. Repertoire
    included Tippett's *The Heart's Assurance.*

178 Pears to Britten

Royal British Hotel.
<u>Dundee</u>

<u>Friday</u> [20 Feb 1953]

My honey bunch –
    This is just a little note to send you all my love, & to hope you may get it
tomorrow somehow –
    Quite a good journey up – not too much sleep but otherwise allright – walked
around Dundee yesterday – do you remember an abend 1840 arch¹ to the Docks
here? rather dreary town & dirty-ish hotel, but lovely weather & quite a nice
concert – Today we go on to Milngavie, & on Saturday to Edinburgh.
    There were lots of good wishes to you here & expressions of regret that you
couldn't come & any amount of hopes for "Gloriana" – The local amateur opera
coy; which is doing "Marta"² next week, is seriously considering investigating the
possibilities of doing "Nelson" some time on the strength of its notices !! Bless them
    Much much love to you honey pot
        P.

P.S.

Rang Seymour[3] on Wednesday & she is trying to get all our jobs in the <u>last</u> 2 or 3 days of Greece – Their Sunday concerts take place in the morning, & if we were performing in the 1ˢᵗ half of the concert on the 29ᵗʰ we could still catch a BEA[4] plane at 1.15. Anyway that's <u>my</u> last plane – it goes to Rome where I'd change for Amsterdam – You all could stay longer perhaps.

> Going on March 16ᵗʰ, there is a plane leaving London 10 or so via Zurich which gets us to Athens[5] that night – Otherwise we have to spend a night in Rome.

P.P.S.

Hope scoring goes well –
much love to Imo

---

1   The Royal Arch, constructed to commemorate an 1844 visit by Queen Victoria and Prince Albert, was demolished in 1964.
2   Probably Friedrich von Flotow's opera.
3   Whinyates (1892–1978), Director of Music at the British Council, 1943–59.
4   British European Airways.
5   Pears and Britten were planning a working holiday to Greece with the Harewoods.

179 Pears to Britten

The Royal Stuart Hotel
Abercromby Place
<u>Edinburgh . 3 .</u>

<u>Saturday night</u> [21 Feb 1953]

My darling –

Here I am again – another concert[1] over (at Milngavie this time) – and a day nearer to seeing you – The concert was allright – I'm not sure how good a programme it is – The first half is very tense, & the 2ⁿᵈ half rather too light – However – they seemed to enjoy it – I had lunch with Alex. Duncan[2] today & discussed our October concerts at their festival – I think I've got you out of the Brahms Horn Trio! but there's quite a lot to play without it!

I'm longing to see you again my bee & to be with you – You are the only person I want to be with, & I want to be with you all the time – Are you well & working well – & not too hard? Much much love to you all the time –

The enclosed has come from Seymour – What d'you think? I suppose we shall <u>have</u> to do it, but it must be in those last 3 days …

I went & coped slightly at BEA with our journey to & from Athens – We can get via Zurich in a day – otherwise we have to stay Monday night in Rome – I've booked via Zurich.

Coming back, I <u>must</u> come at the latest on a 1.15 BEA from Athens on Sunday 29th. We still could do the Orch. concert that morning, if we did our stuff in the first half – You could come back later if you wanted to!

Ever your
     P.

---

1   Pears was giving four concerts in Scotland.
2   One of the founders of the Milngavie Music Club.

180 Britten to Pears

[*Letterhead:* 4 Crabbe Street, Aldeburgh]

Feb. 22nd 1953

My darling Pyje
   – Excuse the black ink, not mourning, only what I use for scoring, therefore my pen is filled with it.

Thank you for your sweet note; terribly happy to have it this morning, & to know you are well & happy. I hope Glasgow was also good, & that you'll enjoy Edinburgh & Karl R. Give him my regards. I did actually try to telephone you twice while you were in Dundee, but you were out each time. I thought maybe that you'd tried to 'phone me on Wednesday evening. You see I heard the telephone ring in the evening – over the roar of the sea – rushed to it, & the operator said that 'they'd cleared' as it had been ringing sometime (it is a curse, this not hearing it ring; but we've now applied for it to be moved). I had expected you to ring about the flat. How is that situation now? Do let me know, because if it (the Harley St) has fallen through, then I've got a plan of flat-hunting which I can set in motion, (friends of Imo's – as you might imagine!).

All goes along here. I score & score – in the middle of Act.I Sc. II now, so it's going quite fast. I played Badminton (very badly!) last night, & enjoyed it. William [Plomer] comes this evening (Saturday). I've seen Billy several times – <u>very</u> low, bored with river walls & crises, so I'm taking him in ten minutes for a drive away from Sea & Aldeburgh. Barbara is coming too.[1]

We've got a Friends meeting to-morrow night. Hope it's go allright. They'll need pushing abit I think, but Stephen[2] is quite keen & energetic. Saw Fidelity yesterday – she's very happy with the programme changes. Just had a note from Mable saying she can't sing Miss Wordsworth[3] – blast her! WHO can we get now – E Morrison? – Gwen Catley? – Lorely Dyer?[4] What do you think?

I've fixed an earlyish luncheon with Decca[5] on March 3rd. O.K? O.K. about the Greece arrangements (visas just come!!) End of News Bulletin – but not end of my love, which goes on for ever–

Ben.

---

[1] Billy Burrell (1925–99), Aldeburgh fisherman, and his wife Barbara. The river wall and sea defences at Aldeburgh had sustained serious damage during the recent flooding.

[2] Stephen Potter, Aldeburgh Festival Friends chair, married to the artist Mary Potter.

[3] Role in *Albert Herring*, for a performance in Wiesbaden and at the 1953 Aldeburgh Festival.

[4] Sopranos Elsie Morison (b. 1924), Gwen Catley (1906–96) and Lorely Dyer (1907–2000). In the end, Margaret Ritchie was able to sing Miss Wordsworth at the Aldeburgh Festival *Albert Herring*.

[5] For talks about recording the Aldeburgh Festival.

181 Britten to Pears

[*Letterhead:* 4 Crabbe Street, Aldeburgh]

Feb. 23rd 1953

My darling P.,

Thank you for your sweet letter – just arrived. Don't worry about the concerts, I am sure they are fine – anything you do will always be that. But however good Noel is, I am certain that you & I together have something very special, & it won't be long before <u>that</u> happens again! I'm getting on well with the score, Act I nearly done, so Gloriana is nearly behind us ___ !

William went off this morning after a busy week-end of work, & walks. It was a glorious spring day yesterday, &inspite of the depressing last of the Floods everywhere the countryside looked lovely when we went for a bit of a drive after tea. I'm soon off to Ipswich to meet George so I'll see some more of it – can't see too much of Spring! How I wish you were coming too, my darling – but it isn't so long now. I hope you'll enjoy some of the concerts this week. My greetings to Karl Rankl.

I'll ring up Seymour about her letter. Yes I suppose we'd better do the King & Queen[1] – only if it can be done in the last 3 days tho'. I'll talk alittle to George this evening about it, & the plans generally.

The enclosed note from Kathleen[2] – rather pathetic & brave, isn't it? But I hope she really <u>is</u> getting better.

I see I didn't put the full address on your letter on Saturday – & so I do hope it reached you & that I don't get a rather doubtful letter returned to me "to the writer of a letter to darling P." ——!

Nice joke from William – the Queen Mum & Princess Margaret who often go around together are frequently referred to as 'Ma'am & Super-ma'am' ___ nice?

Lots of love, my dearest. Take care. See you very soon.

> Lots to Noel too.
>
> Your devoted B.

---

1 Paul, King of Greece (1901–64; r. 1947–64) and Frederica, Queen Consort (1917–81); the UK ambassador (Athens) planned to host a party for the Harewoods, Britten and Pears.

2 Ferrier had been suffering from cancer, to which she would eventually succumb in October 1953, aged forty-one.

182 Britten to Pears

[*Letterhead:* 4 Crabbe Street, Aldeburgh]

Feb. 24th 1953

My darling,

Just a brief note.

George was here last night, & we talked a great deal about this & that, all nice & sympathetic & a good deal useful as well. One thing did however transpire which makes the Greek tour a little doubtful – He's been summoned to see Alan Lascelles[1] to enquire into this thing we're sponsors of (League for Democracy in Greece)[2] – as the Foreign Office take a dim view of it, & the Greeks (inspite of the fact they've given us Visas) are angry. However I gave him the letter I received (with names of Presidents etc.) & he's taken that along, & we can only wait & see what happens. I've rung Seymour & told her to hang on for a day or so. But this, coupled with the fact that the fares each cost the horrifying among of £112 (which I think almost puts George & Marion off), may put the scheme off??

We worked on the Gluck & Rossini programme which I'll show you next week. The luncheon is O.K. for him on 3rd with the Decca people – so can you keep it too. Do we then drive back in the afternoon?

No more now my dear – Jeremy [Cullum] has shingles so I've got lots of letters to write!

Hope things flourish with you as they should.   Lots of love   Ben.

---

1 Lord Harewood's cousin and private secretary to the Queen.

[2]   Established by Sir Compton Mackenzie in 1943 as the Greek Unity Committee; Britten
      signed a petition for the fair treatment of prisoners. The trip to Greece did not occur.

183 Pears to Britten

Edinburgh

Tuesday afternoon [24 Feb 1953]

My honey-pot –

Thank you very much for your letter – What a nice quick service seems to run
'twixt E'burgh & A'burgh! Not quick enough for me, though!

One more concert gone, last night – recital here. Went fairly well, I think. Noel
went off this morning to Manchester, so now I'm alone – On Friday & Saturday I
have Karl Rankl,[1] & on Sunday the Schütz, then night train to London –

I have gone & got a bad eye – something in it I think – I had to wear a shade for
the concert last night & I'm just going off to see a doctor now –

What a bore about Mabel. We may have to have Edna Graham[2] whom we
heard at auditions – quite clever, shrewd hardworking, moderate voice, sang Miss
W. at the RAM.[3] Can sing the notes allright. And what about a Polly[4] at Bideford
too? Oh dear –

Everyone here (Hans, Isobel Dunlop, Ruth d'Arcy Thompson,[5] etc) ask after
you and so do I! Longing to see you –

Much love

    P.

---

[1]   Pears was to sing with the Scottish National Orchestra in Glasgow.
[2]   (1925–2005), New Zealand-born soprano.
[3]   Royal Academy of Music.
[4]   As well as a new Miss Wordsworth for *Albert Herring*, they also needed to recruit a Polly
      Peachum for *The Beggar's Opera*.
[5]   Possibly violinist Hans Geiger, who performed at the first Aldeburgh Festival; Isobel
      Dunlop (1901–75), Scottish composer; and writer Ruth d'Arcy Thompson, daughter of
      noted biologist D'Arcy Wentworth Thompson.

184 Britten to Pears

[*Letterhead:* 4 Crabbe Street, Aldeburgh]

Feb. 25th 1953

My darling,

Just a scribble to thank you for your note just arrived. I am so very sorry to hear about the eye – that is <u>maddening</u> for you. I hope you've got a good doctor who is helping you. Is it madly painful? Do take care of yourself & see Doctors galore (what about a specimen to Mrs B???!!)[1]

Slight plans for the beginning of next week: – I think I'm going to drive up on Monday evening – spend the evening & night with George & Marion, & meet Basil [Coleman] & discuss problems with him on Tuesday morning & then the Decca lunch, & home —— ?? Will you want to stay with the Harewoods too? It would be lovely (& convenient) if you did. I'll (may-be) warn them you want to come. If you <u>are</u> free on Monday evening I wish you'd keep it so, & be able to discuss the Greek question with us. It is rather worrying – & I think we may be forced to think of going somewhere else. The Greeks are obviously fed up about us signing that thing – & I don't want to have our precious 2 weeks ruined by nastiness. Isn't there a nearer British Colony we could go to – or even Sicily? (Morocco?)

I'll be talking over the E.O.G problems with Basil [Douglas] on the 'phone this week, I expect. It is worrying, but I don't think insuperable. Both George & Imo think Anne [Wood] would be an <u>excellent</u> Polly – so <u>there</u>!!

All my love, my sweet. Longing to see you. The house is upside down with electricians re-wiring us. The damp is still coming up, down-stairs. We shan't be able to use that room for ages, I'm abit afraid. Hope the Rankl concerts go well.

    <u>Lots</u> of love, & get well <u>very</u> soon.

          Your devoted

            B.

Imo sends a '<u>great</u> deal' of love. The scores going well. ½ done!! }

---

[1] Mrs G.M. Barraclough, a 'Radiethesic Consultant' who supplied Britten and Pears with homeopathic remedies after analysing their urine samples.

185 Pears to Britten

Edinburgh

Wednesday. 3.30pm [25 Feb 1953]

Darling Fudge.

Just got yr letter. So sorry to hear Jer[y] has sh'gles. Don't b[r] ab[t] lett[rs] – Let them an[r] thems[ves] – Only to me as I'm import[nt].[1]

Was afraid Greece might go that way – v. sorry that Geo. sh'd be fussed into it – Dreary old F.O. [Foreign Office]. Anyway it is fearfully dear – so let's stay at home instead or go motoring somewhere –

Had a small piece of coal cut out of my eye last night – no pain – cocaine. It'll take a day or two to clear – don't worry –

Went out for a drive & lunch to North Berwick – v. pretty, & now I'm just off to Isobel Dunlop's to practise.

Longing to see you – 3ʳᵈ lunch – I'll be at Melbury Rd the previous night I hope – Yes, let's drive down & we might take the Sickert with us from Lefevre's, as well Miss Frink. & perhaps the Steer??![2]

     Much much love honey bee

        P

---

1   'So sorry to hear Jeremy has shingles. Don't bother about letters – Let them answer themselves – Only to me as I'm important.'

2   Artworks – Sickert's *Santa Maria della Salute*, Frink's *Christ bound at the pillar* and Steer's *Harwich Estuary* – from Lefevre Gallery in London.

186 Pears to Britten

Kensington

Monday [?1953]

My darling honeypot –

It was heavenly to speak to you yesterday, though I wish I were with you instead of being far away! Aldeburgh was very nice, Miss H. was v. sweet (She was better – she had been seedy – she's going away today until Thursday) and I had a useful session with Imo who is trying to get on with festival matters – and I had another session with Basil D. late last night after my pleasant dinner chez Terence & Hans.[1]

He was off to Bideford this morning; working v. hard, of course v. disappointed about The Screw[2] but genuinely understanding. We must make some decisions about Stravinsky-Holst now, & hope to have a meeting with Basil C [Coleman], John P [Piper] & John C [Cranko] after I come back from Switzerland. I shall probably come straight back here on Sunday I think or even Saturday night.

When shall I see you? my bee – much much love. & to all of you up there –

     yr. loving   P.

[1] Terence Hodgkinson (1913–99), assistant to the Director at the Victoria and Albert Museum, and his partner, Hans Schneider (d. 1995), designer at Marks and Spencer. Pears and Britten met them in 1940 in Amityville, Long Island, NY.

[2] *The Turn of the Screw.*

187 Britten to Pears

[*Letterhead:* Hotel d'Angleterre, Copenhagen]

[20–1 Sep 1953]

[*Incomplete – only the second half survives in the archive.*]

Schnappy luncheon with Frank Lee,[1] who is quite a dear & got as tiddley as I did! Walked abit in the afternoon, & had a rehersal with the boys[2] in the evening, which I must say was heaven – meaning, of course, the way they sing. Wøldike has trained them beautifully, & I gulped all the time, naturally. Benny & Leif are still in it – Leif singing the top solos like an angel. After that we had a rather awful meal with the Tuxns (the conductor of the orchestra) & Ormandies[3] – all rather exaggerated (I eat lobster & died of it, nearly) terrific compliments, & rather boring – Beth stood up to it manfully. She's a dear & really enjoying herself, I think. To-day we have lunch with the Schiøtzs[4] and record again in the afternoon. One has to fight to get any free time, they are so madly hospitable.

How goes the house and all? I envy you madly being in Aldeburgh this week-end. I'm all for a quiet life – can't take all this really. We must get that farm in East Bridge! I look forward hugely to Wednesday – I think the plane gets in in the afternoon, but don't stay in or anything, I'll just turn up – how wonderful that will be!

Lots of love to you my darling – I miss you very much. Every one sends love – I haven't seen Ingelise yet, but hope to soon.

Your devoted

B.

[1] Artists' Manager for Decca.

[2] Britten was conducting *A Ceremony of Carols*, with the Copenhagen Boys Choir (choirmaster Mogens Wöldike).

[3] Erik Tuxen (1902–57) and Eugene Ormandy (1899–1985).

[4] Danish tenor Aksel Schiøtz (1906–75) and his wife.

188 Pears to Britten

[*Letterhead:* The Central Hotel, Glasgow]

Jan 1ˢᵗ [1954]

Dearest Ben.

    I do hope you are getting on alright & are feeling happy & rested, and perhaps have forgiven me now for being such a very inadequate and uncomforting visitor – It was lovely to be with you and to see you so well looked after and I wish I could have been less dreary & disappointing. You know I <u>am</u> rather fond of you, in spite of all demonstrations to the contrary – It had even occurred to me that if you come over on the 6<u>th</u> night, I could meet you at Harwich and spend a night or two at Aldeburgh, possibly driving over to N'hampton on the Saturday & back on the Sunday – Would you anyhow <u>consider</u> coming back on the 6ᵗʰ night? (I <u>am</u> BBC-recording on the 6ᵗʰ. Arthur O. (with Ernest Lush)[1] & unaccompanied.)

    I shall see Bill Fell today I hope & tell him that you will not conduct – I have already told Emmie your position & she is ready –

    Glasgow is horrid & foggy – It's not Karl [Rankl] but the Chorus master,[2] nice but inexperienced–

    V. much love, dear Ben – come back –[3]

        P

---

1   (1908–88), pianist.
2   Charles Cleall (1928–2015); Pears was singing *Messiah* at St Andrew's Hall.
3   Britten had spent Christmas at Wolfsgarten, with the Hesses.

V

'Why shouldn't I recognise that you are such a large part of my life'

MAY 1954 TO DECEMBER 1959

Britten's relentless schedule of writing and performing began to take its toll on his health. Towards the end of 1953 he received confirmation that an aching, burning sensation in his right shoulder that had plagued him for several months was bursitis. The ailment, he wrote to E.M. Forster, prompted his doctors to forbid him using the arm, which brought a temporary halt to performance and composition. Work on the new chamber opera, *The Turn of the Screw*, was delayed until 30 March 1954, leaving him little more than five months to complete it in time for the premiere in Venice, scheduled for the following September.

There is a pause in the correspondence when Britten and Pears embark together on a lengthy international tour towards the end of 1955. Beginning in Holland, they travelled across the continent to Istanbul, then flew to India and on to Malaysia, Indonesia, China and Japan. The trip included concert engagements in Europe in October and November, and Japan (one of which was recorded by NHK Television, their television debut) in February 1956. Although the trip was intended partly as a holiday, an enforced rest for Britten, the unfamiliar, exotic cultures he experienced proved to be a rich source of inspiration for him. Both musicians were captivated by traditional Japanese theatre, especially the Noh drama *Sumidagawa* that eventually became a model for *Curlew River*, the first of the three Church Parables. The most immediate legacy, however, arose from a visit to Bali, where Britten's experience of the gamelan led him to incorporate its percussive sounds and rich, alien sonorities into his latest project, the ballet *The Prince of the Pagodas*. With a scenario and choreography by John Cranko, the work was finally premiered at the Royal Opera House on New Year's Day, 1957. Later that year the singing of East Anglian schoolchildren inspired him to adapt the medieval Chester Miracle Play for a new type of opera, *Noye's Fludde*. Composed primarily as a work for community performance, it was premiered at the 1958 Aldeburgh Festival by a combination of schoolchildren and professional musicians. Britten was also inspired by the artistry of fellow musicians, for example in 1954 he composed *Canticle III: Still Falls the Rain*, for himself and

Pears to perform with virtuoso horn player Dennis Brain, to verses by Edith Sitwell. They gave the premiere the following January with its companion piece *Three Songs from The Heart of the Matter* (1956). These works proved to be the last of Britten's compositions for Dennis Brain, who was killed in a car accident in August 1957.[1]

The year 1957 was pivotal in the couple's domestic lives. In November they moved further inland from their home of ten years on the Aldeburgh seafront to The Red House. They made alterations to the surrounding outbuildings to suit their lifestyle, first when Britten engaged the architect H.T. 'Jim' Cadbury-Brown to design a composition studio in what had formerly been the hayloft in the upper floor of an adjacent building, which eventually came to be called Red Cottage.

Travel was integral to both musicians' lives and Pears's correspondence of the mid-1950s reveals how active his career had become, independent of Britten. He writes of performances in the Bavarian town of Ansbach to celebrate the music of J.S. Bach.[2] Here he formed a close connection with such emerging talents as Karl Richter and Dietrich Fischer-Dieskau. Pears sang at the Bachwoche Ansbach between 1955 and 1964, and refers frequently in his letters to rehearsals and other performances he attended. His reputation as an operatic performer and interpreter of early music continued to grow, in addition to the success of his recitals with Britten (they toured Belgium and Switzerland in 1955 and Germany in 1956). Pears received official recognition for his work as an ambassador for British culture with the award of CBE in 1957.

At this time Pears also expanded his early music repertoire to include the English lute song, establishing a partnership in the early 1950s with the lutenist and guitarist Julian Bream. During the 1957 Aldeburgh Festival they performed a programme of music by Thomas Morley, interspersed with groups of madrigals sung by the Purcell Singers, at Great Glemham House. They worked often together over the next two decades, including a tour to the US in 1959. Working with Bream gave Pears the opportunity to continue his recital work even when Britten was unable to play, because of either work or illness. Pears's letters include regular reports on these concert tours, a feature of this and the following chapter. Britten showed his support for the new recital partnership with his six *Songs from the Chinese* (1957), for Pears and Bream to perform alongside the songs of Dowland and Morley.

Another significant joint project affects the flow of letters in 1959, when Britten and Pears embark on recasting Shakespeare's *A Midsummer Night's Dream* into a workable libretto. Plans were made to mark the extensive refurbishment of Aldeburgh's Jubilee Hall with a new opera which would be premiered during the 1960 Festival. With time very much a factor they decided to work on an existing text which would not require extensive redrafting. Britten writes to Pears about useful suggestions received from John and Myfanwy Piper, but two heavily annotated copies of the Penguin edition of the play, now held in their Archive, reveal much about their thinking and how they themselves went about reorganising the text.

Although their professional partnership was by now well known internationally, the exact nature of their private relationship continued to remain concealed from wider public attention. As cited in the Introduction, in September 1957 the Wolfenden Report suggested that homosexual acts between consenting adults should not be regarded as a legal matter. Despite the report's proposals, criminalisation would remain in place for another decade. In a letter written during a North American tour with Bream in February 1959, Pears recalled conversations in which Elizabeth Mayer spoke to him with 'philosophic devotion' and 'passionate interest' about her adopted home of America, a subject that urged him to confirm his own sense of where and with whom he belonged. 'Why shouldn't I recognise that you are such a large part of my life[?]' (Letter 227), his choice of phrase implicitly questioning the severe and restrictive laws that refused to acknowledge the basis of his and Britten's relationship.

The year concluded satisfactorily, on an artistic level at least, with the screening of an innovative Associated Rediffusion television film of *The Turn of the Screw*. Produced by Peter Morley, designed by John Piper with musical direction by Charles Mackerras, it remains a pioneering example of television opera, a genre which Britten would later explore with *Owen Wingrave*. A Television Audience Measurement (the equivalent to today's ratings system) recorded that just over 200,000 viewers watched the programme which was broadcast over two nights at Christmas. Britten was particularly impressed with the scenery and effects, as he writes to reassure Pears, who did not appear in the film: 'TV. of Screw was awfully good', a judgement borne out in Morley's memory of the composer personally commending the 'skill, taste and knowledge shown in adapting this difficult opera for television'.[3]

---

[1] See Britten's tribute, 'Dennis Brain 1921–1958' in Paul Kildea (ed.), *Britten on Music*, pp. 158–9.

[2] For a diary of the 1959 Festival see Philip Reed (ed.), *The Travel Diaries of Peter Pears 1936–1978*, pp. 73–84.

[3] Peter Morley, *A Life Rewound: Memoirs of a Freelance Producer and Director*, pp. 63–4.

189 Britten to Pears

I still love the Gwen John. It is a beauty.[1]

[*Letterhead:* 4 Crabbe Street, Aldeburgh]

May 28th (?) 1954

My darling P.

This is just a brief note to send my love to you now in Switzerland – although as I write it, you are still in Brussels. I hope it isn't all too hectic, & that you've met some nice people, & that you got on well with the Fullers.[2] I shall try to listen to P.G. to morrow night, but rather doubt if we shall hear anything. I suppose Lucretia isn't to be broadcast?[3]

All goes well here – the work slow, but (I think) sure. Wish it wern't so slow, but I expect it'll be done in time. Imo likes Act II beginning alright.[4]

The Goble recorders[5] have come, & are lovely – Much nicer than the "monarchs of the plastic" – nice sound, & very (almost too much) in tune. The tenor needs a finger piece (like your bass) I think, because neither Imo nor I can stretch far enough to cover the bottom hole. It is a lovely noise it makes, not too cow-like.

I've just seen Stephen Reiss & he says our little Bonnington is genuinely a B. It is catalogued apparently in the original catalogue – a detailed description – "man with red cloak, before a tomb in a crypt with light coming through the door". Isn't that exciting? A jolly good buy of yours![6]

No other news. The fine weather broke yesterday with big thunderstorms (& a hurricane at Hasketon!), & to-day is sunny but windy & clouds too. I expect to play tennis this afternoon, but otherwise work – work – work.

I miss you dreadfully. It's almost worse you coming for just a day & then off again – but it isn't so very long. I'll try & find a way of collecting you on Whit Sunday.

Much love to you: enjoy yourself abit.

B

Greetings to the Fullers – & to Arda[7] if she's with you

---

1   Gwen John's Study for *The Messenger*.
2   Frederick Fuller (1909–95), baritone, who also translated German lieder. His wife Patricia corresponded with Britten and Pears.
3   Pears sang in two Belgian performances of *Peter Grimes* in May before travelling to Switzerland at the beginning of June for a Geneva production of *The Rape of Lucretia*.
4   Britten had begun work on *The Turn of the Screw* in March.
5   Recorders by early instrument makers Goble & Son. Britten, Pears and Imogen Holst were all accomplished recorder players.
6   Bonington's *Crypt of a Church*.
7   Arda Mandikian (1924–2009), Greek soprano.

190 Britten to Pears

Since writing this, I've talked to you – lovely! – & we are in the middle of yet another thunderstorm – not so lovely! –

[*Letterhead:* 4 Crabbe Street, Aldeburgh]

[Summer 1954]

My darling P.,

Be an angel & read through the proofs for me, & then put them (with letter) in the envelop to Cardus & post it – very soon, as it is already late. Make any alterations you want.[1]

Elizabeth [Sweeting] says is Aug. 20th, 8.15, alright for our recital in Jubilee Hall, & how do we bill it?[2]

Also enclosed is a suggested letter to Green; I think they need a slap back. Should we be more detailed?

Do you want me to pay the enclosed bill to Goble? Or do you want a key fitted to the Tenor – actually it <u>can</u> wait till you get here.

Have a <u>lovely</u> time abroad love to Peter & Maria of course.

All my love

B

---

[1] Britten's contribution to *Kathleen Ferrier: A Memoir* (published by Hamish Hamilton in 1954), edited by Neville Cardus.
[2] Norma Procter (b. 1928), contralto, sang with Britten and Pears at the Jubilee Hall in Aldeburgh on 20 August.

191 Pears to Britten

Not from [*Letterhead:* 5 Chester Gate, London][1]

1 Rue du Rhône
Genève

Tuesday [1 June 1954]

Darling Honey bun –

It was lovely to have your letter last night – & v. very v. sweet of you to write – I miss you very much & wish I were with you instead of Europe-trotting, although with Grimes & Lucretia round my neck I can't feel very far away from you.

Brussels was up & down – A somewhat bumpy flight, in some ways desperate rehearsals – a rather dear M. Daniel Sternefeldt[2] – wild fellow soloists in certain ways – Viccy very graty & breathy – Chorus in agony over the Mad Scene

– Wonderful old Astoria with an influx of French footballers on the last day –
Finally not a wholly bad performance (did you hear it?) which made a great
impression.

Superb steaks each day! Leo & Janet Kersley[3] came over from Rotterdam
especially for the performance, & Peter D. rang up afterwards; it came over well
apparently. Then on to Geneva, again bum-py, v. Frederick & Patricia Fuller
extremely nice & kind, & sweet daughters – The whole performance is in danger of
bursting through the nerves of the Conductor M. Horneffer[4] – but not bad voices
at all, rather lovely Lucretia, sweet Swiss-li Lucia, & a solid Bianca. Men's voices
good but v. young & inexperienced & gittery. We'll see – I am being a father to
everybody & calming them all down – M. le Contrabassiste is old & deaf & the
Bullfrogs are very curious – I shout into his ear "Beaucoup très resonant, Monsieur,
& plus lent! Comme les grenouilles! Gong-ng-ng-ng!" & he smiles & produces a
sound like a packet of needles being dropped onto a rug!

Handsome young American Collatinus with the usual American Knees & a
Tarquin – ex d-p. [displaced person] from Ukrainian Poland, useful voice, good
figure, but mentally a baby. & some odd English sounds –

However we shall see – Mme Ansermet was there last night & they both come
tonight I think – I have a feeling that there is someone that we know living in
Geneva whom I ought to see, but I can't think who it can be. It's quite nice to
be in Switzerland again for a short time, but I wish I were with you. Take care of
yourself, B.

I had a idea (good?) about Janacek – I don't honestly think I can really sing any
of these folk songs – language difficulty too great & no time to translate. Could
we perhaps get our repetiteur chap Martin Isepp (good pianist it seems)[5] to play a
few of those pieces from "Down the garden path" or whatever it was called – "Oh I
say stop" & 1 or 2 more – or should we try Robert Keys?[6] What do you think? We
need a little more than the Women's Folksongs, Cello Piece & Mladi, don't we? He
could also play Women's Folksongs, couldn't he? & you could listen & help more
that way perhaps!

V. good news about the Bonington!

    Much love

        Peter ox ox

Lucretia not broadcast.

---

1 5 Chester Gate, NW1, Britten and Pears's London house from 1953 to 1958.
2 Daniel Sternefeld (1905–86), Belgian composer and conductor.
3 Leo Kersley (1920–2012), ballet dancer and teacher, founder member of Sadler's Wells
    Theatre Ballet.
4 Jacques Horneffer, Swiss conductor and pianist.

⁵ (1930–2011), Austrian-born accompanist and singing coach.
⁶ (1914–99), pianist and repetiteur with the Royal Opera House, Covent Garden.

192 Pears to Britten

[*Letterhead:* The Queens Hotel, Leeds]

Monday. [?10 Jan 1955]

Dearest Bunch –

I am longing to ring you up all the time – I miss you very much & it seems like a thousand years since Saturday morning. Saturday was regulation dreary north country Messiah – Long talk with Norma [Procter], who is a great dear – Sunday largely in bed, then long session (after evensong in Parish Church) with Mr. & Mrs. Knisz (you remember – the man with the stammer) – both great simple Liverpudlian dears – Then a train over here this morning, & rehearsal this afternoon with Norman – Dennis[1] arrives tomorrow & I will tell him about the Bliss (?) idea for Aldeburgh – I will also break it to Norman[2] that he's not wanted at Aldeburgh.

And how are you, my honey pot? I <u>do</u> hope your tummy is better. Well now I <u>have</u> just rung you – so that's better –

It was lovely to hear your voice & nice to know that everything is well – or better – Give Clytie lots of love & also to Roger & the rest – & much much love to yourself –

One lazy day in bed alone in Liverpool is <u>quite</u> enough –
     P.

---

1   Discussion with Dennis Brain about the possibility of a new piece for horn and strings by Arthur Bliss for that year's Aldeburgh Festival, which Bliss later declined.
2   Probably Del Mar (1919–94), conductor.

193 Britten to Pears

[*Postcard:* Down Along, Clovelly, Devon]

[19 Apr 1955]

Spent yesterday afternoon here – an amazing little village, as cute as pie.[1] Went in a boat & Roger rowed; but we are nearly dry now ——! I'm coming up with the family in the car on Thursday; hope to be with you in the afternoon. Hope 'Don G.'[2] was fun & lots of people came. Good luck for the 3rd Missa.[3]

    Lots of love   Ben

[*also signed by Ronald, Roger and Briony Duncan*]

---

[1]   Britten joined Roger Duncan and his family in Devon, while Pears prepared to sing
      Vašek in Smetana's *The Bartered Bride* and Pandarus in Walton's *Troilus and Cressida*, both
      at Covent Garden.
[2]   Mozart's *Don Giovanni*.
[3]   A third performance of Beethoven's *Missa Solemnis*. Pears had also sung in the work on 15
      and 16 April.

194 Pears to Britten

[*Letterhead:* 5 Chester Gate, London]   Hotel Stern
                                                                          Ansbach.

                                                       Saturday 7 A.M. [30 Jul 1955]
My darling Honey bee
    Thank you so very much for your telegram – I do hope you are well and happy &
that your Dorset dash was allright & the car didn't wobble too much –
    Here everything has been really very moving. My concert went off yesterday
morning very well, it seems.[1] It was in a curious rather lovely little old Gothic
chapel, very German, with curious old ugly tombstones all round – very resonant
acoustic, too much, but allright-ish when full. Everyone was, on the surface anyway,
bowled over by your favourite tenor, and I think I sang quite well, although I had
to wait from 10.30 until 12.0 before I sang! owing to a sort of Council meeting
going on & on. Peg & Lu are of course very much here, in very good form, a lot of
late nights! – very sweetly they have asked us (all 3 chaps & me) to spend a night
at Wolfsgarten – We have of course discussed the world tour a lot (Peg's brother
David + wife have been here till today) & everyone advises us <u>not</u> to cross the
Pacific, v. expensive & tiring – Much better they say to come back same way or over
the top. In any case I suggest we agree to cut the Pacific & Mexico etc,[2] & either
come back the way we came more or less, <u>or</u> stay longer everywhere & then dash
back over the old North Pole. But more of that when I'm back.
    This Festival is very instructive – Gosh! What lots of money there is for art
here! The tickets are very expensive & the audience smart, snob to a certain extent,
but Bach is safe that way! Performances frightfully efficient, jolly accurate in every
way & with about as much charm as a type-writer. The great rage is a young man
called Karl Richter, played a complete organ recital by memory on a hideous
organ – The line seems to be straight & narrow Bach with no room to expand
– an occasional, very, ornament played pokerfaced to show we know about them
– Plenty of lively down-beats but precious little living rhythm. My players were as
usual better wind than strings – oboe good, flute young & a bit silly, violin a very
adequate Brucknerian from Munich. Rather sweet girl harpsichordist. But all the
musicians are young and passionately keen, and play for their lives. It is in many

ways curiously touching. It makes me sure that we ought to have our musicians at Aldeburgh for the whole of the week before the Festival – !

Ros and Noreen and Philip[3] are of course wild with excitement – They live in a hostel with 13 East German music students – & the stories are pretty dreary and make them think quite a bit –

Everyone here sends lots of love to you, my B. We think of you & talk of you often – It will be lovely to see you again –

Please give lots of love to Roger and Imo & Clytie –

       & to yourself, my own dear B,

            from a very loving P.

I think NO to Tureck[4] – Too awkward during August Sept Oct.

---

1   1955 Ansbach Bachwoche. Pears sang Bach Cantatas nos. 55, 160 and 189 on 29 July.
2   Plans for their upcoming world tour in October.
3   Singers Rosamund Strode, soprano, Noreen Willett, alto, and Philip Todd, tenor, a former pupil of Pears who later went to teach at the University of Auckland, New Zealand.
4   Rosalyn Tureck (1914–2003), American pianist and harpsichordist.

The Prince of the Pagodas occupied Britten throughout much of 1955, but he took a major break from composition to join Pears on their world tour later that year. This lengthy holiday (which included frequent recital work as well) is the primary reason for the lack of correspondence during this time. Letter writing is resumed as Pears tours Holland and Britten works towards a deadline to complete the ballet.

✠✠✠

195 Pears to Britten

[**Letterhead:** Hotel Kurhaus, Scheveningen, Holland]

                                    WEDNESDAY [?July 1956]

Dearest Honey bee –

I do hope you had a rather very good journey yesterday & that you contacted J. Chr....o and Miss Kremmin gave you some nourishing Berlinese food.

Hier ej mis u w. much.

I sit in Peter's room in Mr. Seilstra's pub looking out at the donkeys on the sand and the wicker hooded chairs and the Dutch flags all streaming south and lots of

frothy white horses. This morning I ran through the Serenade with M. Tomasi –
sketchy little Frog – & a good hornist called Piet Schijt! It won't be very good I
fear.[1] The orchestra were tired after Falstaff last night – which really was very good
indeed – Giulini obviously is very gifted. I don't know Falstaff very well but it was
really a pleasure to have such a well-integrated performance. Beautifully produced.
Spoilt of course by the wrong Meg – though Miss Merriman did very well – the
Alice let her stays down a bit too much as a result, & got out of control.[2] But the 1st
scene was excellent so was Act II Sc I. Ravishing Nanetta – Fenton in poor voice
but a real artist on the stage. Falstaff excellent & young – voice got tired too early.
Rather small scale Ford which was good in a way so the jealousy aria didn't stick
out <u>too</u> much. What a piece! What sounds! I am entirely won to it.

No other news – I rather dread tonight & the Ambassadorial supper afterwards –
Much love to you – wish I were home!

My B –   yr P.

---

1   Pears performed the *Serenade* during the Holland Festival, 11 and 14 July 1956.
2   Nan Merriman (1920–2012), American soprano who sang Meg Page in the 1950
    broadcast recording of Verdi's *Falstaff*, conducted by Arturo Toscanini. The role was taken
    during the Holland Festival (29 June and 10 July) by Fernanda Cadoni.

196 Britten to Pears

[*Letterhead:* 4 Crabbe Street, Aldeburgh]

July 20th 1956

My darling P.,

This is to send my love, & say how I'm thinking of you all the time, hoping the
drive is going well, & not too much rain & traffic, & also not too much of a strain. I
long to know you've arrived, & hope there'll be a message on Monday or so!

Poor old Jeremy is still stuck in London – the blinking old Rolls won't start <u>still</u>!
… what a car; I think I'll buy a Morris 8 Station wagon!

Anne Holt[1] has been here, talked alot with Miss Hudson about the arrangements for August, & seemed very happy with the house. I gave her lunch.

Johnny Cranko has just arrived, plus Clytie – it is nice to have the three genera-
tions together.[2]

Just dashing off to the Festival meeting – hope it goes well, & that there arn't too
many fireworks – but I expect Fidelity will control them.

I'll write properly in a day or so.

Hope the Festwoche goes well – & that you begin to enjoy the pieces. Don't forget to talk to Fisher-Diskauer about the Winter Reise, & mention the possibility of Aldeburgh to Yehudi, will you?

Lots of love, & bon voyage, my honey.

B

Love to Peg & Lu when they arrive.

---

1   Wife of Oliver Holt, teacher and art historian, life-long friend of Pears.
2   John Cranko bred dachshunds and evidently brought his own dog and puppies on this
    visit, one of whom was Clytie, the first of three dachshunds kept by Britten and Pears.

197 Pears to Britten

[*Letterhead:* Wolfsgarten, Bez Frankfurt, Hessen]   Ansbach
                                                           Monday [23 Jul 1956]

Dearest honey –

Thank you so very very much for your letter which arrived Midday today – I arrived here last night about 9.45pm, having lost my way a few miles back & therefore being 45 mins. late. Not that it mattered. The Morris has gone without a hitch – no trouble – in fact the first day (Friday) I drove through to Köln & stayed at the Dom Hotel, then rang Peg in the morning & came to Wolfsgarten for the night. It was lovely to be there again, & to see them, & to talk to you. How I wish I were with you! I am very much the new boy here, and although everyone is really very kind I feel like hiding in my room allday – Why don't I speak German & when shall I learn it? Never. Fischer-D doesn't come till next Sunday night, I think. Yehudi comes on Thursday to play his solo Sonatas, & does 2 more concerts of Sonatas with cembalo & flute. Karl Richter who is very much in charge & is conducting me all 4 times is really rather nice, I think, & musical (in the German way)

The players are very efficient but hard & overplay – Arias with solo are boring because they play so loud! We did Nos 110 & 171 this morning – very difficult – B minor 2 Flutes tempo fearfully hard – no room for breath.

We have 3 rehearsals today – interrupted for meals and sleep – tomorrow 2 – 1 & a concert on Wed –

Tuesday morning,

Rehearsals went allright – Am beginning to enjoy some of it – wonderful music – difficult some of it – but Richter is a terribly efficient & admirable German type – Wish we had more of them. My solo cantata is going quite well & Richter sees what I'm at & appreciates it, I think – My German is ghastly but I hope it will sich verbessern [improve] – My fellow singers might be a whole lot worse as people and as singers – Two nice useful Sopranos, a big Alto, & a Papageno[1] from Hamburg – I'll write again soon –

Much much love & longing to see you on August 4th at Munchen.   P.

Suddenly remembered – <u>Very important</u>. Miss A. Sellstrøm (West d. Konz.) wants pictures of you & me for Berlin.[2] Should be some of us two in my bureau – also some separate ones – 2nd or 3rd drawer. Also please send <u>here</u> an Aldeburgh Prog. book or two to show Yehudi.

---

[1]   Baritone role in Mozart's *The Magic Flute*.
[2]   Britten and Pears were to give recitals in Berlin from 22 to 25 September 1956.

198 Pears to Britten

Neuendettelsau

[25 Jul 1956]

Dearest B –

Well here I am, after the first concert; just got back after a nice meal with Lu & Peg, & writing to you before I go to sleep –

Basically the Bach problem remains the same – String players soar away all year at Beet. & Brah & Bruck. & Bach too let's face it, but really have no idea of phrasing or style – Everything legato; no air. Only the oboists are marvellous, flutes also brilliant but slightly boring – Richter conducting from the cembalo – old fashioned but efficient – A damn good choir of students from Munich. I am expected to make a loud noise, & I do my best. I've got the 2 most difficult arias over. & I look forward to my Solo Cantata – There is some wonderful music in these Cantatas, & there's a lot to be said for a good quiet dose of Bach sometimes. The other vocal soloists are what one might expect more or less good & routiniest. Jauchzet Gott[1] yelled by a fairly efficient Stuttgarterin, A dear old cosy cow alto called Sieglinde Wagner !!![2] and a possible Billy Budd from Hamburg called Horst Günther.[3] He has charm, a high voice, & his figure is not yet quite gone. He is singing Papageno at Edinburgh, so George may hear him.[4] Not perfect but possible.

Yehudi comes tomorrow. Dieskau on Sunday. This back-to-school life is all very well but I find it a bit much – My bad German is a disadvantage & singers are boring people – I'm <u>longing</u> to see & be with you again, my honey – roll on August 4th. !!

I shall probably wander in the Morris between 1ˢᵗ & 4ᵗʰ in Bavaria – perhaps even into France. but will certainly be in Münich to meet you on the 4ᵗʰ. Let me know (and Lu) the time of your plane.

I do hope work is going well –

	Much much love P.	Love to Imo
Bring very warm clothes. & the camera?		& Miss H.
		& Clytie

---

1   Bach Cantata no. 51.
2   (1921–2003), Austrian contralto.
3   (1913–2013), German baritone.
4   The Earl of Harewood was Casting Manager at Covent Garden between 1953 and 1960.

199   Britten to Pears

Afraid we get in very late on 4ᵗʰ – the only possible plane to Munich that day – arriving at 10.50 at the air-port (Luft Hansa) – will come straight to 4 Jahrseiten Hotel.

[*Letterhead:* 4 Crabbe Street, Aldeburgh]

July 26ᵗʰ 1956.

[*In PP's hand:*]
Posted Thursday 6.45pm
Monday
arr 30ᵗʰ midday

[*In BB's hand:*]
My darling,

Your letter has just arrived & I was so relieved to get news of you. I am afraid it is all being abit of a strain for you, but I hope you're beginning to enjoy it now – just relax about your German.. it really doesn't matter making mistakes, & anyhow, as we all know, mistakes are so charming!

Glad the car ran well. You can imagine how worried I was about you, going off in that weather & feeling so tired! But it was jolly good that you managed to get to Wolfsgarten.

Jeremy is doing the chores, photo to Sellström, & sending 2 programme-books in another envelop for you to show (or give) Yehudi.

There are quite alot of things to tell you, but not much time to write fully, because I'm slaving, slaving at the old ballet: trying at the moment to get the music of Act III written. We got Act. I score off last week. Tony's [Gishford] suggestion to Webster of postponing had the usual Webster reaction (nothing at all). But I'm trying to get it done for Johnnie's [Cranko] sake. He is still here; lazing around & enjoying the complete rest, before plunging back into work next week. The weather has suddenly become <u>madly</u> hot. Do hope it isn't too hot with you – because I could imagine that Bavaria could be baking. Here, it has been almost too hot to sit in the garden. You can imagine that working's not easy, with all the little naked figures disporting on the beach to distract me!

We had a <u>ghastly</u> council meeting; but there's nothing really to worry about, & we are in excellent hands: Stephen & Fidelity are in tearing form.

Erwin & Sofie come to-morrow for a long week-end – Erwin to work on the ballet, of course. George & Marion came down last weekend which was terribly nice. They are darlings.

Well, my darling – enjoy yourself abit – remember how good you are (the best ever). & see you very soon. All my love

your – B.   oxxxxoo

200 Pears to Britten

Neuendettelsau

<u>Friday</u> [27 Jul 1956]

Honey bee –

How are you? Have you sent a sample to Mrs. B.[1] yet? If not, <u>do so</u>, because I am at last beginning to feel alive again, through her pills – (and even had an überfluss last night!) This working life here is, it must be said, very good for one – to concentrate on one composer like Bach (& what a giant he is!) & to work hard at these works is something extraordinarily strengthening & soothing. Tonight we have our 2nd Cantata concert, with that <u>wonderful</u> cantata 21. Do look it up. The opening piece is marvellously played by a Swiss oboist, & the chorus which is very good sings it all excellently – Only Richter likes too loud a bass for solo arias – he has 3 cellos 1 Bassoon & 1 DB, for the B.Cont. which is too much – Sometimes cuts it down – is going to for me, I think. There is also another really wonderful oboist from Detmold, who combines the rest of all the oboe players, Lee's phrasing without his exaggeration, Haakon's power yet with a finer tone I think – Really wonderful –. Strings on the whole saw away – no air – no real phrasing, no difference in the sound of 🎵 and 🎵.

Yehudi played last night – & what a programme – all unaccompanied.
>   Sonata in G minor.
>   Partita in E major
>   Partita in D minor.

He is in a pretty bad state – Forcing madly – Fast pieces too fast – no repose – none of the monumental quality of Szymon[2] (let alone Orrea Pernel!)[3] – Saw him afterwards He is a very sweet chap – pathetic – lost – Working much too hard (take warning, Mr B.). Of course he can play awfully well but … the best bits were the familiar Gavotte – & perhaps the Chaconne. But it was a tremendous fight against odds – & he lost.

Saturday morning

Well that's the second of them over – only two more – I am counting the days and ticking off the events. I am afraid I'm not really a great success – They want something bigger – more Deutsch – I hear the word "Häfliger"[4] being uttered in longing tones from time to time. Still, it remains very beautiful music and well worth having done.

I should warn you that, of all things, Yehudi has a daughter at school at Tarasp, and he is coming to give a concert there on Aug. 6th! Peg has asked him to overnight at Tarasp, but he flies off the next day somewhere, & we won't have him for long (& his wife not atall) – and he is really a great dear.

Yesterday for lunch I went over to Rothenburg, which was lovely – The weather is rather better; yesterday very hot. So perhaps it may be lovely in Tarasp.

I must go to the Post –

Much much love

P.

---

1   G.M. Barraclough, the homeopathic physician Britten and Pears consulted.
2   Szymon Goldberg (1909–93), Polish-born violinist and conductor.
3   Orrea Pernel (1906–93), violinist and teacher.
4   Ernst Haefliger (1919–2007), Swiss tenor.

201 Britten to Pears

[*Letterhead:* 4 Crabbe Street, Aldeburgh]

July 28th 1956.

My darling,

Lovely to get your letter just now – I must say it sounds the tiniest bit dreary for you, & such hard work too – I hope you don't have to yell <u>all</u> the time! Don't feel you have to work hard with your dear Teutonic friends & colleagues let them entertain <u>you</u> – try to be a grand & aloof great artist occasionally. It'll probably be nicer when Yehudi turns up & Diskauer too – at least they speak a decent language!

Here all goes to plan, I've just finished on the music of the ballet (Thank God!!!), & now I get down again to the score. Theres a good old row developing between B&H & Covent Garden (Webster is the pink limit (a good term for him, don't you think?)), but no sign yet of postponement alas.

Erwin (to get on with copying) & Sofie are here – Johnnie [Cranko] goes to-night – all nice, but I do wish I could have the house occasionally to myself (with one exception).

The puppies are thriving & adorable – even their puddles are adorable, & Miss Hudson worships them. Alison Pritt[1] has gone mad at the idea of the bitch, & the black …… well, we'll see! Clytie's run-downness is better, & her skin is improving. (We get her away from the pups as much as possible).

I nearly knocked myself out playing tennis yesterday – hit myself on the temple running for a difficult one … don't actually <u>think</u> I've got concussion, but I wonder what complex that means!

I say 'hear, hear' to roll on 4th. So sorry the plane's so late, but it's the only one, & let's pray there's no delay.

Good luck to everything my honey – don't get too tired. Love to Peg & Lu, & see you <u>very</u> soon now. Love you.   B.   x x o o x x

---

[1]   Daughter of hotelier Lyn Pritt, Chairman of the Friends of the Aldeburgh Festival.

202 Pears to Britten

Neuendettelsau

Sunday. [29 Jul 1956]

Dear Mr. Britten –

I hope you will enjoy another letter from Ansbach – We are having such an enjoyable week, all of the music of Bach – violin, cello, orchestra chorus and soloists. There is a very famous tenor from England who is very musical they say and ever so nice but unfortunately I cannot hear him as the orchestra makes so much noise. But tonight he has his Solo Cantata[1] and perhaps I shall be able to hear him.

Last night we had Die Kunt der Fugge[2] (such a funny title don't you think) in the Orangery. There were no oranges although it was very hot. And the Fuggs are very long, aren't they but of course most interesting, and the way Bach turns the subjects upside down and then Fuggs them! What an old Fugger he was, to be sure! Ha! ha!

<u>Monday A.M.</u>
Well, Bunch, the 3rd dose is over and I think it went reasonably well – I was nervous & made one ghastly howler in German, singing 'Lust' instead of 'Last' but

noone seems to have noticed!! and in my small English way seem to have made an impression. After the perf. Peg & Lou & Yehudi & Diana (she's a great dear though never stops talking) & old Mrs. Clews (do you remember? American millionairess from Cannes) & a queer German Baron von & zu Puffstück (or something) & the mother-in-law of the Emperor of Austria and I, all had a very gay party which was great fun. Peg has been terribly kind & helpful all this week – I get fonder & fonder of her – warm amusing sensitive – She's an absolute darling – I may go to Bayreuth on Thursday – Meistersinger!

I have grown to be rather fond of my colleagues who have all meals with me & chatter away in German & I lumber along understanding fairly well but oh! how bad at speech!! I _must_ have some lessons. My colleagues are an attractive bright strongish sop from Stuttgart opera (Friederike Sailer) who sang Jauchzet Gott,[3] rather a dear – Also another sop – Then a very nice warm youngish cow with a good voice which won't be as good as it was soon (?!) who has health trouble – This very agreeable baritone Horst Günther (Billy Budd, he was _asked_ to do it at Wiesbaden & couldn't manage dates) who looks 28 but has a son of 18 – A new tenor has come too called Wunderlich,[4] little black square 25 years old, not heard him sing – very civil, with a mouse wife. The alt is from Berlin where she says they _very_ _nearly_ did Lucretia this year with Ebert![5] – The sop & tenor were at our Stuttgart liederabend – great admirers.

What music this Bach is! Do please look up Cantata 31. The Sonata is one of my favorite bits of music – It really might be Britten! Particularly up to bars 18 & 19! It's heavenly – And then there's a wonderful tiny alto recitative in No 21 – melting.

Richter is a Brahmsian really & so much is _far_ too solid & unimaginative & excited & chuggy. The choir is first-rate.

Yesterday morning Yehudi played the Violin & Cembalo Sonatas – wonderful F minor & C minor. They might be something for Aldeburgh with unaccompanied Bartok. Y. has plans for a chamber music festival in Gstaad[6] where he lives – designs on us I think – he is a dear.

Haven't had a letter from you for a week, B. Got the 2 programmme books in a _very_ torn envelope. Jeremy _must_ pack all mail stronger. They tear it to pieces. _When_ do you arrive München?

If you have not already written please cable here or 4 Jahresreiten Hotel, M.

Much much love   P

---

[1]   Cantata no. 160.
[2]   _The Art of Fugue._
[3]   Cantata no. 51.
[4]   Fritz Wunderlich (1930–66), German tenor.
[5]   Carl Ebert (1887–1980), German director, closely associated with Glyndebourne.

⁶ Gstaad Festival, established by Menuhin in August 1957 with concerts given by Menuhin, Maurice Gendron, Britten and Pears.

203 Pears to Britten

Neuendettelsau

Tuesday [31 Jul 1956] 2pm

My honey.

It was lovely to have your letter yesterday – It arrived just after I had posted one to you. This one, which I will finish tonight after the concert, is the last you'll get from here. I have decided to go forth tomorrow (perhaps after hearing a little of Fournier & Kirkpatrick)[1] and I am going to wander through these parts looking at various beauties, natural and artistic. I'm sorry your plane arrives so late – I almost suggest you changing plans & coming to Zürich instead by an easier plane, but I expect you've decided now – I am <u>longing</u> to see you again, my honey, but <u>longing</u>. I intend to meet you at the Airport.

I am now at the end of 10 days really rather attached to this whole set-up. Weymar (the hon. director) & his wife are both really <u>very</u> nice. Richter is allright & amiable – & the chorus have taken to me it seems, and the orchestra are very appreciative – Tonight after the concert I go to Abendessen with the Choir at Windsback where they live in a big house. They are really very sweet, madly keen. At first the men were all very critical of me (tiny voice! Not as good as our Höfliger[2] etc) but my Solo Cantata won them round – & the girls adore me!

As far as I can make out, I shall hardly see Fischer-Dieskau atall. He is being grand, living in Ansbach – only came to the 2ⁿᵈ rehearsal (last night) ½ way through & left after, This morning (our General Probe)[3] he came at 11 – (we started at 9.30) and left after – I have shaken hands twice – that is all, & I suppose tonight will be the same – He seems very nice, & is very musical, but grand – A pity.

Richter wants me to do Matthäus with him in München though I can't manage dates this year – & they seem to want me to come back to this Bachwoche again – so I can't be quite such a phlop as I thought!

The weather here varies madly: we had 2 or 3 baking heavy days after 3 drenching cold ones. Now its pleasant, cloudy, the sun is warm when it shines & there's a high breeze. The country is beautiful, so are the people – but you are the only person I want to see at the moment. So Komm, Braüt'sam, Komm! Ich want auf dir!

I shall give 1 Aldeburgh Book to Weymar & another to Richter, I expect, so bring another 1 or 2 if you like. I wonder if you could also remember to bring 2 copies of Blessed Virgins Expostulation 1 or 2 of 1ˢᵗ vol. Orpheus. Brit. <u>medium</u> (Mad Bess for the Contralto) (Man man also Job's Curse for Baritone)[4] – They have been so nice that I would like to give them something.

Wednesday morning.

Last night was really very moving. Fischer-Dieskau (He will be in Berlin when we are there.) sang beautifully the Kreuzstab Cantata[5] – & Richter did "Wachet auf" Cantate[6] in mem. of Gunther Ramin (ex-Leipzig Cantor) with great dignity & intensity. It was a good end to a remarkable week. After, I went up to the Choir – very sweet – lots of speeches, toasts, & singing – The Germans are very devoted to music & damned efficient. More of all this later – My soprano Antonia Fahberg was the Lucy in B. Opera in Innsbruck.[7] Do you remember?

Longing to see you, B.

deine P.

---

1   A recital by Pierre Fournier (1906–86), French cellist, and Ralph Kirkpatrick (1911–84), American harpsichordist.
2   Ernst Haefliger.
3   Final rehearsal.
4   Purcell realizations by Britten.
5   Cantata no. 56.
6   Cantata no. 140.
7   Antonia Fahberg (b. 1928), Austrian soprano, sang Lucy Lockit in *The Beggar's Opera* in March 1952.

✠✠✠

The absence of letters until November 1956 was probably because Britten and Pears were working together on the EOG season at the La Scala theatre in London. This included the first performance of Lennox Berkeley's opera *Ruth*, as well as productions of Gustav Holst's *Savitri* and Britten's *The Turn of the Screw*. They also continued to give recitals, such as at Bishopsgate Hall (on 11 October), so kept in close working contact throughout the period.

✠✠✠

204 Britten to Pears

[*Letterhead:* 4 Crabbe Street, Aldeburgh]

November. 7th 1956.

My darling P–

You left these behind – only just discovered them, but I'm hoping that since you never asked for them you haven't needed them. Are you really feeling better, but I'll have talked with you, I hope, before you get this. The enclosed sweet letter came yesterday.

All my love – see you Friday.

Ben.

205 Pears to Britten

Good luck for Ballet rehearsals!![1]

Dom Hotel.

Sunday evening [9 Nov 1956]

My own darling honey –

It was heavenly to talk to you – to hear your voice and have some contact, and your letter was adorable and very welcome – Bless your sweet heart! how I <u>long</u> for Saturday – and let's pray for a quiet Christmas all by ourselves – That would be heavenly! I am flying on Saturday – I really have to – But it won't take long – & I'll be with you all the quicker – It's a LuftHansa which arrives at 11.55 I think – stops at Stuttgart and Frankfurt!

Things are a bit dreary here and I long to get back to Bach – ! René Leibowitz[2] conducting is pretty deadful – v. bad conductor & no ear atall or real feeling – The Stravinsky will be allright – But the Burt is fairly Chaotic – & I <u>can't</u> get all the notes right![3] Francis Burt is here and is rather nice in an over-intelligent sort of way – Interesting company for a bit anyway – He is not <u>very</u> gifted, I fear, but quite competent & works hard at getting to know people, thus getting his works done – He has quite a number of performances in Germany, by this means – & is finishing an opera & having it translated! Oh Germany!

It's been dismal & foggy & damp every day until this afternoon when there was a ray of sunshine but I have been taking it easy spending a lot of time on or in my bed – This morning 10–2 was the General Probe [final rehearsal] & now I have nothing till tomorrow night – then train to Munich.

Much much love to you – take care of your tummy etc – Forgive this scrappy letter.

Your P.

Listen on Friday night (8 München time) to Bach if you can!
No of course you can't!

---

[1] Preparations for the premiere of *The Prince of the Pagodas*.
[2] (1913–72), Polish-born French conductor, composer and teacher.
[3] Francis Burt (1926–2012), composer, whose cantata *The Skull* (1956) is dedicated to Pears.

206 Britten to Pears

[*Letterhead:* 4 Crabbe Street, Aldeburgh]

December 4th 1956.

My darling,

It was one of the most horrid moments I can remember – yesterday afternoon on Frankfurt station. It was unbearable seeing you steaming off into the cold darkness towards Munich, so many hundreds of miles away from Aldeburgh. But one mustn't be silly, it really isn't for so long, & when you get this half the time of separation will probably be over. I am living for Saturday week, and in the meantime you are so very much in my thoughts. It is lovely to think of you singing Bach, & with people around who love & appreciate you. But no one can, or could, more than I do; you are a most adorable man & artist, intelligent, gifted, simple, loving & noble, <u>and</u> with the lightest touch too. I am really very, very luck to be alive with you around – & 'how' around!

My journey was long & excessively boring – train was ½ hr late & I froze on the station, & then boiled in the carriage. With a bad meal after Eindhoven, into the bargain. But the boat wasn't too full, & passage fairly calm after a tossing beginning. Poor old Jeremy dragged himself from a 'flu bed to meet me, & I packed him off back to bed. Miss Hudson & the dogs are in spanking form; Jove's grown tremendously & is excessively naughty & attractive. Clytie gave me a sweet welcome, but looked over my shoulder to see whether <u>he</u> was there too, & was disappointed to find it wasn't the boss himself! I've seen Mary [Potter] for lunch, & she's very excited at the idea of us all being back for Christmas. I shall get on with Christmas arrangements this evening – & see if I can track down a 'conjuror'. This is scribbled off to send you a letter or two – they are mostly <u>very</u> boring.

The best of luck for all the concerts – & all, all my love for always, my honiest of honeys,

Your B.

207 Pears to Britten

Lamontstrasse 8.

München

Thursday A.M. [6 Dec 1956]

Dearest B –

I do hope you had a reasonable journey home – not too dreary and with a sufficiency of porters to relieve you of your bags – and that Jeremy was there to meet you and that everything is lovely at Aldeburgh. I had a pretty dismal slow long journey here, but finally arrived, and was very nicely welcomed by Leslie[1] – There have been parties both other evenings here, so that a bearded B. Council University officer can meet Munich professors! Rather curious gatherings but quite nice –

During the day of course there have been rehearsals of the Weihnachts Or. With Jochum[2] – all pretty heavy and underphrased – all tempi sounding the same – no idea of rhythm – I was very nervous as always to start with, but then knocked everyone out with "Frohe Hirten"[3] – middle florid section especially. they all gaped! I really don't know why! Tonight is the first perf. of 1st ½ – tomorrow 2nd perf of 1st ½ – then train to Köln –

My fellow-singers are nice – Grummer[4] very good really – Alto – is a little fat Kugel-type – jolly useful voice but a bit contralt-stuck. The bass-baritone is a Finn called Kim Borg,[5] jolly useful voice but as yet unused to Bach – whom he finds difficult! The usual balance problem, of modern trumpet, modern strings (oh! how I hate violins!) – but my flautist is good & intelligent.

In between times I walk about & practice a bit & in fact am relaxing a bit – Had lunch with Weymars, & Richter, yesterday – They were expecting me to sing all Narration & Arias in Mat. & Joh. at Ansbach – I gently put my foot down – These people are curiously naive and ignorant and provincial in certain ways – but thorough & have money for music – !

Much love to you my dear – I think of you a lot & am longing to be home – not much over a week now – oh! oh!

dear B – your P.

Look up in your Hardy poems one that starts:

> The day is turning ghost
> And scuttles from the Kalendar in fits & furtively
> To join the anonymous host
> Of those that throng oblivion; ceding his place, maybe
> to one of like degree.[6]

T.H. also said: "my art is to intensify the expression of things, as is done by Crivelli, Bellini etc. So that the heart & inner meaning is made vividly visible."[7]

1   Leslie Sayers, a member of the British Council, hosted Pears during part of his visit to Munich.
2   Bach's *Christmas Oratorio* was sung over six nights, conducted by Eugen Jochum (1902–87).
3   Aria from the Cantata for the Second Day of Christmas.
4   Elisabeth Grümmer (1911–86), German soprano.
5   (1919–2000), Finnish bass-baritone.

6   Thomas Hardy, *A Commonplace Day.*
7   Thomas Hardy, Notebook entry, 3 January 1886.

208 Britten to Pears

Do you want to do a concert with me in Canterbury on July 8th (Festival) – I'm not
mad keen, because it's a work period – but shall I suggest Julian Bream?

[*Letterhead:* 4 Crabbe Street, Aldeburgh]

<u>March 16th 1957.</u>

My darling,
    I do hope you had a nice trip across from Wolfsgarten – that Julian looked where
he was going for most of the time, anyhow. I am so glad you enjoyed the time at
Wolfsg., & that they enjoyed <u>you</u> so much. I bet it sounded ravishing in the big
room. Now I suppose you are in Munich, & preparing for the Passions. I do hope
they go well, & that Richter isn't <u>too</u> Brahmsy for you – or Bach! I'll be thinking
of you.
    We've applied for extra petrol – & got it![1] – so now Jeremy can drive you back
in the Morris after the Birmingham concert, which'll be much quicker than going
via London. We must get you back quick because there have been <u>45</u> entries for the
Blake competition so far, & we'll have alot of work to do![2] There are actually other
reasons for wanting you back quick, but we won't go into those now, & probably
you can guess what they are ……!
    Not much news – Edith has wired 'yes' about the Blake, which is a relief. She
says she's writing about Day Lewis. Nothing yet about Marjorie Thomas, or Dennis
Dowling,[3] but I'm agitating.
    It was nice having Maurice[4] for 2 days; he is a dear, & a jolly good 'cellist now –
played a Bach Suite really well – but he's ever such a teensy bit boring, he do go on
so about his loves, & his problems, etc. etc. – I forget to listen, occasionally. To-day
I've got Barbara & Vlado H.[5] coming; that'll be less intense, I daresay! Poor Mary
is depressed about the Red House-Studio problems, but I daresay we'll solve them.[6]
    <u>And</u>, much, love – I'm <u>very</u> devoted – all my thoughts are in Munich – see you
soon, I pray —— B.

---

1   Fuel rationing was in force at this point because of the Suez crisis.
2   The Aldeburgh Festival marked the bicentenary of William Blake's birth with a compe-
    tition for the best new setting of one of his poems, and with a concert of Blake readings
    by poets Edith Sitwell (1887–1964) and C. Day Lewis (1904–72).
3   (1923–2008), contralto, and Denis Dowling (1910–96), New Zealand-born baritone. Both
    were being considered for the forthcoming Aldeburgh Festival production of *Albert Herring.*

⁴ Gendron (1920–90), French cellist.
⁵ Vladimir Habunek (1906–94), Croatian opera producer, who had recently directed *The Rape of Lucretia* in Dubrovnik.
⁶ Mary Potter moved to Crag House, Britten and Pears's former home, when they took residence in The Red House. She eventually moved into a bungalow, Red Studio, built for her in the grounds of The Red House, in 1963. Her (undated) correspondence to Britten and Pears suggests lengthy delays in the building process and difficulties in agreeing the settlement with her ex-husband, Stephen.

209 Pears to Britten

München

Monday A.M. [18 Mar 1957 – dated below]

Dearest B.

Forgive this scruffy paper but the Hotel Eden Wolff doesn't seem to provide any of its own – not up here in the room anyway –

It was lovely to talk to you in Wolfsgarten, where we had a lovely short stay – Peg & Lu were in very good form – They had invited about 40 people to hear us (Kugel,¹ Sellner,² Betta von B.,³ lots of semi-familiar faces) including my oboist from Detmold, and a young tenor admirer of mine – It was a v. sweet occasion – Julian played beautifully & it sounded prima in that room. Altogether lovely – Then the next day on towards here – stopped the night at Ulm where there is a splendid late Gothic Dom surrounded by destruction – but a beautiful rich tower. Then on to here where we did our "auf nature" on Saturday afternoon, & the balance man who is a dear dotty old enthusiast but very insistent, got across Julian because of his grunting when he plays – It was a pity, but was just allright – rather tense.⁴ Nice Hans Ludwig came & I went out to lunch with him & family yesterday & went on to see his church which is v. simple but nicely done. Tomorrow Julian goes off to Basel, & I had thought I might go with him, but have decided not to – Too far – So I shall stay with Leslie [Sayers] from tomorrow – I may ring you tonight or tomorrow morning early. Longing to see you again – Will you get Jeremy to find out if there is a late B'ham-London train on Saturday? Otherwise could he bear to come to B'ham & drive me back after to Aldeb.? or is that silly? No – it is not.

I do hope you are well & taking it easy-ish, & that Vlado & Maurice were nice to have & not tiring – Give lots of love to Imo & Miss H & Jeremy & Clytie & Jove – I wish I were with you, though I must admit that it might be much worse here – München is one of the better places to stay in –⁵

ooooxxxx Much much love xxxxoooo

yours sincerely Peter Pears   18/iii/57

1   Unidentified.
2   Gustav Sellner (1905–90), German director later to produce the German premiere of *The Turn of the Screw* (Darmstadt, December 1957).
3   Unidentified.
4   Pears and Bream recorded a radio programme in Munich on 16 March 1957.
5   Pears was singing in the *St John Passion* at the Lukaskirche in Munich on 21 March 1957.

210 Britten to Pears

Jeremy is fixing the gas, electricity & Telephone for Chester Gate

Will you send your <u>old</u> driving license so he can get your new one!

[*Letterhead:* 4 Crabbe Street, Aldeburgh]

July 13th 1957

My darling P.,

    I do hope the journey wasn't too 'bumpeh'. When I saw all those thunderstorms coming up I got abit worried for you. We escaped most of the rain, & had the hood down most of the way. A nice journey, across tiger country, with tea at Beth's about 5.0. Roger is well, rather tired by his exams but enjoying being here. We had a nice but cold bathe this morning.

    This can't be a proper letter because I want these letters to catch you at Wolfsgarten.

    Do what you like about Detmold – but don't be bullied by Fineman – or me!

    Elizabeth [Mayer] <u>is</u> coming to Stratford,[1] which is very lovely, & also means we can be free not to go to New York after the season, but I'll find out about boats from there in case there are other ones than Cunard/White Star.

    I am only sending on important letters. I'll write to you at Munich C/o Leslie Sayers. so get in touch with him, will you?

    Think of me on Wednesday lunch-time, at Buckingham P. won't you! & after at the American Embassy … What a day![2]

    I do hope the concerts go well, & that Wolfsgarten is a great occasion. Hope weather is more settled than it is here now. Are you feeling livelier now; I am sure you will be, now you're back at work you love.

    Much love, my dear, longing to see you in Ansbach ——   Ben.

1   A music festival in conjunction with the Stratford Shakespeare Festival in August 1957, featuring a performance of *The Turn of the Screw*.
2   Britten was to go to Buckingham Palace and then the American Embassy, to be elected an Honorary Member of the American Academy of Arts and Letters.

211 Pears to Britten

[*Letterhead:* Wolfsgarten, Langen]

<u>Tuesday A.M.</u> [16 Jul 1957]

Dearest Honey B.

Thank you so much for your letter "mit Einlage" [with enclosure] which arrived yesterday – It was lovely to hear from you – I hope everything goes allright with you – I wish I were with you although I must say that so far things have gone very nicely really, except of course that last night here the weather murdered the concert! which was in a way very sad but showed quite conclusively that one cannot make open-air music here – The whole day had been showery & thundery but it looked as if it w.' hold off in the evening – Concert at 6: shower at 5.30: chairs etc put out after shower: players begin with Mozart Horn 5tet O.K: Julian & I begin: at once the largest Turbo jet slowly drifts over, destroying 'Amarilli'; we gallantly continue, quite hopeless: then Thank God the rain returns & we go indoors. The final question remains in fact: When you have an adorable Saal like this, why bother about the courtyard? & we all settled happily down to make real music, without thunder or bombers.[1] Courtyards must be surrounded high with buildings like Aix or Menton, this one is no good. It was a bit shattering for Peg & Lu, but I think they were quite well pleased finally.

I heard yesterday that our Baden-Baden date is off today. Dr. Gräter away on holiday, hadn't had my letter, & in any case apparently, not having had prog. suggestions earlier, they didn't expect us. Why Finemann hadn't buttoned it up, I don't know. I presumed that they wanted us whatever we were doing. However, it doesn't matter; we have an extra day here which is very nice, & then go on to Munich.

Holland was really very nice too – a tiny room in a medieval castle, candles etc. Peter & Maria very sweet & nice, looking forward to Ansbach. I told them to ring you. You will have to leave here on 29th, very early in order to get to Ansbach, ~~by~~ between 3 & 3 1/2 hours away; Peg says 6.A.M. but that's unnecessary I think. I'm not sure how mad keen Peg is to start off so early: she would as soon miss our concert, I fancy. So don't worry about that too much.

I have now met all the Geddes brothers[2] – The 2nd Baron was here between the House of Lords & a directors meeting in Brussels (or something) – rather a dear in a way, as they all are, but ein bisschen zu viel [a bit too much] – Alexander was also here (is still) – attractive in a way & compelling, big business – All very strange & remote but in a way like bright prep. school boys, bouncing with energy, must be doing something.

2nd Baroness also here – rather nice slightly intimidated sister-type – marriage rather precarious –

1st Baroness (old lady) here too – rather fond of her but I can see she could be a trial.[3]

Last night there were the usual room full of royalty – Lobkowitzes, Rassamofsky, Liechtensteins (I think), Kinsky – I couldn't help feeling somehow that we were playing the wrong composers – !

Philip of Hesse[4] here – curious – but his ancestor was Mozitz of Hesse who was a great friend & patron of Dowland so we had a link there! Julian has been marvelous – playing v. well & charming every one by being his natural self. The big lute Schemelli[5] went very well in Holland – I was awfully pleased –

Must stop, my B – I send you all my love & shall be seeing you in Ansbach – Everyone asks after you & sends love.

Please give my love to all – Wish I were at Aldeburgh.

Peter OXOX

---

[1] Pears and Bream planned concerts at Wolfsgarten and Baden Baden before Pears went on to Ansbach.

[2] Brothers of Princess Margaret of Hesse: Ross Campbell Geddes, 2nd Baron Geddes (1907–75) and Alexander Campbell Geddes (1911–72).

[3] '2nd Baroness' refers to Ross's wife Enid Butler. '1st Baroness' refers to his mother, Isabella Gamble Ross (1906–62).

[4] Philip of Hesse (1896–1980) succeeded Prince Ludwig as Head of the House of Hesse in 1968. His connections with the German National Socialist movement may be the source of Pears's observation.

[5] Georg Schemelli (1676–1762), musician and hymnologist. Pears and Bream performed a programme of lute songs at the Holland Festival on 13 July.

212 Britten to Pears

Sorry I opened Iris' letter – but didn't recognise the writing, especially as she addressed it to <u>Craig</u> House!!

[**Letterhead:** 4 Crabbe Street, Aldeburgh]

July 18th 1957.

My darling old thing,

Lovely to get your letter & to hear news at last. It seems an age since you went away, & not always knowing where you are is abit horrid. How <u>sickening</u> about the weather at Wolfsgarten; that kind of thing is so upsetting both for Peg & Lu, & you two as well. The rain here has been colossal too, cloud-burst after cloud-burst. Poor old Roger's week-end was abit washed out – the Saturday was lovely, we went & bathed at Covehithe,[1] & then played tennis – but the Sunday was ghastly. He was very sweet, & affectionate, but worried about his exams I think —— felt sick (familiar feeling ——??!!) going back & all. Otherwise things have been madly hectic – crises in every direction, & one hasn't had a moment to think of work (except that I've completed the Dido edition to for printing, at last).[2] The Opera School was thoroughly on the rocks, but was salvaged at the very last moment by the Arts Council, Covent Garden (!), The Elmhirsts, & the E.O.G. Association (our suggestion, very much backed b up by Stephen [Reiss]).[3] The Canadian visit is intolerably boring still – The E.O.G. situation maddening. But they'll all be over soon. I've got the Screw cast coming for the week-end, but had to have invite Jimmie Lawrie too, to talk over all these things, which will complicate matters abit.

The Red House has been a nuisance abit too, Stephen [Potter] has behaved very poorly towards Mary, & into the bargain written really spoiled-child letters. But Isador's being good, & I hope by the week-end that a valuation will be made, & then Leslie P. is coming down next Tuesday to discuss it all with me (& Mary too).[4]

I spent 2 days in London. Heard Ab. & Isaac at Decca (really <u>wonderful</u> record).[5] Then went to the 'Chairs' at the Court, which I agree is very interesting & moving. Extraordinary performance by that girl. Devine is pleased at the idea of coming here, I gather.[6]

Spent the moring on Grimes with Kubelic,[7] & then my Palace lunch … Rather boring, because so formal, but nice people there (v. nice ex. Minister – Edward Boyle, friend of Georges – Freya Stark – Group-Captain Cheshire (anti-atomic pilot))[8] about 6 altogether – but alas little time or opportunity to talk to them. The Queen is a real dear I think, & awfully easy to talk to! Philip I find difficult, I think resents us abit vis a vis Peg & Lu. <u>Then</u> the American Embassy for the 'Citation'. A nice ambassador, badly arranged reception, rather silly people invited (Leslie & Ethel Boo[9] – David Webster etc.) – but Marion came along & held my hand. I've got a nice large certificate, <u>but</u> at last something to wear in my button-hole, a little knobbly thing – very swell! Then home with Stephen & Jeremy, in pelting rain – stopping at Harlow for a meal in Maurice Ashe's restaurant – not bad, but v. expensive.

Robert Ponsonby[10] has been down to-day. He's really rather a dear, very keen, but got so <u>few</u> ideas. I think he'd really rather like us to run Edinburgh for him! But nice to have a sympathetic person in that possition. He's just gone, & I'm going to have a bathe then Francis Bennett[11] (here for a few days) comes in for a drink, & then to Mary's for dinner —— so you see, even the stay at homes have busy lives!

Sorry about Baden muddle, but at least you'll have a day off. I do hope that Ansbach goes well & pleasantly. Take it easy, my darling – don't worry. Give my love to Julian. I'm <u>delighted</u> that Schemelli begins to go well, & by hook or (Harwich) crook I'll be there to hear you on the Monday.

Much much love (all of it) —— your devoted B.

---

[1]   A small village near Southwold, Suffolk.

[2] Britten and Imogen Holst completed a realization of Purcell's *Dido and Aeneas* in 1951 and later revised the work for publication in 1959.

[3] The Opera School was established in 1948 by Joan Cross and Anne Wood and administered by the English Opera Group.

[4] Following the house 'swap' that occurred when Mary Potter left The Red House, a formal settlement had to be made that would satisfy her ex-husband Stephen.

[5] Britten recorded *Canticle II: Abraham and Isaac* with Pears and Norma Procter on 25 February.

[6] Eugène Ionesco's *The Chairs* (1952), an absurdist farce, was produced at the Royal Court Theatre, London in 1957, starring Joan Plowright and George Devine.

[7] A live recording by Rafael Kubelik (1914–94) at Covent Garden, featuring Pears, was made on 6 February 1958.

[8] Edward Boyle (1923–81), MP; Freya Stark (1893–1993), explorer and travel writer; Group Captain Geoffrey Cheshire (1917–92), RAF pilot who resigned following the nuclear bombing of Nagasaki.

[9] Britten's publisher Leslie Boosey (1887–1979) and his wife Ethel.

[10] (b. 1926), Director of the Edinburgh Festival, from 1956 to 1960.

[11] E.K. 'Francis' Bennett (1887–1958). Long-standing friend of E.M. Forster.

213 Pears to Britten

Munich

Saturday [20 Jul 1957]

My darling Honey bee –

How are you & how was the Queen? I am longing to hear all about it – I expect a letter is on the way – Thank you for your note with enclosures.

We left Wolfsgarten on Wednesday & came uneventfully over the Autobahn hither – On Thursday we had lunch at Leslie's [Sayers] after rehearsing in the morning, & the Nymphenburg concert in the evening – I must say it was in its way very lovely – beautiful Baroque hall, with a very good acoustic, a little big maybe for us but not much – wonderful audience, lots of young chaps, who wouldn't go away, so we sat down surrounded by them & did lots of Lute songs – very sweet! After that a reception at the Somers-Cocks (Consul General) – quite nice. Then yesterday we did the hour's music in Hans Ludwig's Church, which was really very lovely again – He is such a dear & his family awfully sweet. It was a huge occasion for him & he was touchingly happy – We went to their home after, & met some friends, architects etc. very pleasant.

Hans Oppenheim[1] who is convalescing not very far away rang today & wanted us to go out to him but I thought I didn't want to drive about again today – so refused. He sent lots of love to You. Today is lazy for me! Lunch with Leslie who is very helpful & nice – Tomorrow Julian is driving me to Ansbach & leaving me there.

Then I start to rehearse – & before long you will be coming – That will be especially lovely, my honey – Don't kill yourself to get here for our concert. Don't forget to bring the Donne + Purcell Sonnets + Schubert etc. I have only my own part of Bach & Telemann –

Longing to hear from you and see you –

      Much much love –

           P.ox. Pox.

---

[1] (1892–1965), German pianist and conductor who worked with the English Opera Group in 1946.

214 Pears to Britten

Ansbach

Monday. [22 Jul 1957]

Honey bee –

It was lovely to have your nice letter and hear all about Buck. P. and all that. I had read about it in The Times in Munich on Friday! also the announcement about the Malayan Nat An![1] also about the Am Am[2] and the nice things he said about you – In fact for about 2 days the Times was entirely occupied with you and your doings. Quite right too. my bee.

I arrived here, driven by Julian yesterday; he went back to Munich. I wasn't wanted for rehearsal yet; but I had a half-hour run with Richter on the St. Mat. last night. It has the weaknesses that I have already bored you with – too excited & not enough style. But I heard the rehearsal for a Cantata concert this afternoon & the Choir really is most awfully good! Exciting young voices. I do think we should have the Choir over one Festival to do Bach Motets. (with Richter inevitably.)

One the 29th afternoon I have a Johannes P. rehearsal; & in the evening there's Musikalischer Opfer played by a Kammerorch. from Munich which I think we needn't attend. 30th. I am free: there's Kirkpatrick at 11.A.M. and Yehudi & Brandenb. 3.1.& 4. in the evening, which we must go to. 31st. I have Generalprobe at 10. & Joh. P. at night. Otherwise I'm yours.

Yehudi was here this morning but I didn't see him – Shall see plenty of them later!

Don't forget to bring Scores of Johannes P. and Brandenburgen for yourself!

I enclose my driving licence which you asked for earlier.

Could you possibly ask Jeremy or Leslie or both if they can find any trace of this money from Zürich being paid to me in my bank account (3.300 SF.) and <u>when</u>? After November/55

         Much much love to you, my honey – I count the hours.

                 P.ox P.ox.

I hope Jeremy has done the dog licence for me.

---

1   The Chief Minister of the new Federation of Malaya requested, via Leslie Boosey, a new national anthem from Britten. He composed the anthem in July 1957, but it was eventually rejected.

2   American Ambassador.

215 Britten to Pears

[***Letterhead:*** 4 Crabbe Street, Aldeburgh]

<u>Monday</u> [22 Jul 1957]

My darling P.,

Your letter arrived this morning & did me a whole power of good. You are an angel to have written, when you are so rushed, but the effort was worth it from my point of view! I am so glad the concerts have gone well. Nymphenburg sounds quite specially enchanting. I would love to have heard it, & seen all the young chaps listening & surrounding you both – lucky young things! I must say I am fired to write some guitar songs for you both. So glad too the Ludwigs were so nice. And now for Ansbach. I shall be thinking of you. I've talked to Peter & Maria, & we are going to get to that Sonderkonzert somehow, even if it means getting up <u>really</u> early – for them!

I must say I've just staggered thro' one of the most strenuous, complicated & in many ways frustrating week-ends of my life – & feel pretty whacked. I can't, & won't bore you by trying, to describe it all. But what was going to be a simple week-end rehearsing the Screw was complicated by I) having to have J. Lawrie too (on account of the Opera School crisis which thank God is now solved, but Jimmie wanted to discuss it, & the E.O.G. too, & could only manage <u>this</u> week-end) ii) Cadbury-Brown, with nice plans for the Studio,[1] & wanted to discuss them <u>on</u> the plot – naturally – but they are <u>fearfully</u> expensive, & may be prohibitative iii) Michael Hartnett,[2] having infinite complications with Mother, London digs (tears & homesickness too!), worries about Canada, finally leading up to a bed-wetting, poor kid – & being so good too in the rehearsals iv) Basil C. <u>really</u> digging his heels in about those bloody blocks for Canada, <u>and</u> Television – so long letters have had to be written …… o, etc. etc. & with weather ghastly, & you know picnics to entertain the chaps getting washed out. Miss Hudson was a brick of course. but the dogs hated it, especially the thunder. To-day we've had James Fisher[3] down, but that was painless & we got on well. To-morrow Leslie Periton. I'm thinking of moving to North Scotland so as to be able to work abit …!

It'll be heaven to see you, my darling. Good luck to everything – & love to Julian. Loads to yourself

xxxxxoo Ben xxoo

---

[1]   H.T. 'Jim' Cadbury-Brown (1913–2009), architect who designed Britten's composition studio (completed in 1958) in an outbuilding adjacent to The Red House.
[2]   Treble who sang Miles in *The Turn of the Screw* directed by Basil Coleman at the Stratford Festival in Ontario, Canada.
[3]   (1912–70), naturalist and broadcaster.

216 Britten to Pears

Red House

Sunday. [15 Dec 1957]

My darling,

Just off – so sorry that you are having such a terrible time; iI was distressed that you sounded so tired on the telephone at lunch time. But I must say you don't sound <u>abit</u> tired at this moment – Ruth is meandering her pleasant & rather dull way along, enlivened by you, my darling, at the moment a nice lot, but not at all in the first scene, to its detriment.[1]

Miss Hudson & I have tried the yellow silk in the dining-room & it looks lovely. It needs a backing to bring out the yellow in the silk, we feel, otherwise it looks abit faint. I think the room will be beautiful. I think the other pattern for the drawing-room. too – you are a clever thing, & but I hate to think all time & energy you must be taking up rushing around for the house & me.

Have a good trip up North – wrap up well – it is <u>bitterly</u> cold here.

All my love, darling – see you very soon

B –

---

[1]   An English Opera Group production of Lennox Berkeley's opera *Ruth* (in which Pears sang Boaz) was broadcast on 15 December.

217 Pears to Britten

[*Postcard:* image of boys doing cartwheels, 'Düsseldorfer Radshläger
In alder Zick wird dat jedonn, für eine Pfenning Rad jeschlonn'.]

[postmark 24 Mar 1958]

Greetings from Düsseldorf. This is an old established custom in that city, it appears.
Give us a pfennig, mister!

Love P.

218 Pears to Britten

[*Postcard:* image of landscape, WINORT Umweg BEI BADEN-BADEN,
Gasthaus 'zum Weinberg']

[postmark 20 May 1958]

Dear Ben – wir trinken zusammen "Your good health", ihre Ellen und ihre Junius
von Karlsruhe und auch ihre "Illuminations-Tenor. und schicken ihn unsere
Grüsse![1]

Aufwiedersehen: Peter P.

[*Additions in German in two unknown hands – illegible*]

---

1   'Ellen and Junius from Karlsruhe and the tenor who sings *Les Illuminations* drink to "your
     good health" and send our greetings.' Pears performed *Les Illuminations*, conducted by
     Eugène Bigot, on 18 and 19 May 1958.

219 Pears to Britten

Dartington

Monday 6 p.m. [4 Aug 1958]

My darling old honey bee – It was lovely to have a chat with you this morning and
I am v. sorry if I rang you rather late. I'll ring you earlier another time, but I had
been trying to for 10 minutes or more –
     I am settling down quite well for a new boy and all the younger chaps who
have been here for ages are being jolly decent – Johnnie Amis being very helpful,
William Glock[1] all over me in a magisterial way. It's nice having George M. &

Julian & Raymond Leppard[2] here. & a lot of the young things are keen & touching. A soprano sang to me this morning and I helped here for an hour. & then an infant whom we met at Sherborne, came & tried to yell Verdi arias at me. Quite absurd & very sweet in a bovine way. And now I have just finished 3 sets of tennis with John A. & 2 others, in which in spite of a pale grey hard court which bounced oddly & against which one couldn't see the balls, & a high wind, I appeared to be the best of a poor lot. Now I sit in my bedroom hearing Brahms Clarinet Sonata being practised below me. (Noone makes a clarinet sound so soupy & soapy as Brahms) & Busoni piano music next door (nicely spaced piano writing) –

The concert on Saturday was fairly allright – My voice wasn't quite at its best all the time – it got froggy & tired – but it wasn't too bad. Tomorrow night we are doing the Chinese songs again & I hope I shall be in better voice.[3] Also doing a v. beautiful Purcell song "the Fatal Hour" which please set some time. It would be v. useful to us.

There are lots of the v. earnest composers working away in corners with bass clarinets or tapes. I shall hear some tomorrow. Now I can hear someone tuning a piano in the Hall or perhaps it's a young composer. Had tea with Peter Cox & his mirror of a wife yesterday. Julian & Juliette Huxley[4] there. Good bread & home made rosehip jam! scrummy.

Leslie Sayers was over for the concert – he's at home now – & I go over to him on Wednesday for lunch.

A nightmare character from the days of Ursula N. has turned up called Pamela.[5] Do you remember? I have to hear her sing on Thursday. oh dear. All this chatter & I haven't asked about you. Write & tell me lots of troubles which I can comfort you about.

Much much love   Poxoxox

---

[1]   (1908–2000), music critic and Director of Music at Dartington.
[2]   (b. 1927), harpsichordist and conductor.
[3]   Pears performed Britten's *Songs from the Chinese* with Julian Bream on 2 August.
[4]   Sir Julian Huxley (1887–1975), biologist.
[5]   Unidentified.

220 Britten to Pears

[*Letterhead:* The Red House, Aldeburgh]

<u>August 5th 1958.</u>

My darling P.,

Several letters to-day, but this is the only one I opened in case it was important. However it's only poor old Gustaf bumbling away – what a bore for you!

Things are going along here – miss you alot – ghastly weather; a few hours of sunshine, & then rain and gloom (poor old holiday-makers). I work away, slowly &, I think, well. The oil-burner is an endless trouble; the starter will be replaced to-morrow. The dogs are well, but bored with all my working, which means fewer walks – Mary[1] & the boys & I took them to Ely yesterday afternoon for an outing, & they enjoyed the open car (& I think appreciated the cathedral; Clytie likes Norman arches). Much love – hope all goes well – good luck for Nic.[2] longing to see you.   B.

---

[1]   Mary Potter and her sons.
[2]   *Saint Nicolas* was performed in the Totnes Parish Church on 8 August.

221 Pears to Britten

[*Postcard:* ~~Richard Wagner-Museum~~
~~Tribschen – Luzern~~
~~Wagner in seinem Heim~~
~~Gemälde von W. Beckmann (1880)~~ *Crossed out by Pears*]

[postmark London, 28 Aug 1958]

BENJAMIN BRITTEN MUSEUM
ALDEBURGH – SUFFOLK

"The Master at Home" – reading the text of his new opera "Sammie", the seventh
evening of his cycle "The Thing of the Drivelinghams" (after H. James) to a circle of
admirers consisting of, on the left in the gym tunic, Imogen Holst; by the window,
the singer Peter Pears, who later took orders and became Archbishop of Beccles,
and Stephen Reiss manager of the 27th Aldeburgh Festival.
(Oil painting by Mary Potter. 1975)

222 Britten to Pears

[*Letterhead:* The Red House, Aldeburgh]

Oct. 9th 1958

My darling P.,

Here are one or two rather dreary-looking letters which I thought you'd better
have – Just off to London for rehearsal with Schwatz[1] & the BBC Soloists – hope
it goes well. I've done some more Hölderlin (6 in all now) & I think not bad – can't
wait to hear you sing 'em Don't be too gloomy about the Nocturne – you already
really know it & do it beautifully. Hope all goes well – & that you like Horenstein[2]
– & that you can eventually get to bed …!

My love to everyone – see you very soon, & take care of yourself

B

---

[1] Rudolf Schwarz conducted the premiere of *Nocturne* at the Leeds Festival, 16 October
1958, with Pears and the BBC Symphony Orchestra.
[2] Pears sang in Beethoven's *Missa Solemnis* on 11 October at the Leeds Town Hall,
conducted by Jascha Horenstein.

223 Pears to Britten

[*Telegram*]

[9 Feb 1959]

DEB 308 GB RT065 AO TC191 NEWYORK 7 9 2038=
    BRITTEN MAIDAVALE 0112 LONDON=

OKAY WHY PETEROX

224 Britten to Pears

[*Letterhead:* The Red House, Aldeburgh]

Feb. 10th [1959]

My darling Peter,

It was lovely to get your telegram – if abit confusing. I'm arguing with myself about the "why?" – whether it meant that you had a hell of a journey & that you were amazed at being 'Ok'; or that you'd arrived but couldn't make out why you'd ever decided to go (hope that isn't true); or that the bloody authorities had made a fuss on your arrival. Well, I shall know one day; & in the meantime the major thing is that you <u>have</u> arrived. It seems a year since you left yesterday – hope you didn't have too much of that dreary Major Walker! My tooth business is being a bit dreary, but with luck should be all tidied up this afternoon. Only these two letters since you left, besides a long joint one (<u>very</u> useful) from Isobel Dunlop Re Burns,[1] which I can't send because I must work on it with Stephen. Much love to Elizabeth – I hope she's well – & heaps to yourself – come back safe & soon —— B.

---

[1] Isobel Dunlop (1901–75), Scottish composer, who with Hans Oppenheim and Eric Crozier wrote *Rab the Rhymer* (1953) about the life and songs of Robert Burns.

225 Pears to Britten

c/o Elisabeth Mayer
1 Gramercy Park N.Y.C

Thursday. [12 Feb 1959]

My honey darling.

I do hope you weren't too mystified by the curious cable which I found I had sent. In my efforts to be succinct I foxed the operator it seems. "Why" was simply Y, the last letter of an old American work OKAY which I thought he couldn't spell, and spelt out for him. Anyway, even if it was nonsense, it showed that I had arrived – and very quickly. The comet goes awfully fast.[1] Once you're up it's like any other plane. but it roars to get up and climbs very steeply, out of consideration for the neighbours, they say. Fortified by any amount of food & drink, we arrived an hour early here in a snow storm, which has since all melted. Michael [Mayer] came to meet me which was very nice, & one was soon back in the familiar traffic of parkways, much quieter & slower than it used to be. Elisabeth is in amazing form, just the same & wonderful to be with. We have had long long talks about everything as you can imagine. On Tuesday I spent all afternoon & evening with John & Clytie & go there again tonight. In good form they are & very sweet & they gave me fabulous martinis & jumbo lamb chops English style! You never saw such joints! On Tuesday it rained all day and as I wandered about old familiar avenues in the rain I felt very depressed, but yesterday & today are crisp & sunny. I went into the Museum of Modern Art & looked around; it's still as avant garde & muddled as ever with wonderful things there. Yesterday I went & arranged for my flight to Halifax on Monday via Boston. I shall pick Julian up in Boston I hope, arriving there 10 am o'clock from N.Y. & leaving in the same plane as he I hope at 11.30 am: If you have a ~~amount~~ moment & get this in time, perhaps you could ring him.

Last night my dear E. & I went round to see Wystan & Chester [Kallman] at Lincoln's house[2] – just round the corner. It was a very odd evening, with me inevitably being goaded into sulky defiance & behaving odiously. Wystan looking like Oscar Wilde painted by Picasso or somebody was just the same as always, dogmatic laying down the law about opera translations & librettos, Chester puffy & gossipy & Lincoln nervous & sensitive & dotty, with a nice wife. I got furious & the whole affair was hateful to me. I can't bear to see them again, tho' Chester threatens to ring & arrange a gossip! You would have adored it! Today I have lunch with nice Sidney Shaw (you remember Salzburg?)[3] tea at Arda's [Mandikian], & supper with John & Clytie. Tomorrow we go to Beate's at Bay Side which will be nice I hope.

It is lovely to see Elisabeth & friends, but oddly enough I miss you v. v. much & wish I were home. How was the dentist & are you allright? Let me have a line. I count the days.

Much much love, my h d   yr Peteroxox.

---

1   The De Havilland Comet 4 airliner.
2   Lincoln Kirstein (1907–96), American author and founder of New York City Ballet.
3   Shaw is mentioned in a recollection by Pears in his travel diary of a recital that he and Britten performed at the Mozarteum on the 17 November 1955.

226 Britten to Pears

[*Letterhead:* The Red House, Aldeburgh]

Feb. 13th 1959

Darling P.,

Just a few letters, nothing important. Let me know if you want any of them answered – especially the Elmau one![1] There was a very sweet fan-letter about your Festival Hall business, (talking of McCormick!) which I stupidly left in London.[2] I'll send it on when I next go up there (week after next).

All goes well here. Decorators arn't in yet, but we are chasing them. We go to fetch Clytie this afternoon. The teeth have been a bore but are better now. All is well on the Festival front. The Dance went well, sorry, Opera Ball, last night. Paul R.[3] has just arrived, & is very sweet, but very curious & vague in manner —— poor dear, it'll take him some time to settle down, I fear. I do hope you enjoyed your time with Elizabeth. I long to hear about it; & now I'll be thinking of you starting the tour – do hope the coat is warm enough! All my love OX

B.

---

[1] Britten, Pears and Julian Bream performed at Schloss Elmau, 6–14 January 1959.
[2] Pears sang in a Sunday Concert at the Royal Festival Hall on 8 February 1959.
[3] Rogerson (b. 1935), a friend who was staying with Britten.

227 Pears to Britten

Shall be at Basil C's. from late next Sunday night for 5 days or so.

[*Letterhead:* The Carleton, Halifax, Nova Scotia]

Monday. 16th. [Feb 1959]

My honey bee. It was lovely to get your long & rather involved telegram about Basil C. & thank you v.v.v. much for your letter. I count the hours the minutes the seconds – one quarter of the month has gone already – Some of the time will now go quicker because of concerts and functions, but it is still a terribly long way off. Please I needn't do this again – need I? Apart from our darling & beloved Elisabeth & Clytie & John I never want to see anyone here again – No except Beate whom E. & I went out to visit on Friday & spent the night there. She is just the same & a very sweet person indeed. I stayed in Michael's guestroom; he is chaplain at a children's hospital round the corner from Beate, very tubby, rather lazy, nice & getting more like William every day – dropping in for 2 minutes, full of minute statistics, having to go off suddenly, etc.! Beate's children are Mukki very attractive & lively & Jewish & intelligent, & Monica 100% American neurotic v. curious. Max[1] nice – worried about his mother who has depressions: Beate is grand, contra- dicting Elisabeth as always working hard, coughing, smoking, very fond of a drink, awfully warm & dear: & Elisabeth – well of course she is a <u>great</u> woman – we have sat for hours together, talking & not talking, translating Hölderlin[2] & sharing news – it has been the greatest joy to be with her & she is in wonderful form – no younger of course but not older either in most ways. One of her most wonderful qualities is her philosophic genuine devotion to America & passionate interest in it. She has to live there. & it is much better that she should love it, but for me, there is only one place I want to be in at the moment & that is just where you are. Why shouldn't I recognise that you are such a large part of my life that without you my life is dry and stupid and dull. We don't have such long lives that we can afford to waste so much out of them –

I came here from New York today; flew to Boston, found Julian there, & we came on together. Here we are in a wretched hotel with the plaster off the ceiling, & no drink as far as I can make out. Very warmly welcomed, nevertheless, by a man who interviewed us at Michael Langham's[3] house in Stratford, Ont: & also by an old boss of Julian's in the army band! Very sweet & enthusiastic. We are going to have supper there in a few minutes. Tomorrow there's a T.V. interview, & on Wednesday the concert; then on to Ottawa & Montreal. Barwick[4] wrote to me – at last – in New York: a v. curious letter full of "unfortunate references" to things here in Halifax: apparently we shall have no audience as there is another concert on – Barwick sounds less & less competent: we shall see.

On Saturday I went to Clytie & John (I had been there on Thursday to hear 3 young singers) for supper & there were two old English singers, David Brynley & Norman Notley,[5] the former the most boring old queen who didn't stop talking all night. It was hideous – Meg & Dino were also there. Thereby hangs a tale –[6]

Please will you write me a long letter telling me exactly what you are doing every minute of the day, exact details of the weather, the garden, Miss Hudson's feet, Clytie's lactation, Jove's character, Imo's states, Stephen's blunders, Dolly & George[7] – I love them all & want to be <u>kept</u> <u>in</u> <u>touch</u> with the important things of life – Your back for example, your teeth, your wrist, your tummy, your ~~btm~~ b-t-m, everything –   my own h. b. I l y

Poxox Poxox

---

[1]   Dr Max Wachstein, Beata's first husband (d. 1965).

[2]   Pears worked with Elizabeth Mayer on an English translation of Britten's *Sechs Hölderlin-Fragmente*.

[3]   (1919–2011), actor who became company leader of the Stratford Festival in Ontario, Canada.

[4]   Jack Barwick, a concert agent based in Ottawa, Canada.

[5]   David Brynley (1902–81), tenor, and Norman Notley (1891–1980), baritone. Both sang in the New English Singers and worked for CEMA during the war.

[6]   Meg Mundy (1915–2016), actress daughter of John and Clytie, married opera director Konstantinos (Dino) Yannopoulos (1919–2003) after divorcing her first husband Mark Daniels.

[7]   Dolly was on the domestic staff at The Red House, and George, Miss Hudson's brother, was the gardener.

228 Britten to Pears

[*Letterhead:* The Red House, Aldeburgh]

Feb. 17th 1959.

My darlingst P., It is wonderful to get your letter, just arrived. I'd been hoping to hear fairly soon, but letters clearly take a long time, even from N. York. I wonder, did you get 2 I've already sent – 1 from London on 10th to N.Y., & one end of last week c/o Barwick (couldn't get name of your Halifax hotel in time)? Your picture of N.York was alarmingly clear – especially the ghastly evening with Wystan etc. – what is one to do about him? Nothing, I suppose – just keep away. But thank God you had Elizabeth & Clytie etc which must have been lovely. Now you are all set in Canada, & I hope everything goes well – that you manage to keep warm. It has been cold & dreary here – practically no sun, just cloud & fog. Things tick over – still not started on the Basel piece[1] because of delayed text, but hope it'll arrive soon. Paul Rogerson came last Friday – a poor pathetic dear; I'm afraid, rather hopeless. I'm afraid I can see why they chucked him out; the mind is almost gone – quite childish – but of course a sweet person still.[2] He's happy helping George [Hudson] in the garden, & practising the 'cello (which he plays quite hopelessly – I'm trying gently but firmly to ~~tell~~ make him realise he's not up to being a professional!). Alan (nephew) came for week-end, quite the reverse – bright, quick, intelligent, interested – abit super-ficial, but very nice to have around. Looks abit too much like his Mum, I fear, with very short legs. Morgan (inspite of Gout) comes for 2 days to-day. We've had long talks with Stephen & Imo; all goes well with Festival – bit of a problem over Otto K. for Tarquinius still.[3] Stephen's own future is abit doubtful,[4] but everyone's taking it calmly … just means he'll have to be more in London. Imo good, but pretty wild – I'm doing my best to keep my temper! One big thing has come up, which I'm afraid you'll be cross about!, & that is the BBC transcription of Dido. They've given the EOG carte blanche, dates & all (except should be first half of year to enable them to get it out in the Purcell year). I've agreed to do it (conduct, not play) on condition convenient dates can be found, Claire Watson[5] ~~avable~~ available, also a certain tenor, & if someone can completely rehearse it for me; it'll then take two days only. Suggested cast (apart from two above mentioned!), Elsie Morison, Lauris Elms, Studholme & Kells for witches (they sound nice & edgy on the records for P.G.) & Pat Clark as 2nd lady.[6] Comments please! (but I'm not arguing about Aeneas – remember it's a recording). By-the-way I listened to the broadcast of our Schubert-Wolf prog. – & enjoyed it enormously. You really sang divinely, & generally it was very good. I must say, we are pretty good together! and what divine music too![7] Winterabend was surprisingly convincing, & the Wolf too – I wish we could record some.

Not many letters – altho' Madame C.[8] forwards very regularly. We go up 23rd-24th, & hope to clear up Chester Gate then. I shall finish off P. Grimes then,[9] see McCready & Taralrud (tooth business better, but not quite finished yet),[10] pop down & see Roger (that dreary business is abit clearer – a 'separation' now, which – thank God – means no ~~legal~~ court case).[11] Then probably shan't go up again till you're back.

Give my love to Julian, & thank him <u>very</u> much for doing the Chinese songs fingering – I'd never realised what a task it was. Could you ask him or tell him one or two things about them? 1). Old Lute, bar 13 – last note, bottom line, <u>should</u> be E. 2) Dance Song bar 11, don't see why last 2 D♮'s should be tied? 3) Dance Song, bar 13, can't we possibly keep G♮ in 3rd chord? I do hope the concerts go well. I'll be thinking of you – but probably <u>not</u> at the time of the concerts, which is when I shall be fast asleep, I hope!

Clytie is back & in terrific form. She was quite horrid to Jove for 1st day, but is very fond of him now. She's fond of her uncle too … can't think why. Hurry up the days till March 8th – I can't wait! Much love, my darling – take care of yourself, & come back quick.   B.

Clytie is back & in terrific form. She was quite horrid to Jove for 1st day, but is very fond of him now. She's fond of her uncle too … can't think why. Hurry up the days till March 8th – I can't wait! Much love, my darling – take care of yourself, & come back quick.   B.

---

1   *Cantata Academica.*

2   Paul Rogerson had only recently left the Jesuit order he had entered in 1953.

3   Otakar Kraus (1909–80), Czech-born baritone, Tarquinius in the premiere of *The Rape of Lucretia* and at the 1959 Aldeburgh Festival.

4   Probably a reference to the extra responsibilities assumed by Stephen Reiss on becoming General Manager of both the English Opera Group and the Aldeburgh Festival.

5   (1927–86), American soprano.

6   1959 (BBC/IMG, released 1999) EOG recording of *Dido and Aeneas* (realized and edited by Britten and Holst), conducted by Britten. Despite his mentioning Elsie Morison, Lauris Elms, Marion Studholme and Iris Kells, in fact Pears, Watson and soprano Patricia Clark were the only singers suggested by Britten to join the cast.

7   First of seven programmes of songs by Schubert and Wolf, broadcast by the BBC Third Programme, 29 January 1959.

8   Mrs Chauveton, who looked after the Chester Gate house.

9   The Decca *Peter Grimes*, recorded the previous December, was due to be released in September.

[10] Britten refers to his London-based doctor, Michael McCready, and dentist, Mr M. Taralrud.

[11] Separation of Roger Duncan's parents Ronald and Rose Marie.

229 Pears to Britten

Thursday [19 Feb 1959]

My h.b. So far when I have written to you, a letter comes from you by the next post. Here's hoping that this will bring one quickly again! Thank you v. much for your last. I do hope the tooth is going along easier. I have written to Oppie [Oppenheim] at Elmau giving Julian's & my dates in case he wants us: we can't be there together except early in Jan. I didn't think you would want to come again somehow! I don't think we <u>can</u> do a concert with Mabel; what could we sing?

We had our first concert last night which was allright; people seemed to be pleased; & we were up till 3.45 being entertained by enthusiasts & friends – then our plane was 5 hours late starting from Halifax.

<u>Next day.</u>

Arrived at Ottawa – staying with a very nice pair of English diplomats. Had a party last night – nice people mostly diplomatic including one pair who heard us in Delhi. Now we are off to have a business talk with Barwick. Tomorrow to Montreal.
    Much much love   P.

What do you think of the enclosed Hölderlin trans? The fruit of hours of discussion between Elisabeth & me

230 Pears to Britten

[Incomplete – missing the final quarter of the page]

Montreal.

Saturday [21 Feb 1959]

My h.b. I wrote to you yesterday & sure enough before I had posted it, along came a bundle from you – I hope my letter did get posted finally (with Hölderlin translations) but may not reach you before this. We reached here today at noon, & Julian has just gone off to record a 1/2 hour recital. Tomorrow I should have done the Serenade but owing to a Radio strike (of balance & control men, I think!) I shall do a 1/2 hr recording with Julian. Tonight I have to go & drink cocktails with that nightmare woman from here who was at the Festival, do you remember?

Unpronounceable name & only speaks French. The weather continues on the cool side; it was 20% below zero last night in Ottawa, but my new coat is lovely & warm & Julian has bought himself a fur-cap.

    We were staying in Ottawa with so [*missing*]
who were very sympathetic. […]
just before the end. <u>BY</u> […]
been booked back on BOAC […]
at 22.00 arriving London 14.2 […]
Canada Plane leaving at 6. pm […]
this, unless you object, I propos[e] […]
quite a lot more hours with […]
meet me at Heathrow (at 10, say), or […]
to Ipswich – whichever you d[…]
I count the hours. Your letter […]
Schubert, but I think we ought to re[…]
certainly love to sing the Sailor in Dido. […]
or Geraint? Other suggestions v. good exce[…]

    Much love will write again so[…]

[*on reverse*]
I go to Basil [Coleman] tomorrow Sunday p.m.

231 Britten to Pears

Love to Julian – hope the   We are in London
old foxes stand the cold.   Monday & Tuesday

Chester gate situation in hand – Jeremy in touch with
Caplan & ordering movers. No important letters to send to day

[*Letterhead:* The Red House, Aldeburgh]

Feb. 21st 1959

My darling,

    Your letter from Halifax just arrived – so <u>very sorry</u> it seems so gloomy there, but I honestly expect by now it'll have cheered up abit – & even if it hasn't, remember when you get this there'll be less than 2 weeks before we come to the Airport to meet you home! This can't be a long letter because I want to get it off to-day so there's some chance of getting it to Basil's in time to reach you there. I some how don't trust old Barwick to get letters to you (I've already sent two, so ask him for them!) – Do hope he doesn't turn out quite so inefficient as you fear. My honey – it

is difficult to tell you every thing that happens or doesn't happen here – but so much
of the routine you know – Miss H's feet (not so bad) Clytie's Milk (coming on, I
fear) Jove's barking (ff staccato), Imo's panics (about the same), George Hudson
wanting a new lawn-mower (£~~110~~ 120!!), Jeremy (coping with oil heating going
out, driving splendidly & forgetting letters) etc. In addition to all that we've had
abit of a time with dear Morgan Forster. He was here for 2 days very happily, rather
interuptingly, gossiping, showing me a very moving play about a Public School,
sympathetic & intelligent – not like our Wystan at all! – but not awfully well. Then
Thursday evening his nose started to bleed – from an Alde, to a Thames, a Rhine, &
then a <u>Niagara</u>! It coincided with the thickest fog ever, & it was ages ~~since~~ until the
dear Doctor Stevens[1] could grope his way up. Nothing serious, but with him at 80,
both Miss H. & I were worried stiff. However we coped with bowls, towels, hankies,
sheets, & Dr. S. stopped it finally. Yesterday he was pretty sick – should have gone to
London, but Dr. S. said better not. He may go this morning, & Bob will meet him.[2]
He's pretty doddery now of course, & but still too stingy to have some one to look
after him.// Paul went up yesterday because his mother has tonsilitis – otherwise in
his sweet vague meandering way he'd have stayed for months, perhaps ever …! I'm
pretty worried about him – dear as he is, I can't see him coping with life outside the
Monastery – altho' he <u>did</u> improve here quite abit, & was gently useful. We've seen
dear Bill quite abit – Barbara's still waiting for Baby no. 2.[3] // Don't worry about the
Dido idea because Claire Watson can't manage it & I refuse to do it with someone
inadequate … Sylvia Fisher, Söderstrom[4] – any ideas? // Give lots of love to Basil
& Merle[5] (? what's his name). I do hope all is well with them. I ought to have
written to Basil, I know, but I can't quite remember what about. I must stop now
– Imo is just coming to work on Dido, Seymour Whinyates[6] is bringing a Polish
Conductor to lunch (he is doing P. Grimes in Russia! – perhaps), & I want to post
this.   I.l.y … lots & lots, take care of all of you –
        B.

---

[1] Dr John Stevens, Aldeburgh general practitioner.
[2] Bob Buckingham (1904–75), policeman, with whom Forster had an intimate relationship
     for many years.
[3] Billy (a local fisherman) and Barbara Burrell, friends of both Britten and E.M. Forster,
     lived near The Red House and were expecting the imminent arrival of their second child.
[4] Sylvia Fisher (1910–96), Australian soprano; Elisabeth Söderström (1927–2009), Swedish
     soprano.
[5] Basil Coleman's partner, interior designer Melville Doty.
[6] (1892–1978), Director of Music at the British Council, discussed a possible (but
     unrealised) Russian production of *Peter Grimes* with Britten and conductor Zygmunt
     Latoszewski (1902–95).

232 Britten to Pears

[*Letterhead:* The Red House, Aldeburgh]

Feb. 27th 1959.

My darling Peter, I am sorry that it is nearly a week since I wrote last, but one way
& another I have been fully occupied. I spent 2 days in London, & then George
Malcolm was here, & I've been getting on abit with the Basel piece too. I was so
pleased with your two letters from Ottawa & Halifax, & also the Hölderlin translation; It seems awfully good, & I've only got one or two comments – but how
fearfully difficult it must have been. I bet Elizabeth enjoyed doing it with you. Of
course we'll meet you on the earlier plane from Canada – direct; I do hope there's
no delay – if this perfect Spring weather goes on (we've had nearly a week of sun)
you should come home nice & quickly! Everything is beginning to sprout up in
the garden, a wonderful show of show-drops, & bulbs pushing up too – however,
I'm sure we'll have snow & gales in March to pay for it! I had two sort of usual
days in London. Saw Mde. Chauveton who is getting on well. Jeremy has seen
to all the stuff from Chester Gate, & it's arrived down here to-day. He's in touch
with Isador so I hope all is well. I saw Roger who was very low – RoseMarie is
now talking about going back to Ronnie & I think it may be the reaction. Also a
bloody Matron is gossiping about his friendship for Ian (I'm very glad he's given up
'Garth'!) – & he's worried & defiant. However I cheered him up abit. Then I had
a most desparate evening at Covent Garden. Lucia[1] has been the <u>wildest</u> success,
& dear Joan S. has become a prima donna (very good for George [Harewood],
of course) – but it was the most horrid experience. It is the most <u>awful</u> work;
common & vulgar, very boring, no subtleties, poor tunes (the Old Sextet is the
best – Donald Duck & Clara Cluck), just as if Mozart, Gluck & all (written in
1835) hadn't existed. Apart from Joan (who sang it well, it suits her perfectly, but
to my taste with no real musicality or warmth – she'd been taught a̶l̶l̶ the Italian
style like a dog is taught tricks) & Geraint, the singing was poor, the orchestral
playing feeble (Serafin isn't interested in the pit), & it looked like an Italian copy of
Landseer, even to the gauzes matching imitating old dirty varnish. Hideous! At the
first interval I saw Gilly C.[2] & rushed to her for sympathy, but she was loving it; at
the 2nd I fled to Anne W. in a box with Joanne etc.[3] & Martin Penny,[4] & they were
revelling in it too! The audience screamed & roared – everyone out of step except
our Benny, but I have a feeling that our Peter would have been out of step as well.
It's abit awkward with George [Harewood], but he's a dear & I think understands.
T'other George (Malcolm) was here for 2 days, & it was nice having him. He's a
complicated difficult one, but full of interest & gifts, & very sympathetic too. I must
tell you about it when you're back (only just over a week now!) I went over to a
sweet rehearsal of Let's Make at Wolverstone[5] – & go to a performance to-morrow

night. They are remarkable kids – especially the slung-mug chap doing a complete Jimmy Blades Act![6]

Festival things are abit problematic, but Stephen is being good Fidelity helpful & we'll scrape thro' I think. Claire Watson can't do Dido for the moment, & we have to see if the BBC can postpone it all, otherwise who … I've got so interested inthe work completing our edition that I'd hate not to do it now.

I think about you all the time – follow your movements with my diary. To-morrow you are in Saskatoon, I suppose flying to-day. I hope you don't freeze. It's curious to think of your 20° below zero is in this spring weather! I had a lovely walk down to the river this afternoon with the dogs – absolutely ravishing, blue rippling water, with swans, shell-duck, cormorants, & loads of lapwing.

Give my love to Basil & Mell – I am so glad you are staying with them in Toronto. I wonder if you are meeting any of the Stratford chaps. A pity about the Serenade recording – but it mightn't have been too good, I suppose. Decca want us to do it again, by the way, with the Nocturne, & I think perhaps we ought to.[7] Miss Hudson is well & cheerful. Jeremy is in his new room. Clytie is, alas, starting a phantom preggy I'm afraid. I'm not so bad; back & all getting on – teeth forgotten about – wrist having more treatment – the rest perfect & waiting …… Much love to Julian. I hope the he's standing the strain, & you too – my honey.

Good luck, & bon voyage, & see you soon –   xxxoxxoxx B.

1   The Zeffirelli production of Donizetti's *Lucia di Lammermoor* at the Royal Opera House featured Joan Sutherland (1926–2010) as Lucia, Geraint Evans (1922–92) as Enrico, and was conducted by Tullio Serafin (1878–1968).
2   Gillian Collymore, soprano in Imogen Holst's Purcell Singers and sister of the architect Peter Collymore.
3   Anne Wood and her partner Johanna Peters (1932–2000), mezzo-soprano.
4   (1912–2000), pianist who later worked with Britten as a copyist.
5   Woolverstone Hall School near Ipswich, who performed *Let's Make an Opera* at the end of February.
6   James Blades (1901–99), legendary percussionist.
7   These proposed Decca recordings eventually took place in September 1959 with Britten conducting the London Symphony Orchestra. *Serenade* was not released.

233 Pears to Britten

[Toronto]

[27 Feb 1959]

My old h-b. I am starting this sitting on my bed, waiting for the guests to arrive at a drinks party which Basil is very sweetly throwing for me. Tomorrow early (Sat.) we fly off to Saskatoon, so I want to post this before we go West! It is lovely being with Basil, he is such a great dear, so full of appreciation for every thing one is & does. We arrived here on Sunday – Monday was a day of T.V. rehearsals in & out of the studio with long breaks – Tuesday the same but with more rehearsals, dress rehearsals & finally performance at 9.30. It went quite well & people were pleased, it seems. The rest of the programme varied from dotty to stinking, but the fee is <u>v. good</u>!! Everyone at T.V. very full of the Grimes performance on T.V.[1] which sounds rather curious & baddish – Wednesday we went by train over to Kingston, where we arrived 1 ¾ hr late, & gave a nice concert in a big hall on an enormous stage, which we diminished, by turning off all lights except one standard lamp & a spot on us – Mercifully a lovely acoustic – & a very nice audience – a little nice party afterwards – Thursday (yesterday) we drove back to Toronto (4 hrs) & gave our lecture recital at 3 – & our concert at 8.30, terrific success, a party after where I met lots of familiar faces, the Wrys, Lou Appelbaum, the Jocelyns, Arnold Wolte (??)friend of Imo to whom many greetings, Boyd Neel, Terence Gibbs,[2] etc. Ghastly accident – Julian's guitar is cracking through the dry heat & cold, & he had to borrow another for the concert – He managed it marvellously – Everyone talks of you & our concert 10 years ago. I wonder if you remember what happened at Toronto 19 ½ years ago? It is a place which cannot help having a certain importance in my life. Today I have been seeing modern Canadian pictures, & giving an interview on CBC, & we have now had our very nice party here (Aksel Schiotz, Süsskind, Boyd, Terence etc)[3] & have had a good steak & I am in bed – We have to be ready at 7 A.M. to fly off to Saskatoon – !

Much much love hb   your PoxPox

---

[1] The Canadian Broadcasting Corporation (CBC) broadcast *Peter Grimes* on 13 January 1959.

[2] Gordon Wry (1910–85), Canadian tenor, sang Bob Boles in the Canadian premiere of *Peter Grimes* (12 October 1949); Louis Applebaum (d. 2000), Canadian composer; Gordon Jocelyn, Administrator for the 1957 Stratford Ontario EOG performances of *The Turn of the Screw*; Arnold Walter (1902–73), Canadian musicologist; conductor Boyd Neel and Terence Gibbs (1921–73), music producer for CBC.

[3] The guests included: Aksel Schiøtz (1906–75), Danish singer; Walter Susskind (1913–80), Czech conductor; Boyd Neel and Terence Gibbs.

234 Britten to Pears

London flat was fine on the way thro'
& left money for MdeC. [Chauveton]

[*Letterhead:* The Red House, Aldeburgh]

<u>April 15th 1959.</u>

My darling old thing,

I had a good journey – hope the same with you, but I fear yours may have been rather hot. The weather broke on the way over & I landed in cloud & rain! To-day has been lovely, but a cold wind rather, blowing the blossom about. The garden is coming on well – the Magnolia is out, but rather disappointing, it's quite white. But when we move it to a better position it will probably look fine. Cherry tree not out yet – I've told it to wait for your return. <u>Nightingales</u> galore! – but no cuckoo, altho' I heard one at Wolfsgarten before I left. The re-decoration of the rooms is done, & they all look lovely – the bathroom especially; I think they've done it well.

Many letters, but nothing really urgent. Much muddle over dates in Holland, & irritating, pleading letters from Meikie & the Concertgebouw. I was going to ring Peter D. about it, but then noticed the death of Van Beinum inthe papers so obviously they'll be upside down now & there won't be any urgency about it. (They ~~still~~ wanted us to change our German dates).[1] Thrilled letter from Nigel Fortune about the article.[2] Rather anxious one from June Gordon – could you drop her a line about dates or something ——?[3]

I've maddeningly got to go up to London to-morrow again to see the Gulbenkian.[4] But I hope it'll produce some £50) Dido has blown up ~~for~~ again, for middle of May, but I've rather sat on it ~~because of~~ for many reasons, notably that it's Whitsun, & also getting too close to the Festival. One or two problems re the latter, but Stephen & Imo are coping well.

I've been thinking abit about Schöne Müllerin.[5] Don't you think it might be a good idea to cut a few (very few) verses to make it less tiring in a big hall – in a strenuous tour? Think about it, old thing. Give my love to Julian. Hope he's in good form. Hope you enjoy Malta & Rome – longing to have you back. Excuse scribble but I want to get this off.

xxxxxoooxxxxoo   B.

---

[1] A concert tour of West Germany was planned for March 1960, but Britten had to withdraw because of tendonitis.

[2] Musicologist Nigel Fortune corresponded with Britten about his contribution to Imogen Holst's recent volume of essays on Purcell.

[3] June Gordon, Musical Director of the Haddo House Choral Society, wrote asking if Britten and Pears could perform in Bach's *St John Passion* in 1960.

⁴   Calouste Gulbenkian Foundation, charitable organisation, established in 1956.
⁵   Song cycle by Schubert.

235 Pears to Britten

Alas! not at [*Letterhead:* The Red House, Aldeburgh]

Écu de Genève Hotel.

April 18th? 19th [1959]

My honey old bee – It was lovely to have your letter here on arrival today at midday. Since then we have had our concert at the Conservatoire – do you remember – a lovely hall with a perfect acoustic – & it is 3.A.M. I have just got to bed & Julian is having a night cap somewhere else. The concert went very well & was a great success, it seems. A nice M'lle Lombard putting it on. I arrived here at lunch time from Paul & Maja,¹ where I had 4 very nice sympathetic rather boring days – doing Handel fairly well – very well looked after – heavenly food etc. But a bit boring not being at home with you –

The magnolia is supposed only to be white, I think, but should be in front of everygreens – to be shown off best. Good that there was some rain for the garden. In Bale we had two more baking summer days, but now it's broken. Your most passionate admirer Jacques Horneffer was at the concert tonight; he is putting on a series of Britten performances on the radio, & wants to bring the whole C.G. cast of Peter Grimes over for 2 performances! Ansermet was also there & <u>adored</u> the Chinese Songs. & sent v. much love to you –

10 A.M. Just had breakfast! Jimmie Walker of Decca also is here & I'm going to have a cup of coffee with him in an hour. It seems years since I saw you, h.b., the days are going very slow & boringly. They always do when you don't want them to, & t'other way round – I am longing to be back. My plane on Saturday BE 143. leaves Malta at 10.10 & should arrive at the airport Central at 17.00. Will the Standard be in London?² I might stay the night in London & drive down on Sunday – or drive down straight away, depending on flight & weather.

My hotel in Malta is the Phoenicia.   oxoxoxo
much love   P.

---

¹   Paul Sacher (1906–99), Swiss conductor and patron, and his wife Maja.
²   One of the cars that Britten and Pears owned was a Standard Vanguard (YRT 453).

1. Benjamin Britten (c 1942).

2. Peter Pears (c 1940).

4. Publicity shot for recitals in Vienna, while on an Austrian skiing holiday with the Harewoods (March 1952).

5. On the train to Rome as part of a recital tour (April 1949).

3. At the Old Mill, Britten's home in Snape, Suffolk (c 1943).

6. On tour with the English Opera Group (August 1947). From left: Britten, Pears, Joan Cross, Otakar Kraus, Lesley Duff and Anna Pollak.

7. In recital, their television debut on NHK, Japan (9 February 1956).

8. On a picnic in the Suffolk countryside (mid-1950s).

9. Playing recorders at Crag House, their home on the Aldeburgh seafront (1954).

10. With Clytie the dachshund at Crag House (c 1954).

11. In a street cafe in Siena, Italy (May 1957).

12. In Venice, their favourite city (September 1954).

13. Pears performing with Julian Bream at Great Glemham House, Suffolk (17 June 1957).

14. Pears with Julian Bream
at Ansbach (July 1957).

15. Pears singing Bach in Germany (late 1950s).

16. Outside Snape Maltings Concert Hall before the start of the Aldeburgh Festival (late May 1969).

17. In the ruins of Snape Maltings, the morning after the Concert Hall was destroyed by fire (8 June 1969).

18. Rehearsing for the BBC film of Schubert's *Winterreise* (1970).

19. Pears as Aschenbach
in the first production of
Death in Venice (June 1973).

20. Britten rehearsing *The Burning Fiery Furnace* in the library at The Red House (spring 1967).

21. In the garden of The Red House, at the party to celebrate Britten's peerage (June 1976).

22. With Mstislav Rostropovich and Marion Thorpe at the Aldeburgh Festival (June 1976).

23. At Snape Maltings (May 1975).

I've just listened to a re-broadcast of Winter Words (something like Sept. '72) and honestly you are the greatest artist that ever was – & every nuance, subtle & now over-done – those *great* words, so sad & wise, painted for one, that heavenly sound you make, full & always coloured for words & music. What *have* I done to deserve such an artist and *man* to write for? I had to snatch Us before the Folk songs because I couldn't anything after – "how long, how long". How long? – only till Dec. 20ᵗ – I think I can *just* bear it

24. Britten's letter to Pears in America, and Pears's reply (Letters 349 and 351, November 1974).

My dearest darling
No one has ever ever had a lovelier letter than the one which came from you today – You say things which turn my heart over with love and pride, and I love you for every single word you write. But you know, Love is blind – and what your dear eyes do not see is that it is *you* who have given *me* everything, right from the beginning, from yourself in Grand Rapids! through Grimes & Serenade & Michelangelo and Canticles – one thing after another, right up to this great Aschenbach – I am here as your mouthpiece and I live in your music – And I can never be thankful enough to you and to Fate for all the heavenly joy we have had together for 35 years.

236 Britten to Pears

[*Letterhead:* The Red House, Aldeburgh]

<u>July 21st 1959.</u>

My darling P.

This is a tiny note, written in the few hours I've got here before going back to London again, to welcome you to Neuendettelsau, to send my love, & hope all goes well with you. I presume that since there hasn't been a wire summoning me to Nymphenburg that that naughty Julian <u>has</u> turned up. I was very worried when Sue [Phipps] told Jeremy that ~~the~~ he hadn't arrived in Rome <u>at all</u> —— but I'm hoping no news is good news.

We go on baking here – not a sign of rain, & the weather forecast chaps have now given up bothering to predict it. It is of course lovely, & I had a lovely bathe last night, if one could only forget the state of the garden! I watered the trees etc. this morning with the bathe water of course!

It was lovely to see Walter[1] who was very sweet & came over to Noye at Lancing with us. Would that he hadn't, actually, because it was unadultered HELL. John Alston[2] is quite, quite hopeless – he hasn't a clue as to how to beat the simplest bar, & that coupled with the fact he's totally unmusical, got no sense of rhythm, & found the music impossible to remember (when he took his eyes out of the score) etc. etc. made the performance as agonising as any I yet remember. Ditto the production, which was inane & incompetant – & really made no ~~news~~ use of that lovely place. What was doubly infuriating was that the material was <u>excellent</u>, the kids knew it backwards, were really gifted; & to see their efforts so sacrificed made one mad. Poor Norman Lumsden was quite bad – really no voice left. Nancy Thomas did her best in an impossible situation.[3] – and so on. But oh, Hell, Hell, Hell – why must children always have the 5th rate to guide them? That's what makes the Westminster Choir so exceptional. One good ~~ther~~ thing – it has brought all those schools ~~together~~, state & private, girls & boys together for the first time; and they are doing 8 performances, all sold out!

We went back for the night to Chichester, & that cheered one up. Left early for London, saw McCready, very nice, & were back here soon after 2.30 after a lovely drive. I go to the Festival party this afternoon, & then to London & stay with the Harewoods, & then Mass,[4] & to the Pipers to morrow to discuss something <u>really</u> important.[5]

Much love, old thing – I think ~~af~~ about you every moment, & hope it all goes well – have you got the car yet? Drive carefully!   Much, much love,

come home soon & quick —— B.

---

[1] Hussey (1909–85), arts patron and Dean of Chichester Cathedral.

²   John Alston (1914–96), son of Britten's viola teacher Audrey Alston and Director of Music at Lancing College from 1948 to 1974. The performance of *Noye's Fludde* took place at Lancing on 19 July 1959.

³   Norman Lumsden (1906–2001), bass, played Noye, and Nancy Thomas, mezzo-soprano, played Mrs Noye.

⁴   The first performance of Britten's *Missa Brevis in D*, performed by the Boys of Westminster Cathedral Choir conducted by George Malcolm, 22 July 1959.

⁵   Britten and Pears's plans for adapting Shakespeare's *A Midsummer Night's Dream*.

237 Pears to Britten

Alas! not at [**Letterhead:** The Red House, Aldeburgh]

Neuendettelsau.

Friday. [24 Jul 1959]

My darling – It was heavenly to have your letter when I arrived here yesterday with all its news. I am <u>sorry</u> John A. [Alston] was so awful. I was afraid he couldn't be anything but. Can you tell him so ? or not? How awful. By now you'll be back at home having seen John P. I long to hear all that.

This end, I've got over the first stretch allright – Julian was on the plane with me! He had been hiding incog. in London! I blew him up quite a bit; but on the one hand I see his point, and on the other one will never change Julian. He will always be hopeless in certain ways, I'm sure. He was disturbed when I told him you were worried about his playing, but he played pretty superbly at Nymphenburg, which as always with that fabulous acoustic & wonderful décor & adorable audience was a wow again! And I have agreed to sing "Orfeo" there next year – but only "Orfeo" – & only 2 days rehearsal & 2 performances – so not too bad! but not Ansbach – that's sure!

I hired my car quite successfully in München – an Opel Olympia – & drove up here without difficulty – no accidents – not too much traffic on the Autobahn. Rehearsed here for the first time with Richter, wonderful music, performed very much as usual, with virtues & defects. Today more rehearsals – This is a sweet spot, & the country is adorable but oh God how I wish I were back home – I count the days. Häfliger was here yesterday recording the Arias I am doing on Sunday, for DGG.!¹ Lots of people send greetings to you – Weymar, Hans Ludwig, Phillipine Schick, Richter, Nicolet.² I found I had not realised there was an aria for me in one of the Cantatas; I sightread it & to my great joy found it was a very beautiful one, just up my street. A relief, as some of the others are corkers. Richter accepts that curious passage, takes the whole aria v. fast!   Much much love, my own honey –

Keep well – & it won't be long.   P

[1] Ernst Haefliger recorded Cantata nos. 8 and 45 for Deutsche Grammophon Gesellschaft; Pears performed both at Ansbach on 2 August.

[2] Carl Weymar; the architect Hans Ludwig; Phillippine Schick (1893–1970) German composer; Karl Richter; Aurèle Nicolet.

238 Britten to Pears

Saw Romantic Ex. at Tate – which
is <u>v</u> exciting.[1]

[*Letterhead:* The Red House, Aldeburgh]

<u>July 24th 1959.</u>

My darling P.,

No news yet, but I expect you've been too busy to write. I do hope Nymphenburg was OK. & that you didn't swelter too much in Munich. It was certainly baking in London on Wednesday & Thursday when I was up, & fear it may have been like that with you. However, I expect you are at Ansbach now & hope that may be cooler. Have you started the cantata series yet? Hope they are interesting & not too strenuous. Try to drop a note even if brief, because I long to hear.

I went up to London after the Glemham 'Festival' party, which was very nice & successful. Fidel was very good & gracious & everyone adored it. I stayed with George & Marion – very tense, & I thought, worrying but they both seem to feel the corner's been turned – which is certainly true in one way – but I hope that the scars will heal. They came to the Mass [*Missa Brevis in D*] with me which was really most beautifully done – the children sang divinely. Quite a nice lot of friends turned up. Tony [Gishford] came to lunch, & we had a useful Group & Covent Garden discussion. Then I went off to Henly & had a nice evening with John & Myfanwy. They were thrilled with the idea of Midsummer Night's Dream, & we discussed it endlessly. I'm just sending off to Myfawny our projected scheme for it; she has some good ideas about it. John was most useful & full of suggestions about the look of it, but we couldn't really settle on the producer – Basil Coleman & Johnny Cranko the first choices (latter slight favourite) but John was quite keen on the Sellner[2] idea. We'll talk more when Stephen & I go there for the T.V meeting on 30th next week.[3] Then I spent morning in London, mostly at B & H, had nice lunch with Leslie P. (he is coming here in September), & then ~~could~~ caught train down in afternoon, & almost fell into the sea to get cool! All the same I'm going to brave London again for 2nd (& I suppose last) Mass performance to-morrow morning.

Not many letters, only these two of importance.

The Mauds[4] are all coming for August bank holiday week-end, which will, I hope, be nice. They seem excited at the idea. Roger comes on Monday, & then I drive him down to Devon when I go on 5th. So I shan't be alone, altho' not with the person I love & with whom I feel happy – still, I've got a-lot to do, & roll on the days – ! I'll send you another scribble in a day or so. Much love, keep well, & drive carefully.

Your devoted B.   XXXXOO

---

1   *The Romantic Movement*, Tate Gallery, London, 10 July–27 September 1959.
2   Gustav Sellner, the German producer whose recent *The Turn of the Screw* at Darmstadt had impressed Britten.
3   The Associated Rediffusion television production of *The Turn of the Screw* was recorded at Wembley Studios in October 1959.
4   Humphrey Maud with his parents and sisters.

239 Pears to Britten

[*Letterhead:* The Red House, Aldeburgh]

[Ansbach?]

Tuesday [28 Jul 1959]

My darling – Your 2nd letter just arrived – Thank you so much – Lovely to have all your news – so glad the Missa went well & nice visits to John P. &c. Very sorry I'm behind in writing – It's curious here – one gets into a tremendously relaxed frame of mind which tends to make one concentrate on nothing but Bach & one self. Wonderful to have a quiet time etc. but lazy making in certain respects. I'm trying to do a diary auf Deutsch in the Lu style! I thought it might amuse them.[1]

Bach goes on – He is quite wonderful & monumental – Richter has improved – not so overpushing – more modest – makes mistakes, sometimes big ones – it is of course German but this solidity is very useful to build up & away from! The first Cantata evening Sunday went well enough – Marvellous music – including the Cantata "Meinen Jesum lass ich nicht" 124 we did at Bideford years ago. v. beautiful with oboe d'amore. (I want to direct some of these Cantatas!) Tonight comes the next lot.

Yesterday was free – so I went over to Nürnberg for the 1st time – terribly bombed – but 3 v. beautiful rebuilt churches & the Germanisches Museum full of lovely things – How terribly coarse & crude the German Renaissance must have been in many ways & how lifting when it went to the Baroque. Last night Richter had an organ concert at Heilsbronn the organ misbehaved – an ugly brute anyway – but he played quite well.

It is extremely hot here – My room is on a corner & seems to get an awful lot of sun – The church gets sweltering & we all stream – There was a thunderstorm on Saturday which cleared the air a bit but not very mucch. This is rather a sweet village filled – as all southern Germany – with honey coloured creatures of extrarodinary beauty. and how much music is part of the whole life – A party of girls have just been singing catches & rounds etc extremely well in the adjoining house for 2 hours without repeating themselves. The Ansbach audience (snobs & all) sit like mice in the Gumbertus oven, or the Orangerie frying pan, bathing in Bach. I had a nice meal with Hans Ludwig after the 1st concert here. He has largely altered the Johannes Kirche here, & I shall hear the Liepsig Thomanerchor[2] there on Saturday.

Tomorrow & ~~Wed.~~ Thurs. are free days for me, & I had thought of driving to Wolfsgarten for the night but I believe they have already gone to Tarasp. I come back to hear Keilberth conduct orchestral Bach on Thurs. with Nicolet & Szeryng (Yehudi's successor) –[3]

My colleagues are very amiable – nice bright Soprano – good Hertha Töpper alt – & respectable if American Keith Enghen.[4]

Not many days more, my bee – Much much love PoxPox

---

[1]   The Prince of Hesse's diary *Ausflug Ost* was written during the holiday to the Far East he and the Princess shared with Britten and Pears. Pears presented his own diary as a gift to the Princess in 1963.

[2]   St Thomas's Choir of Leipzig.

[3]   Joseph Keilberth (1908–68), German conductor; Aurèle Nicolet and Henryk Szeryng (1918–88), Polish-Mexican violinist.

[4]   Hertha Töpper (b. 1924), Austrian contralto, and Kieth Engen (1925–2004), American bass.

240 Britten to Pears

Greetings to Weymar
& Richter!

Red House. [*Letterhead:* 4 Crabbe Street, Aldeburgh]

<u>July 28th 1959.</u>

Darling P,

Only a scribble – no time for more – to send you a few letters which have arrived – people seem to have got wind that you are away & aren't writing much, or else they're all on holiday.

I g couldn't resist going up to London for the 2nd Mass performance, & was rewarded by a good performance, & also a sweet presentation by George [Malcolm] & the choir of a lovely 'Liber Usualis', all the Gregorian chants, signed by all of of them! Otherwise as usual here, except that the weather has <u>broken</u> to-day, terrific rain & thunderstorms all the morning – so exciting I could scarcely bear it! I

Inscription in the 'Liber Usualis' given to Britten by the boys of the Westminster Cathedral Choir and their conductor, George Malcolm – dedicatees of the Missa Brevis in D (Letter 240). The volume remains in the Britten–Pears Archive.

wonder now what has survived this extraordinary drought. I was so very relieved to have your letter & to know that all goes well. I long to talk to you next Monday night. Hope journey goes well. I'll be down in Dartington on Wednesday. Roger comes to-night. The Mauds on Friday. Had 2 games of tennis – wrist not too bad. Only a few bathes because of jelly-fish, horrid!

   Much love, my Honey.

    B.

241 Pears to Britten

[*Letterhead:* The Red House, Aldeburgh]

                [Ansbach?]

           Thursday. [30 Jul 1959]

Dearest B.

  Another letter! Lovely. They take 2 or 3 days. This last one (express) 2 days.

  The Second Cantata evening went quite well – Lovely arias for me – fair, not fizzing – Wonderful Soprano one. What a lot of Tenor Arias are with Oboe

D'Amore, nice player from Baden baden who remembers our visit (with a Bach Cantata) very happily.

Was in Bamberg yesterday & a flat tyre <u>just</u> as I arrived there, having driven for an hour over Lappish roads trying to find Pommersfelden – unsuccessfully. Thank God it came when it did. It was changed while I saw the Cathedral & had lunch.

Tonight I go to hear Keilberth to see what he is like, also to hear Szeryng, & Nicolet play the B minor Suite. There's a party afterwards by the Bavarian something or other Minister.

I expect this will be the last letter – I drive back to Munich (Hotel am Hofgarten) after Sunday night & fly early Monday morning.   Much much love   Pox Pox

SUNDAY NIGHT Cantatas 45, 27, 8, 79. IS BROADCAST – 8.0 (MUNICH? F'furt? Stuttgart? Don't know)

✠✠✠

Having worked together preparing the libretto for *A Midsummer Night's Dream*, Britten and Pears were able to concentrate on recording projects in the latter half of September. They also enjoyed a holiday in Venice with Mary Potter in October, but then Britten suffered a recurrence of bursitis which impeded his ability to write, and the letters, as well as his work on *A Midsummer Night's Dream*, were not resumed until December.

✠✠✠

242 Britten to Pears

[*Letterhead:* The Red House, Aldeburgh]

Dec. 9th 1959.

My darling P.,

This isn't a real letter – you've only just gone, & there's no news – but only to send my love & every good wish for Friday night, & all the other nights. I do hope Paul does Purcell nicely – teach him how, won't you![1]

I hope the flight wasn't too frantic. It was a ghastly night here – I was disturbed by moans & shrieks all night, just like animals or children being slaughtered (the latter to be eaten, of course, like my dream!). It is just as bad to-day, but I dragged the dogs out for a good long walk round the river-wall this afternoon, to collect ideas for Act II.[2] Imo is up here all of these days, doing the vocal score of Act I, so it's good company, & stops me fretting for – you know who – !

I haven't got things worked out yet about the TV. Show on Thursday – they'll obviously be very upset if I <u>don't</u> put in an appearance, but on the other hand, they see my difficulties. We'll see.[3]

Let me have some addresses where I can write or forward letters. Perhaps just the hotel in Zürich if you go on straight there after Freiburg.

Lots of love to M. & P.[4] – & infinite apologies for having let them down; but I'll make it up to them sometime.

Lots of real love to you, old thing, I miss you very much indeed – it's horrid when you go away, so come back soon!

Your

B

---

1   Pears was rehearsing for a concert performance of Purcell's *The Fairy Queen*, directed by Paul Sacher, in Basel on 11 December.
2   Britten was at work on the score of *A Midsummer Night's Dream*, which he had begun in October.
3   The Associated Rediffusion production of *The Turn of the Screw* received a London preview on 10 December at Television House.
4   Maja and Paul Sacher.

243 Pears to Britten

Schönenberg

Thursday p.m. [10 Dec 1959]

My old honey –

It was heavenly to talk to you last night & lovely to have your letter which I got this morning – I do hope your visit to MacCready and T.V. has gone off successfully and not too tiringly. We talk about you a lot here with much sympathy and understanding & if love can cure you will be O.K. very soon – Things go on quietly & efficiently – lots of rehearsals, lots of rest, lots of food – very easy & unexciting – Tonight is Pre-performance. It will not be the finest most varied performance, but there are nice things. Pat Clark is doing well – & Elsie is a good girl & has a v. useful voice & is much more intelligent & sympathetic than most Australians! John Whitworth[1] is efficient if dim, but we trumpet away together in "Let the fifes". Tom H.[2] is in good voice & is <u>v.</u> interested in Demetrius & thinks he will most probably be able to do it, if he can go back to Düsseldorf for a week or so in May – He is owed a lot of leave which he can take then. Good news, I think!

I have been thinking about the Orch. Concert, & I must say I am worried about juxtaposing Haydn and Fricker next to tiny-group-chamber-music of Henze &

Petrassi. Might it not be better to include Henze in the Schubert Melos programme – His piece lasts 10 minutes & is for Flute, viola, cello, bass clar., piano, marimbaphone, celeste & percussion (4 players) The Petrassi (20 min) is for flute, violin, c.bass, cembalo & percussion (1 player.) Could we perhaps sell Hans conducting his piece & Petrassi to the BBC (for studio pre-perf.) but only use Hans' piece at Aldeburgh?[3]

They speak here v. highly of the conductor for the Zürich Nocturne – Santi? – we shall see.[4] He is apparently rather successful already – though young. I am booking rooms at the Neue(s) Schloss Hotel in Zürich from Monday – & shall go to Freiburg on Saturday. c/o Egel, Müllheim/Baden, Hauptstrasse 131 –

I am already longing to get home – so what shall I feel like next Friday? I am doing bits of Christmas shopping, and have already got 6 ties & a pair of cufflinks! When I get to Zürich, I shall really start!

I am trying to read Erwin's book but it is rather difficult & I only have vague ideas for presenting it – Perhaps they will crystallize but will they be any good?[5]

Much much love my old bee – oh so white o so soft --
                    deine P.

The enclosed arrived at 59ᶜ. & I forgot to readdress it. Sorry.

---

[1] Patricia Clark and Elsie Morison, sopranos, and John Whitworth (1921–2013), countertenor.

[2] Thomas Hemsley (1927–2013), baritone, who was to sing Demetrius in the premiere and 1966 recording of *A Midsummer Night's Dream*.

[3] Pears's suggestions relate to the programming of the 1960 Aldeburgh Festival. Hans Werner Henze's *The Emperor's Nightingale* was tentatively scheduled to appear in a Melos Ensemble programme on 16 June but in the end was not included. The Fricker and Petrassi works were also not performed.

[4] Nello Santi (b. 1931), Italian conductor who was appointed Musical Director of Zurich Opera in 1958.

[5] Erwin Stein, who had died in 1958, had been working on *Form and Performance*, leaving an incomplete manuscript draft. It was finished by Britten (who wrote the Foreword), Pears, Donald Mitchell and Stein's daughter Marion, and published in 1962.

244 Britten to Pears

[*Letterhead:* The Red House, Aldeburgh]

<u>Dec. 14th 1959.</u>

My darling P.,

I only just got your letter this morning – 5 days coming; I suppose it's the Xmas posts starting up – & so I'm only scribbling a note hoping that it will reach you before you leave for home, & it having reached you that we'll be talking as soon as you are back – very soon now! I'm similarly not sending any letters on in case they get lost, or don't catch you. There's nothing madly important, but the mass of Xmas cards is starting to descend on us. Ours haven't gone off yet, as Jeremy has had 'flu, but there's time yet.

No particular news – situations the same. TV. of Screw was awfully good, scenically rather than musically, actually. Peter Morley[1] is really quite a chap (the producer) & John [Piper] has done some spiffing new designs. He & Myfanwy come to-day, Johnnie Cranko & Bill Bundy[2] to-morrow so I expect we'll have some useful discussions: Wish you were here for them. I am awfully pleased about Tom Hemsley – that'll be excellent, I'm sure. No news yet from McAlpine[3] – but how I wish another singer were available for Lysander! Still I'm having fun with Thisby now – well into the 2nd Act, & going fairly well, I think.

I long to hear about the concerts & things. I'm glad it was nice with Paul & Maja, & hope it hasn't been too dreary at Zürich.

I'm sending this off quick now – hoping it will catch you –

All my love, darling P.

Longing to see you, & talk to you.

B

---

[1] (b. 1924), filmmaker.

[2] William Bundy (d. 1991) was Technical Administrator for the Royal Opera House.

[3] William McAlpine (1922–2004), Scottish tenor who had sung the Novice in the premiere of *Billy Budd*, was considered for Lysander (eventually sung by George Maran). Pears, whose schedule prevented his singing Lysander, sang the comedic dual role of Flute/Thisbe.

245 Pears to Britten

[*Letterhead:* Hotel des Bergues, Geneva]

Tuesday [15 Dec 1959]

My old honey –

It was heavenly to talk to you & it will be heavenly to talk to you on Thursday & it will be heaven itself to <u>see</u> you on Monday. But please be quite well by then – all sinuses (sini or sinūs or sinera?) clear – poor old thing – es tut mir so furchtbar leid – je suis désolé – non so che lingua io pailo – each one worse & worse – my French! I have just given an interview, in which I said the Jubilee Hall held 30 people!

Yesterday Lausanne was Illuminé[1] – It went all right & people were happy I think – Ansermet's tempi are a fraction unreliable – Thou tun'st this world was rather slow and so was De-vant ' un-e nei-ge ' and Villeswasveryveryfastindeed. However!

Tonight I go with Pat Fuller & friend to Amateur Dramatic performance of Noel Coward!

Marion & Topazia[2] were there last night – M. being released by the change, I think. They go off to Yugoslavia on Monday for 10 days. She is a little nervous about it. Such a sweet! Topazia is not a bad old hardboiled egg; useful.

Much much love
    Pox Pox

Thought you should have the enclosed.

---

[1] Where Pears sang *Les Illuminations*.
[2] Topazia, wife of composer Igor Markevitch. The trip was evidently a respite for Marion Stein from problems in her marriage to George Harewood.

246 Pears to Britten

[*Letterhead:* Hotel Neues Schloss, Zurich]

Thursday pm. [17 Dec 1959]

My darlingest old honeybunch, I was so saddened by your poor old voice this morning and everything gloomy and dismal that I have been thinking of you all the time and wondering what I can do. Thank God I shall be back on Monday & shall have all the week with you as I needn't go back to Munich till Sunday afternoon – What can I say except that I love you very very much with all my heart – Take courage my bee – you are so unbelievably loved by everybody – All your friends in Switzerland and there are many admire you and what you stand for so intensely and steadfastly – Your ears should have burned all the time – dear Ansermet and Madame – who has been having a foot operation & only came out to day – and Jacques Horneffer who asked me to salute you "He is a great genius" – and many more people that you won't remember. "Les Illuminations" and its composer went straight to the heart of these stolid French-Swiss – Let all the love that comes to you from so many directions dry those sinuses up and lift your spirits My spirto ben nato, my spirto leggiadro – I have been singing these words a little just now, as I have an idea for improving the top of my voice, and perhaps one day I shall be able to sing those words well again for you. – for you my honey for that's really only what makes me go on singing – you. and your music –

I am beginning to sing the Nocturne & I can sing some of Rimbaud – Will I ever be able to manage Fruit[1] My darling – oxoxoxo Pox Pox

---

[1] Possibly either a hasty misspelling or private joke relating to Flute, the role Britten was writing for him. Alternatively, a misspelt reference to *Les Illuminations* 'Départ dans l'affection et le bruit neufs'; an indication of Pears's imminent departure for home.

VI

'Far away as you are, at least I feel there is contact!'
JANUARY 1960 TO MARCH 1968

The correspondence in this chapter continues to chart Pears's career as a recitalist on the continent and in the US, as well as his final appearance at Ansbach in 1964. But it also takes account of the personal and artistic connections Britten was forging with other musicians. On 21 September 1960, the composer attended the British premiere of Shostakovich's Cello Concerto no. 1 at the Festival Hall and established what would become a life-long friendship with the soloist, Mstislav Rostropovich. At Rostropovich's request Britten composed the Sonata in C major for cello and piano for them to perform together. It received an enthusiastic reception at its first performance in the Jubilee Hall in Aldeburgh in July 1961. The Symphony for Cello and Orchestra followed in 1963 and the three suites for solo cello in 1964, 1967 and 1971; all demonstrated Britten's complete awareness of Rostropovich's exceptional musicianship, and were gifts that functioned as 'lifebelts', as the cellist described them. Rostropovich and his wife, the soprano Galina Vishnevskaya, were frequent guests at The Red House and they accompanied and hosted Britten and Pears's visits to Russia; their enduring relationship remaining unaffected by the surrounding tensions of the Cold War. Music drew them together, but perhaps it was because the Rostropoviches also felt themselves to be outsiders, eventually defecting from the Soviet Union in 1974, that they became so close. Britten had kept Vishnevskaya's voice in mind as he wrote the solo soprano part of his *War Requiem*, which he began composing in April 1961. Dietrich Fischer-Dieskau, for whom Britten composed the baritone part, also joined the select list of artists to whom Britten dedicated works, premiering the *Songs and Proverbs of William Blake* in June 1965. The composer admitted to Pears the difficulty he experienced in writing for other singers (see Letter 290), although Pears had his own connection with the piece, having made the selection of texts to be set from Blake's work. Julian Bream, by now well established as an alternative recital partner for Pears, was also the recipient of a work written for and dedicated to him. *Nocturnal, after John Dowland* (1964) was based on Dowland's song *Come, Heavy Sleep*, from the repertoire in which Bream specialised.

Nocturnal was composed at the culmination of Britten's long connection with his publisher Boosey & Hawkes. The relationship that had benefitted from the guidance of mentors such as Ralph Hawkes and Erwin Stein, both now dead, had by this stage become less cordial, as the composer worried about what he perceived as the company's growing indifference towards him and his work. The ensuing 'squabble', as Britten understatedly described it in a letter of April 1964 to William Plomer, effectively brought about a withdrawal from renewing his contract, a decision that led to the eventual establishment of a new publisher, Faber Music, of which he became a director (*Nocturnal* was one of its earliest publications), and with whom he would remain for the rest of his life. The year also saw more international recognition of Britten's standing as a musician when he became the first recipient of the award bestowed by the Aspen Institute of Humanistic Studies, prompting an acceptance speech in which he would describe some of the most important duties, as he saw them, of a composer within society. His credo is partly summarised in the overarching desire to write music that will 'be of use to people, to please them, to "enhance their lives"'. When writing to Pears, Britten calls the address, which Faber published as a small booklet, 'our speech' (see Letter 287), indicating that it was a joint effort. In fact the draft, still held in the archive, is written by them both – as ever, Pears's influence was key. His facility with and understanding of literary texts is evident in his notes and articles for Aldeburgh Festival programme books, assessing material for publication and drafts for talks about the relation between text and music.

The letters of this period also emphasise Britten's continued reliance on Pears for moral and emotional support. The effects of his recurrent health problems and intermittent attacks of depression are evident in their exchanges during the early 1960s, when the pressure of work and sickness prevented him on occasion from participating in concert tours. His self-esteem was undoubtedly sustained by Pears's thoughtful reassurances throughout these letters ('I do hope things are allright with you – Work going well – not too much worry of all sorts' Letter 251). Holidays often involved thinking about work, but changes of scene brought some relief. Between January and March 1965 they once again journeyed to India with the Prince and Princess of Hesse, and later in August to the USSR to stay with Rostropovich and Vishnevskaya, with whom they then travelled to Armenia. Their companionship inspired Britten to write a cycle to texts by the Russian poet Alexander Pushkin, published as *The Poet's Echo*. Notably, anxieties were also eased, if only temporarily, by young visitors to The Red House who renewed Britten's connection with childhood. Through friendships such as those with Roger Duncan (son of librettist Ronald Duncan), John Newton, who sang treble in productions of *Curlew River* and *The Turn of the Screw*, and Stephen Terry, who appeared on Decca recordings as Harry in *Albert Herring* (1964) and Puck in *A Midsummer Night's Dream* (1966), Britten was able to partly escape some of the pressures of his professional world. As John Bridcut has observed, and as Britten's letters to Pears indicate, such friendships allowed him to be more at ease, more natural, to re-encounter and recharge himself.[1]

Britten and Pears made judicious use of the space available to them at The Red House. In the late 1950s they commissioned the installation of a swimming pool for the frequent bathing that the North Sea, no longer in such close proximity, had allowed so easily. Architect Peter Collymore had known both musicians through their connection with Lancing College, where his father had been a Master, and had grown up listening to their music. Under his guidance new building projects were undertaken on and around the site. These included The Red Studio, the cottage and artist's studio built for Mary Potter which she occupied in 1963. Another major project was the conversion of a disused barn into a Library and Music Room, beside the swimming pool (Britten comments on the delay to its full completion in Letter 287). A stable block was also converted into staff offices, and three years later Collymore made alterations to allow for a new porch on the north side of The Red House. Significant changes also took place amid Britten's personnel. Imogen Holst, wishing to spend more time writing, composing and cataloguing the work of her father, Gustav Holst, gradually passed on her role as Britten's assistant to the assiduous and equally devoted Rosamund Strode. Holst continued her work for the Aldeburgh Festival and her vast contribution to the musical life of the town. Strode remained in the composer's employment until his death, taking a leading role thereafter in the organisation of his and Pears's archive.

By 1965 operations had ceased at the Maltings, the large industrial building where malt-drying had taken place at Snape for a century – along with the River Alde it had formed a significant part of the landscape over which Britten looked from his balcony at the Old Mill during the 1930s and 1940s. Local investor George Gooderham purchased the site that year with the idea of using some of the available room to store stock feed, but he also had ideas for other types of usage. Initial discussions soon took place with Aldeburgh Festival Manager Stephen Reiss and Britten about the conversion of the largest of the Malt Houses into a concert venue that would accommodate both full orchestral forces and large audiences during the Festival, a problem that had worried the directors for several years previously. The long-term lease that followed witnessed the reconstruction of the Maltings' interior in preparation for its official opening by the Queen and Duke of Edinburgh in June 1967: an event preceded by their visiting Britten and Pears at The Red House.

In early 1968 Britten writes to Pears, then engaged in a recital tour in America, on progress with the third Church Parable, *The Prodigal Son*, some of which he composed while in Venice. Still troubled with illness which would occasionally prevent him from fulfilling concert engagements, he speaks excitedly about exploring the sights of his favourite city, the art and architecture stimulating his imagination. The only qualification is the longing for Pears's companionship.

---

[1]   John Bridcut, *Britten's Children*, p. 5.

247 Britten to Pears

[*Letterhead:* The Red House, Aldeburgh]

Jan. 7ᵗʰ 1960

My darling P.,

It was sweet & comforting to hear your voice from Munich. I'd been having rather a rough evening's telephone between Pipers ([*inserted with an arrow:*] I think this situation will be cleared up), Stephen [Reiss], & Johnnie [Cranko] & it was nice to talk sense for abit! I do hope all goes well at Elmau, that it isn't as cold there as it is here![1] Give'm all my love, & let me know how it goes. I got back yesterday aft. – good sessions with McCready who encourages me to do the next concerts, but rather wants me to have a rest for a month before Germany – but we'll see abt that.[2] Roger [Duncan] is here, very nice & easy. Tony G.[Gishford] comes to-day, & the Hesses on Saturday, but come what may work <u>must</u> go on! Only one note so far for you, which I enclose, I'll send more later.

Thank you for being so angelic & patient these last days – one day I'll be adequate again – All my love, my darling

Xxxoo B.

---

1 Pears gave recitals and sang the Evangelist in a performance of Schütz's *St Matthew Passion* at Schloss Elmau between 8–14 January.

2 Britten consulted Michael McCready about his worsening health on 6 January. He and Pears were scheduled to perform in Liverpool and Oxford at the end of January, but Britten had to withdraw from the intended tour of Germany in March.

248 Pears to Britten

Friday. Elmau –

[8 Jan 1960]

My sweet old honey bun –

I do hope you had a satisfactory session with McCready – I want to hear about it please – Everyone here is asking most anxiously & lovingly after you, so please let me know, even though you may think <u>I'm</u> not interested, and of course I'm <u>not</u>, I've got to have something to tell other people! Did you have a good journey to Aldeburgh? I came up here on Wednesday midday – It's snowing all the time and I literally haven't been out yet. We had our first 2 concerts – one with just some unacc. carols for me, & last night with Julian (Lute songs & the Chinese) – which went really very well. Julian has a new guitar which is quite noticeably better than the old one, and the songs sounded better & it was a great relief to have a printed copy which didn't involve turning over every 20 seconds!

You will probably have heard from George M. about his May dates[1] – He very badly wants to do his T.V. offer – it's extra good money – Do you think he can? I would have thought he probably could. We shall have to have a 3rd coach-conductor type won't we? Many scenes can be rehearsed simultaneously as far as music is concerned in different rooms. I know you will be bored at having to work out May when you are still on Act 2, but it must be done soon, & I daresay this is as good a moment to start as any. I have been thinking about Johnnie C. We mustn't be foolish & throw him over too soon. Suppose you played him over as far as you'd got at the beginning of Feb. and talked about the rest, could he then spend a considerable time with John P. working out the basic stage shape. Then presumably every so often further conferences. I don't know how long John P. needs or how many consultations & when, but would after April 24th be long enough for costumes? There is no doubt that after that would be more than long enough for actually stage production. One mustn't forget that this sort of behaviour is what one might have expected from Johnnie [Cranko]; it is really a question of whether the present situation is actually impossible or not; & of course if there is even a faint chance that his première might go still later. Oh dear – no, I suppose he's hopeless – We'd better forget him. Do you think a tactful, affectionate letter to Fred. A[2] would get him? He might do a very lovely job of it.

WEDNESDAY

How awful that I have been so long in going on with this. It was partly that I intended to write down some festival (particularly Mendelssohn ideas) & didn't quite get them clear, & partly laziness & stupefaction & rehearsals! We have now had 1000 concerts conducted by Oppie or still worse with O. at the piano,[3] than which there can be nothing more howlingly depressing – Julian went off on Sunday & we have had Abe & Ike (wow!) & Monteverdi in O's realisation play'd by himself. Indescribable. George Malcolm in very good form playing very well on a troublesome harpsichord. Tonight comes Purcell, Poulenc & Schubert with him. I wish it were someone else. There is much talk of next year of course, but I am absolutely not going to commit myself or still less, you – Bobbi[4] is a very sweet person & there is a lot to be said for the whole music week, but the great fly is O. You shouldn't be asked to listen to him. The singers are not so bad, but he!

Thank you v. v. much for your two letters – very welcome. I am longing to see you needless to say & count the days – Tomorrow I have the Copland songs at 5 o'clock & immediately rush into Munich for a Weinachtsoratorium rehearsal with Richter – I fly Sat. morning & shall be at Marjorie Collymore's[5] for Saturday night.

John Amis has been here which has been nice for me, as I like John. He recommends strongly Ossian E.[6] for the Apollo. Therefore he should not be in

Mendelssohn – I have had long talks with George M. about M.sohn. The real snag is that there is <u>no</u> music of faintly dramatic character, for a situation. To my mind therefore, all drama etc. must come from outside the music i.e. incidents with dialogue – which means we must get someone to write a $^{play}_{script}$}.[7] (I have an idea for the little story) – What about Paul Dehn? Eric Crozier? Lance Sieveking?[8] Morgan even? / John A. says there is a late piece by Grieg for chorus 2 horns & something (which Percy Grainger says is G.'s masterpiece). Might this fit with Brahms for Bardgett?[9]

     Very very much love –
      oxo Peter oxo

After Schütz, Flute is feeling rather deep. Bass Flute <u>not</u> doubling Piccolo

---

[1] George Malcolm coached the children's chorus for the first production of *A Midsummer Night's Dream*.

[2] The choreographer Frederick Ashton (1904–88), director of the *Albert Herring* premiere, 1947, was also considered as producer of *A Midsummer Night's Dream*.

[3] Conductor Hans Oppenheim (1892–1965) accompanied Britten's *Canticle II: Abraham and Isaac* on 9 January, and played continuo for Monteverdi madrigals on 11 January at Elmau.

[4] Sieglinde Mesirca (1915–2009), cultural events director at Schloss Elmau.

[5] Wife of Eric Collymore, a physics teacher at Lancing College; their children were Peter and Gillian.

[6] Osian Ellis (b. 1928), Welsh harpist; played with the Melos Ensemble and premiered a number of Britten's works.

[7] 'A Mendelssohn Soirée', devised by Paul Dehn and directed by George Malcolm, was subsequently organised for the 1960 Festival.

[8] Paul Dehn (1912–76), critic and screenwriter. Lance Sieveking (1896–1972), BBC producer.

[9] Herbert Bardgett conducted Brahms's *Fest- und Gedenksprüche* with Grieg's Four Psalms at the Aldeburgh Festival, 25 June 1960.

249 Britten to Pears

The wire arrived a propos nothing (unless it was a broadcast of the Nocturne recording in N. York?) – but rather sweet!

[*Letterhead:* The Red House, Aldeburgh]

                   Jan. 9th 1960

My darling,

  This isn't a proper note, only to send you heaps of love & to enclose a few letters that have arrived & which I thought might interest you. I hope all goes well, that you are enjoying the place & the snow – <u>We</u> have some snow this morning – not probably as much as you, but enough to make the cabbage patch outside my studio look nice & romantic.

All goes well here – I struggle on with Act 2, sometimes good, sometimes not so – Festival things progress, but some big questions still outstanding. I still don't know plans about next week-end as we can't get a decision about the Massine boy coming over.[1] I'll probably send a telegram to you – when you are in Munich – Eden-Wolff Hotel? Peg & Lu come to-day which will be lovely – but <u>wish</u> it were you! All my very best love
B.

----

[1]   Leonide Massine II sang Puck in the premiere of *A Midsummer Night's Dream*.

250 Britten to Pears

[*Letterhead:* The Red House, Aldeburgh]

Feb. 16th 1960

My darling P.,

We've had the letters sent down from Marlborough Place,[1] but there are only a very few so far, & I'm sending them on quick so as to catch you in Stockholm. Do let me have addresses in Switzerland so we can be in communication again![2]

I hope all goes (& went) well. How was Winifred[3] or whatever his name was in Frankfurt? I expect you are in the middle of the Swedish stuff now. I hope Julian turned up all right! Is it as cold as it is here?– too cold for snowing they say. But the rest of England is deep in it. I have a cold to end all colds – a legacy from Sir David[4] who was streaming when he came down – which makes working difficult if not impossible. I stay in bed for breakfasts but stagger up & potter around gloomily all day. I'm abit afraid Miss Hudson's got it too – Jovey was even coughing this morning! It's just good old February gloom, I suppose – but spring will soon be on the way, & you will be back for a few days in March – won't you?

By-the-way, you went off with the letter from Denis Matthews[5] about lending the Sickerts or Steers for China – could you send it back or scribble a line yourself, saying no, I presume?

The 2 chaps – Strowger & Wythe[6] – have been over to Snape & collected about 6000 bricks (quite cheap, it seems) so we can almost build a mansion. I'll try & delay them doing the Summer House till you're back, since they've got lots to get on with.

Much love, old thing, longing to see you – hope you are surviving
B.

1   59c Marlborough Place, NW8, Britten and Pears's London residence from 1958 to 1965,
    was the top section of a house owned by Anne Wood.
2   Pears had travelled to Frankfurt and Stockholm, and was going on to perform with the
    Orchestre de la Suisse Romande in Geneva.
3   Winfried Zillig (1905–63), German composer, conducted Pears in Britten's realization
    of a Suite of Songs from Purcell's *Orpheus Britannicus* for broadcast on Hesse radio
    (Hessisches Rundfunk) on 14 February 1960.
4   David Webster had received a knighthood in the New Year's Honours list.
5   Denis Matthews (1919–88), pianist and musicologist.
6   Aldeburgh builders who installed a summerhouse to the east of The Red House using
    bricks from nearby Snape.

251 Pears to Britten

Grand Hotel
<u>Stockholm</u>

[16–17 Feb 1960]

My old honey darling –

How are you, my pie, & I do hope things are allright with you – Work going well – not too much worry of all sorts – Snow? Like in yesterday's Times? Dogs liking it? How I wish I were with you.

Here everything is very Swedish – frozen-in ships on the canals – Aquavit required frequently. I spent yesterday rehearsing "Nocturne" with nice radio conductor & orchestra – not bad – & I begin to be able to sing it – It is a <u>very beautiful</u> <u>work</u>. At last I have said it! Thank you my own sweet heart for having written it – & for me – Oh dear I am a lucky duck –

Last night the Blomdahl opera "Aniara" was on – so I went – a marvellous performance, excellent voices, singing it, I thought, superbly – It's a funny mixed piece, all about life on the planets, lots of effects, tape-noises, etc. But not without considerable dramatic effect, & some good ideas not always very well carried out. Very well staged. Excellent chorus singing frantic things – Boring finally because not enough stuff to it, & the people didn't come alive mostly.

This morning we will go off to T.V. Julian arrived last night. Tomorrow is "Nocturne" taping – Friday our recital, Saturday to Geneva.

Gustaf has called me 50 times. It looks as if I shall come back to London after the Henze in Zürich,[1] probably on Monday morning 29th & will have to fly back to Münich on Sunday March 6. You can't guess where I shall be between those two days!!

Much much love, my dear

Pox Pox

Wolfsgarten was heavenly. The concert went allright.

[1]　Probably Henze's *Kammermusik 1958* for solo tenor, guitar and ensemble.

252　Britten to Pears

We've got the Snape bricks 6000 of them!

[*Letterhead:* The Red House, Aldeburgh]

Feb. 18th 1960

My darling P.,

I wish I knew your movements in Switzerland – but I am hoping it's safe in sending these few letters via the Swiss Romande.

I hope all goes well with you in Sweden, that you are enjoying the concerts a bit; that they play the Nocturne nicely for you. I wonder if you've seen the King & Queen – hope you gave them my love, or what was tactful!

I am afraid I'm still very much under the weather here – oscilating between bed & drawing-room. The cold's got into the sinuses, & I stream from nose & eyes, & can't breathe or hear – a charming sight! I had the doctor who's given me pills & inhalants, & sniffers – abit disloyal to McCready but he did nothing from a distance, & I got panicky about not being able to work. However I'm pushing on with the score. But these colds are the most loathsome things, albeit not important.

I long for news of you, P. darling, nothing would cheer me like a note – but I realise how busy you are. Love to the Ansermets. And heaps, all to you – B.

253　Pears to Britten

[*Letterhead:* Grand Hotel, Stockholm]

Saturday morning [20 Feb 1960]

My own darling –

It was heavenly to have your letter.[1] Thank you so much for it – But why has Webster dared to give you a cold? I am so sorry & I do hope it's better now & Miss Hudson has recovered. I suppose Jeremy will get it & Mrs. Goddard & Mrs Manning[2] & Jove & Clytie – oh dear. <u>Do</u> take care –

Well – today we leave Stockholm & I arrive in Geneva tonight & will probably ring you tomorrow morning & then this letter will be stale buns when you get it. Never mind. We have had a nice time here. They have been immensely hospitable – the Radio people – Mr Brodin is really a very sweet man – First there was the T.V. on Wednesday, which was quite a sweat but very successful – & a very pleasant little programme. Nice people who took us out to dinner (v. good) after & then to the new Ingmar Bergmann film[3] – extraordinarily impressive & terrible & shattering

& moving & Swedish & well-done & gloomy – but a real experience. I didn't sleep
that night. Then Thursday came "Nocturne" recording which was goodish from
orchestra & conductor, & fair from me. Party in the evening at David Thomas,
ex-British Council-at-Oslo, do you remember? now BC here. Nice faintly pompous
man, with other pleasant guests, also Elis. Søderstrøm[4] who sent v. many greetings
to you. She will come to Aldeburgh at the drop of a hat. Just back from the Met.
which she didn't care for too much.

Then yesterday was our recital – Not a very large audience, but I must say very
very sweet. A great success – Chinese Songs not our best performance but very
much taken. Then afterwards a very pleasant party with the Brodins & a nice
balance & control man & wife – Lots of Aquavit – what a good drink.

Brodin very happy about our coming back this time next year – We talked about
programme. They want Spring Symphony – & another half hour or so –

The voice is standing up allright – I have been madly trying to make up a
programme for Munich where we have sung everything we know – However I dare
say it's allright –

I look forward v.v. much to seeing you again, my bee. Just over a week now. It
will be heavenly.

   Do look after yourself –
Much much love
    Pox Pox
How's Thisne?[5]

---

1 Letter 250.
2 Both office staff at The Red House.
3 Probably *The Virgin Spring*, which was released 8 February 1960.
4 Elisabeth Söderström (1927–2009), Swedish soprano.
5 Thisbe, the part in *A Midsummer Night's Dream* which Britten was writing for Pears.

254 Britten to Pears

[**Letterhead:** From Benjamin Britten, The Red House, Aldeburgh, Suffolk.]

[?Feb 1960]

My darling – not much mail to be sent on – thought Kathleen Davies'[1] letter might
amuse you, she's abit of an old bore but she did send an extra gift to the Jub. Hall
Fund because she was so moved by our Birmingham Concert! I shall, I hope, have
talked to you again before you get this so no news now – just to say how I'm longing

to see you next Monday – I think it's going to save my life, if it's worth saving – the mouldy old thing.

Much much love (all of it, in fact)   Ben.

---

1   Mrs Davies donated to the fund to support the Jubilee Hall in Aldeburgh after hearing Pears and Britten performing *Nocturne* and *Spring Symphony* with the City of Birmingham Symphony Orchestra on 11 February 1960.

255 Pears to Britten

[*Letterhead:* EDEN-HOTEL-WOLFF, MÜNCHEN 3]

Tuesday. A.M. [8 Mar 1960]

My own honey – It seems like a thousand years since I saw you on Ipswich station and it will ten thousand years before I see you again. I hope you got back allright & by now are settling into routine of work again without at goings & comings to upset you – It was heavenly to be with you and I cant wait for the next time.

Here we had our concert last night.[1] Julian arrived by plane yesterday about 3 with 2 changes of plane. He is being awfully sweet about everything, since the poor old thing right thumb nail has gone groggy and really got him down – He was in despair last week, not sleeping at nights etc, & just before he left England he felt so worried & knocked up that he wrote Emmie[2] cancelling 7 English concerts from next week! & he is proposing to go on to Italy for 6 weeks from here. His nail has grown crookedly; half has sunk or something & it throws his whole plucking out. It is v. decent of him to carry on here. Last night was fairly allright. Enormous Hercules saal – dotty really – very warm & sweet audience – endless encores. Claire Watson[3] was there the darling – Then there was a party at the new Consul Gen. HALFORD[4] – very nice & easy with nice wife – mad Noh enthusiasts, in Japan for years – Knew all the Kabuki actors personally. Very keen on music. Studio for New Music (& Radio) wants to engage us next season to do a whole <u>Britten</u> concert – with horn or whatever if needed – what do you say? Mr. Vedder wanted us again (Sch. Müll. [*Schöne Müllerin*]) next year, but I have put him off until the next year after. We have a very faithful public here.

Tomorrow to Regensburg. For lunch today, Oppie & Bobbi.[5] For supper tonight, chez Ludwigs. Tea with Desmond Clayton & wife.[6] Uh-huh! It's snowing here.

Could you tell George [Hudson] that he can make a list up to £3 of the things he wants from what I marked in the Kathleen Hunter catalogue?[7] Jeremy had better order them & pay with order, I think? May I?!

*I enclose another bit for [Hans] Keller. Could Jeremy type it & express it to him? Also a letter which was at 59ᶜ [Marlborough Place]., I readdressed it & forgot to post it. Only faintly important, it seems to me.

Just as I came back to finish & post this, chaos ensued – but you know about that!

                Much much love   Peter ox Pox

*Coming later.

---

1 Julian Bream replaced Britten (who, in addition to working on the opera, was suffering from intense shoulder pain) on a recital tour of Germany with Pears.
2 Emmie Tillett was also Julian Bream's agent.
3 (1927–86), American soprano.
4 Aubrey Halford (1914–2000), Consul General to Munich. With his wife Giovanna he published *The Kabuki Handbook* (1956).
5 Hans Oppenheim and Sieglinde Mesirca.
6 Desmond and Louise Clayton, translators.
7 Order for imported seeds to be made by George Hudson, gardener at The Red House.

256 Britten to Pears

Yes let's do a New Music concert in Munich

Red House

[11 Mar 1960]

Honey darling,

It was so lovely to get your letter this morning, & also your nice (relieving!) telephone call on Wednesday, that somehow I feel you arn't so very far away! I wish you were <u>much</u> nearer, but you soon will be back, & I'll come up to London to see you: What a bore you can't get down even for 24 hours. All the chores you said are done, except that I think there's some blithering fresh form to fill up for the Customs which I think Jeremy will enclose. All goes well here – things buzzing along.

Stephen went away & lots of things were settled before he went. I've had a long meeting with Muffett[1] & the programme notes are all more or less under control now (I've done all mine except for the queries – 2.b. the Bach Oboe & Vl. Concerto, & the Schubert Adagio & Rondo[2] – do ask Peter D. if that's the same as a Zonzertstück Deutsch mentions), thank god – what a job! You were marvellous over them, but that's nothing new ...... Clytie is being taken this afternoon to her husband, a <u>long</u> haired dog, who after much discussion was decided to be the best (he is the <u>smallest</u> & Mrs Moore (owner) thinks we oughtn't to risk a <u>large</u> dog) – but I think there's only a small chance of getting a long haired pup..

I was in London yesterday – usual gloomy day, dentist (except Taralrud is so nice), doctor (McC. [McCready] has new plans for tests etc. re. arm), B&H (situation <u>not</u> really too worrying about the opera; I've been over the complete time schedule with them & it seems not to be impossibly panicky, so I'm relieved), lunch with George & Marion, the latter radient, in excellent form, she is a splendid girl, the former ghastly, filthy behavior, & looking awful; the situation isn't changed. Poor David's[3] had a tennis ball in his eye & is rather under the weather, poor kid.

Viola & Martin[4] come to-day, & I hope they'll get on alright with the score, but I expect so, & I'll be nice having them.

I hope all has gone & is going well with the German concerts – no more slips of memory: you poor darling, I was so worried for you.[5] I'm dreadfully sorry about Julian; give him my love & tell him I'll write him a lovely piece to celebrate his complete recovery, & a thank you for doing these concerts (but not quite <u>yet</u>..!)

Take care of yourself, my honey – & ring up at the <u>slightest</u> provocation! Love to all Dutch friends.

Ben oxoxoxoxxoox.

---

[1]   Mary Harrison (1912–99), editor of the Aldeburgh Festival programme book from 1957 to 1971.
[2]   Both pieces to be played by the Netherlands Chamber Orchestra at the Aldeburgh Festival on 12 June.
[3]   David Lascelles, the Harewoods' eldest son (b. 1950).
[4]   Viola Tunnard (1916–74), pianist and repetiteur, and Martin Penny (1912–2000), pianist, were working on the vocal score of *A Midsummer Night's Dream*.
[5]   Pears would sometimes forget his lines on stage and Britten's reference is probably to one such occasion.

257 Pears to Britten

München

Saturday. [12 Mar 1960]

Darling B.

I shall be ringing you tomorrow morning but maybe this will reach you Monday with my love and oxes! Ingolstadt as I told you was allright, then on we went to Coburg, a little remote town, very sweet and sweet audience. Dotty hotel – then onto Regensburg – all through beautiful country – Regensburg is old & lovely & the concert was allright & the audience sweet & warm, & then yesterday we came back. Julian went to bed with a temp. but he seems better today & tonight we go to Augsburg & that's that. Bremen is off at Julian's request,[1] & I shall fly to Amsterdam tomorrow evening (Pay Bas Hotel) – Poor old Julian is really in rather a mess – sleeps all the time – his nails & fingers are worrying him. He badly needs a holiday & is going to have one. But he has no idea of how to look after himself in any way – badly needs a wife to look after him. I don't see how he can carry on for long as he is at present. He isn't as lucky as I am!

Longing to be back – oh dear. It's been rather hectic – 5 concerts in 6 days <u>and</u> travel.

Longing to see you.

      V. much love.

          PoxPox

Enclosed is for Keller – it's the rest of it. Hope Jeremy can read it. Please express it to H.K.[2]

---

[1] Performances of the *Spring Symphony* and Handel's *Acis and Galatea* were scheduled with the Philharmonische Gesellschaft Bremen on 21 and 22 March.

[2] Possibly text for a BBC radio programme 'Problems in Translating Bach', broadcast on 3 April 1960.

258 Britten to Pears

[*Letterhead:* The Red House, Aldeburgh]

                        <u>March. 15th 1960.</u>

My darling,

I am not sending on letters (there's nothing urgent) incase you decide to fly back on Thursday & then might miss them; but I'll send them to London to wait for you. It'll be lovely to think of you at anyrate in England, tho' I should have preferred Aldeburgh! I am planning to come up for 2 nights or so on Sunday, & can bring up the Citroën if you'd like it – but we'll talk about this when you arrive.

All goes to plan here, & we get on slowly but surely. Martin & Viola have been here, the former still is, & they're getting on well, at least he is – she is abit wild & much of what she's done has to be re-written. But with luck they'll have done ½ the Act by the end of the week & then will wait until the end to complete.

Very sad news – Kurt Hutten[1] died suddenly – yesterday. After a terrible winter of illness. Sad for poor Gretel.

I hope all goes well with the Concertgebow – who is the conductor?[2] I hope it'll be as good as our records, which we've played again & I find <u>wonderful</u>: You particularly are superb, but then you always are, even when you think you arn't!

I hope you feel abit less tired. Sad about Julian – he <u>must</u> get himself into order somehow.

Rusdjak[3] is o.k. for Tarquinius – hope he'll be good. No more now, as I must post this – it is only to send all my love, & to say how I long to be with you again – my own honey.

Lots of love

<u>B</u>

---

[1] Kurt Hutten (1893–1960) – often credited as 'Hutton', German-born founder photographer of *Picture Post*, who spent his last decade in Aldeburgh, photographing Suffolk and the Festival.

[2] Britten's diary notes that Pears performed *Nocturne* on 15 March. The Concertgebouw concerts actually occurred on 16 and 17 March and were conducted by Willem van Otterloo (1907–78). Pears sang *Les Illuminations* with the Concertgebouw, conducted by Bernard Haitink (b. 1929), on 25 March.

[3] Vladimir Ruždjak (1922–87), Croatian baritone; appeared in the 1960 Aldeburgh Festival production of *The Rape of Lucretia*.

259 Britten to Pears

[*Letterhead:* The Red House, Aldeburgh]

[around 3 Apr 1960]

My darling,

Not a letter – no real news, since you left yesterday – only a note to send my love & hopes (rather faint!) that it isn't too painful a performance, that it isn't too Jochumesque.[1] Don't worry, we'll put on the best Passions ever at the Festival each year, even if it costs us all our Aldeburgh Fees!

Work's going quite well – I should be finished in a day or two, & hope & pray it's not too bad.

John [Piper]'s sent photos of the sets which look <u>ravishing</u>! Full of leaves, & twigs, & branches – a real deep thick wood. Martin leaves to-night, Viola on Thursday – they are both working splendidly but Imo, just back is trying to get rid of them both, but I'm not having any of <u>that</u>! Sofie's just arrived, & had a good cry, but otherwise seems fine. <u>Longing</u> for Saturday. Ring up?   All my love   B

---

[1] Eugen Jochum (1902–87), German conductor, regularly worked with the Concertgebouw in Amsterdam where Pears was to sing in Bach's *St Matthew Passion*.

✠✠✠

Britten was preoccupied during this period with the final preparation of *A Midsummer Night's Dream* for its premiere in the refurbished Jubilee Hall. During the summer the opera was performed again at the Holland Festival before he revised it. Pears was recording Handel's *L'Allegro ed il penseroso* for Decca during the latter part of September, but after this they were able to take a holiday together in Greece from 10 to 29 October. A busy schedule followed in November with Pears in the revised *Billy Budd*, for radio, then *Peter Grimes* at Covent Garden. In early December they embarked on a recital tour of Germany before Britten returned to start work on the cello sonata he had promised to write for Mstislav Rostropovich.

✠✠✠

260 Britten to Pears

[*Letterhead:* The Red House, Aldeburgh]

Jan. 17th 1961

My honey – just a scribbled note with a few letters to send on – I do hope the journey wasn't too bad & 'bumpey' with all that wind, & that all the connections connected.[1] I hope now, too, that the cold is really clearing up & that you'll be able to sing to-night. What a bore for you it has all been; & it was incredibly noble of you to try & record with John on Friday.[2] I only hope you didn't harm yourself.

I got down allright on Sunday, but felt pretty rotten & tired – I think I had a kind of inverted 'flu. But I went to a sweet little tea at the Aldersons,[3] & came back soon & went early to bed. Yesterday was a gorgeous day here & a long walk in the Sun & East Wind made me feel better. As far as I can I've got the cello piece[4] in order – at least I <u>must</u> stop fiddling with it & get on with something else. I played it to Imo who was quite impressed, &, as if an omen, as soon as I'd played it over, the telephone rang & there was 'Slava' from Paris, & I had a wild & dotty conversation in broken German (<u>very</u> broken) with him. But he is a dear, & his warmth & excitement came over inspite of the bad line & crazy language. He is going to come to London on the way to South America early in March to work with me, which is a good thing.

Not much in post. I've written a note to the Behrends (dear things). I cabled poor silly old Duvauchelle saying the programme & texts were chez Valmalite.[5]

As soon as I hear from Hans Keller Okaying the new Thursday programme & the singers (Harper, Norma, you & Hervey) I'll write to Hervey.[6] Norma had a nice notice in The Times for Orfeo, so I hope it went well & that she was happy. I sent a wire & some flowers.

Much love, & to George [Malcolm], & the naughty Julian, & Bobbi & Hans et al. Take care of yourself: don't ski too violently. Hope Sofie enjoys it all – love to her too.

                 & loads to you, my honey – B

---

1   Pears was in Schloss Elmau to perform in the 'Anglo-German Music Days', a concert series inaugurated in 1959. Sophie Stein travelled with him.

2   Pears recorded *Canticle II: Abraham and Isaac* with John Hahessy (alto) and Britten in January 1961.

3   Peter Alderson, a young pianist, and his family lived in Woodbridge, Suffolk.

4   The Sonata in C for cello and piano, for Rostropovich.

5   Probably Pierre Duvauchelle (1906–2000), French conductor, for whom Pears would perform with Julian Bream in Rouen at the end of January, brokered by the Paris concert agents Valmalète.

6   A BBC 'Thursday Invitation Concert' for the Aldeburgh Festival performed by Pears, Heather Harper (b. 1930), soprano, Norma Procter (b. 1928), contralto, Hervey Alan (1910–82), bass-baritone, with Britten and the Melos Ensemble, took place on 29 June.

261 Pears to Britten

[Elmau]

Wednesday pm. [18 Jan 1961]

[*Letterhead: ~~The Red House, Aldeburgh~~*] Oh dear no

My darling honey – How are you? and are things going allright? Is Morgan with you or not yet? & Roger? Much love to them and to your dear self whom I very acutely miss – You are so much a very part of me, that when I am away from you (and I know we can't always be together & perhaps shouldn't always be together) I am not complete – just that – there is a large piece missing, & though I may be beastly and foul to that piece of me, I need him. & not only to be beastly to him. but to try and help him so that he may feel that I am part of him and can be of use to him. I shall be telephoning you probably before you get this letter.

The great thing about life here at the moment is that since I arrived on Sunday evening after a good journey with Sofie, the sun has shone all day & has only gone down because the mountains in front of my room are in the way! There's lots of snow on the ground & it is very cold but heavenly. I do wish you were here. Then I would ski – but not now – Things are the same as always – Great kindness from Bobbi & Bernard[1] – Frantic programmes – Oppie ill and not yet appearing – Sigrit Schlieffen[2] is here – & various other familiar faces – I rang with Peg who has had a further catastrophe with the death of her cook.

I finish singing on Sunday & I think I shall fly back on Monday – I will talk to you about it; if I do, the plane is due at London Airport at 18.25 & it would be worth while driving to Aldeburgh wouldn't it? (I should go to Rouen on the Saturday for a Sunday concert.)

George M. says Jo Ward[3] was not good in "Phobus & Pan" for which George had chosen him on the strength of M.S.N.D. He would prefer Tom H.[4] to Jo. He is prepared to accept Hervey Alan as Christus –   Much much love   Pox Pox

---

[1]   Bernhard Müller (1916–2007), co-director with his sister Sieglinde Mesirca at Schloss Elmau.

[2]   Countess Sigrid von Schlieffen, first came to Wolfsgarten with her two sons as refugees from East Germany.

[3]   Joseph Ward (b. 1932), who played Starveling in the first performance of *A Midsummer Night's Dream*. He sang Phoebus in Bach's secular cantata *Phoebus and Pan*, broadcast by the BBC on 28 November 1960.

[4]   Thomas Hemsley (1927–2013), baritone, also sang in the first production of *A Midsummer Night's Dream*.

262 Britten to Pears

[*Letterhead:* The Red House, Aldeburgh]

Jan. 19th 1961

My darling,

Only one or two letters, which I send on. Hope to get news soon from you to say you're feeling better. All goes well (fairly well) here. Morgan didn't come because of gout. Roger came on Tuesday & goes to-morrow – very nice, very bucked because he's got into Cambridge, & just off to Aix for 6 months. Jeremy's back, rather piano [quiet], & I've given him a good 'pep talk'.

Stephen's had an EOG. meeting at Cov. Garden – rather disturbing – but that will keep.[1] The Victorian painting idea for Ald. Fest. Exhibition has fallen thro' for this year (probably next). Arts Council suggests alternatives 1). Etchings from their permanent collections (British & Foreign). 2).Sculptures ditto. 3). Osbert Lancaster is doing an exhibition of collected cariacatures & cartoons for Bath which we might take on. 4). The Harrisons have a connection with the Watts collection at Guildford who might lend us an exhibition (5) alternatively there is the old Douglas Cooper[2] Freud drawing idea. What do you think? Our first reaction here was combination of (1) & (4) or (5).[3] but I've not asked Mary [Harrison].

I've given details of Elizabeth [Sweeting]'s letter to Stephen.

I hope all goes well, that you enjoy at least the place if not the concerts.

Please thank <u>Julian</u> for his very long (sic!) letter – Details of Morley Consort[4] thankfully received & noted – very nice. Tell him I'll write in time about his other suggestion —-!!

I may ring you one of these days – it would be nice to have a talk. Jeremy's getting on with measuring the pictures for Wakefield.

Much love, my honey.

                    B

                              The Kouros book[5] has come & is fabulous – makes one
                              long to go back to Greece!
Love to Sofie

---

[1] In January 1961 Covent Garden proposed taking over administration of the EOG. The Royal Opera House was preparing the first London performance of *A Midsummer Night's Dream* for February.

[2] Douglas Cooper (1911–84), art historian.

[3] The 1961 Aldeburgh Festival included an exhibition of works by George Frederic Watts (1817–1904), as well as Edinburgh Tapestries, Contemporary Drawings and a selection of musical instruments arranged by Millers of Cambridge.

[4] Bream supplied an essay, 'The Morley Consort Lessons', for the 1961 Aldeburgh Festival programme book.

[5] A recent purchase: G.M.A. Richter, *Kouroi: Archaic Greek Youths*, still in The Red House book collection.

263 Britten to Pears

[*Postcard:* Hesse Museum, Darmstadt. 'M. v. Schwind, Wien 1804–71 München. Die Morgenstunde, Olgemälde um 1860'. The figure depicted is reminiscent of Imogen Holst.]

[14 Mar 1961]

Just seen this charming v. Schwind in the Gallery here. Probably, as usual, I'll be back before this p.c. Hope week-end in Alde wasn't too wet-painting, & w-papery. Sun went in almost as soon as I arrived here, but it is lovely to be here.

    Much love from all

        B.

264 Britten to Pears

[*Typed*]

22nd July, 1961.

Dear Peter,

  The enclosed cheque for £10,000 is a gift from me to you which I hope you will accept.[1]

With best wishes.

Yours ever,

Benjamin Britten

Peter Pears Esq. C.B.E.
The Red House
Aldeburgh
Suffolk.

---

[1] This unusually formal letter was written to transfer funds from Britten to Pears, part of the financial rearrangements to cover the purchase of The Red House.

✠✠✠

The 1961 Aldeburgh Festival was held from late June to early July, from which Britten and Pears went on to festivals in Dubrovnik in late July, Edinburgh in August and Hereford in September. Concert tours of both Germany and Poland followed before the EOG season of *The Turn of the Screw* at the Rosehill Theatre, London. In April Britten had begun composing the *War Requiem*, which he completed in December. After Christmas he and Pears travelled together during the early months of 1962, holidaying again in Greece with friends Imogen Holst and Mary Potter, and embarking on a concert tour of Canada in March to early April. An EOG tour in Sweden took place before focus centred on the premiere of the *War Requiem* at Coventry on 30 May. Their relentless schedule then encompassed the 1962 Aldeburgh Festival followed by a working holiday in France, Basel, Dubrovnik, Tarasp and West Germany. As we see in his letter of 28 July, Britten was once again troubled by severe pain in his shoulder, forcing him to withdraw from a number of commitments.

✠✠✠

265 Britten to Pears

[*Letterhead:* The Red House, Aldeburgh]

July 28ᵗʰ 1962

Honey darling,

It was wonderful to have those few words with you. I'd been wondering how far you'd got, & how it all was. Didn't ask about weather, which was lovely here Sat. & Sunday, but to-day has, as usual, turned to rain. But I don't mind too much since it helps one to work on correcting the [War] Requiem score, which is boring but got to be done. I go to London to-morrow. Lunch with George H. McCready & Neurologist in afternoon & then evening with dear Leslie P. Auditions Wed. morning & back here in afternoon I hope, unless I have to stay up for treatment. Do tell them all how sad I am about not coming,[1] but there is <u>no</u> sign of a miracle, in fact the ruddy old shoulder has never been as painful. Still let's hope that this new man will find something, or perhaps it's the last dying kick!

Just these few letters. Dear Clifford … but I wish playing with him <u>were</u> more fun.[2] But I <u>should</u> do some Fauré if you like the idea – nice to have a <u>2</u> arm pianist for a change …

Much love, my p. take care, drive carefully & see you just in a week's time – lovely!   Your B

---

¹ Pears was giving recitals at Dartington with Julian Bream.
² Britten, Pears and Clifford Curzon performed together a month earlier during the Aldeburgh Festival (19 June) in a programme including Debussy piano duets.

266 Pears to Britten

<u>Dartington</u>

[30 Jul–5 Aug 1962]

Honey bee –

Only a loving note to hope you are not <u>too</u> bruised and sore and battered – Take it very easy – stay in bed – or lie in the sun (if any) – Keep warm – (Helene's gadget?)[1] And above all remember now you can have a lovely convalescent rest – Relax and indulge!

And just to show you there is a future for us both, I am going to agree to sing the W Requiem in L'pool on October 29, 1963 & you & I will do a concert for I. Keys[2] at Nott'ham on Oct 31/63. OK? Something to look forward to, ahem.

Much love to you from all here who are full of concern –
                              oxoxoP.

[1] Probably Helene Rohlfs (1892–1990), widow of the artist Christian Rohlfs, whose corre-
     spondence sometimes included homeopathic advice.
[2] Ivor Keys (1919–95), composer and Professor of Music at Nottingham University.

267 Britten to Pears

[*Letterhead:* The Red House, Aldeburgh]

Aug. 29th 62

My darling P.,

This letter (from I think the <u>daughter</u> of Frau v. L.)[1] has just come – & it's so sweet (&right about <u>you</u>) that I send it on – with my love, & real hopes that you'll enjoy some of the Edinburgh week. I feel terribly sad not to be coming up with you, but I don't think it would have been wise, all that going to performances & meeting people. Besides at the moment I can scarcely walk, stand or sit, so the journey wouldn't have been much fun, much less going to all those functions, and being polite.

I've written to George [Harewood] – another blow for him I fear, but this'll teach him to run Festivals![2]

Much much love, my honey, see you soon and then – Venice!

B

[1] Unidentifed. The enclosure has not survived in the archive.
[2] Britten wrote to the Earl of Harewood on 30 August to cancel plans for a production
     of Mozart's *Così fan tutte* at the 1963 Aldeburgh Festival, in part because Janet Baker (b.
     1933), contralto, was to have sung Dorabella but felt the role was too high for her voice.

268 Britten to Pears

[*Letterhead:* The Red House, Aldeburgh]

Sept. 1st 1962

My darling P.,

What a lovely lot of surprises in the post this morning.[1] First the Henry James which I am <u>most</u> grateful for – how clever of you to find it. And how <u>clever</u> of the BBC. to know I'd be interested in R. Firbank, but I suspect the Corporation was well-advised by P.N.L. Pears. I was also sent 2 volumes of School-boy howlers by an unknown admirer to cheer me up (curious how one's tastes get around) – including quite a funny one – "B.B. is our most famous contemporary composer. It is difficult to be contempory because a composer isn't alive until he's dead" (I quote from memory). At the moment being jolly nearly dead, or feeling it – as stiff and raw as you could imagine – I supposed I'm slowly coming alive. I hope I'll be really alive in time for Venice.[2]

I shall be thinking of you & Julian this afternoon & hope you'll enjoy it, I know the audience will.[3] And I do hope the Screw goes without hindrance.

Have you heard that the Slava crisis is off? After Stephen telephoned, Hochhauser decided to take S. out of the Sunday concert – very nice of him, & a great relief for us.[4] I had some wild words with dear Slava on the telephone from Marion's yesterday – but I don't think much got across except a great deal of love. I told him about the Baltika,[5] but to make sure I'm writing to him at once.

I am sure you'll like being at Dalmeny.[6] I'm glad Tony [Gishford] is there to drive you – but tell him to be careful, especially for boys riding across cross-roads!!

I don't do much at the moment – except proofs of course. I'm getting in a bit of a muddle over the Good Samaritan,[7] & badly need your help … In fact I badly need you. Come quickly, my beloved P.,

—— your B.

---

1   Gifts (unidentified editions of James and Firbank) sent in compensation for Britten's enforced absence, owing to ill health, from the Edinburgh Festival, where he was to have given recitals with Pears and Rostropovich and conducted *The Turn of the Screw*.
2   A trip to Venice was planned for September.
3   Julian Bream accompanied Pears in recital, replacing the programmed performance of Schubert's *Winterreise* on 1 September.
4   Victor Hochhauser (b. 1923), agent for Rostropovich and Galina Vishnevskaya. His action enabled Rostropovich to perform at the 1962 Bach at Long Melford weekend.
5   Soviet passenger vessel.
6   Pears was staying near Edinburgh at the home of Eva Primrose, Countess of Rosebery (1892–1987), arts patron.
7   *Cantata Misericordium*.

269 Pears to Britten

[*Letterhead:* Dalmeny House, South Queensferry, West Lothian.]

Monday [3 Sep 1962]

Dearest Honeypot,

Just a line to thank you for your sweet letter this morning & to hope you are slowly unstiffening. Everyone up here is asking after you most tenderly & very sorry that you aren't here. We had a Dress Rehearsal yesterday which went medium well, not too well – The stage lighting is fearfully behind, as we haven't had nearly enough time, but it does look very well in spots, & John & Myf are pleased – Sylvia is fizzing, also Fretwell v. good, Jenny over-singing but I talked to her about it. Kevin good.[1] The Theatre is really rather hopeless, nice atmosphere – but too wide & the pit dotty of course – It is real Britten-Edinburgh weather – yesterday drizzle, today it's teeming solidly. I am off to Edinburgh this morning to hire a car. I can't bear being dependent even on Tony – sweet as he is – for taxi-ing to & fro.

The Borodin yesterday playing your [Second String] 4tet was v. interesting – I will talk at length to you when I see you, as I did to Hans Keller afterwards – & he to me!! <u>Basically</u> they didn't really cotton on, though a lot of it was damn well played. They are young-sounding & still immature, I think.

I have supper with Isobel Dunlop tomorrow. MacTaggarts on Thursday, Tertia Liebenthal on Friday![2] So I am well looked after. It is v. lovely here but a bit wild & grand. Eva is a sweet woman –

Much much love

P

Lots of curlews, oyster-c's, etc.

---

1   The EOG production of *The Turn of the Screw* took place at the King's Theatre, with cast including Sylvia Fisher (1910–96), Australian soprano, Elizabeth Fretwell (1920–2006), Australian soprano, Jennifer Vyvyan (1925–74), soprano, and Kevin Platts, treble.
2   Isobel Dunlop (1901–75), Scottish composer; William MacTaggart (1903–81), Scottish artist; Tertia Liebenthal (1889–1970), concert organiser at the National Gallery of Scotland and dedicatee of *Who are these Children?*

270 Britten to Pears

[*Letterhead:* The Red House, Aldeburgh]

Sep 5th 1962

My darling P.,

Only a brief note to say that Ian T.[1] has been & examined the poor old thigh again, & he's <u>sure</u> there's nothing wrong. This kind of gigantic bruising <u>does</u> produce this pain & ache (if you're unlucky!). But he wants me to have some short-wave treatment, & so over to Saxmundham I go at 5.15 to-day! I'm fed up with doctors, X-rays, examinations, short-waves & all! only Ian is really very sweet. I've asked him & his v. nice little wife to dinner next Tuesday. Hope you approve.

Love to everyone. Sorry about the 'Screw' black-out – that was mouldy for everyone. Do give them my sympathy. It does make one think again about

appearing under those dotty circumstances. Hope all goes well this week. Love to
Tony & Eva. & Slava if you see him.

& loads to you xxxoxxx darling P. – dein B

1   Ian Tait (1926–2013), Britten's Aldeburgh GP.

271 Britten to Pears

[*Letterhead:* The Red House, Aldeburgh]

October 29th 1962

My honey darling,
I am so dreadfully sorry I'm being such
a broken reed at the moment – it is the bloodiest
nuisance from every point of view. But I promise you
that it is only a bad patch this, & I'll get it all coped
with & promise to be a worthy companion for you from
now on! I suppose one can't help having weak
spots, and being a jumpy neurotic type – but at

My honey darling,

I am so dreadfully sorry I'm being such a broken reed at the moment – it is the
bloodiest nuisance from every point of view. But I promise you that it is only a bad
patch this, & I'll get it all coped with & promise to be a worthy companion for
you from now on! I supposed one can't help having weak spots, and being a jumpy
neurotic type – but at least I'm determined now not to be such an infernal nuisance
to everyone – including myself, because it isn't fun to feel like the wrong end of a
broken down bus for most of the time; I don't <u>like</u> spending most of my life sitting
on a lavatory seat, because it isn't comfy, nor pretty. But from now on you'll see a
new me – I hope –, & one that's not a drag on you, a worry for you, & a bit more
worthy of my beloved P.

It is a curse about Russia & those concerts. Honestly given our first pick of
people they could have been fun – but now, it all seems so mediocre & pointless.
<u>What</u> a first concert – Elgar (well, not <u>so</u> bad, I suppose), Fricker, Bliss, & V-W

[Vaughan Williams]! I'm jolly well going to get hold of those programmes & see if I can't think of something abit brighter. I'll ring Sue & John C.[1]

I enclose a nice letter from Hayward – so you just put <u>that</u> in your pipe & smoke it, after what you told me about the 2nd performance![2]

Much love my honey; hope things arn't too dreary with the old Cantata. Thank God <u>you</u>'re singing it, & Heather – that'll brighten poor old J.P. up abit I hope.[3] <u>Do</u> get some life into him –

From your devoted, feeble, but determined,

<u>B</u>

---

[1] Concerts proposed for the 1963 'Anglo-Soviet Music Festival'. Britten spoke with Sue Phipps (who became Britten and Pears's agent in 1965) and John Cruft from the British Council who co-organised the Festival.

[2] Heywood Hill (1907–86), founder of the booksellers in Mayfair. The 'second performance' may refer to the Covent Garden revival of *Peter Grimes* in October and November.

[3] Pears was singing Britten's *Cantata Academica* conducted by John Pritchard (1921–89) with fellow soloists including soprano Heather Harper and bass John Holmes in Liverpool on 30 October.

272 Pears to Britten

[*Letterhead:* The Adelphi Hotel, Liverpool]

[30 Oct 1962]

My darling Ben –

Your letter simply makes me go hot with shame – That <u>you</u> should be asking me to forgive you for being ill, when it is I that should be looking after you & loving you, should long ago have thrown my silly career out of the window & come & tried to protect you a bit from worry and tension, instead of adding to them with my own worries and tetchinesses. God! I think singers over the age of 14 should be wiped out. They are not worth it – I can see why they used to try & keep them that age artificially. But it obviously didn't really work! It wasn't just a question of vocal chords –

My honey, you <u>mustn't</u> worry about me & my affairs – & if you don't feel like coming to Switzerland on Sunday we jolly well won't go – It won't kill the Swiss or Louise-A[1] to miss us again – You are <u>far</u> more important. And the Krauts too can get on without us – perfectly easily. So don't worry – !![2]

I have just bought J.J. Rousseau's Confessions. Marvellous book! beautifully written & fascinating – probably too long (2 fat vols.) but at present very readable!

I have just talked to you – I love you –

P.

1   Unidentified.
2   Britten and Pears were due to perform Schubert's *Winterreise* in Geneva on 5 and 8
    November.

✠✠✠

Britten recovered sufficiently to travel to Berlin with Pears for the German premiere of the *War Requiem* at the Deutsche Oper in November, then embarked on a recital tour together, including performances of *Winterreise*. The *War Requiem* received its first London performance in November and was recorded by Decca in January 1963. Towards the end of January Britten and Pears returned to Greece for a holiday and then joined the Prince and Princess of Hesse in Schloss Tarasp before venturing to the Soviet Union to participate in the Festival of British Musical Art, then later on to Holland and France. Britten journeyed to Wolfsgarten while Pears made a television recording before going to Munich on 19 July, and Britten came home to work on the *Cantata Misericordium*.

✠✠✠

273 Britten to Pears

[*Letterhead:* Wolfsgarten, Bez Frankfurt, Hessen]

[mid-Jul 1963]

My darling P.

Here are some letters either to us both or which concern us both. I hope to have spoken to you before this so I won't write more except send you all my love. It's <u>v</u> hot here, but since you are working all night hope the TV. thing isn't too gruelling (literally).[1]

Hope you are enjoying having Sally[2] with you, & that she's enjoying it too.

It's heavenly here, but I must go back on Thursday. I want to get down to the old work

All my love,
        B

1   Pears was filming Bach's *Christmas Oratorio* for German television.
2   Britten's niece Sally Welford.

274 Britten to Pears

Love to Hans & Belka

[*Letterhead:* Wolfsgarten, Bez Frankfurt, Hessen]

July 18th 1963

Honey darling,

I am just starting off for Aldeburgh. It has been a lovely, quite relaxed 4-days here. I've done little but sit about, write letters, try to do this Observer article,[1] sun & water-bathe (but too many horse-flies for pleasure), & a couple of tiny excursions with Peg & Lu – Johannisberg & Darmstadt. It has been fiendishly hot & muggy – sleeping at night not too easy & I've taken too many sleeping pills, I fear. I've missed you quite frightfully, & thought & got cross for you with those bloody T.V. hours. I hope at least that Munich will be abit of a rest for you before you plunge into Ansbach.[2] Don't worry too much about Ansbach – you need never go back – in future you must never do a damn thing that you don't want to – see? Life's too short for all this TV. & bad conductor business. Let's build up Aldeburgh into a real centre, & do all the things there we want to.

Lu hasn't been awfully well in this heat. Got scared & worried about his heart. Peg has been dashing around Red X'ing. I've thought alot about our reactions to the great Bourges quarrel – & was amused to learn from Peg that their (principally her) reactions were the same – that we are too different & can't go on as close friends, only to regret it the next day. Actually altho' we are such very different 4 people (in 1000 ways), I think that we have so much in common – in aims if not means – that it would be a great pity to break up. I am awfully fond of them, & I do admire really quite colossally what Peg has done. She is so very different from all these other dreary HRH's, you know – these hopeless misfits who go around condemning everything new in their snobbish way. (Tatiana[3] also is pretty remarkable, tho' not nearly so sympathetic). Oddly enough I've got on very well, particularly well with Lu. He has talked openly & freely to me, as never before. I am also so sorry for him – so consciously out-of-date, & end-of-line, & yet with such vehement points of view. We must clearly be careful & ration our trips together, but I think it would be quite a sadness if they stopped altogether.

My darling – I live for 28th-or 30th whenever I'll see you next. Let me know what you want me to do about things. I'll fuss abit about the Berkeley songs[4] – but actually what with these asinine TV hours & Ansbach coming up you know there wouldn't have been much time for working at them.

Give lots of love to Sally. I hope she'll enjoy Wolfsgarten. I'm glad she'll have 2 days in the house before the children arrive – but warn her to steel herself against the poor creatures; I can't stop crying when I see them. All my love (need I say that?)

B.

1 Britten was drafting a response to criticisms of an interview he gave to *Pravda* in March which he felt had been widely misinterpreted. He never in fact finished the article.

2 Pears sang in Bachwoche concerts at Ansbach between 24 and 27 July.

3 Princess Tatiana von Metternich (1915–2006), who with her husband Prince Paul took refuge at Wolfsgarten during the war.

4 First performance of Lennox Berkeley's *Four Ronsard Sonnets* (Set 2) at the Proms on 9 August.

275 Britten to Pears

[*Letterhead:* The Red House, Aldeburgh]

July 20th 1963

My darling P.,

It was lovely to talk to you to-day. I've talked to Willcox immediately & have, I think, squashed the Italian orchestra idea.[1] I've also paved the way for you to get out of going, so think about it, will you, & I expect to ring you with definite news on Tuesday or Wednesday about whether it is on or off – I mean, the whole thing.

Stupidly we didn't complete what you wanted me to do about Winifred Radford[2] on 29th. Will you wire me about that?

Good luck for Ansbach & all those Cantatas – bully Richter to do what you want, won't you?

Much love, come back soon.

I'll be in London 29th & 30th.

your B.

1 David Willcocks (1919–2015), Director of Music at King's College, Cambridge, was planning the Italian premiere of the *War Requiem*. This took place in Perugia with Pears, Heather Harper and Donald Bell, Britten conducting the Melos Ensemble and David Willcocks conducting the Bach Choir and LSO, on 28 September 1963.

2 Winifred Radford (1901–93), soprano with whom Britten and Pears had worked for CEMA.

276 Pears to Britten

[*Letterhead:* Grand Hotel Continental, München]

Sunday [21 Jul 1963]

My dearest darling

It was heavenly to have your letter last evening written just as you were off home. I am so glad that you had a nice relaxed time with Peg & Lu. I fear really that I am the one who is the edgy surface in the Quartet. I am too stupid and selfish and incapable of exerting myself for other people – otherwise one would really never have trouble with such fine good people as Peg & Lu, nor indeed with good if flighty HRH's like Tiny.[1] They are admirable people in their own sphere – The reason for such tensions is complex, but we are after all queer & left & conshies which is enough to put us, or make us put ourselves, outside the pale, apart from being artists as well. I fear I am in a way continually saying "leave me alone; I am outside the pale"! which is not v. helpful. But you – well – you are just you, dearest honey, – marvellous & adorable & loving & much loved – and I only really want to tag along – occasionally pulling (boring!) and occasionally pushing (irritating!) but mostly sleep-walking at your side – which is where I belong & am happy & am <u>longing</u> to get back to!

We have had a nice time here – arriving Friday evening – having given a lift from Birnau to that touching fan of ours, the girl who brought us the carnations at Aldeburgh, who is engaged to an English student-teacher, & mad about England. Then Hans Ludwig took Sally & me out to supper, & again yesterday for a lovely drive through Niederbayern, seeing Asam churches[2] etc, beautiful country, & with of all people Julian B. who turned up here on his way to Elmau. Then last night to supper at Hans', where Belka had arrived looking rather tired, I thought. Today we drive slowly off to Ansbach via some lovely Bavarian places, I hope, & tomorrow start work on chugging through Bach. The first Cantaten Abend is the only alarming part of the week, with these frantic Arias, 1 in particular, & somehow Richter must be persuaded to get <u>my</u> tempo exactly right! I do really think it would be wonderful if we could build up Aldeburgh (& Suffolk churches) into a real centre. I am only too willing to cut down foreign excursions. There's only one unquestionable joy here just now & that is the sun – One does need a fair dose of it each year – & if only England. —— ah well! It wouldn't be the same –

My bee, I live for the 28th & then the 30th – & how heavenly to be at A for a few days. Could one be driven down after the War Requiem[3] or is that ausge-schlossen [out of the question]? I may have to go to London Aug. 13th to rehearse with Julian B.

Much much love my dearest dear.

P.

1 Princess George of Hanover, the former Princess Sophie of Greece and Denmark (1914–2001), older sister of the Duke of Edinburgh. She and her children took refuge with the Hesses at Wolfsgarten in 1945.
2 Late baroque churches by the Asam brothers – Cosmas (1686–1739) and Egid (1692–1750).
3 They were performing the *War Requiem* at the Proms on 1 August at the Royal Albert Hall.

277 Britten to Pears

[*Letterhead:* The Red House, Aldeburgh]

July 22nd 1963

My darling P.,

Just a few letters. The receipt from the A.A. [Automobile Association] hasn't come yet, but Jeremy has rung them & they say that the ticket will be given to you any how, but we send the duplicate of the reservation which will make it doubly certain. I also include the extra day's insurance if necessary.

I hope you are not too boiling hot. It's been terrific & wonderful here – so much so that work has been difficult, but Imo. Ros. & Stephen & I have had good discussions. Also got lots of little things done. The dogs have been sweet – good company, but get very cross if I go out & leave them. I can't wait till you get home – I miss you horribly … I hope we'll speak on the 'phone the next few days. No news yet from the Bach Choir – L.S.O.[1]

All my love –   Ben

----

[1] Regarding the Italian performances of the *War Requiem* with David Willcocks.

278 Pears to Britten

[Ansbach]

Tuesday. [23 Jul 1963]

Dearest B.

Here is just another loving Blatt from Ansbach with no particular Einhalt und auch wirklich kein Zweck wenn es ist nur ein Liebesbotschaft zu schicken, auf Flügeln der Liebessinn zu fahren, so schnell wie möglich zu dir mein Herz zu bringen, als ein Taubenpost zu funktioniesen.[1]

Yesterday I started rehearsals with Richter on these v. difficult Cantatas for Wednesday, & he is in good form, friendly and sympathetic. He enjoys working with me, I think, and everyone is very kind. The Weymars are all smiles. My colleagues are Ursula Buckel, nice gay whom we thought of once for Aldeburgh or Melford, & her husband also decent; Hertha Töpper, growing older & slower with a v. much older husband professor: Keith Engen, amiable & helpful, ditto Mrs.;[2] and Sally, who though a trifle dazed by it all does very modestly & quietly.

Last evening we drove over to Rothenburg do you remember – very Gothic – too touristy, but splendid.

This morning I rehearsed my Solo Cantata "Meine Seele"[3] with the little Cembalist conductor Hans Martin Schneidt, who later in the week is playing all 48 by heart, I believe[4] – He is very agreeable & lively & sympathetic, so that will be no great trouble.

5.pm. Tonight is the general probe [final rehearsal] for the 1st Cantatas (Tomorrow's perf.) and as Helene [Rohlfs] is arriving today I may try & see her afterwards & perhaps have a meal.

I have managed to get the Ludwigs seats for tomorrow so they will come; he designed the new organ in the JohannisKirche which Richter will play on on Thursday.

Thursday & Friday are both busy with Solo cantäta rehearsals; we always give an extra one up here for the Nuns etc & sick people. Saturday is Johannes P. & Sunday —— ah well! one must not think too far ahead.

Lennox's songs have arrived. V many thanks to Jeremy, please. They look v. different with accompaniment. Quite agreeable, I hope.

    Much much love to you
        Everlastingly your   P.

---

1 'No real purpose at the moment other than to send a message of love to ride on wings of love to get to you as quickly as possible my heart, like a pigeon post'.
2 Ursula Buckel (1926–2005), German soprano; Hertha Töpper (b. 1924), Austrian contralto; Kieth Engen (1925–2004), American bass.
3 Bach Cantata no. 189.
4 Hanns-Martin Schneidt (b. 1930) was to play the forty-eight Preludes and Fugues from Bach's *The Well-Tempered Clavier*.

279 Britten to Pears

Peg rang & they want to come for Birthday week-end after all

[*Letterhead:* The Red House, Aldeburgh]

                        Oct. 2nd 1963

My honey darling,

    I do hope you have survived the last few days – that the Scala wasn't too big & cold for the piece, that our dear fear friends the Venetians turned up in numbers that the treck worth while, that D.W [David Willcocks] conducted not too badly etc. etc. And I hope you don't feel too tired & depressed. I wish I were in London to greet you – this bloody life of separation is boring & frustrating, & we must plan it differently, even <u>after</u> 1965, that blessed year! But I hope to talk to you before you go off to Dorset etc, which I imagine will be Friday? Do you stay with Cecily?[1]

    It is nice to be back & to be doing a little work. The weather is absolutely arctic, dull, cold & occasional rain. But the house is nice & warm & the dogs are pleased to see me back & have some walks. Not much news. A few letters are sent on – most of which answer themselves (especially about more work!). I hope you've been taking your pills properly. McCready wants to see you as soon as they are done, I believe, so go along to Chester Street for a mauling!

The leaves are turning & beginning to fall – & we are settling into a nice long cold winter I suppose. How I wish we could hibernate (together) like sensible animals do.

The Edinburgh Festival has been flapping about next year, unaware that you'd written to George. I suppose his letters just lie about when he goes off like this. However Jeremy told Michael Whewall[2] that you'd said no.

Much, much love, my darling. Let's talk as soon as possible. Take care of yourself. Love to Julian – 'Come Heavy Sleep'[3] is a beautiful song.

xxxx   Ben

---

[1] Pears's older sister, Cecily Smithwick (1897–1982).
[2] Michael Whewell, Deputy to Lord Harewood at the Edinburgh Festival.
[3] Britten was writing a guitar piece *Nocturnal, after John Dowland, Reflections on 'Come, Heavy Sleep'* for Julian Bream.

280 Britten to Pears

[*Letterhead:* The Red House, Aldeburgh]

Oct. 3rd 1963

P Darling,

Thought you might like to have Helene's [Rohlfs] sweet letter which has just come. I've put the Duck[1] in the garden & I think it looks nice, but I expect you'll find a better place when you come home!

I hope by now I'll have talked to you & found out how it all went.

Filthy rainy day here – hope at least the morning is better in Venice to-day where I can imagine you wandering around, unless you are busy looking at houses!

Much much love my sweet, see you before not so long I hope,

B

PS. Sweet note from Michael Roll who badly wants to play in the Festival next year. But what?[2]

---

[1] Bronze by German sculptor Philipp Harth who specialised in casting animal figures. The Duck is still by The Red House garden pond today.
[2] Michael Roll (b. 1946), pianist, played in two concerts during the 1964 Aldeburgh Festival.

281 Pears to Britten

[*Letterhead:* Park Hotel, Düsseldorf]

<u>Wednesday</u> [18 Dec 1963]

Dearest B

I was shocked to have your telegram yesterday – How awful for poor Dieter – and what a misery for the children. Poor Irmel[1] – How can it have happened? These things don't have to be, nowadays, do they? I am <u>so</u> sorry. In her context, she was a very remarkable & necessary creature – one had got fond of her. It is really very sad.

I sent off a telegram to Dieter and I will try to write a letter too, – if I can find the right things to say – never easy.

B. please look after yourself – I don't want telegrams of sympathy – I prefer to have you, honey – !

Well – last night[2] is over – and it went allright, I think – my Düsseldorf public is really very kind and warm, even when I am singing low baritone parts! The Xmas Story is a very sweet piece & we ought to do it one day – but with a v. good boy angel, [John] Hahessy–type, as most of it lies between middle C & the C above. A soprano female (as last night) is worse than useless. It c^d be adorable.

Gustaf is coming to see me to-day. (6 pm). So I am not going to Freiburg bis morgen [until tomorrow]. I have bought for Peg that "Primo Uomo" book[3] & hope to find a tie or something for Lu.

Helène [Rohlfs] has been v. sweet as always. She came & spent Monday night in the Hotel & then went back to Essen after the concert last night. Thomas[4] came looking dazzling but v. hag-ridden! awfully sweet but needs a boarding school! I am burdened with presents from Helène – a v. fine CR [Christian Rohlfs] woodcut, a pair of cuff links, a scarf, home made biscuits! What can one do?! (as well as 3 packets for you, 1 for Julian & 1 for Miss H [Hudson])

In about 24 hours I shall have had more than enough of hotels – Roll on, Monday – quick!

Much love oxoxoxP

---

[1]   Irmgard Poppen, wife of Dietrich Fischer-Dieskau, had died whilst giving birth to their third child.

[2]   Pears sang the Evangelist and tenor solos in Schütz *Magnificat, Symphoniae Sacrae* and *The Christmas Story* at the Bachverein Düsseldorf on 17 December.

[3]   Alex Natan's 1963 book *Primo Uomo: große Sänger der Oper* (Great Opera Singers).

[4]   Unidentified.

282 Britten to Pears

Hope you enjoyed Wolfsgarten

[*Letterhead:* The Red House, Aldeburgh]

[?around 21 Dec 1963]

My darling – I do hope these manage to reach you – that your schedule <u>is</u> correct &
that you are going back to the Dom Hotel.

    Is your weather as arctic as ours? I do hope not, because the roads are icy &
snowy & I hate the idea of your driving on the Autobahns. The snow doesn't lie yet
here, but looks very pretty when it's falling (like now). Things are all right here –
work slowly progressing, & very difficult but worth doing (I hope!) Miss Hudson is
well, & the animals. The Cullum family more or less ill, & poor Jeremy looking like
a ghost – but he usually does in this weather. Come home soon honey – we need
you! Love to Julian. Get him to tell you how the Nocturnal goes – Much, much
love

        HB ['Honey Bun']

In January and February 1964 Britten and Pears were in Venice, where the composer
was working on his first Church Parable, *Curlew River*. In March, Pears sang Bach
in Oxford, Edinburgh and Amsterdam but towards the end of the month and in
early April he and Britten recorded *Albert Herring* for Decca in the Jubilee Hall.
They then toured together, first in Germany and then Hungary, where they met
Zoltán Kodály (who would attend the 1965 Aldeburgh Festival). Britten's final
break with his publishers Boosey & Hawkes occurred in May when he signed a
contract with Faber and Faber. After the Aldeburgh Festival, he and Pears went on
to Holland, where, as part of the annual Festival, an EOG performance of *Curlew
River* was recorded and televised at the Westerkerk, Amsterdam.

✠✠✠

283 Pears to Britten

Neuendettelsau

Tuesday 7.45 a.m [21 Jul 1964]

My darling honey –

I think of you in wonderful hot sunshine in the garden sunbathing & then cooling off in the pool surrounded by Miles's and such. Am I quite wrong? Here it is extremely hot, a boiling sun, and no sign of a break – We all sweat and swear – unmöglich zu singen [impossible to sing] – How was your journey? and how is everything? I caught my plane, changed in Paris, found a young lady in Stuttgart waiting to give me a brand new white Taunus (German Ford) and carefully drove up the Autobahn, arriving here to the usual room in the Schwesterhaus at 6. o'clock. Since then one rehearsal yesterday & some quiet practice; 2 more to day; in between, sitting quietly in one's room, hearing (as now) a clutch of little girls singing the old 100th and other hymns – Just across the road in the Church, and the bell that strikes the quarters sounds A, and the hour bells sound E, which is all very helpful to an old not-perfect pitcher such as me. Several people have enquired after you, Weymar & Frau, Nicolet (George [Malcolm] comes here tomorrow) Richter, F⁼ Buckel.[1] My altistin with whom I sing two duets (nearly all the duets for A & T [Alto & Tenor] that exist in the Cantatas) is Hilde Rössl-Majdan who sang with me in Wien Matthäus?[2] Do you remember? Actually a rather nice woman. The S & B [Soprano & Bass] had not arrived so I saw quite a lot of A. Otherwise everything very much as usual, except more lorries, cars, noise. Autobahn <u>not</u> too bad, even on a Sunday, but of course I wasn't on the North-South one.

We are off the main road here and I enjoy looking out of my window at the locals pushing vegetables in barrows here & there, old inhabitants of the various almshouses etc hereabouts sitting in the sun or watering their gardens; it gives me a delicious foretaste of what <u>we</u> shall enjoy next year and many years after! When the aeroplanes go and we do less concerts?!

Much love to you always and take it as easy as you can – let me know of any news and I will try & get through on the phone some time – at the week-end

ewig dein [forever yours]

P.

---

[1] Ursula Buckel.
[2] Hilde Rössel-Majdan (1921–2010), Austrian contralto, sang with Pears in Bach's *St Matthew Passion* in Vienna.

284 Pears to Britten

Neuendettelsau

Mittwoch 11 am. [22 Jul 1964]

Dearest B.

Sei nicht böse dass ich schreibe dir noch einmals, aber du bist sehr teuer zu mir und ich mäg mit dir zu sprechen – gleich wenn es nun auf papier sei!

Wie war es in Sandringham? Hoffentlich nicht zu langweilige leute mit der Königen mama? Sybil Ch? aber Kein Ruth! Und die Proben in Aldeburgh?[1]

Don't work too hard, my poppet, leave that to the others who have less complicated lives –

We have had two more rehearsals here – last night was a general probe for tonight's concert, which was quite crazy in the Richter manner, stopping the chorus & orchestra time + time for tiny invisible points, but missing the major stylistic ghastlinesses which the strings in particular like to perpetrate – Is there a filthier sound than 30 powerful German strings sawing away at a simple 4 part string accompaniment like the Alto Aria in Cant. 20 O Ewigkeit? It breaks the sound-barrier; this dreadful solid over-resonance. And then he won't phrase my Ewigkeit aria ♩ ♫ ♪ ♩ / ♫ ♫ ♩ as Bach writes. It is just sostenuto ff throughout. What can one do? One suggests & if the suggestion is not taken, one can only shrug one's shoulders. However Aurèle plays divinely in my Aria in Cant. 180, which makes up for a bit.

Otherwise here everything goes on. The heat is excessive – sehr schwül [very humid].

Keith Engen & wife arrived last night – very nice people – all the German papers were full of Curlew River at Amsterdam apparently.[2] Much interest. I had to explain all about Noh and Curlew auf deutsch. Sehr anstrengend aber gut für mich [very exhausting but good for me]. I have developed a passion for Yoghourt – I have it here every meal – very agreeable, & much nicer than Kalbsbraten mit Kartoffeln und Suppe [roast veal with potatoes and soup], in this heat.

Do you remember the Tenor Aria in "The Seasons" [Haydn] – Exhausted nature, sinking wilts – or something? So is it here.

Jeremy

Could you be kind & remind him to contact Brown Jenkinson & Co Ltd

Dunster House

17–19 Mark Lane EC3

about our Glass from Prague,[3] which arrived on M/S Titania on July 9th – if there is no news before long. Needless to say, I found the letter I wrote to them in London still in my pocket here!

They are rather bitchy here about Münchinger[4] – They say he has never done the Matthäus! I am used to this! The choir is to be the Windsbacher Knabenchor it seems!

      Much much love

          P.

---

[1] 'Do not be angry that I am writing to you again, but you're very dear to me and I like to talk to you, even if it is only on paper! How was Sandringham? Hopefully there were not too many boring people with the Queen Mother? Sybil Ch. [Marchioness of Cholmondeley (1894–1989)]? But no Ruth [Lady Fermoy (1908–93)]!

And the rehearsals [for *The Turn of the Screw*] in Aldeburgh?'
[2] The EOG performed *Curlew River* at the Holland Festival, 7–9 July.
[3] Possibly a Bohemian glass decanter which remains part of the original collection. Britten and Pears, who visited Prague for a recital in April, often collected mementoes during their trips overseas.
[4] Karl Münchinger (1915–90), German conductor.

285 Pears to Britten

Neuendettelsau

Thursday 10 am. [23 Jul 1964]

Dearest B.

    Well the first third of my contract is accomplished – Our Cantata Abend I took place last night – wonderful music – very good healthy choir, singing much too loud, painfully at times – Richter himself was perhaps slightly less wild than at the rehearsals – But still – those strings! What a Chap Bach is – No 20 O Ewigkeit (Long Melford) preceded by Nun ist das Heil then Bleib bei uns 6[1] – very beautiful. We must do it – Oboes and Cor ravishing – & to finish, marvelous Whitsun Cantata 34, O ewiges Feuer. I just managed 2 top B♮s in a little recit – but it was not v. impressive, I fear. I think I sang alright but was not "inspiriert". Today is an important day – a holiday – ! I am going to hear George [Malcolm] and Nicolet play a Partita & 3 Sonatas in the new Hall which they have just (?re)built in the town – Onoldia Saal named after a local St. Onold whose bones did some good work in the middle ages – After the concert, I shall drive Helene [Rohlfs] over to Rothenburg for lunch & sightseeing – & then tonight Die Kunst der Fuge [The Art of Fugue] – perhaps –

    I do hope things go well with you, my dearest dear.

      All my love

          P.

P.S. After the Cantatas came a party in the Schloss (v. pretty) given by Bavarian Minster of ? Culture – where was that admirable Bishop Lilje – a brave good musical man.[2] Nice to meet him again.

---

1   Cantata nos. 50 and 6.
2   Johannes Lilje (1899–1977), Bishop of the Evangelical Lutheran Church, Hanover, imprisoned for his faith by the Nazis during the war.

286 Pears to Britten

Neuendettelsau

Friday 6 pm [24 Jul 1964]

Dearest B –

Just a scribble, as the bells summon the Sisters to Church, to send you my love and hope that all goes well – Is the sun shining? I have not seen a paper, but George M. who gave a stunning concert with Aurèle N. yesterday told me of frightful floods in London. I do hope they didn't come near you. Please never go out for a walk without your life-belt. Here we have had storms & the weather is more agreeable – warm enough but not humid or heavy.

I had a lovely Hauptprobe [dress rehearsal] for tomorrow, this morning, of my Aria with Nicolet from Cantata 180. Heavenly piece, he plays it divinely & I wasn't wholly displeased with myself even – I believe our concerts are being broadcast but I suppose only in Germany.

Hans Ludwig comes here tomorrow & I have lunch with him. Hélène & I had a nice drive to Rothenburg and Wolframs Eschenbach where I posted you a letter. It was very pleasant & relaxed.

I will be calling you on Sunday morning.

much much love
P.

287 Britten to Pears

[*Letterhead:* The Red House, Aldeburgh]

July 28th 1964

My darlingest P,

I am so sorry not to have written before. But until this week-end there hasn't seemed any point – the strike had gone on & on, & they had announced a <u>complete</u>

strike for Saturday – only cancelled at the last moment. I'd hoped you would have been able to get through on the telephone, but obviously it was difficult for you – or you couldn't get through. It was lovely to have your letter. I bet it was hell having to work in that heat. It's been very hot here, but looks like breaking today … I hope that doesn't mean you've got to drive back & forth from Stuttgart in the rain though. (Be <u>Careful</u>!)

This can't be a proper letter – I'm writing it before breakfast – the only moment, as we rehearse & discuss all-day & late evenings – the odd moments I work on my speech (<u>our</u> speech!)[1] which I think you've done marvelously for me, & I'm very grateful. I've worked on it hard, & read it to Basil [Coleman] who was moved, but made some useful comments – Jeremy typed it to-day.

The rehearsals[2] go well – with some great problems – but I've enjoyed working on ~~it~~ the old piece. Basil's done very well. Colin came yesterday to help him. Baulkwill has been here, but is pretty dreary, I fear. April is <u>lovely</u>. The Miles' are all sweet, but vocal problems (I'm afraid the blond Robin won't do, as I feared). I went to Sandringham[3] – very nice Queen Mum, but the whole set up rather juvenile & irritating (one has to behave so stupidly with Royalty). Performance so-so – showing the effects of London. Bob does quite well as Quint, tho'

Slava has had his operation, but successful & is now out of hospital. I speak to him each day. The Harewood thing has now come to its inevitable dreary climax – all very sad & infuriating. (The children are being told this week-end)

I had the whole company up for tea yesterday – lovely day & they enjoyed themselves – tennis, croquet swimming etc. – bit exhausting – but I'm clinging on by my eye-brows, ~~prob~~ praying to get thro' till Aug. 4th[4] – my, how we shall enjoy it then!! Oh for some quiet ——

The library is getting a move on, & they know they must be out by then – hope they will![5]

I think so much of you – my old P – & pray for next week. Do hope the St. M. pass. [Bach] isn't too boring for you – walk out if he's a nuisance.

All my love
Your B
xxx

PS.

Your <u>two</u> new letters – just came, so I've reopened my scribble to thank you. How I understand about the strings in Bach – but <u>we'll</u> do it better in Long Melford, won't we. Inspite of what you say, I'm sure you were wonderful & I wish I were listening to you instead of flying off to Aspen!

The enclosed telegram has just come from Georg[6] – very sweet of him. I've written to Arts Council about the boy but not mentioned price.

xxx

1   The address Britten would give on receiving the Aspen Award.

2   For a forthcoming EOG production of *The Turn of the Screw* touring from September
    through November; produced by Basil Coleman assisted by Colin Graham. Britten
    shared conducting duties with Bryan Balkwill (1922–2007). Robert Tear (1939–2011)
    played Quint, April Cantelo (b. 1928) the Governess, while Robin Seaman alternated as
    Miles with John Newton (b. 1951).

3   Britten was due to visit Sandringham, the Royal Family's Norfolk retreat, on 21 July.

4   Proms performance of the *War Requiem*.

5   Building work on the library was not in fact to be completed until November.

6   Georg Ehrlich (1897–1966), Austrian sculptor. Britten and Pears collected a number of
    his works.

288 Britten to Pears

[*Letterhead:* The Red House, Aldeburgh]

Nov. 2nd 1964

My honey darling,

I was so sorry to hear from Sue about your wild dash to the air port. Since we none of us had any news we imagine you must have caught ~~sell~~ some plane that evening – I only hope it wasn't too worrying for you! – but knowing of course you <u>never</u> worry ......!

It is nice being back here, although the weather yesterday was abysmal: it never got light all day. Still I did a bit of work, & now I am going to see if it will do – at least it is a lovely sunny day, but bitterly cold. Not much news. One or two Festival matters – Stephen is trying to sort out the Philomusica thing, with BBC too. Did you ask Helene R. about a possible Rohlfs exhibition?[1] Do try & ask her if you see or talk to her. The Orford meeting seemed to be a triumph for sanity – with Sherlock[2] behaving admirably, I gather. Saw Muffett & Arthur Harrison[3] for dinner last night which was very nice. Meeting with Imo and Ros. to-day. Barbara comes for week-end on Sat. So life goes on nice & normally, but I only wish you were here too. However – next year –. Just had a letter from New Philharmonia orchestra asking whether you & I would do a tour with them next Summer to U.S.A., Mexico & S. America – inspite of our Sabbatical! An easy one to answer – that! We've been trying to work out L. Melford & Aldeburgh dates – 1966. But we don't know which week-end Ulm is – do you? Is it the 10th or 17th? Could you find out, somehow?[4]

Give my love to Julian – I hope the concert last night went well. I keep track of you thro' the itinerary. Do ring sometime if you want a chat!!

Much much love – honey – v. looking <u>forward</u> to 11th

B

¹ Philomusica of London were to premiere Witold Lutosławski's *Paroles tissées* (written for Pears) at the 1965 Aldeburgh Festival. An exhibition of Christian Rohlfs's work also took place that year.

² Reverend G.H.K. Sherlock (1901–90), who gave permission for the use of Orford Church as a Festival venue.

³ Mary and Arthur Harrison, Aldeburgh Festival Programme Book editor and Hesse Fund administrator.

⁴ May refer to a proposed festival appearance in Ulm, West Germany.

289 Britten to Pears

[*Letterhead:* The Red House, Aldeburgh]

Nov. 17ᵗʰ 1964

My honey darling,

Here are the few letters I told you about – nothing much. The circulars & packages will be waiting for you in London.

I am so glad that you are feeling better. I was worried that you seemed coldy & depressed in London – ~~but~~ and naturally rather tired – & it is marvellous that you've recovered so quick. Good old Ansermet for doing the Nocturne so well.¹ I hope the other two went well as well.

I've been madly low & depressed – you being away mostly I expect, but worried about my work which seems so bad always. If I could only have a longer stretch at it – these "Screws" are a ruddy bore – but I fear the fault lies really in me. I <u>must</u> get a better composer some how – but how —— but how ——? However little John [Newton] has cheered me up a bit. He is a sweet affectionate child – makes one feel rather what one has missed in not having a child. But one must remember the Butler (notebook) bit – about choosing the mother & 'Besides, he would probably be a girl.'² But John is a little bit of a substitute & I'm really lucky!

I hope Denmark is nice – it should be, but sad that the Tivoli isn't open! Greetings to the Wøldikes.³

It'll be heaven to have you back next week – wish it weren't such a beastly busy & formal week, tho'.

Much, much love, my h. d..

See you soon.

B

¹ Pears was in Switzerland performing *Cantata Misericordium* and *Nocturne* with Ansermet and the Orchestre de la Suisse Romande.

² 'My Son' from Chapter 24 'The Life of the World to Come', *The Note-Books of Samuel Butler* (1912).

³ Mogens Wöldike (1897–1988), founder and choirmaster of the Copenhagen Boys Choir.

290 Britten to Pears

[*Letterhead:* The Red House, Aldeburgh]

March 16th 1965

My dearest Honey darling,

I hope York was interesting, absorbing, & not too agonizingly difficult to decide.[1] I also hope you weren't too rude to the other judges if you disagreed with them – as I expect you did! You went away just in time because I woke up on Monday with a streaming cold! However, with Vitamin C, cold baths & long walks it's better now! But I miss you a lot. I'm getting on quite well with the Blake[2] – but finding it pretty difficult & doubtful. Frankly I find <u>other</u> singers rather non-inspiring to write for – I'm too choosey about the performers I ~~want~~ fear! Talking of that – I had the sweetest, long letter from Slava to-day, from Tel Aviv, so I feel much better about him. He's rather desparate I fear, but things seem to be all right (?) with Gallia – I wonder … He likes my piece, & approves of the programme, & looks forward to our holiday in Russia – ! and wants another 'Cello piece – he calls them his life-belts![3]

The enclosed notes to us both I send on – Jeremy <u>should</u> have forwarded loads of stuff for you. But I'll ring you to-morrow when you're back – one or two queries from Backhouse[4] – & Janet[5] (have you seen Stephen's letter yet?)

Much love, my darling – it will be nice to talk to you, but nicer still to have you back at the end of next week.

B

love to Basil – what Billy Budd news?[6]

P.S. Imo loves the idea of a Long Melford – Bach & Sons evening in the Hall.[7]

---

[1]   Pears was an adjudicator at the 1965 BBC Singing Competition, held in York.
[2]   *Songs and Proverbs of William Blake.*
[3]   Rostropovich premiered the First Suite for Cello on 27 June.
[4]   Possibly E.J. Backhouse, a local builder.
[5]   Either the singer Janet Baker or Janet Stone (1912–98), photographer and wife of artist Reynolds Stone.
[6]   Initial plans for a BBC television film of *Billy Budd*, directed by Basil Coleman, in 1966.
[7]   'The Bach Family', Melford Hall, 11 September.

291 Pears to Britten

<u>Friday</u> [19 or 26 Mar 1965]

Dearest B,

Two things I forgot to mention

1. I heard the contralto Eliz. Holden. It is a v. useful voice in the Kath [Ferrier] line. I gave her useful advice BUT <u>did</u> talk about Long Melford. She ^{wd} be as good as any young singer. Sings Bach perfectly OK to a point – & goes up & down. I think we sh' have her. (The little Sop Cath Crawshaw BBC 2nd Prize was a little disappointing – scoopy – I told her off!)

Julian's telephone No:
    DONHEAD 451.

2. Could you pass the enclosed on to Stephen? I <u>did</u> say that 2 tickets w' be OK for Jacques Horneffer[1] & his friend Peter Hartmann.

    love oxox
            P
I suggested to Basil the day at Aldeburgh on Sunday – He might ring up tomorrow.

---

[1] Swiss conductor and pianist.

292 Pears to Britten

59^c [Marlborough Place]

Saturday 7.45am [20 Mar 1965]

Dearest old H.B.

Just in case we don't speak this morning (& I fear I may be gone by 9.45) this sends you as ever and ever my dearest love – Did Leicester[1] go allright? I am sure it did – there's no reason why not. Now relax a little – & be comfortable at home!

My cold is being kept at bay by drugs of all sorts and I am fairly confident. I get back Thursday morning & will be around until Saturday. I have not looked up trains for Saturday – but we can talk later about that. Thursday evening is EOGA Committee here – Friday rehearsal with Steinitz.[2] The performance on Sat. is being BBC recorded for future reference. It seems the Munchinger St. Mat. is out & v. successful![3]

                Much much love oxoxPPox

---

[1] Britten received an Honorary Doctorate from the University of Leicester, 20 March.

² Paul Steinitz (1909–88), organist and conductor, conducted Bach's *St Matthew Passion* on
   27 March.
³ Decca recording of the *St Matthew Passion* conducted by Karl Münchinger at Schloss
   Ludwigsburg in July 1964.

293 Britten to Pears

[*Letterhead:* BENJAMIN BRITTEN, The Red House, Aldeburgh]

[after 23 Mar 1965]

Darling P–
    I opened this letter from Sat (with a sweet photo of you, & a typical one of me!)
incase it was about arrangements – so here it is to cheer you up. I hope Geneva
wasn't as dreary as Lausanne.¹ What a <u>pity</u> I didn't come & conduct; we might have
made sense of it. But I've got on quite well with the Blake.
    The enclosed, if you have a chance to see Sue you might ask her about. But I
haven't answered it yet – it only arrived this morning – so could you bring it back?
Thank you for your sweet note – most comforting.
    The OM storm has broken, but I'm keeping my head above it!²
                    All, all my love, B

<hr/>

¹ Pears performed the *War Requiem* with Heather Harper, Thomas Hemsley and the
   Orchestre de la Suisse Romande, conducted by Ernest Ansermet in Lausanne on 22
   March and Geneva on 24 March.
² Britten was awarded the Order of Merit on 23 March 1965.

294 Britten to Pears

[*Letterhead:* BENJAMIN BRITTEN, The Red House, Aldeburgh]

[before 4 Apr 1965]

Darling P,
    Here are a few letters which arrived to-day & which Rosamund is bringing up
with the Schütz.¹ I expect we'll have had a talk after I've written this so no more
now – except a great deal (all of it, in fact – had you guessed!) of love. Good luck for
Sunday & ignore bloody old Dart (I wish he was a Darter–Indian!) as much as you
can.² I <u>think</u> the Blake is OK – but what poems! I'll pay these book bills if you like.
                    B

1 Pears was singing Schütz's *St John Passion* in Liverpool on 12 April.
2 Pears gave several performances of Bach's *St Matthew Passion* throughout April. Britten refers to a concert at the Royal Festival Hall on Passion Sunday at which Thurston Dart (1921–71) played the harpsichord. (His reference is probably to an Oriental Darter Bird, or 'snakebird'.)

295 Britten to Pears

[*Letterhead:* BENJAMIN BRITTEN, The Red House, Aldeburgh]

[?around 16 Oct 1965][1]

Darling P.

Just to send my love with these few letters to be sent on (there are some packages etc. which will go to London to await you there). Hope all is well & that Kurtz is not too hellish. Take it easy: you'll soon be back! Just had a draughty visit to Lowestoft cemetary – <u>not</u> my favourite form of amusement.

All my love
                B.

1 This short letter is very difficult to place in the chronology, but the reference to Britten's visit to the cemetery is probably for maintenance of his parents' graves about which he was in correspondence with his brother Robert in October 1965.

296 Britten to Pears

[*Letterhead:* The Red House, Aldeburgh]

Jan 19th 1966

Darling P–

This is only a note to put in with some letters to be forwarded to Hamburg. I hope Sweden wasn't too hectic, that Gibson[1] wasn't too bad or over awed by you or Slava. I was broadcasting rays of luck to you over it all, as I am sure Lucie[2] was too! I long to hear about it – perhaps you'll have telephoned sometime.

Here things go on the same. I work pretty hard in the mornings – the tum feels really much better, so I hope to be quite ok for Feb. 14th. Johnnie [Newton] went back to school, & is very proud now that he has been made a Monitor. He's a dear boy, & was very sweet to me here. The weather remains bitter, but no more snow. Gilda is very cheerful. She saw the vet about her bald patch over the eye, & he agrees it's teething, but has given her some ointment. She adores the snow. Beth is back & cheerful, but worried about the divorce – so am I, I must confess. But that dear Joan Wynn Reeves[3] is helping her a lot. Much much love, my honey – all my thoughts are with you.   B

---

[1]   Alexander Gibson (1926–95), conductor.
[2]   Pears had embarked on singing lessons with Lucie Manén in October 1965.
[3]   Author of several books on psychology and close friend of Beth Welford.

297 Britten to Pears

[*Letterhead:* The Red House, Aldeburgh]

Jan. 21st 1966

Darling P.,

Just a note to put in a few letters Jeremy is sending on. Nothing important to say. We struggle on – in every sense – & on the whole symptoms are clearing up. Don't see many people – just Mary [Potter], Beth, Reisses. Work as hard as I can, & it is slowly coming on I think. Mrs C.[1] up & down, but really very good. Gilda angelic altho' her eye (the little bald patch) hasn't cleared up yet. Snow nearly all gone, & everything's looking drab & grey – fog horn going all day & night.[2] Fidelity & Stephen come to lunch to-day & we sign letters in aid of Snape Kiln.[3]

I was sorry not to speak to you again before you left Sweden, but imagine you were all very busy. I was very happy with the wire – please tell everyone. I do hope Gibson did all right – I'll write him a note. Did you see Slava again? – O yes, of course at lunch, but I'll hear all news from Sue. Just had a packet of sweet photographs from Erevan[4] – terribly nice, & happy – a marvellous one of my P (beside my bed now – cheering me up!) All my love – B

---

[1]   Ludmilla Cooper, Austrian-born cook who worked at The Red House. She became housekeeper in 1972.
[2]   Horn of the lightvessel Shipwash, anchored off Orfordness, near Aldeburgh.
[3]   The New House (Kiln No. 5) was the largest of the Malt Houses at Snape. Plans were taking shape to raise funds for its conversion into a concert hall.
[4]   Yerevan, the capital of Armenia, where Britten and Pears holidayed in August 1965 with Rostropovich and Vishnevskaya.

298 Pears to Britten

[*Letterhead:* The Red House, Aldeburgh]

Tuesday [?Feb 1966][1]

My darling B

Only the briefest of notes to say Arpeye larpuv yarpu and I do hope it isn't too miserably uncomfortable – As I write you are just having a cup of tea, so your nice Sister ?Mills said, and she seems very happy to have you back with her! I don't blame her.

Rosamund drove me to Wickham Mt. for the 9.50 & I am awaiting Lucyie at the moment. I just let Dr. Assher in to see Sue who is not well still. (we last saw him in Bariloche!)

No other news – There's a splendid line of washing next door but one – I have got most of the Schütz into my head now. Will it stay?!

V.v. much love.   <u>U NO Hoo.</u>

---

[1] This letter is extremely hard to place in the chronology, but the stationery used and references to Britten's operation and Pears's lesson with Lucie Manén indicate February 1966.

299 Britten to Pears

[*Letterhead:* The Red House, Aldeburgh]

April 3rd [1966]

My darling Peter,

I do hope you <u>really</u> don't mind too much about Morocco.[1] I felt miserable & guilty about the decision – but I am determined to give you a lovely Easter here, & am pulling every string I know about to get the weather fine – shaking the Barometer, & guiding the Barograph – & it will be nice having Viola[2] & Colin [Graham] here – rain or fine.

I am sorry I have been such a drag on you these last years; with so much to think about, it has been wretched for you to have the extra worry of my tum. However, having to-day had the first taste of ease & efficiency in that quarter, I am determined that all this has not been in vain, & that you'll never have to give my health (or that part of my anatomy) another thought – !

It may not seem like it to you, but what you think or feel is really the most important thing in my life. It is an unbelievable thing to be spending my life with you: I can't think what the Gods were doing to allow it to happen! You have been so wonderful to me, given me so much of your life, such wonderful experiences, knowledge & wisdom which I never could have approached without you. And above all – your love, which I have never felt so strongly as in the lowest moments, physically & spiritually, of that old op.

What's all this gush in aid of – only, really to say sorry for having mucked up your Easter plans, & to make quite sure that you realise that I love you!

B

---

1   Britten was going to Morocco with Anthony Gishford from 13 to 23 April to recover from his recent operation for diverticulitis.
2   Tunnard (1916–74), pianist, who now worked for the EOG.

300 Pears to Britten

[*Letterhead:* The Red House, Aldeburgh]

[16 Apr 1966]

Darling Honey Bee,

This is only just to send you my love, and all my thoughts to Aberdeen & back will be with you – I do hope you are not too miserably uncomfortable and rotten.[1] I count the hours till I see you again, my own darling

P.

---

1   Pears's pocket diary indicates that he travelled to Scotland for a performance of the *War Requiem* at Haddo House just as Britten had arrived in Morocco.

301 Britten to Pears

[*Letterhead:* The Red House, Aldeburgh]

August 17th 1966

My darling P.,

I hope the visit to Innsbruck was a success – journeys not too bad & the time with Lucie as valuable as you'd hoped. I also hope the weather wasn't too typically Austrian & that you had a bit of sunshine like us! It is maddening that on Sunday it suddenly improved here – the glass roared up to the top & is staying there. There has been an icy N.E wind of course, which made the Carnival rather a strain, but there's always some snag – some defect … The Carnival procession actually was rather fun – very long, & quite amusing – a very good Tableau of B.F. Furnace &

a smaller 'decorated pedestrian' of Curlew River both winning 1st prizes. Fame at last![1]

Stephen Terry is being a good, if voluble, little visitor, but very helpful for errands etc. We work hard at Puck (coming along well).[2] Mary gets him to pose at the pool, & while I get a certain amount of work done![3]

I've relieved my conscience about Beth etc. by having them up here, & going down there, & giving them dinner last-night, before Roguey leaves to-day. Fairly calm atmosphere, but hard work to keep things going amicably!

I'll hope to have a word with you over the 'phone to-morrow & hear all your news.

> All my love, my dearest
>
> B

---

[1] The Aldeburgh Carnival, with its parade of floats and revellers in costume, is still held every August. The 1966 Carnival featured entrants celebrating the first two Church Parables, *Curlew River* (1964) and *The Burning Fiery Furnace*, which had premiered on 9 June 1966.

[2] Stephen Terry (b. 1951), treble, was preparing the role of Puck for the Decca recording of *A Midsummer Night's Dream* in September and October.

[3] The painting by Mary Potter, *Boys at the Pool*, is part of the art collection at The Red House.

302 Britten to Pears

[*Letterhead:* 99 Offord Road, London]

Oct. 6th 1966

My darling Peter,

Here I am sitting comfortably at your desk, using your writing paper, to send you my love with the few letters of any interest which have come since you went.

I am going back to Aldeburgh this afternoon, after a session (in an hour's time – ugh!) with the dentist, & a quick lunch with Colin, having achieved the Dream last night, after a marathon double session, with overtime, 7 hours! Satisfactory I hope, but can't really say. I heard most of it ~~rol~~ roughly put together on Tuesday & was mostly <u>very</u> happy. A lot of it is excellent – lovers (marvellous quartet!), Deller (<u>very</u> impressive). Children not so good, & Harwood very disappointing, I fear.[1] The latter last night little short of disastrous: we did her aria (2nd Act) endlessly, but it was always sloppy & scoopy. However the miracle – working Decca chaps may be able to make something over it. She is a silly little thing, you know, but with a sweet voice, perhaps ……

We have had Slava around, as sweet & touching as ever. <u>He</u> played well at the dreadful rehearsal of the Shostakovich, but that is <u>another</u> story which will save till you come back … (I am about to go into arms about the BBC orch and Colin Davis – so help me.[2] ~~Ma~~ But I forgot, of course you saw Slava at breakfast – that must have been a saga, for you, with Lucie <u>and</u> catching the plane!

I do hope you are enjoying some of the tour[3] – not got cold, or too tired; but I expect you have found marvellous friends everywhere, & that the countryside is beautiful, & I hope you have seen sweet creatures made of butter around the place!

I shall be in London I think when you come back – it's a little difficult to work out rehearsals at the Wells,[4] & I want to be up for the Spring Symphony.

Much love, my honey; I miss you dreadfully, but it isn't so long now. My greetings to anyone you happen to see whom I <u>ought</u> to remember!

   Dein
        <u>Ben</u>

P.S. Basil Coleman <u>is</u> coming down for the week-end, (but of course with lots of work to do) – Triumph!![5]

---

[1]   Alfred Deller (1912–79), countertenor, sang Oberon and Elizabeth Harwood (1938–90), soprano, Tytania on the Decca recording of *A Midsummer Night's Dream*.

[2]   Rostropovich performed Shostakovich's Second Cello Concerto the previous evening at the Royal Festival Hall, with the BBC Symphony Orchestra conducted by Colin Davis (1927–2013).

[3]   Pears was touring Sweden and Norway with a programme that included *Les Illumina-tions*, the *Serenade* and works by Bach and Handel, before returning to sing in the *Spring Symphony* at the Royal Festival Hall on 16 October.

[4]   The revival of *Gloriana* at Sadler's Wells in October.

[5]   Basil Coleman had directed the recent film of *Billy Budd* for the BBC, which aired on 11 December.

✠✠✠

There is no obvious explanation for the lengthy interruption from this point until the beginning of 1968, other than the usual busy schedule of performing and composing commitments. Britten and Pears holidayed together early in 1967 in the Caribbean and on their return Pears took further singing lessons with Lucie Manén before embarking with Britten on a tour of Germany in late February. He went on to sing the *St Matthew* and *St Luke Passions* of Schütz in March and then prepared for a season of *Peter Grimes* at Sadler's Wells as Britten concentrated on completing the second Church Parable, *The Burning Fiery Furnace*, which was rehearsed in the Library at The Red House and recorded in Orford by Decca under Britten's musical direction at the end of May. The 1967 Aldeburgh Festival was the first to feature the new concert hall after the conversion of the Maltings at Snape. This event was recorded in Tony Palmer's BBC television documentary *Benjamin Britten and his Festival*, a film that also provided some insight into Britten and Pears's working partnership.

From September to October they travelled together through the US as well as Central and South America and to Montreal, Canada to give recitals and a number of EOG performances. They made recordings of *The Holy Sonnets of John Donne* at Snape and *Billy Budd* at the Kingsway Hall in November and early December, then performances of the *War Requiem* (in Norwich Cathedral) and Bach's *Christmas Oratorio* in London. After Christmas, the thread of correspondence resumes as Britten continues work on *The Prodigal Son* and enjoys sightseeing in Venice.

✠✠✠

303 Britten to Pears

Palazzo Mocenigo [Venice]

Feb. 6th 1968

My darling P.,

This is only a scribble to catch you (I hope) before you leave for those bloody old Stati Uniti.[1] There is no news that we haven't talked about on the telephone this morning (how lovely to hear your voice!) – except that we really are getting on pretty well – I get a little irritated, but they are so sweet & enjoying it so much, & being so good & helpful that one can't help loving them. We had a nice afternoon yesterday at Murano – got into St. Donato (the Romanesque church) full of splendid things – wonderful floor like S. Marco, covered with ~~fre~~ mosaics & ~~quite~~ just as rough a sea! A lovely mosaic of the BVM[2] in the apse & quite a few other bits & pieces. They are just off to the Academia now – we've had an omletty salady lunch, & I'm staying to write to you & then will go for a solitary thinking walk. The work[3] goes very fast (too fast – I left out a large bit yesterday by mistake), & I am enjoying it a lot, but I'm sure there'll be lots to rewrite. I shall be up to where I'll need William again by the end of next week, so I'll definitely come back on 19th. It'll ~~will~~ be useful to work with a decent piano, much as I'm fond of this one! Well, honey – I shall be thinking of you all the time. I expect you'll enjoy the first part of the time with dear old Julian (give him my love) – & I hope you won't take the other concerts <u>too</u> seriously – enjoy them if you can, but if you don't – don't mind, you need never do that kind of thing again! Come home nice & quick & I'll whizz back from Geneva as fast as I can to greet you.

Love to all the friends you'll see, but particularly to Elizabeth.

Thank you for looking after me so sweetly here – I'm afraid it wasnt the happiest time for you, altho' you did lots of <u>very</u> useful stuff, & we <u>did</u> see lots of marvellous things to-gether. It has been a fabulous time for me, though – mostly because you were so sweet & self-less. It was (& is) marvellous to work so peacefully. Please give lots of love to Sue & Jack – & tell S. I'll write in a day or so about the Grimes problems[4]

All my love, my dearest P., goes with you on your travels. Roll on March!

Your B – XOXXXOX

---

1   While Britten remained in Venice, Pears had returned to the UK and was leaving on 10 February for a recital tour of America with Julian Bream.
2   Church of the Santi Maria e Donato features a thirteenth-century mosaic of the Blessed Virgin Mary.
3   Britten was working on *The Prodigal Son*, his third Church Parable, to a libretto by William Plomer.
4   The composer was in negotiation with the BBC about filming *Peter Grimes* under his musical direction and with Pears in the title role. The BBC was initially sceptical about his intention to film in Snape Maltings.

304 Pears to Britten

[*Incomplete – only the first half survives in the archive.*]

[*Letterhead:* The Red House, Aldeburgh]

Wednesday [?7 Feb 1968]

Dearest B.

I may not get through to you today, so I send my love in ink instead and hope you are happy & well & <u>not</u> hag-ridden nor jet-propelled (plenty of jets here) – A soft day thank God, here – yesterday cold gales of wind. We had a very sweet meal on Monday here with Imo, Beth [Reiss] & Stephen. Lots of things discussed. S. took all our points about the Snape leaflet. I went over with him to Snape yesterday – & looked at it all on the spot. I don't think Derek[1] has done a good job on the new bit. You <u>don't</u> want to be at the end next to the tall Barn, & I don't think his ideas elsewhere are specially good – also expense is hideous – So I think Stephen will probably knock two doors inter and do a minimum of wall building & fire-regulation – for this year. He wants to knock two doors in in time for St. Mat.[2] The rest can wait for a bit. The ventilators are leaking like mad; they will have to put in metal trays we have had gails of rain to catch the drops, which will then evaporate. Gooderham[3] has cleared the big ditch – no water in pit now.

I talked to Stephen about Long M. (see enclosed, arrived to-day) He is going to ring Herbert – S. is <u>rather</u> against doing anything there – but would agree to Slava Richter[4] if the Vicar & Ullah w' organise extra chairs in the Church & so on. He thinks we are rather committed to ECO, & wants a Bach Concert at Snape – same prog. as K. Lynn ± Edinburgh.

Arrau[5] wants to change from Schubert Sonata to two of the three Klavierstücke not yet clear which – All lovely music, anyway!

<u>Thursday</u>
Spoke again to Stephen. He has rung Melford & has definitely decided to let Melford adrift;[6] and he has, I think, told

[*remainder missing*]

---

[1]   Derek Sugden, (1924–2015), the engineer from Arup Associates responsible for the acoustic and structural design of Snape Maltings Concert Hall, which had opened in June 1967.

[2]   A performance of Bach's *St Matthew Passion* was scheduled for Good Friday, 12 April.

[3]   George Gooderham (b. 1937), owner of the lease on the Maltings site since 1965. The site was sold by the Gooderham family to Aldeburgh Music in March 2015.

[4]   Sviatoslav Richter (1915–97), Russian pianist, performed at the Bach Weekend (7–8 September) at Blythburgh Church, playing *The Well-Tempered Clavier* Book I.

[5]   Claudio Arrau (1903–91), Chilean pianist, was scheduled to perform three Schubert concerts at the Aldeburgh Festival that year, but his final appearance on 22 June was cancelled and John Ogdon (1937–89) played instead.

[6]   Concerts for the Bach Weekend were performed at alternative venues closer to home – Snape Maltings and Aldeburgh Church.

305 Britten to Pears

<u>Palazzo Mocenigo</u>

Feb. 11th 1968

My darling Honey,

This is Sunday & I suppose you got there after a long & boring journey last night. Anyhow I hope you have had to-day to relax in, & get yourself adjusted, & ready for the concert to-morrow night. I hate to think of you over there, but it's good to think that Julian's with you & that the concerts will be as lovely as they always are. // Donald [Mitchell] arrived yesterday, & it is very good to see him. He is a very dear & intelligent man, & it is good to have a <u>male</u> around! – But I must say that the two girls[1] have been very sweet & I <u>hope</u> I haven't snapped their heads off too much! But al actually the time is very full, & whizzes by, what with hard work at Prod. Son, eating, wandering around … well, the pattern as before, which you know so well – my darling! Weather has been poor, except for 2 days of sun, since you went. We went to Padua in the pouring rain, but that didn't spoil the Giottos![2] We had a lovely, cold but sunny day to-day at Torcello, picnic, & a Stock at Murano on the way home. The cathedral there wasn't quite as cold as before & so, one had the stamina to look at those touching beautiful mosaics – especially the chapel south of the altar with its Lamb, & animals & all. As usual we called at St. Giovanni Grisostomo on the way home – the Bellini & del Piombo are still there![3] Unfortunately there was a service at SS. Apostoli so we didn't see sweet St Lucy.[4] I'm taking Donald to see on a Tiepolo crawl to morrow morning – discovering that he's as mad as we are about him. So life ticks over – & the opera goes very (too) fast, but I think I can make it good. It certainly has impetus now! I shall be thinking of you, all the time (a cliché I know, but I think you've no idea how much I do think of you). I'll try & catch you at certain places with letters, if I can. (Graham[5] comes for 2 days on Wednesday. He rang up from Florence.).

    All my love —— & <u>some</u> to Julian

        Your B

---

[1]   Mary Potter and Rosamund Strode joined Britten in Venice on 3 February.

[2]   Cappella degli Scrovegni, Padua, features a series of frescoes about the lives of Mary and Christ by Giotto.

[3]   Giovanni Bellini's bas-relief of the Coronation of the Virgin and an altarpiece depicting Saints Jerome, Christopher and Louis of Toulouse; Sebastiano del Piombo's painting over the high altar of Saints and Mary Magdalene.

[4]   Santi Apostoli altarpiece, *Last Communion of St Lucy* (1747–48), by Giovanni Battista Tiepolo.

[5]   Nicholson (b. 1949), son of friends John and Pat Nicholson, who worked occasionally for Britten and Pears as a driver.

306 Pears to Britten

Very Cold. | Sending this to A. Safer.

[*Letterhead:* Hotel Algonquin, New York]

C/O Hurok Attractions !
730 Fifth Ave
NYC19.

Wednesday AM [14 Feb 1968]

My dear old Honey –

We have had our first concert (Princeton) and tonight we have another in Connecticut – So the ice is broken – Julian is being very sweet – He is very much a Royalty at Hurok & they also treat me very kindly – So you needn't <u>worry</u> about me! just occasionally <u>think</u> of me & later on when I go to the Mid-West alone, a prayer or two will be welcome! Our Hurok man, Harold Shaw,[1] is very agreeable – Anglo-phile New Englander flew off to London yesterday along with John S-Q who had his Town Hall début on Monday – Very nice notice – Janet Baker is touring here & has a Recital on March 1st, & Bob was & has now gone too – So there has been an English invasion[2] – ! Stephen R. is in this hotel, & is going about his (& our) business in his own way – Harold Shaw made a number of helpful & willing suggestions, but Stephen thinks in terms of Trusts – He may well have to come back here later on, or someone – I saw Norman Singer & his friend Geoff,[3] & have spoken to Betty Bean, and on Sunday I went out to see Elizabeth – and Beate & Michael were there – She is indomitable & obviously proving quite a task for Beate, who looked awful but very dear. E. has recovered 80% but is an old v. old lady, but just the same. & strong meat – ! <u>All</u> send love to you. So do I

Are things OK with you, B? Happy? Work going well? Oh for Venice & the Mocenigo & you –

Bless you   oxoxP.

---

[1] Harold Shaw (1923–90), Artistic Manager at Hurok Attractions Inc., concerts agency.

[2] John Shirley-Quirk (1931–2014), bass-baritone, contralto Janet Baker and tenor Robert Tear; all singers from the UK with strong connections to Britten and Pears.

[3] Norman Singer (1921–2001), American teacher and arts administrator, with his partner Geoffrey Charlesworth.

307 Pears to Britten

[*Letterhead:* Hotel Algonquin, New York]

[around 17 Feb 1968]

My dearest old thing.

This is really No 2 letter, but the other hung around & didn't get posted so I am asking Stephen to take this with him.

1000 Grazie per la adorabilissima telegramma. Posso vedere che la tua Italiana è molto migliorata![1] Very Sweet of you & lovely to have your letter. –

Things go on alright. Last night at the Met. Mus. was a great success[2] – v. nice notice in the Times – <u>v. important</u>!

As I write this you are

<u>in the air over ? Verona</u> !

Saw Betty Bean, Terry McEwen, old faithful Ruth Patterson from Amityville[3] – who else? Norman Singer & his Geoff. I go off to mid-West now, & come back in a week – Then from Sunday 25th I shall be c/o Richard Vogt 316. W. 79. for 5 nights before I go West. The Great News is that I can catch a plane from Chicago after my concert on Friday 8th ∴ arrive London on 9th instead of 10th. TW.770.

How I long for it!   oxoxoP

---

[1] '1000 thanks for your most adorable telegram. I can see that your Italian is much improved!'

[2] Pears and Julian Bream gave a recital at the Metropolitan Museum of Art. The programme included songs by John Dowland and Britten's *Songs from the Chinese.*

[3] Terence A. McEwen (1929–98), Canadian manager at Decca; Ruth Paterson, a friend from their time with the Mayers in Long Island.

308 Pears to Britten

[*Letterhead:* The Edgewater hotel, Madison, Wisconsin]

Sunday AM [18 Feb 1968]

Dearest Ben–

Did you get back allright? & not too tired after the flight? Heavenly to be back again? & Gilda to greet you? & Miss Hudson & Heather[1] to bring you a nice meal? How I envy you – & Gilda licking you all over, dear B.

We flew hither yesterday evening – & I have to say that the Americans have made flying <u>very</u> painless – <u>Real</u> service, with drinks, care over instruments, efficient ticketing etc. I was v. impressed.

Here we are in a pleasant hotel on the edge of a frozen lake, & the sun blazes. A really lovely spot – We came here didn't we in '49 – or was it in 39 already? Didn't Tony Brosa[2] teach here? A University with 33,000 students! The American Universities are <u>vast</u> & <u>rich</u>!

I shall be staying in N.Y. when I get back with Richard Vogt[3] 316 W 79th which is close to Norman Singer – which will be nice. Betty Bean is also being very hospitable and warm. So I shall be well looked after. Don't <u>worry</u>! Just pray for me in Oklahoma City, though apparently the conductor is a very nice old Briton. & maybe it will be just lovely –[4]

There was talk of another recital (Town Hall NY) being pushed in but we can't manage it.

I count the days but at least there is one less to count than there was –

      All my love   P

---

[1] Heather Bryson (later Grant) had joined the staff as Miss Hudson's assistant in 1961.

[2] Antonio Brosa (1894–1979), Spanish violinist who premiered Britten's Violin Concerto in 1940.

[3] Richard Vogt (1930–95), American choral conductor. He performed at the Aldeburgh Festival in 1976 and 1985.

[4] Pears was singing with the Oklahoma City Symphony Orchestra on 3 and 5 March, conducted by Guy Fraser Harrison (1894–1986). The programme included Britten's *Serenade* and folk-song arrangements.

309 Britten to Pears

[*Letterhead:* The Red House, Aldeburgh]

                                   Feb. 20th 19698

My darling P,

Your two very sweet letters, & above all your telephone call from Madison Wis., have cheered me up no end. Far away as you are, at least I feel there is contact! and you didn't sound too bored or mis. I am glad things go so well. Stephen [Reiss] was lyrical about your Met. concert, & I'm glad the press (!) was also. The last two weeks will go very quickly & I am hairing (haring?) home as ~~quiet~~ quick as possible from Geneva to see you when you get home – John M.[1] is being very nice & shifting sessions around for me, so I can catch early plane.

The end of Venice was OK. Weather remained pretty poor, but we had one more picnic. Graham Nic. [Nicholson] was really sweet – gentle, & enthusiastic, & a help against the female domination! Ros. is a good girl & very helpful but just abit of a bore, & a chatter box. I snapped a few times, but she took it very well & did enjoy herself. Mary painted away like mad, & was adorable – quite at her very best.

She managed to walk quite a lot. Donald Mitchell's visit was a success too – & I proudly showed him all <u>our</u> Tiepolos![2] We went to Moses[3] – & the ballet part (a full 7 minutes!) was excellent: Sampsova was really lovely. The opera, a nonsensical story, with dull routine music (always a ~~rat~~ real composer) most of the time, but with one <u>marvellous</u> ensemble, & a few bits only when he got interested. Scenically deplorable – (except for <u>excellent</u> Red Sea!) singing, better than Le D.C.,[4] but not distinguished – an elderly USA bag (Elinor Ross) & a v. good young Italian tenor were the only two who made any effort to sing less than mff – & as for Tagliavini, my ear drums still ache!

Journey back was good, & Sue & Jack met me, & then came down here on Sunday morning: thereby hangs a story, but it must wait, & is <u>nothing</u> to worry about. Miss Hudson is sweet, & in good form, & v. pleased to see me home – so is Zilda (Ros's idea for new spelling – Sant Anzolo style!).[5] Stephen, Beth [Reiss] & Imo came to dinner last night – rather like a repetition of <u>your</u> dinner – party, but sadly inferior in the host, I fear. We discussed America of course, & S. was v. aware of problems. I personally don't think we should touch it, but I may be over-persuaded.[6] He is up in London to-day & to-morrow, but we'll be over to Snape when he's back to discuss Derek's [Sugden's] plans.

I hope it will be nice at the Vogts – it will be much nicer I'm sure than in a hotel, & I'm sure you can sing & work as much as you wish. My work is going well – I've redone most of the Venetian stuff, but it is 90% v. ℘ good. I'm about ¾ there, & should be done in time for William [Plomer] to come here on 29th to put finishing touches to the words. Then I'll play it all (<u>very</u> slowly & softly) to you, <u>very</u> soon after!

Much much, all of it in fact, love – my P. Greet any greetable USA friends – & come home v. soon, please

    <u>B</u>

---

1   Mordler, Decca Records producer. Plans to record the *Scottish Ballad* with Bracha Eden, Alexander Tamir and the Orchestre de la Suisse Romande were in the end not realised.

2   Britten and Pears owned two prints by, and three books about, the Venetian painter and printmaker Giovani Battista Tiepolo (1696–1770).

3   Rossini's *Mosè in Egitto* at Teatro la Fenice. Russian ballerina Galina Samsova (b. 1937) danced in the ballet section, and the singers included Elinor Ross (b. 1932), American soprano, and Franco Tagliavini (1934–2010), Italian tenor.

4   Ermanno Wolf-Ferrari's comic opera *Le donne curiose*, which Britten and Pears had attended at La Fenice the previous month.

5   Venetian spelling for Campo Sant'Angolo. Rosamund Strode had suggested the same spelling technique be applied to Britten and Pears's youngest dachshund, Gilda.

6   Possibly a reference to Stephen Reiss fundraising in America for the Snape Maltings Concert Hall.

310 Britten to Pears

[*Letterhead:* The Red House, Aldeburgh]

Feb. 21st 1968

Darling P,

This is only a little Coda (di Rospo?) to go in with Jeremy's batch of stuff – because there are two things I forgot to mention in my letter of yesterday, slightly important.

1) Snape Easter Monday concert;[1] – Heather <u>does</u> rather badly want to know what we suggest for her to sing (selecting from her choice, that is). Either Duparc, or Schubert for her solo group, & do you think the Bridal Duet from Lohengrin makes sense? Apart from the final Purcell bit, Imo wants to do two 2 groups – 4 light Madrigals, & 4 of her father's folksong arr. Do we want 2 solo groups from H. & you (or just one big mixed one?)? Imo & the singers should start the two halves & Purcell obviously at the end. I did suggest a big Schubert group of her & you & ending with 'Nur Wer die S. Kennt';[2] she didn't seem too happy, but when I said it was v. straightforward, I think she would agree. I'm <u>not</u> v. keen on Duparc because of lack of rehearsal time. If you <u>could</u> react fairly quick about this I'd be happy because she'll be here around March 1st.

2) Mozartiade.[3] I think Sue told you that the b. old Fest Hall has booked Dieter for a recital that same night – & the general feeling is that it is such a bad coincidence (they say he'd be v. upset), & might affect audiences, that we should postpone till the Autumn. Que crois-tu, mon ami? I don't mind much, except I'm a bit snowed under with work then, but I don't imagine the Autumn would be completely thawed –

If you want to telephone I shall be out Sunday evening (going over to Johnnie's play),[4] & <u>possibly</u> going up to London for 2 days (Tues. – Thurs.) <u>if</u> the opera's finished —— but the mornings are always OK because I'm hard at work – <u>if</u> you can work the time out! – we are <u>6</u> hours ahead of you now.

Much love —— XOXXOX
<u>Ben</u>

Love to Elizabeth, Beate etc if you see them.

---

[1] Concert in aid of the Aldeburgh Church Tower Appeal on 15 April, featuring Britten, Pears and Heather Harper.
[2] Schubert's song *Nur wer die Sehnsucht kennt.*
[3] Britten was to have performed with Pears and the Amadeus String Quartet in a Mozart concert at the Queen Elizabeth Hall on 3 May, but Britten was unable to take part due to illness. Viola Tunnard and Gervase de Peyer (b. 1926), clarinettist, performed in his place.
[4] Possibly a play at John Newton's school.

311 Britten to Pears

[*Letterhead:* The Red House, Aldeburgh]

Feb. 24th 1968

My darling P.,

I fear this may not catch you before you leave for Oklahoma, but perhaps R. Vogt will have an address for forwarding. I will any how see if Sue knows your Hotels there or in Chicago, so I can send my love to you ~~there~~. I hope the Julian tour has come to a triumphant end. It was good that so far it had made such an impact – the request for a repeat in N. York was quite a compliment! Now just these other two, & you'll be back here! Nothing much to report from here except that I write from bed – but don't worry, the worst is over. I'd been feeling awful for 2 or 3 days, then suddenly, yesterday, I went down with a high temperature & had a horrid day with deliriums – John Stevens[1] came (Ian [Tait] was away) – couldn't find anything wrong – gave me some nice, nasty-tasting green medicine (just the right kind) & here I am to-day, much better, & sitting up & reading abit & writing to my darling P. I won't go to London as I had planned next week because this will g set my work back a lot, & William is coming on Thursday to work on the libretto – & I must get some more ~~opera~~ done before he arrives. I suppose it was just 'flu, or if one wants to be grand: 'a virus infection'. I must say, John S. was awfully nice & comforting. It's so nice I can write & tell you that I'm really better.

Philip (& Mary) Ledger[2] came over to talk about the 'Seasons' on Wednesday – interpretation & translation etc. We made a few changes in the latter, but still no solution for "O God" which produced shouts of delight from his university lot when he rehearsed it! Any ideas? 'O Heav'n'? (The German is 'Weh Uns')

Love to friends – Mayers, Betty B., Norman [Singer] etc – & so much to you my dear that I can't express it.

Your B

---

[1]   Aldeburgh general practitioner, from the same practice as Britten's regular GP, Ian Tait.

[2]   Philip Ledger (1937–2012), Director of Music at the University of East Anglia (and later of King's College, Cambridge). He played piano in Haydn's *The Seasons* at the opening concert of the 1968 Aldeburgh Festival on 8 June.

312 Britten to Pears

[*Letterhead:* The Red House, Aldeburgh]

Feb. 29th 1968

My dearest darling P,

I expect I shall have talked with you after I've scribbled these lines & this may be redundant – if love can ever be redundant? – at the moment, I miss you so dreadfully that I feel that it is the only thing that matters! & I know I'm ~~ghite~~ right. Whoever invented the beastly old USA, esp. Oklahoma & Chigago? Well, I know they are going to enjoy you, lucky blighters, & if they send you home pretty quick I suppose I musn't complain. I'm feeling very low, as I write this, maybe there'll be a different story when you get it, & I'll be getting better – but it's <u>awfully</u> frustrating just to lie here & feel wuzzy & sweaty, hot & cold, & <u>not to be able to work</u> at all. Everyone's very kind, but everyone's not you … William [Plomer] is supposed to be coming next Thursday (7th) & going Saturday, but I am afraid I shan't be well enough. // I hope you enjoyed New York, didn't get too bored; I wish I could send you a little vodka in this letter, but I hope you'll have kind friends –

All my love, & a lot more besides, roll on, 9th.   B.

313 Pears to Britten

[*Letterhead:* Hotel ~~Algonquin~~, New York]

Oklahoma

[postmark 5 March 1968]

Here are some new friends to have by your bed-side!
All well here – sweet people – rehearsal OK. good hornist.
        Much much love
                oxoxoxP.
    Be good
What is Tamino told to be?[1]
    Schweigsam – tüchtig?! und gehörsam
            obedient – yes!

---

[1] Pears's advice refers to the instructions given Tamino by the Three Spirits in Act I of *The Magic Flute*: 'Sei standhaft, duldsam, und verschwiegen!' ('Be steadfast, patient and silent!').

314 Britten to Pears

[*Letterhead:* BENJAMIN BRITTEN, ~~The Red House, Aldeburgh~~]
                                                                    Ips. Hosp.[1]

[around 25 Mar 1968]

My darling, This is just to bring my love to Canterbury, & to wish you lots of good things for your Gerontius[2] – I'll be thinking of you, & <u>that</u> ought to help, plus Adrian's conducting! Give my love to Janet & John, & remember to keep your eyes closed reverently!

You have been so sweet to me – coming up & down to see me, & it has helped me over these rough passages more than I can possibly say – you are so calm & wise, as well as being beautiful & good & intelligent & the rest of the long list! If you have the slightest doubts about coming down on Friday – <u>please</u> don't! I should hate you to tire yourself, & I'll be in very good hands I know. Beth [Reiss] & Stephen are just coming so I must stop this –

All, all love
        B.

---

[1]   Britten had been admitted to Ipswich Hospital on 29 February with a serious infection found to be endocarditis.

[2]   Pears sang Gerontius in Elgar's *The Dream of Gerontius* with Janet Baker, John Shirley-Quirk and the London Philharmonic Orchestra conducted by Adrian Boult (1889–1983) at Canterbury Cathedral, filmed by the BBC at the end of March for broadcast on 14 April.

VII

'It is you who have given me everything'

JANUARY 1970 TO JUNE 1975

Following Britten's four-week stay in hospital in March 1968, we see a change in the pattern and nature of the letters. There is a gap until January 1970, and then only very sporadic correspondence, with nothing at all from Pears until 1973. There are a number of possible explanations – the most obvious being that they had begun to communicate much more regularly by telephone. This was made easier by the advent of international direct dialling in 1970, as well as the installation in 1969 of a second, private line in The Red House for their personal use (as distinct from the office line, which would have been answered by assistants). Letters were therefore no longer the easiest or most discreet way for them to communicate when apart. During this period we see mainly short greetings from Britten at home when forwarding mail to Pears, as well as birthday cards, or cheerful postcards from Pears while on his travels – and more often than not they make mention of a recent or planned phone call.

Another reason for the lack of correspondence in these years was simply that they were busy and together for much of the time. The establishment of Snape Maltings as a hub of musical activity following its inaugural concert at the beginning of the 1967 Festival saw an expansion of events throughout the year – the concert series Spring at the Maltings and Summer at the Maltings, in which Britten and Pears were involved often as organisers as well as performers, began during this period. It was also a favoured recording venue for Britten in his longstanding relationship with Decca. Then the destruction of the Hall by fire in June 1969 dealt them a huge blow personally as well as professionally, and their full attention for the next year was focused on financing the rebuilding, including a fundraising recital tour of the US from October 1969, as well as Britten's acceptance of new commissions. He reports briefly to Pears from Wolfsgarten in January 1970: 'I slog away at O.W.' (Letter 315) about his progress on the television opera *Owen Wingrave*, a BBC commission which would help fund the building work, intended to be filmed in the reconstructed Maltings after the precedent had been set by the recording there of *Peter Grimes* for television in February 1969. Other work for television kept them together until the end of the year, with the filming of a staged version of Schubert's *Winterreise* (with Pears as soloist but Britten accompanying out of shot) in September and the completed *Wingrave*, in which Pears took the role of General Sir Philip, in November 1970. These and more joint projects mean another considerable gap in the letters from June 1970 until December 1971.

In January 1972 Britten confesses that he continues to rely upon Pears for support, declaring that just the thought of Pears 'inspires me to work' and 'keeps me going in the moments – which I admit I do get – of rather flat homesickness, & Petersickness' (Letter 322). After the 1972 Aldeburgh Festival he went with Pears, Princess Margaret of Hesse and her brother David Geddes on holiday to the Shetland Islands. The experience proved invaluable to both men: for Britten it was a necessary break from the physically taxing pace of the Festival, and Pears later said: 'There are many things about the two weeks which I shall always keep locked away in my memory with other treasures.'[1]

The year 1972 proved to be the culmination of Britten's career as a performer. A recording of Schumann's *Scenes from Goethe's Faust* at the Maltings in September was his last conducting engagement. On 22 September they gave what would be their final Pears–Britten recital in the UK at Snape Maltings, and then their last ever joint recital, where they performed *Winterreise*, in January 1973 at Schloss Elmau in Germany. On 2 April 1973, Britten wrote to Princess Margaret of Hesse recalling celebrations of her sixtieth birthday at Wolfsgarten, suggesting that his time at the Schloss had given him the same restorative and inspiring qualities that he found in Suffolk: 'how boring ailments are […] Anyhow, they were wonderful days at Wolfsgarten. It was wonderful how the house & its happy inhabitants rose to celebrate you; everything (& everyone) had a special bloom on it! They were treasured memorable days, & I am so glad to have been able to take part in them, & felt set up by them to face the future.'[2] Along with Wolfsgarten, Chapel House in Horham, which Britten and Pears acquired in 1970, became an important place of refuge. A simple brick building in the garden allowed him to work without disturbance, offering particular relief from the military planes from Bentwaters airbase in nearby Rendlesham that often flew over Aldeburgh.

In the summer of 1972 Britten was diagnosed with chronic heart failure that required a valve replacement. He was by now at work on a new opera with librettist Myfanwy Piper, an adaption of Thomas Mann's novella *Death in Venice*, and delayed the operation until his work was finished. Despite his rapid physical decline, and knowing the possible consequences, Britten as ever put his music above all else, including his own health.

Once scoring of the opera was complete, in May 1973 Britten was admitted to the National Heart Hospital in London, where five days later he underwent surgery to replace a failing aortic valve. Despite the surgeon's best efforts, it was not a total success and was complicated by a stroke that impaired Britten's use of his right arm and leg. In effect, the composer became a virtual invalid, never fully recovering strength and unable to play the piano in public or conduct. His capacity to work was severely reduced – his physical frailty is all too apparent in his handwriting in many of these final letters – and he was unable to compose for over a year after the surgery. Rita Thomson, who had nursed Britten in hospital and had formed a close friendship with him, left her post in London to come and care for him full-time in Aldeburgh. It was Rosamund Strode who came up with the idea of cutting Britten's large-format manuscript paper in half, and Thomson who suggested supporting it on a board so Britten was able to compose while sitting up in bed. This method allowed the composer to return to work, as far as possible, in July 1974. Although Thomson's presence meant that Pears could continue with his career knowing Britten was well cared for, it also confirmed that their relationship had changed permanently. Pears later said 'we'd faced up to what was going to come a good deal earlier'.[3] It is no coincidence that *Winterreise* and Elgar's *The Dream of Gerontius* had been such a significant part of the repertoire they performed together in the past few years.

The pace of their dialogue regains some momentum when, just over a year after the first production of *Death in Venice* during the 1973 Aldeburgh Festival, Pears sang Aschenbach in the American premiere of the opera in New York, making his Metropolitan Opera House debut at the age of sixty-four. But the pattern of the letters has changed. As Pears begins to write longer and more descriptive correspondence, essentially a truncated version of the detailed New York diary that he kept during *Death in Venice*,[4] it is the critically ill Britten whose voice begins to recede into the background. Frustratingly, the letters themselves shed no light on the reasons behind any silence, at this point or elsewhere. In one sense, this lack of detail about Britten and Pears's relationship reflects the privacy they so often secured throughout their lives. Not everything can or perhaps should be explained.

The New York *Death in Venice* proved highly successful but Britten was too frail to attend and relied on Pears's day-to-day account of the progress of rehearsals and performances. The physical difficulty Britten encountered in writing is expressed in Letter 344, where he is unable to send a 'real letter […] because I've been writing quite a lot to-day & the arm's abit stiff' and in his sign-off to Letter 346: 'I've done a lot of work to-day & the hand won't do any more – sorry!' An exchange of letters in November 1974 serve as a poignant reflection on what each had gained from the other both personally and artistically during a period of thirty-five years. After listening to their recording of *Winter Words*, Britten asks, in an amazingly confident hand for this period, 'What have I done to deserve such an artist and <u>man</u> to write for?' (Letter 349). Pears responds, 'No one has ever ever had a lovelier letter than the one which came from you today,' and admits, 'it is <u>you</u> who have given <u>me</u> everything' (Letter 351).

---

1   Quoted in Christopher Headington, *Peter Pears: A Biography*, p. 244.
2   Letter from Britten to Princess Margaret of Hesse, 2 April 1973, *Letters*, Vol. VI, p. 559.
3   Pears, interviewed by Donald Mitchell in Tony Palmer's film *A Time There Was …* (1980).
4   Philip Reed (ed.), *The Travel Diaries of Peter Pears 1936–1978*, pp. 183–200.

315 Britten to Pears

Just sending the Horham cheque to Isador
– completion date Feb. 6th[1]

[*Letterhead:* Wolfsgarten, 607 Langen, Hessen]

Monday [26 Jan. 1970]

Honey darling,
     This has just come from Bettina[2] & I hasten to 'eil-brief' it on to you. Actually
I've talked it over with Peg & more-or-less OK'd it; but if you do have any last
minute ideas ~~do rn~~ ring up & say. because she (or Bettina) is going to meet
Reynolds, & discuss it fairly soon.
     I hope the journeys haven't been too boring this week-end. The weather here
remains foggy damp & cold – still <u>snow</u> – but I think it is fairly local. Anyhow it
is not tempting one to go out, & so I slog away at O.W. [*Owen Wingrave*] Going
fairly well, except for one bad s bit.
     I practised the Schubert last evening – what marvels they are, but <u>so</u> difficult!
Went to a Barlach[3] play last night – long, boring, but very interesting (if you see my
point!). I'm abit jealous of you going home, but it is really quiet, & lovely being with
Peg, & I can get on with work.   All my love & miss you dreadfuly —— Ben

---

[1] Britten and Pears were in the process of buying the cottage at Horham, Suffolk.
[2] Bettina Ehrlich (1903–85), illustrator, who was married to the sculptor Georg Ehrlich,
     many of whose works are in the collection at The Red House. She was consulting Britten,
     Pears and Princess Margaret of Hesse about an engraved plaque by Reynolds Stone
     (1909–79) for a joint memorial to Prince Ludwig and Georg Ehrlich on Ehrlich's 'Bull'
     sculpture at Snape Maltings.
[3] Ernst Barlach (1870–1938), sculptor and German expressionist playwright.

316 Britten to Pears

[*Postcard:* image of Tiepolo fresco from the Kaisersaal at Würzburg]

[Frankfurt am Main]

[postmark 30 Jan 1970]

Couldn't resist sending you this, altho' you know it pretty well! You'll be glad to
know it's as good as it ever was – even better in some bright winter sun (for once!)[1]

Lots of love – & greetings to Gilda (if she remembers me)
Love –
    B

---

¹ The Würzburg Residence had suffered bomb damage during World War II and had
  undergone restoration.

✠✠✠

During March and April, English Opera Group performances of the Church
Parables took place at the Adelaide Festival, after which Britten and Pears
undertook a brief tour of New Zealand.

✠✠✠

Reynolds Stone (1909–79),
Britten–Pears Library Bookplate
(1970) (Letter 317)

317 Britten to Pears

[?22 June 1970]

P from B

OXOX (60 times)

(Only a token – the other 4994[1]
are <u>following soon</u>)

---

1   Britten encloses proof copies of his gift for Pears's sixtieth birthday – the new bookplate
    for the library collection, engraved by Reynolds Stone.

✠✠✠

Very few letters exist for the year 1971, revealing the extent of their joint projects,
including recordings of Bach's *St John Passion*, a trip to the USSR in April, during
which Britten gave cellist Mstislav Rostropovich a copy of his newly composed
Third Suite for Cello (completed in March), and the broadcast of *Owen Wingrave*
on BBC2 on 16 May. The 1971 Aldeburgh Festival featured a Pears–Britten recital of
Schubert's *Winterreise*, and Elgar's *The Dream of Gerontius*, in which Pears sang the
tenor solo and Britten conducted. By early July, tensions with the Aldeburgh Festival
manager Stephen Reiss had escalated, ending rancorously with his resignation and the
appointment of William Servaes to succeed him. The remainder of July was taken up
with recording *Gerontius* at Snape Maltings for Decca. In October, they went together
to Venice for Britten to begin work on *Death in Venice* with the Pipers, unaware of the
progression of his cardiac problems. In December, Pears travelled to Amsterdam to
sing Witold Lutosławski's *Paroles tissées*, which had been composed for him in 1965.

✠✠✠

318 Britten to Pears

[*Letterhead:* The Red House, Aldeburgh-on-Sea, Suffolk]

Tuesday Dec. 7th 1971

My dearest Honey,
    Not much in the post these 2 days – the usual lot of circulars, advertisements of
course, & they can wait of course.
    I do hope the journey over was good, not too many people, & an adequate
amount of Genefa (?).[1] I've been thinking of you during the rehearsal this morning,
& hope Lutoslawsky[2] was helpful & good, ditto the orchestra.

I've started my 'gout' pills! The effect hasn't been too awful, but I've felt rather as if my head was going to blow off – but perhaps that was Rosenkavalier[3] of which I played one side (it's <u>dreadful</u> music, & really rather shocking). Rosamunde will deliver this to the most efficient P.O in the district, "Express" & all, so I hope it reaches you … It is attached to so much love that it can't fail to ……   B.

---

1   Jenever, traditional Dutch gin.
2   Pears was in Amsterdam to perform Lutosławski's *Paroles tissées*, conducted by the composer at three concerts at the Concertgebouw (8, 9 and 12 December).
3   Strauss's opera.

319 Britten to Pears

[*Letterhead:* The Red House, Aldeburgh-on-Sea, Suffolk]

Dec. 8th 1971

Darling honey,

Do hope you were pleased with last night – but I expect to have talked with you again before you get this. It was lovely to hear your voice this morning

Here are some copies of letters for you, & one or two others which have since arrived. Lots of Xmas cards of course!

Much, much (all my) love,

B

320 Britten to Pears

[*Letterhead:* Wolfsgarten, 607 Langen, Hessen]

Thursday Jan. c. 14. 1972.

My darling P.,

This isn't a proper letter – and I'll write soon – but only to say what is uppermost in my mind all the time – Arpi, Larpove, Yarpu, & wish I were with Yarpu.

It's very nice here, tho', very well looked after – Peg is off in Bonn, but I'm just off to that great Metropolis Langen to cash some cheques. Elizabeth (Brosch) & Heinz[1] are having a lovely time seizing my underclothes, & handkerchiefs (after one sneeze) & washing them. I hope the W. Requiem[2] goes well … Greetings to all & sundry, & love to Sue – I feel at the moment that I could face hearing even that old W. Req. if you were singing in it.

Lots of love –

Your devoted old B. XXXOXXO

¹   Staff at Wolfsgarten.
²   Pears was singing in a performance of the *War Requiem* at the Royal Festival Hall on 18 January.

321 Britten to Pears

[*Letterhead:* Wolfsgarten, 607 Langen, Hessen]

Jan. 20th 1972

My darlingest darling,

I miss you dreadfully and want to come home <u>soon</u> – still Peg is being awfully kind & work progresses¹ – (don't know how well, though) & anyhow you'll be here in less than 2 weeks & I must stick it out. Your letter still hasn't come² – blast it, but I hope on, from day to day. You sounded sad on the telephone yesterday – but don't exaggerate about that frog, I'd rather have you with a frog than all other tenors!

I'm going out to lunch with Peg to-day – rather to get away from Siggrid³ who is really rather a drip – tears & all: comes of living alone, with nothing to do but to think about herself. I hope you find Aldeburgh all right, & that Horham progresses – how I long to get back there. It's a bit less cold to-day, but everyone expects snow. Back to-work now, I've just got you on to the Lido!⁴

Arpi larpove Yarpou
Dein
B.

¹   Britten was at Wolfsgarten to work on *Death in Venice*.
²   An envelope addressed by Pears to Britten at Wolfsgarten and postmarked 15 January 1972 survives in the archive, but unfortunately the letter itself does not.
³   Countess Sigrid von Schlieffen.
⁴   Referring to Aschenbach, the role Britten was writing for Pears in *Death in Venice*.

322 Britten to Pears

[*Letterhead:* Wolfsgarten, 607 Langen, Hessen]

January 24th 1972

My dearest P.,

Now you are off to Manchester,¹ & it make not be always possible to telephone you each morning – so here, signed sealed & witnessed (not actually, except by me) is the same old news; that I love you, & think about & with you all the time, that it inspires me to work for you, & very soon with you, & keeps me going in the moments – which I admit I do get – of rather flat homesickness, & Petersickness. Actually it <u>is</u> nice here, & at the moment I am working happily with Myfanwy – getting a lot done, & rewriting earlier bits which have worried me, & ~~of~~ over which she has been helpful indeed. Peg & Tittu[2] have gone off – poor Domenic is quite seriously ill up in Woltersen & won't be home this week, Tittu's brother Dicky is going off to shoot (bang, bang) in Sandringham on Wednesday, so when Myf goes off (on Wed morning) I shall be solitary, except for 500 servants of course. But they are nice creatures & I'll be working jolly hard!. I have had long letters from Rosamund so I'm pretty ~~welll~~ well up with the news from Aldeburgh. Tyger[3] has written a very mad letter, returning the tip I sent him – he is in a strange state, & I'm not sure exactly what to do with him. Charles,[4] on the other ~~had~~ hand, has written a sweet note saying his prep's going better, so I expect I'll be taking up child psychiatry soon. I can't wait for Feb. 2nd – hurry on the day when I'll be meeting you at Frankfurt Airport – it'll be nice that all these bloody airliners buzzing around over Wolfsgarten will be doing something sensible for once, & bringing you to me! Good luck for Schwartz[5] and the Nocturnes – hope the harpists don't pass out with nerves. Good luck for the St John[6] – if you do it even ½ as well as those records it'll be spiffing – love (well – kind of) to the Mellerses.[7]

And all the love the world has ever known to my sweetest of P's,

    Dein

      <u>B</u> XXXOX

---

[1] Pears was to appear on *Face the Music*, a BBC Television production.
[2] Possibly Princess Beatrix of Hohenlohe-Langenburg (1936–97), companion to Princess Margaret of Hesse, and unidentified relations.
[3] Ronan Magill (b. 1954), a young pianist whom Britten was mentoring.
[4] Charles Tait (b. 1958), son of Aldeburgh GP Ian.
[5] Rudolf Schwarz (1905–94). Pears was about to go on tour with Schwarz and the Northern Sinfonia performing Britten's *Nocturne*.
[6] Bach *St John Passion*.
[7] Wilfrid Mellers (1914–2008), musicologist, and family.

323 Britten to Pears

[**Letterhead:** The Red House, Aldeburgh-on-Sea, Suffolk]

                                            19.2.72

Honey darling,

Here is the little fan letter from Jonathan G.[1] You must have sung marvelously: I do wish I'd been there to hear. Good luck for to-morrow.[2]

Work goes pretty well. I've timed it all, & it is now reasonably consise – no need for worries, but I must keep a watch on length now all the time. I've written something this morning which I <u>hope</u> you'll like singing: I can hear you doing it most beautifully. I'm getting rather attached to Aschenbach, not surprisingly!

I've listened to Awake sweet love – it's certainly usable, but I do so love the Morley Come Sorrow Come[3] that I'm going to see whether they'll use that instead, but it may be too long.

Lots of love & luck for next week. I hope it won't be too grisly – don't forget warm clothes & torch – any addresses???   XXXOX Ben

---

[1] Unidentified.
[2] Pears was to perform at the Wigmore Hall, London.
[3] Lute songs by John Dowland and Thomas Morley.

324 Britten to Pears

[*Letterhead:* BENJAMIN BRITTEN, The Red House, Aldeburgh]

[around 24 Feb 1972]

Darling P.,

Just a line as Leo[1] is waiting to take this to the post. Good luck to the concerts[2] – hope no. 1 has gone well & that the French conductor liked your French as much as he liked mine (? I wonder). I'll try to ring you one of these mornings.

Lots of love XXXOOX
     B.

---

[1] Kingston, a hired driver.
[2] Pears was performing *Les Illuminations* on tour with the City of Birmingham Symphony Orchestra and conductor Louis Frémaux (b. 1921). The Birmingham concert on 24 February was broadcast live on BBC radio.

325 Britten to Pears

[*Letterhead:* BENJAMIN BRITTEN, The Red House, Aldeburgh]

[?22 Mar 1972]

Honey darling,

Here are those two tributes – richly deserved, <u>I</u> know! I am delighted that last night was so tremendous.[1] I feel very sad to have missed it – I miss everything lovely these days – & deeply disappointed I didn't speak to you last night.

> Good luck to Mozart & Bach in Scotland[2]
> & come back quick to
> Your waiting & loving
> B.

----

1   Probably Schütz *St Matthew Passion*, which Pears sang in London, conducted by Roger
    Norrington on 21 March.
2   Performances of Mozart's *Requiem* in Glasgow, and Bach's *St Matthew Passion* in
    Edinburgh.

326 Britten to Pears

[*Letterhead:* The Red House, Aldeburgh-on-Sea, Suffolk]

[?early 1972]

My darling ――
    Just to send on this note – don't remember who she is, but I expect one of those
lively 90 year olds! I hope you are happy, & not too cold & obscure. It's dull &
dreary here to-day, but I'm going to cheer myself up by working in your study: the
library is a bit cold, & I'm going to get some inspiration from sitting on your chair –
    I'll probably ring you mid-day to-morrow.
            All my love (did you guess?)
                 <u>B</u>
                        XXX

327 Britten to Pears

[*Letterhead:* The Red House, Aldeburgh-on-Sea, Suffolk]

[?1972]

Darling P,
    Here are the letters that came this morning. It's lovely to know you are back
with Sue & that she can keep an eye on you!
    Good luck for Sunday – wish I were there to cheer. Try & keep warm
        XXXXXOOO Ben

✠✠✠

In January 1973, Britten and Pears went to Germany for their final recital tour together, writing to Anthony Gishford on 18 January, 'a 'flu-ridden 10 days in Bavaria—about the nastiest visit ever'. On 17 April 1973, Britten was admitted to hospital for a diagnostic coronary angiogram, as noted in his diary. He then returned to Aldeburgh during the last week of April, before being readmitted on 2 May for his heart valve operation.

✠✠✠

328 Britten to Pears

[*Letterhead:* BENJAMIN BRITTEN, ~~The Red House, Aldeburgh~~]
CHAPEL COTTAGE HORHAM

[around 22 June 1973]

MANY HAPPY RETURNS ——

from an addled old, wobbley & feeble old (<u>but</u> improving!), propelled entirely by love for a dashing, ever younger, tenor with ever more triumphs to his name, & who mustn't forget to go and choose one of those K. Vaughan's[1] (~~reged~~ regardless of price)

XOXOXOXOXOXOXOX

---

[1]   Keith Vaughan (1912–77), painter. Three of his works are held in the art collection at the Britten–Pears Foundation.

329 Pears to Britten

[*Postcard:* images of Igls, near Innsbruck]

[?10–11 Jul 1973]

Viele Grüsse aus Igls –[1]

[*written by Lucie Manén*]
Lucie, Peter was a very good boy!

[*written by Otakar Kraus*][2]
Good luck from Otto to B

[*written by Pears*]
& I shall soon be back.   Much love to Peg

---

1   'Many Greetings from Igls'.
2   (1909–80), Czech-born baritone.

330 Pears to Britten

[*Postcard:* Jacobello del Fiore *Leone di San Marco* (1430) from the Palazzo Ducale, Venice]

[Venice]

[postmark 26 Sep 1973]

Much love to you from the Winged Lion and all his fellow citizens. P.[1]

---

1   Pears was singing in three performances of *Death in Venice* (20, 22 and 23 September) at the Teatro la Fenice.

331 Pears to Britten

[*Postcard:* Image of Romanian folk costumes]

[Bucharest]

[postmark 1 Nov 1973]

I hope you will like a post card from Bucharest. It is a charmless dump.[1] They call it little Paris, a fair comment except that the food is not so good. I met last night the P. Pears of Rumania, who has sung Albert Herring etc, etc., rather nice and sympathetic. See you in about 1 year of waiting at the Airport.

PPox

---

[1] Pears was performing with the Warsaw National Philharmonic Orchestra in Romania. Interestingly, he writes the first several lines of this postcard far more clearly than his normal handwriting, perhaps hoping that it could be read by Bucharest's postal employees.

332 Pears to Britten

[*Postcard:* statue of Hans Christian Andersen, Cophenhagen]

[Copenhagen]

[Postmark 16 Feb 1974]

I wonder when this will reach you – Easter, perhaps? Rather a sweet picture of a dear chap, don't you think? It was nice to get back to sunny Copenhagen after rain & slush in Stockholm & Oslo.[1]

P.

Much love – see you long before this card

---

[1]   Pears was touring Scandinavia with harpist Osian Ellis (b. 1928), performing Britten, Dowland, Schubert and Schumann in a recital at Copenhagen on 5 February.

333 Britten to Pears

[*Letterhead:* Post Office Telegram]

[postmark 7 May 1974][1]

B16 11.18 STRADBROKE NC 48
PETER PEARS 8 HELLIFORD SREET LDNN1

DEAREST PETER I KNOW GENERAL SIR LUARD WINGRAVE[2] IS NOT THE LONGEST OF YOURE BRITTEN OPERATIC PARTS BUT LONG OR SHORT WHATEVER YOU DO FOR ME IS ALWAYS THE KING PIN AND I AM ETERNALLY GRATEFUL YOURE HUMBLE AND DEVOTED BEN+

---

[1]   For the first night of the revival of Colin Graham's production of *Owen Wingrave* at the Royal Opera House, Covent Garden.
[2]   A conflation of Pears's role, General Sir Philip Wingrave, with his mother's maiden name, Luard.

334 Pears to Britten

[*Postcard:* Image from the Isenheim Altarpiece by Mathias Grünewald, from Unterlinden Museum]

Strasbourg[1]

[postmark 13 May 1974]

A consort – concert of Angels it may be, but how do you bow like this? Most unsatisfactory surely – Adorable place and of course la belle France – oh yes! green countryside, little rivers – smashing lunch & all OK.

Much love
    PPox

---

[1] Pears was in Strasbourg for a recital with harpist Osian Ellis on 13 May.

335 Britten to Pears

[*Birthday card:* Maurice Pledger *Grey wagtail and forget-me-nots*]

[?22 June 1974]

Dearest Peter
    Many happy returns. No
objets d'art this time (until the
bill for English Baroque comes
in), but some objets domestiques[1]
which I hope will be handy.
            All my love
                B.

---

[1]   Probably a gift of cooking utensils.

336 Pears to Britten

[*Postcard:* image of Schloss Tarasp]

[Tarasp, Switzerland]

[postmark 17 Aug 1974]

[*written by Princess Margaret of Hesse*]
Peter – in good form – beat Dolf[1] at Dominoes & at boule! Dave[2] arrives to-day.
Miss you very much. Peg OX

[*written by Lidwine von Clary*]
Yes indeed! – much love and thanks for good wishes Lidi

[*written by Alfons von Clary*][3]
and <u>from Alphy</u>

[*written by Pears*]
Guten Tag!
    Gustav von Aschenbach

[*written by Princess Margaret of Hesse*]
Golo[4] arrives to-morrow.

---

1   Sternberger (1907–89), German philosopher.
2   Probably Princess Margaret of Hesse's youngest brother, David Campbell Geddes (1917–95).
3   Friends of Princess Margaret of Hesse, Lidwine von Clary und Aldringen (1894–1984), 'Lidi', and Duke Alfons von Clary und Aldringen (1887–1978), 'Alphy'.
4   Mann (1909–94), German historian and writer, and son of Thomas Mann, author of the novella *Death in Venice* (1912).

337 Britten to Pears

[*Letterhead:* The Red House, Aldeburgh-on-Sea, Suffolk]

                                            1.9.74

My darling P.,
    Excuse this v. felty pen (it seems to be weeping) – but I wanted to put this in with a few letters that have arrived. It was so ~~great~~ good of you to ring on your arrival & I was so glad to hear all was well (if not!) I've got a call booked to you to-day (Tuesday) because I am keen to know about rehearsals etc. We go to Horham to-day – wish you were coming —— back on Friday, then off to Peg's on Tuesday. I miss you dreadfully, & am very jealous of all ~~the~~ our friends coming over, but I'm working <u>hard</u>[1] & thinking of November
                      B. OXOX

---

1   On revisions to *Paul Bunyan*.

338 Pears to Britten

[*Postcard:* image of Grand Béguinage – Leuven, Belgium][1]

[around 10 Sep 1974]

This is really a very sweet place – all goes well – Lucy in good form – few but nice students, keen and enthusiastic – weather varies – Sun shining just now on pretty pink De Hooch brick – Hope M. Roll[2] went ok.
  Much love to all
    P.

---

[1] Pears was in Belgium for the Flanders Festival, where Lucie Manén was giving master-classes and he was singing with the Wilbye Consort.
[2] Probably Michael Roll (b. 1946), pianist.

339 Pears to Britten

[*Letterhead:* The Red House, Aldeburgh-on-Sea, Suffolk]

[29 Sep 1974]

My darling –
  I am just off and when I see you next I am going to be able to say that I have done the most marvellous performances of your Aschenbach[1] that anyone including me has ever done – I shall be with you all the time – Have a quiet happy time with Peg and give her lots of love
    Your loving   P.

I enclose a billet très! Doux [a love letter, very much so]

---

[1] Pears was on his way to New York to begin rehearsals for his Metropolitan Opera debut in *Death in Venice* on 18 October; Britten visited Wolfsgarten, home of Peg Hesse, from 7 October to 5 November.

340 Pears to Britten

The Mayflower Hotel. [New York]

Thursday 3rd Oct. A.M. [1974]

Darling Ben – Just a note to send you so very much love. It has been marvellous talking to you and sounding so near and clear – Everything here is as you might expect, but I think with luck D in V should go on OK. Steuart is pleased with the Orchestra, though I think the percussion Dept. was slightly dazed! The small parts are excellent mostly, and taking v. well to Colin. No <u>great</u> voices but good and enjoying rehearsals, I think. The Met. is a total warren of corridors, lifts, desks, & I have not yet the faintest idea how to get anywhere where I am called. But that will come! A **v** useful pianist for me, not yet quite in the picture, but I shall grab him from time to time. I have a nice room overlooking Central Park – lovely dawns – The weather is warm, rather too warm, and of course not easy to get one's room the right temperature. But at least the central heating is not on! I have been rung by Harold Shaw,[1] Clytie, Betty Bean, Claire Reis,[2] Michael Burt[3] (a pupil from London) but haven't been social as my voice has been a worry, and yesterday I went to a ENT Doctor prvided by Harold Shaw & he said I have a throat infection & has put me on Antibiotics. Already after 4 doses, the throat is rather better – but I shan't sing today and I go to the Dr. again tomorrow. Then I should be alright. I am keeping a diary you will be pleased to hear! No great excitements yet –

I <u>do</u> hope you are getting on alright and working away at Christmas. and not getting too tired or depressed – What's the weather like? It really is rather glorious here, thank goodness. When I arrived in $\genfrac{}{}{0pt}{}{\text{your}}{\text{my}}$} fur-coat and cap, I almost died of heat; they are firmly put away in the "Closet."

<u>American Words and ACCENT!</u>

At the Doctors yesterday waiting to be called, a large black man burst in, looked at me and said "'re you Rush'n?" So I said "No! I'm English!" He nearly died of laughter. He meant "was I in a hurry?!"

Betty Bean is taking me to the 1st night of Wozzeck[4] on Monday – Peter Glossop[5] as W.

The only two performances sold out quick were the opening night of the season and 1st D. in V. So there! Everyone wishes you were here. But I think you are better off where you are. You would be deeply depressed by every single thing you see in the street!

Much much love_ honey –

and much too to Rita and all

our dear staff –   PPox

1 Harold Shaw (1923–2014), founder of the Shaw Agency, manager of Julian Bream.
2 (1888–1978), music promoter.
3 (b. 1943), bass-baritone.
4 Opera by Berg.
5 Peter Glossop (1928–2008), baritone.

341 Britten to Pears

[*Letterhead:* The Red House, Aldeburgh-on-Sea, Suffolk]

4 .9 10.74

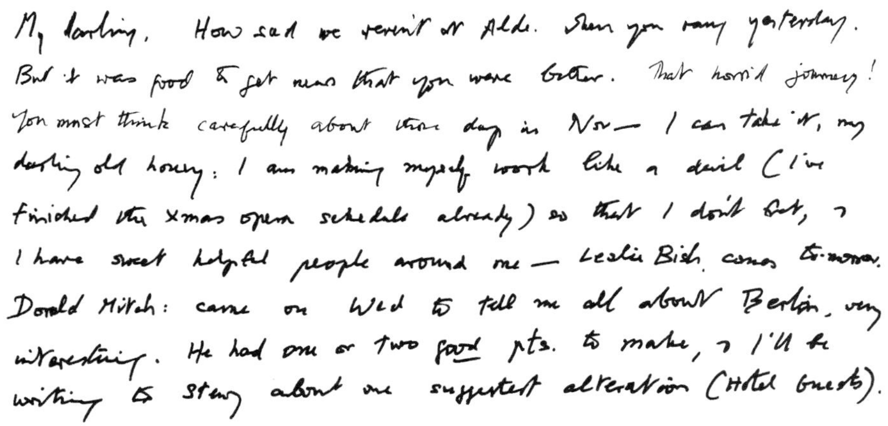
My darling, How sad we weren't at Alde. when you rang yesterday.
But it was good to get news that you were better. That horrid journey!
You must think carefully about those days in Nov – I can take it, my
darling old honey: I am making myself work like a devil (I've
finished the xmas opera schedule already) so that I don't fret, &
I have sweet helpful people around me – Leslie Bish. comes to-morrow.
Donald Mitch: came on Wed to tell me all about Berlin, very
interesting. He had one or two good pts. to make, & I'll be
writing to Stewy about one suggestest alteration (Hotel Guests).

My darling, How sad we weren't at Alde. when you rang yesterday. But it was good to get news that you were better. That horrid journey! You must think carefully about those days in Nov – I can take it, my darling old honey: I am making myself work like a devil (I've finished the xmas opera[1] schedule already) so that I don't fret, & I have sweet helpful people around me – Leslie Bish.[2] comes to-morrow. Donald Mitch: came on Wed to tell me all about Berlin, very interesting. He had one or two good pts. to make, & I'll be writing to Stewy about one suggestest alteration (Hotel Guests). One major trouble is that Grobe[3] (& the rest) treated the recitatives like 'secco' and they were therefore v. boring (they made 12 cuts in them!). No one does them like you, can ever do them like you. When he'd gone I played some of the records to check these points, &, my God you do sing it wonderfully. Don't try & sing the Hymn too loudly; take time & sing it just fully & smoothly. I've fussed you stupidly about it: Asch. isn't a heroic Wagnerian tenor!! // We tried to get thro' to you this morning, but the internat. services were engaged. We'll try properly to-morrow. We've had Beth here these days, very good & nice – a bit on the rough side! And now Barb. for the week-end – I must <u>try</u> not to get cross! Rita sends lots of love. Rene,[4] giving me a smacking kiss, said – 'now one week has gone – he'll soon be home'. Hooray! XXXXOOOXX

---

1   Britten had been drafting a sequence and libretto for a Christmas opera for children, suggested by Kathleen Mitchell (b. 1916), schoolteacher and wife of Donald Mitchell. The work was not completed.
2   Leslie Brown (1912–99), Bishop of St Edmundsbury and Ipswich, the Church of England diocese that covers Suffolk.
3   Donald Grobe (1929–86), American tenor who sang Aschenbach in the German premiere of *Death in Venice* in Berlin.
4   Rene Whatling, one of the caretakers of the Horham house.

342 Britten to Pears

Peg & Rita
send loads of
love

<u>Wolfsgarten</u>

October 12th 1974.

My darling P, This will probably take weeks to get to you, & in the meantime I hope I'll have spoken several times to you, & you'll even have had premiéres & parties, but somehow I want to send my love & wishes in my awful old scrawl & say some of the things I ~~wa~~ always forget to say on the telephone. All goes well here. Every one (Heinz[1] especially) is kindness it-self. Peg wizzes in and out, people come & visit, sometimes R. [Rita] & I take part, sometimes we don't, but everyone understands. I ~~warh~~ work hard, still on this old libretto but I hope to get on to some music soon – possibly the Folk song suite.[2] The weather is fairly beastly – in fact v. wet & windy, & everyone has colds (I've had my first taste of one to-day (Sunday) which means I'm staying in bed, but R. looks after me hand & foot as you'd imagine). Heinz is sweet to me, & has seemed older & more assured since his affair with the physiotherapist across the way. Stephen Runciman[3] came last night & Rainier[4] to-night etc. etc etc. But my thoughts are west-ward, West 61st,[5] & if they & prayers can help & strengthen you ought to be 101%. I wonder if you've seen friends yet. The British contingent should be arriving now (14th) & I hope they help rather than hinder. I hope Bill[6] & Sue will get on after an incomprehensible letter she has written to Peg. O women, women! But <u>dont</u> get involved, my love. I shall be with you in soul & spirit on Friday,[7] hold my thumbs (& every bit of my anatomy tenable). I know you'll be your own wonderful Asch.

XXXOOXXX

---

1   Member of staff at Schloss Wolfsgarten.
2   *Suite on English Folk Tunes 'A time there was …'*, completed in November 1974.
3   Steven Runciman (1903–2000), historian and friend of the Hesses.
4   Probably Prince Rainer Christoph Friedrich of Hesse (b. 1939).
5   The address of Pears's hotel in New York.
6   Servaes (1921–99), General Manager of the Aldeburgh Festival.
7   18 October, the first night of *Death in Venice*.

343 Pears to Britten

[*Letterhead:* The Mayflower Hotel, New York]

12 Oct. Sat. [1974]

My old honey –

    It has been marvellous to talk to you and know that you are safe at Wolfsgarten with Peg & Rita there and all ready to look after you. and thank you for a letter before you left England. Things are going alright here, I think – up & down & the stage-lighting rehearsals are always a bit tiring. Stop – Stop – Stop & start & wait & stop etc etc. But Steuart is doing v. well with orchestra which is good and happy. Percussion getting better every day, really rhythmic and sure, and the bigger number of strings <u>is</u> better, sounds so much richer – Colin working v. hard, changing some labyrinth scenes for clarification, rightly, I think. Lighting going ahead; much better leaves in grave-yard scene. I can't really see it properly, as I am too near. However Myf [Piper] Donald & Kath [Mitchell] arrived last night & they will see rehearsals. I miss Bob Huguenin[1] <u>very</u> much. This boy Bryan[2] is a much better dancer; he is from Balanchine's Co. & as light as air, very fine movements, & the new dance is v. elegant & fine. But he has <u>not</u> got <u>IT</u> at all!! Oh dear! I <u>wouldn't</u> dream of looking at him for more than 5 seconds. A sweet chap and all that, 19 or 20 years old, blond from N. Carolina, but no Bob. I have written to Bob to tell him so, it might cheer him up a bit! Tadzio's mum is no Deanne!![3]

    Last night after a long day at the Met, Act II on stage, costume & make-up with orch., which went well, (lighting – timing complications, & the gondola not properly charged) I went with Betty Bean to Julian's concert at Town Hall packed with mostly young or youngish people – He played a new (to me) Dowland arr. of Walsingham.[4] beautiful. He was in medium to good form. Bach Chaconne[5] a bit too much for him in places. Looks rather plump & bald but still so much charm and dear artistry. They adore him. Saw him briefly after –

The trees in the park are yellowing and browning v. beautiful. Today cloudy but warm; it was 64° at midnight as Betty & I walked up 6th Avenue!

With this scribble comes all all all my love – but spare a little, if you will, for Peg and Rita and Wolfsgarten.   oxoxoP.

---

1 (b. 1953), danced the role of Tadzio in the original production of *Death in Venice* at Snape Maltings.
2 Pitts, from the New York City Ballet.
3 Bergsma (b. 1941), South African dancer who created the role of Tadzio's mother, 'The Lady of the Pearls', in the original production.
4 'Walsingham', a popular Renaissance air.
5 Possibly the Chaconne, transcribed for guitar from Bach's Violin Partita no. 2 in D minor.

344 Britten to Pears

[*Letterhead:* Wolfsgarten, 607 Langen, Hessen]

26.10.74

Darling P., This is not a real letter, ~~but~~ because I've been writing quite a lot to-day & the arm's abit stiff – but I wanted to put my visible love into Rita's m letter. <u>My</u> work (like yours!) is going rather well – the first 1½ pages of sketches are quite promising. I've heard a lovely lot of 1st hand news from our friends who are all slowly returning home —— long talks to-day with Bill [Servaes] & Myfanwy, & of course we had those lovely days with Kath [Mitchell]. I can't say how thrilled I am with all I'm told. It must have been exciting for you, my darling, to be received like that —— & I'm delighted that people seemed to rise to the old work: There is something in the P-B combination still! // Suddenly the weather is cooler, with even some sun (altho' rain of course from time to time) – & this afternoon Tittu (Peg is in Wexford) took us for a ravishing drive thro' the Odenwald: glorious autumnal trees. Marion's just rung up full of excitement because there are head lines in the Times 'PP.'s New York triumph.' She's a dear to tell me. I'm feeling better because work is going well, but it's quite a time to Dec. 20th! Hurry up, time! Hope concerts with J.B. & M.P.[1] go well like everything else ——

All love my honey, we'll talk soon, I hope   OXOXOOX B

---

1 Julian Bream and Murray Perahia (b. 1947), American pianist; both frequent accompanists to Pears.

345 Pears to Britten

The Mayflower

Monday 7am [28 Oct 1974]

My dearest old darling –

It is lovely to be able to talk to you – it is I think – bi-diurnally – or does that mean twice a day – and yesterday you sounded in good form and working well – lovely. Now the dawn is just over, with the sun coming up from behind the grey blocks and lighting the tops of the trees in the park – How I wish the sun had been shining on you – perhaps it did after all for a change. So sorry about that bloody rain. It must stop eventually.

Yesterday I went up to see Beata in West End Avenue. It was <u>terribly</u> nice. just as if we had left off a few days ago. and we talked & talked. She looks <u>very</u> like what she did. Not a grey hair in her head. The marriage with Wolfgang Sauerlander a total mistake, he's an alcoholic, & now back in Austria with his sister. Beate in a new flat in Manhattan working for the New Yorker & in very good form. She sent lots of love to you & we talked about the old times. Many fascinating things, Wystan, Elizabeth etc etc. We had lunch at the Met. Museum & walked back across the park, past the steel bands and the jugglers and the people who just want to play or sing to anyone who will hear him. This is an extraordinary city and I am rather fond of it

The evening before last I was fetched by Dick Vogt[1] for ~~he~~ a drink up at his (not far from Beata) just him & his room mate, and a bass singer[2] came in who had just ~~then~~ sung Arkel[3] at the NY State Opera (Lincoln Centre) for the first time, and had totally dried up in the last bars of the Opera. Talked a lot about it, very upset, for quite a bit. Then someone asked me something about D in V, & the bass was silent for a long time. As I was going a few minutes later, he started to apologise for talking! He hadn't realised he was in the presence of the great PP & was about to go down on his knees! He had been at the second performance & was knocked sideways.

On the way back from Beata yesterday, I stopped at a church a few blocks from here, & went in & listened to a Bach Cantata they were doing – with orch & chorus. Respectable clear singing, rather stiff conducting, "The Russian Father" was in the choir.

Tonight is No. 3. Death in Venice: sold out of course! I shall have to buy up some tickets for later on. Julian should arrive in NY today. I must start with him tomorrow.

Much much love to you, honey

I love you, I love you   Pox

¹ Richard Vogt (1930–95), American choral conductor. Pears often stayed with Vogt and his family while visiting the States.
² Ara Berberian (1930–2005), American bass.
³ King Arkel, a role in Debussy's *Pelléas et Mélisande*.

346 Britten to Pears

[***Letterhead:*** Wolfsgarten, 607 Langen, Hessen]

29.10.74

My honey, It was so lovely to talk to you. Sorry we rang so early, but it's difficult with rest hours & meals. Here are the 2 very nice bits about you. Don't forget that if you give all that there must be some perfs. slightly less terrific than others, & you may be sure that ~~most~~ there is a standard below which you <u>never</u> fall!

Peg is back & we had a nice drive with ~~the~~ her in spite of the rain & near – snow. Will this ~~wl~~ weather never stop? I had a word with Bill this morning, but nothing really to report, except that Reggie [Goodall] had a great reception at the Malting on Sunday. Good luck for the shows with Julian – give him lots of love & all to you – I've done a lot of work to-day & the hand won't do any more – sorry!

XXOXOXX   B.

347 Pears to Britten

[after 29 Oct 1974]

Dearest B.

I thought you might like to see this![1]

Two lovely concerts with Julian – a most extraordinary public.

Much love

P. ox

¹ Possibly Pears was enclosing a press review, but this has not remained with the letter in the archive.

348 Pears to Britten

711 West End Ave.

Wed. [written 13 Nov; postmark 29 Nov 1974]

Here I am, my darling honey, and I have just been talking to you from here for the first time – It is a very quiet flat, nicely done, comfortable bed, nice dog, and Dick [Vogt] is a dear quiet nice chap & so is his friend Tom who has an office here (he is the NY John McCarthy[1] choir fixer) but lives en famille 6 blocks away. More relaxed than the Mayflower in a way, fewer fires, murders etc, I think. A few blocks away from Beate of whom I have re-grown very fond. Musicians of all sorts quite near, Murray [Perahia] not too far. etc. Dick is out all day at his church, & I am having a few quiet days not doing much.

The concert with Murray on Monday[2] seems to have been well received – yes of course it was – dear youngish audience, v. enthusiastic, and after, Beate & Brigitte Steiner[3] & Murray & his Sophie & Vlado Habunek[4] came back to Betty's for a very nice cosy eat & drink! V. nice occasion. Murray now gone off to Cleveland for a concerto date. I know if no one else does & I think Murrays does, how many hundred miles away it was from the music-making of you and me. However Poet's Echo went well, perhaps better – yes certainly better – than the Haydn or Schumann – We make the 1st Song very free – pause after each crunchy chord before I take off – and a strong long dim. to ppp. Also No2 (my heart) much better now. The last also goes very well now I think. How difficult the Schumann are. And I was really full of frogs and cracks all the time. However the enclosed tells you what a press man thought, and another. I am not sure that I should send you them, in case they make you cry. – But don't forget each day is one day nearer December 22nd. I am still trying to decide which route to fly. Can I really face a 10 am. flight the morning after the last night arriving London 9 pm your time (?too late to drive down to A.)? or fly 10p.m. arriving 9a.m. & then drive to A in time for lunch? I must take advice.

V.V. much love, my honey
oxooxoP.

---

[1] 'Tom' unidentified, but Pears refers to John McCarthy (1919–2009), conductor of the Ambrosian Singers.
[2] The recital was at the Lincoln Center on 11 October.
[3] Brigitte Steiner (b. 1910), a German émigrée and friend of the Mayers.
[4] (1906–94), Croatian theatre and opera director.

349 Britten to Pears[1]

Sunday Nov 17th 1974

My darling heart (perhaps an unfortunate phrase – but I can't use any other) I feel I must write a squiggle which I couldn't say on the telephone without bursting into those silly tears – I do love you so terribly, & not only glorious you, but your singing. I've just listened to a re-broadcast of Winter Words (something like Sept. '72) and honestly you are the greatest artist that ever was – every nuance, subtle & never over-done – those great words, so sad & wise, painted for one, that heavenly sound you make, full but always coloured for words & music. What have I done to deserve such an artist and man to write for? I had to switch off before the folk songs because I couldn't anything after – "how long, how long". How long?[2] – only till Dec. 20th – I think I can just bear it

But I love you,

I love you,

I love you ——   B.

P.S. The Folk Song Suite ("Up she goes"?) is just finished – good I hope.

---

[1] See the plates section for a reproduction of this letter and its reply, Letter 351.
[2] A reference to the final song of *Winter Words*.

350 Pears to Britten

Monday [postmark 18 Nov 1974]

Dearest Ben –

One little thing of importance which I forgot to say on the phone this morning was that on Saturday (the Montauk Pt. non-day) I was taken to the Riverside (St. Rockefeller) Church for the Carillon Playing at noon (biggest carillon in the world – 76 bells), and was taken into the playing-room (Victor Parker[1] knew the Carilloneur) and – (nice – man) – he insisted on ending his recital with a transcription by himself on this giant carillon, 300 feet up at the top of the Tower, of BB's The Plough Boy![2]

Wasn't that lovely?

Much much love oxoxoxoP

I am going to see the Turn of the Screw on Sunday – The Rape of Lucretia comes two weeks later.

¹ (b. 1944), photographer – one of Pears's friends in New York.
² Folk-song arrangement.

351 Pears to Britten

[postmark 21 Nov 1974]

My dearest darling

No one has ever ever had a lovelier letter than the one which came from you today – You say things which turn my heart over with love and pride, and I love you for every single word you write. But you know, Love is blind – and what your dear eyes do not see is that it is <u>you</u> who have given <u>me</u> everything, right from the beginning, from yourself in Grand Rapids! through Grimes & Serenade & Michelangelo and Canticles – one thing after another, right up to this great Aschenbach – I am here as your mouthpiece and I live in your music – And I can never be thankful enough to you and to Fate for all the heavenly joy we have had together for 35 years.

My darling, I love you – P.

352 Britten to Pears

[*Letterhead:* BENJAMIN BRITTEN, The Red House, Aldeburgh]

[early Feb 1975]

My darling, I am so sorry that your temp. is up again – but you must try to be very patient.¹ Can you read? I am sure there'll be nice books around you. Or what about going on with that diary? —— don't be shy about saying what happened in N.Y. at the Met!

It is lovely that you are with the Ellis' – how glad I am you arn't stuck in a hotel – St Enoch's!

I hope that by some miracle you can get here & we can look after you! In the ~~ment~~ meantime just Love – love – love –

B.

¹ Pears developed a very high fever (his diary states 'FLU' from Sunday 2 February onwards) while staying with Osian Ellis in London – they had been preparing for a number of recitals which had to be cancelled. On 8 February he returned to Aldeburgh to rest.

353 Britten to Pears

[*Birthday card:* Beatrix Potter, Illustration for *The Tale of Jemima Puddle-duck*]

[?22 June 1975]

P.P.

With All Good Birthday *Wishes* & lots
of love —— for use at Horham.[1]

B.B.

---

[1] When first uncovered in the archive, this Beatrix Potter card was bent as if it had been wrapped around a wine or spirit bottle.

VIII

'My days are not empty'

JANUARY TO NOVEMBER 1976

In these final months of Britten's life, Pears continued to pursue his successful international career, performing and teaching. As well as the imperative to continue singing, an important motivation for his frequent overseas trips was fundraising and recruiting new students for the Britten–Pears School[1] they were working together to establish at Snape Maltings. The School was, in a real sense, their child, and would occupy Pears professionally for the remainder of his life.

In June the composer was made a life peer in the Queen's Birthday Honours list, becoming Baron Britten of Aldeburgh. Britten was reluctant, and disclosed to Rosamund Strode that he accepted the honour because 'he felt it was marvellous for music'.[2] There is a hint at Britten's discomfort over the peerage in Letter 355 from Pears, who feels the need to underline that he is 'proud and touched but in no way resentful or jealous' – the acceptance cannot have been a straightforward decision, given their shared left-wing principles, and Britten would certainly not have taken the decision alone.

Now mostly wheelchair-bound and wholly reliant on Rita Thomson, Britten was too frail to write himself, but in these final letters (356–65), Pears sends home a set of vivid and entertaining descriptions of his time in Los Angeles while giving masterclasses at the University of Southern California. Similar to the narrative diaries he kept on earlier trips, they relay impressions of people and places, effectively sharing his experiences with Britten. Unsurprisingly, both the intimacy and the rushed urgency of the correspondence from earlier years is gone, but the self-deprecating warmth and occasionally trivial, anecdotal tone persists. Pears worried the letters were 'silly', but Thomson writes to assure him that they are of great comfort: 'Your letters 2 and 4 arrived first but today 1 & 3 came so Ben had a lovely time reading the four of them. He reads me the amusing bits like when the handle came off the Gin carton!! They do cheer him up immensely and makes you feel so much nearer.'[3]

Pears journeyed on to Toronto from Los Angeles to perform and raise money for the Britten–Pears School and the Aldeburgh Festival. On 14 November, Thomson telephoned with the news of a rapid decline and he returned immediately, cancelling the remaining masterclasses and a scheduled performance of *Saint Nicolas* in Canada. Pears was certain of the support Britten was receiving from his carers at The Red House, including Thomson, his physician Ian Tait, cardiologist Michael Petch ('all the good people who are looking after you so devotedly' – see Letter 365), but his absence from Aldeburgh at this time would trouble him later (and left him open to criticism, of which he was very aware). He later reflected on his decision to be in America during such a critical stage, stating 'My regret is that I did not spend more time with him in those last months of his life.'[4] Britten's sixty-third birthday on 22 November was marked by a quiet drinks party where family and friends each visited him in his room to speak with him, knowing it would be the last time. In the early hours of Saturday 4 December, Susie Walton, the nurse on duty, called Pears and Thomson to Britten's side. The composer died in Pears's arms. In his diary for that day, Pears recorded the end of their life together, simply writing '4.15 am BB †.'

1   Now the Britten–Pears Young Artist Programme.
2   Quoted in Humphrey Carpenter, *Benjamin Britten: A Biography*, p. 580.
3   Rita Thomson to Peter Pears, 9 November 1976, unpublished letter, Britten–Pears Foundation Archive.
4   Pears, interviewed by Donald Mitchell in Tony Palmer's film, *A Time There Was …* (1980).

354 Pears to Britten

[*Letterhead:* The Pick-Congress, Chicago]

Tuesday early [27 Jan 1976]

Dearest B – Here I am, safe & fairly sound – A perfectly good flight 8 ½ hours in a ¼ full Jumbo – Met at the airport in a great Cadillac supplied by the Symphony Orchestra, driven very smoothly & quietly. How much quieter American traffic is! You can see where the oil goes here – This dotty v. American hotel, built about 1900, lots of carpet. I am on the top floor with a nice view over the trees onto the Lake (?Michigan) which is mostly frozen still. It was just over freezing when I arrived, then on Sunday which I spent wholly reacting to the jet-lag by doing nothing except a visit to see the pictures at the Art Institute, there was a small blizzard, strong wind, snow, and rather cold. Since then it is better, and at the moment it looks like being a lovely day.

Yesterday I had the first (piano) rehearsal with George[1] – It went quite well, he seemed pleased, but I was still a bit jet-laggy and the voice takes some time to adjust. My colleagues include Jo Veasey as my Jocasta and Gwynne Howells[2] as Creon, beautiful voice but not Stravinsky enough perhaps! George in good form and asked tenderly after you – I began on the Maltings, trying to lure him – I don't know, we'll see. I forgot what a strange colour he is, a sort of milk chocolate – He must have some Turkish blood in him – He is madly busy doing Sessions, it seems, even here. I couldn't quite follow.   Perhaps I misunderstood
                                                                   & was confused by
                                                                   Sessions and sessions!

Along with Oedipus they are doing a piece of Roger Sessions, setting of Walt Whitman "When the lilacs at the barndoor bloomed"[3] – Can't remember exactly. I shall hear a rehearsal today. I made two calls to members of A F of A F[4] and shall dine with them tonight and tomorrow. The University also contacted me – Then I gave an interview yesterday to a nice Tom Willis,[5] music critic of the Ch. Tribune. And so we go on! I do hope you are behaving yourself, honey; not worrying, not overdoing it, not getting depressed, not working too hard, not working too little, in fact leading a perfectly balanced emotional life! I think of you v. much. By the time this gets you, I will have spoken to you – <u>Much</u> <u>much</u> love, honey.

P.

---

[1] Georg Solti (1912–97), conductor of the Chicago Symphony Orchestra. Pears was singing the title role in Stravinsky's *Oedipus Rex* from 29 to 31 January.

[2] Josephine Veasey (b. 1930), mezzo-soprano; Gwynne Howell (b. 1938), Welsh bass.

[3] Sessions had set Whitman's *When Lilacs Last in the Dooryard Bloom'd*.

[4] American Friends of the Aldeburgh Festival.

5   (1928–2004), American journalist and musicologist. He gave Pears and the whole production a glowing review in the *Chicago Tribune* on 31 January 1976.

355 Pears to Britten

[7 Jul 1976]

My honey darling

I am writing this at the Airport while I wait to be Shuttled to Edinburgh[1] – and it is only & simply to say that I love you, I love you and I love you – and that in the middle of all those worries which you can't get rid off, don't – please don't – include one that in any possible way makes you think that I "mind" about the Lordship.[2] I am proud and touched but in <u>no</u> way resentful or jealous – I repeat over & over again – In no Way !

I should so love to think that you enjoyed some of the time in Norway, but I'm afraid you didn't, and can only just hope that in retrospect when you're back at dear Horham, they may not seem so painful & that some few things may appear rather lovely.

Oh, my honey –
       all my love
           P ox

---

1   Pears was to receive an honorary degree from the University of Edinburgh on 8 July.
2   Britten had accepted a life peerage in the Queen's Birthday Honours on 12 June.

356 Pears to Britten

[30 Oct 1976]

I.

My darling – Well here I am, 35000 ft up or thereabouts over Greenland – having been put down by Sue and Martin[1] at Departures two or three hours ago – and having gone through passport and customs quite serenely, with half a dozen Gordon's Gin in a cardboard carton of which the handle almost immediately came off in me hand, so I have to carry it over my shoulder or under my arm! The plane is a DC 10, i.e. Jumbo, and rather full. I have by me on my left a 50-year-old Lady going home to Los Angeles – her heavy accent and her fair broad face & high cheekbones make it clear that she is still Russian whatever passport she has. Reminds me a bit of Furtseva,[2] not such blue eyes. She has just been in Moscow, where the snow has come very early before the trees had turned – rather a dear – maybe in another nine or ten hours I shall get to know her better. <u>5:30pm.</u> We have now had tea-cold salmon, fruit salad & a piece of cake – but welcome as I had no lunch, & I am taking Sue's advice <u>not</u> to eat and drink too much & so arrive <u>bright</u> as a button. Now we are going to have a movie, a Hitchcook called Family Quarrel[3] or something & I shall pay £1.42 to hire a stethoscope-listener. I can see one brilliant great star to the right over the North Pole. Now I pull the blind down. Out it goes.

———

The film – a comedy thriller – was quite good in a dotty way, though the stethoscopes are v. uncomfortable! Then came dinner – predictable. And so we dragged on for 10 ¾ hours over icy and snowy landscapes, totally uninhabited, and having lost the sun earlier it suddenly reappeared in the west – We had turned south over Canada & caught it up.

We bumped down in L.A. with a big bang, shook everybody – And then baggage & passports & customs – I was found to lack an essential document & was kept ½ hour & allowed to go on condition I report on Monday – So here I am, after a sandwich & beer, in the Hilton Hotel ready to sleep, having been met & transported by nice Margaret Schaper, Head of Voice at USC.[4]

Love

Pxxx

1   Sue Phipps and her son, Martin (b. 1968).
2   Ekaterina Furtseva (1910–74), the Soviet Minister of Culture from 1962 to 1974.
3   *Family Plot* (premiered April 1976) was Alfred Hitchcock's final film.
4   Pears was in Los Angeles to give masterclasses at the University of Southern California.

357 Pears to Britten

[*Letterhead:* The University Hilton, Los Angeles]

Sunday morning [31 Oct 1976]

II.

Honey – I hope you have had a good night, and not quite such an extended one as mine – I went to bed after a sandwich & beer at about 11 pm (i.e. 6 AM Aldeburgh time) and slept till 7 A.M. – naturally – hoping to start making a cup of tea! – to find that the clocks here went back (or on?) an hour & it was 6 am. Later, at 8.30, I ordered a Continental Breakfast & it took well over an hour to come, brought by an apologetic smiling Mexican! My room is comfy, tho' not cosy, with a whole keyboard of hot & cold air, fans, switches. So I have turned them all off & opened the window. U.S.C. has presented me with a huge basket of fruit including a whole pineapple, most of a vineyard, part of an orange grove, as well as a very pretty bowl of flowers. Nice hosts! I am just across the Univ. from here, so transport for classes will be v. simple. Margaret S. [Schaper] gave me an envelope full of lists and songs and singers – Lovely American names like Pam Kuhn, Vanessa Vandergriff, Cathy Fiasca, and Daisietta Kim – also a baritone called Rusty Saylor![1] I can't wait! I just couldn't quite face going to Midsummer N's D. last night. I was told that musically it was good – orchestra and conductor especially so – but rather tiresome designs. By 9.45, when I arrived at the Hotel, Bed seemed more attractive than MSND, I fear. Sorry, B.

Later.

Today turned out to be very pleasant indeed. The weather of course is wonderful, lovely sun without being too boiling and not too much smog – Margaret Schaper invited me to hers for the day. She & her husband (their children are married & away) live in the most beautiful position you can imagine, high up in the mountain overlooking Pasadena – very nice house – with swimming pool on the edge of the hill & I must say that to sit there quietly sipping gin & tonic was a very restful way of defeating jet-lag. Nice husband who has links with Detroit (motor-cars?), decent simple people, grace before food, nice Californian wine, splendid steak grilled over charcoal, just not too big! (My teeth? OK!) Much talk of you, dear Ben, and waves of love and admiration were sent whizzing East. Most of my Singers this week have been singing in MSND – My hosts are very anti-Ford and will vote for Carter,[2] whose politics do seem much more civilised & liberal. But they think not more than 50% of the electorate will vote & that Ford will probably win, on account of the big business backing him! I do hope you are in good form. It was lovely to talk to you.

Give my love to Rita & lots to you P$_{ox}^{ox}$
$_{ox}$

---

1 Students enrolled in the vocal programme at the university.
2 The 1976 presidential race, pitting Gerald Ford, Republican, against Jimmy Carter, Democrat.

358 Pears to Britten

Tuesday A.M. [2 Nov 1976]

III

Dearest honey – I shall be ringing you before long & it will be lovely to talk to you – Rita is back now. I hope she has had a good time & is refreshed & that you were happy with Susie.[1] I wonder if you have gone to Horham yet.

Yesterday morning Margaret took me along to the Immigration office downtown, to get the form which I should have had before. She is very angry about the whole thing & is writing to her Senator! We found out from a boring but decent official that my bad mark comes from the American Embassy in Frankfurt!! How extraordinary. What <u>can</u> that mean? Next time I am in Wolfsgarten I must try and find out. I'll go to the US Embassy & ask, & try & clear my name!!

Last night was my first class – I heard about 8 singers of varying quality – only one of outstanding promise, but quite sweet things. The songs were yours, On This Island, Winterwords, Poet's Echo etc. (Two V.W. [Vaughan Williams] at the end, really awful). They are well informed, these kids, e.g. I was told that <u>Let the Florid Music</u>[2] originally started with a gliss. instead of an arpeggio. I had totally forgotten that. I suppose it is true. The best girl is doing Poet's Echo for a recital, & sang No. 2 (My heart ——) very beautifully after a word or two from me. I have got some quite interesting literature about this place. What a vast, rich country. & problems too – This city is <u>full</u> of Mexicans; before long, 80% of Californians will have Spanish names. And yet at night you can hear the coyotés ——! So near the desert.

The students were all a bit exhausted after having worked very hard on 4 performances of MSND – & last night I had Helena & Hermia & Lysander & Bottom & Snug. Quite well cast, I should judge, & mad keen about their parts. I was asked why we had changed Shakespeare – 'odious' 'odorous' – I couldn't remember if we had, nor if so, why! Oh dear!

The weather yesterday was fabulous (so is today) & somewhere up in the 80° F. But very dry and therefore not exhausting. I am slowly getting adjusted to jet lag and woke up at 4.30 this morning – nearly normal. Are we in the tropics here? Dawn seems to be about 5.30, and dusk nearly the same.

Well, dear Ben, I think of you so often & you are constantly talked about & loved & admired. Your ears must be boiling! How's work?

v.v. much love to you & to Rita.   oxoxPP

---

[1]   Susie Walton, a retired ward matron who acted as relief nurse for Rita Thomson in caring for Britten.

[2]   'Let the Florid Music Praise!', the first song from *On this Island*. The composition draft shows the piano part did originally began with a glissando.

359 Pears to Britten

[*Letterhead:* The University Hilton, Los Angeles]

Wednesday [3 Nov 1976]

IV

Honey BB – I have done my second class, got rather cross, and Carter is president – I don't know which of these events is the most important! Actually the best part of yesterday was a visit to the fabulous Huntington Art Gallery & Library. The Blue Boy looked very well, I had forgotten how country-tanned his cheeks are, really sunny – and he still hasn't done up all his buttons – Next to him is a wonderful portrait by T. G. of Lord Ligonier & his horse, very strong & manly & cool brown colours; & opposite of course is Abel & his gamba![1] I was taken to the Library & have bought a catalogue. They have a wonderful music Collection, Lutenist Books, Madrigals etc. & lots of Songs. Very enviable. I left a Leaflet of ours, & hopefully am going back to do some browsing there, later on this week. The Gardens there are glorious & superbly kept up. It was 95° F. but so dry that one didn't notice. The whole thing (free entrance, helpful civil librarians etc., kindly information) was typical of the prettiest face of American Capitalism. One is charmed. Blake, Turners, Salisbury Cathedral, half of England's heritage!!

I got rather cross in my class because a stupid tenor had chosen a terrible Beethoven song with a v. hard piano part, & hadn't seen his accompanist till that afternoon. She was hard loud & brittle; also unmusical & stubborn. The piano is a perfectly ghastly Baldwin which everyone hates, & the combination of Beethoven & Baldwin & a Tenor & a Loud Brittle girl was too much, and I shouted and cursed. Bad form but rather salutary! The adrenaline flowed & I felt better. No special voices this time – the Demetrius sang strongly but dully & the Tytania sang Strauss 'Ständchen Mach auf mach auf'[2] – ever so coy – and a <u>girl</u> who did <u>Puck</u>! sang some guitar songs by Thea Mus.[3] Not up to much really, in spite of discernible influence of Yr. L^dship.

At 5 o'clock I went for a Radio Interview with a station on the Campus & talked a lot of stuff about the Maltings, & the Los Angeles "germ" of P. Grimes, & you & me etcetera. And I have promised to have breakfast on Friday with a man who is writing a book about Edith S![4] So my days are not empty.

Things one notices about US, and L.A in particular. The coffee is <u>so weak</u> you can't taste it & you have to take cream & sugar. Oh! for Mrs. Cooper's.[5] The traffic is <u>very</u> polite. Pedestrians are holy, & if you run down a pedestrian you are hung, drawn, quartered, exiled and never allowed to drive a car again. Everyone is instructed in driving in school & must pass an exam – a very good idea. The Univ. is just across the road, but I am getting into the habit of waiting to be picked up & driven 180 yards to a parking place. Crazy!

Very very much love, my dear old thing, from yr. old friend PP

¹   All portraits by Gainsborough.
²   From Strauss's Sechs Lieder, op. 17.
³   *Five Love Songs* by Thea Musgrave.
⁴   Edith Sitwell (1887–1964), poet whom Britten set in *Canticle III: Still Falls the Rain*, and in his final (unfinished) work, *Praise We Great Men*.
⁵   Ludmilla Cooper, Austrian-born cook and housekeeper at The Red House.

360 Pears to Britten

University Hilton Hotel

Thursday AM [4 Nov 1976]

V

Honey – I shall be talking to you in a few minutes probably, which will be nice – and meantime I am sitting on a small terrace of the hotel in the baking sun – somewhere up in the 90°s but always dry and really very agreeable. I have just rung Christopher [Isherwood] and I am going to dine with them tonight. I have my class (No. 4) at 3.30 this afternoon.

Yesterday's chief novelty was a broadcast interview over lunch (and a very good lunch too) at the big new Music Centre here, very splendid & grandly glossy. The Radio Station which specializes in Classical Music puts on a "personalized" lunch, & Neville Marriner¹ came along and we talked to the interviewer (Martin Workman,² v. ordinary) about you & Les Illum. & Albert Herring and so on. How I bask in the shadow cast by you and enjoy it! I am no longer quite sure if what I am telling is truth or invention. It doesn't matter very much anyway, does it?

My class to-day yesterday was rather good. They are getting used to me and I to them. A little Chinese girl is going to sing Les Illum. & I worked with her. Bright & clever. Also some Debussy and Poulenc. How decadent the early-ish lush Debussy is! Those Baudelaire songs and the Proses Lyriques – I really rather hate them.³ yet of course for Americans who start from an operatic approach they are at home & they can let fly a bit. (It is too hot. I am going upstairs!) I have just rung you and I do hope you are looking after your self and keeping warm How I wish you could have a little of this sun, but not too much. This hotel is fairly dreary, tho' convenient for classes, & on Saturday evening I shall go & stay at huge villa in Beverly Hills belonging to a music loving millionaire where Neville stays.. Everything is there, pools, pianos, music rooms, gardens. Better than this!

Much much love, dear heart   Poxox

¹   (b. 1924), conductor and Music Director of the Los Angeles Chamber Orchestra.

361 Pears to Britten

VI

University Hylton Hotel.

Friday [5 Nov 1976]

Honey, It was lovely to talk to you yesterday & know that you were at Horham. How I wish I were there with you. Good that you have some sun. There is plenty here to spare – Apparently at this time it is very rare to have it <u>quite</u> so hot. Still up in the 90s!

My classes go on nicely – Each one is better (from me and, I think, from them). Rusty Saylor has turned out to be a very sweet chap – a graduate of something else who wants to sing and actually has very good potential high baritone, but really musical, I think, and a pleasant rather tough personality. Rusty is short for something, & often means redheaded which he is not really – There's a promising lively Soprano (Wendy Zaro)[1] and indeed the actual standard of vocal material is high as it so often is in the States. And I am looked after very well.

Last night I had dinner with Christopher I. and his Don.[2] which was very nice. They are dear people, inquired much after you and sent you lots of loving messages – (Unfortunately I ate something or other, a hot sauce to a salad, I think, which has "stayed" with me since rather too much – I am sucking "Tums"!) They welcome Carter on the whole, but are very sad to have lost a good Governor of Calif., son of Gene Tunney (boxer, remember?) and instead they have a Tory Japanese ~~instead~~.[3] Christopher has written a book about the Thirties, but has "left out all the names".[4] Don wants to do a drawing of me! So if there is time ⸻ ! I am slightly nervous as he is very exact – All my wrinkles and chins?!

Very very much love to you, dear B. I must go & have a salad before my class!

Bathsheba has sent that Valentine to Boldewood! Oh dear … poor Gabriel Oak![5]

PoxPoxo

---

1   Wendy Zaro-Mullins, who went on to teach at the University of Minnesota.
2   Don Bachardy (b. 1934), a portrait artist, and Isherwood's partner from 1953 until the writer's death in 1986.
3   Samuel I. Hayakawa, Republican, narrowly defeated John V. Tunney, Democrat, for one of California's senate seats.
4   *Christopher and His Kind, 1929–1939*, published in 1976.
5   Pears was evidently reading Thomas Hardy's *Far from the Madding Crowd*.

362 Pears to Britten

<u>Univ-H. Hotel</u>

[6 Nov 1976]

NO VII (?)

<u>Saturday</u>

Lovely to talk to you, honey, but I am sorry you are to stay in bed for a week, except that maybe you are more comfortable and easy, and save energy a bit. Keep warm. Have lots of honey. & yoghurt. I'm sure that's good.

Yesterday started with a breakfast with a girl who is dramatising the life of Edith Sitwell! She & her chum wanted to pick my brains, but I really couldn't help her much, and as always with Americans, she was much better informed than I. I told her a certain amount about thumping old Edith on the shoulder to keep her in time in Façade![1] My Façade is v. popular, it seems.

Then I had my class which went well & I told them all about the Pushkin Songs & our Armenian Holiday etc.[2] Very sweet kids. very keen and appreciative.

After that, a very nice old Canadian accompanying professor threw a party in her house up in Hollywood – very sweet occasion but it tooks hours to get there. We drove & we drove & we drove! This is an absurd city – so enormous, and getting from one part to another is a day's journey. After the party, Margaret Schaper (a v. nice woman) drove me and Michael Sells (tenor & teacher who came to the Festival this year) up to her house among the Coyotés and owls, and we had an omelette, and talked and talked about you and your music – They are both passionate devotees & worship you. Michael got me to hear him, & he is good & v. musical – "Winter words" v. well done. He has sung <u>every</u> thing of yours except perhaps "O that I'd ne'er been married".[3]

I am sorry that my first letter failed to arrive. I hope it will. Not that there is really very much news, other than just going on, and counting the days till I am back!

Very much love to you my dear dear darling –

oxoxP.

---

[1] Work by William Walton, written to poems by Sitwell.

[2] Britten's song cycle *The Poet's Echo* and the August 1965 trip taken in the company of its dedicatees, Rostropovich and Vishnevskaya.

[3] Michael Sells recorded a number of Britten's works, and went on to teach music at Butler University. *O that I had ne'er been married* was not published until after Britten's death.

363 Pears to Britten

VIII (I think!)

[*Letterhead:* The Red House, Aldeburgh-on-Sea, Suffolk]

<u>Los Angeles.</u>

Sunday. [7 Nov 1976]

Honey, are you getting bored with my Silly letters? I wouldn't blame you. So just tear them up & don't bother! Yesterday started with going up and spending the morning at the Huntington Library. I was trying to get copies of as many ~~copies~~ songs as I could of "songs sung by Mr. Beard".[1] & they have a lot there – a lot of other things too, just about all the Madrigals and Lute-songs and endless 18th Century Stuff – all magnificently catalogued, and serviced by gentle Yankee spinsters – We had lunch there too in the superb gardens. Then came my last class which was good; everyone very sorry it's over – except me! The enthusiasm and keenness has been very endearing – In the evening Christopher came & collected me, & drove down to his place where Don cooked. There were also David Hockney & his engraver chum.[2] He is a very nice direct open unspoilt person, and we had a v. nice evening, although the pork chops were so tough that I <u>did</u> think I had lost a tooth! But it survived – When I got back to my Hotel I found eventually a message inviting me to Mr. Colbourn's[3] mansion in Beverley Hills for Sunday & Monday nights. So I shall be <u>very</u> quiet and <u>very</u> luxurious for the next 48 hours, which is rather a pleasant change after the endless music in every corridor and elevator in all the public rooms of the Hilton!

Very very much love. I shall be ringing tomorrow.

oxoxPP

---

[1] Collection of songs by Thomas Arne.
[2] The painter David Hockney (b. 1937) with Maurice Payne, who printed many of Hockney's etchings.
[3] Richard D. Colburn (1911–2004), amateur violist and benefactor of music in Los Angeles.

364 Pears to Britten

IX

p.m. <u>Monday</u> [8 Nov 1976]

Honey, here I am living (only for 36 hours) in a super millionaire establishment, built by a Mr Richard Colbourn who is away & I haven't met – His wife, very much younger, is a nice bright American personette who reigns over this little kingdom very sweetly. It consists of three sizable houses (Tuscan style) linked by a large swimming pool (much too hot) and a grass courtyard

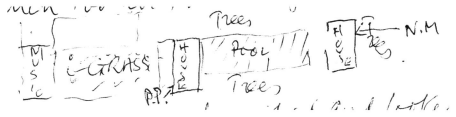

Very handsomely furnished and looked after – with two Chinese servants, very difficult to understand, not a consonant among them – An enormous Music room, with a HUGE fireplace which belonged to Randolph Hearst,[1] two Steinway concert grands, harpsichord, and a collection of Strads. He is mad about music, & the notes I heard were a broadcast LA performance of Cantata Academica![2] Neville Marriner lives in a large house (not <u>many</u> rooms but v. <u>big</u> ones) & I in another smaller. Norma Shearer[3] lives next door one side, and to the North is Darryl F. Zannuck![4] All very wild but quiet & undisturbed & let's face it, quite comfy! One meal produced some super Chinese food, lunch today was tender steak, & my teeth stayed in.

We had a good rehearsal today, and yesterday, & Neville is very adequate, players good & with any luck it should be a good perf –

Did I mention in VIII my afternoon by the Ocean at Malibou Beach? A very pleasant Restaurant on a pier like Brighton only smaller & of course endless young things bathing, & one can see that the Sun is j. nice & beautifies. There is a very sweet efficient girl who manages the Chamber Orchestra – fearless, energetic, who has driven me miles here & there in L.A. <u>Someone</u> has to. You couldn't walk these distances!

Much much love for now.

will write again tomorrow   PoxPox

---

[1] (1863–1951), American newspaper magnate.

²   Britten's choral work.
³   (1902–83), film actress.
⁴   Darryl F. Zanuck (1902–79), film producer.

365 Pears to Britten

NO X, I think.

<u>In the Train on the way to Kingston</u>[1]

Nov. 11th Thurs.? [1976]

Honey, It was lovely to hear your voice clear and strong this morning. I had been worried yesterday – It is good that Janet was so helpful and I hope Mike will find some new treatment which will relieve your breathlessness a bit.[2] I am thinking of you all the time and transmitting waves of love and strength all day and night, probably confusing all the TV sets in Toronto. And there are plenty of them! The set in the Suttons' house has 15 different TV stations obtainable, only one of which is non-commercial!

The Suttons are v. sweet kind people. He works in a big Oil firm & goes to work at 8 a.m each morning. Very gentle, quiet, unobtrusive, sensitive. She is firm Parisian, efficient, but most sympathetic. They are good friends of JSQ and he lent them Amelia di Liverpool[3] soon after we had it, and we swapped stories about the horrors of Banbury Lock! They had just the same sort of agony that we had there. They have three sons (one away at University 20-years old) two at home seventeen and thirteen, nice quiet and non-American. Their house is built round a courtyard on ground floor only, each room running into the next, rather nice.

The weather is crisp and cold (27° F.), some light snow which has disappeared – a rather violent change from L.A. but more seasonal and normal. The flight from L.A. was superb, over long stretches of barren mountain, & certainly v. Rocky. What a vast country & so much barren. The Canadians like one to know that tho' their country <u>is</u> vast & empty, most of it is barren rock or simply ice covered with snow. They can't feed too many people. True, I suppose.

Last night was a party in my honour at the Br. Consul-General. V. good food, I ate too much! Lots of people whom one had met once twenty years ago. Boyd Neel of course, & names like Godfrey Ridout, John Beckwith, Nick Goldschmidt[4] (of course). Well disposed people to Can. Friends. The Suttons have done well, raising money. We must publicize Benson & Hedges more. People are impressed by them backing us.

In Los Angeles I had been fidgetting & nervous about settling US tax matters and getting a Sailing Permit, having visions of being held until it was all OKayd by

Washington. But I had forgotten that they are perfectly happy to let you <u>go</u> – no difficulty there – it's just entry which is so troublessome –

Canadian entry no difficulty at all! Sweet customs lady – "B.E. is British Empire, I guess, but what does C. stand for?"

Had two Press interviews yesterday. Nice young man John Fraser who was at East Anglia & a Hesse Student, intelligent. The other a Prof. at the University, painless. Outskirts of Toronto just like Mosow, huge blocks standing up looking in different directions in the middle of deserted prairies. It turns into a new University, grey and square.

Sorry about my writing but the train is not perfectly smooth.

Much much love to you dear honey and to Rita and all the good people who are looking after you so devotedly so that I can come back quite soon now and see you sparkling & welcoming.

Your one & only PoxPox

---

1   Pears had travelled on to Canada, where he was staying with Francoise Sutton and her family in Toronto. He was performing with Osian Ellis in Kingston in the evening of 11 November.

2   Janet Tait, Aldeburgh GP (married to Britten's doctor, Ian Tait); Michael Petch (b. 1941), Britten's cardiologist from the National Heart Hospital.

3   A narrow boat belonging to the baritone John Shirley-Quirk (1931–2014) on which Britten and Pears holidayed in 1975. The Liverpool-born singer named the boat after his mother, Amelia, and was also making a play on the name of Donizetti's opera *Emilia di Liverpool*.

4   Canadian composers Godfrey Ridout (1918–84) and John Beckwith (b. 1927), and conductor Nicholas Goldschmidt (1908–2004).

Personalia

First Names and Nicknames

Anne WOOD
Arthur OLDHAM
Aurèle NICOLET
Barbara BRITTEN (often Barbara and Helen)
Barbara PARKER
Basil COLEMAN
Basil DOUGLAS
Beate – Beata MAYER
Bertus van LIER
Beth BRITTEN (later Welford)
Betty BEAN
Boyd NEEL
Christopher ISHERWOOD
Clifford CURZON
Clytie MUNDY
'Clytie' the dachshund
Colin GRAHAM
David WEBSTER
Dennis BRAIN
Dieter – Dietrich FISCHER-DIESKAU
Donald MITCHELL (often Donald and Kath)
Eddy SACKVILLE-WEST
Elisabeth – Elizabeth MAYER
Elizabeth SWEETING
Emmie TILLETT (née BASS)
Enid SLATER
Eric CROZIER
Erwin STEIN
Esther NEVILLE-SMITH
Ethel or 'Eth.' BRIDGE
Fidel – Fidelity CRANBROOK
George Lascelles, Earl of HAREWOOD
George MALCOLM

'Gilda' the dachshund
Gustaf FINEMAN
Hans LUDWIG
Helen HURST (often Barbara and Helen)
Humps – Humphrey MAUD
Imo – Imogen HOLST
Iris HOLLAND ROGERS
Isador CAPLAN
Jeremy CULLUM
Jetty BOSMANS
Jimmie – James LAWRIE
Joan CROSS
John (sometimes Johnnie) AMIS
John (sometimes Johnnie) CRANKO
John PIPER
'Jove' the dachshund
Julian BREAM
Karl RANKL
Kath – Kathleen FERRIER
Kit WELFORD
'KWHS' – Wulff SCHERCHEN
Lennox BERKELEY
Lesley (sometimes 'Leslie') DUFF
Leslie PERITON
Lu – Prince Ludwig of HESSE
Lucie (sometimes Lucy) MANÉN
Mabel (sometimes Mable) – Margaret RITCHIE
Margot BAKER
Maria CURCIO (often Maria and Peter or the Diamands)
Marion STEIN (later Harewood then Thorpe)
Mary BEHREND (often Mary and John)
Mary POTTER
Michael MAYER
Michael TIPPETT
Montagu SLATER
Morgan – E.M. FORSTER
Myfanwy PIPER
Nancy EVANS
Peg – Princess Margaret of HESSE
Peter COX
Peter DIAMAND (often Maria and Peter or the Diamands)
Piers DUNKERLEY
'PNLP' – Peter PEARS
Ralph HAWKES
Rita THOMSON

Robert BRITTEN
Roger DUNCAN
Roguey – Rosemary WELFORD
Ronnie – Ronald DUNCAN
Rosamund (sometimes 'Ros.') STRODE
Sally WELFORD
Sebastian WELFORD
Sofie – Sophie STEIN
Sophy – Sophie WYSS
Stephen REISS
Steuart (sometimes 'Stewy') BEDFORD
Sue – Susan Pears PHIPPS
Tony – Anthony GISHFORD
Tony – Tyrone GUTHRIE
Ursula NETTLESHIP
William MAYER
William PLOMER
Wulff SCHERCHEN
Wystan – W.H. AUDEN
Yehudi MENUHIN

Personalia

This Personalia is a list of the friends, family and associates of Britten and Pears who appear most often in the letters. We have included people who are referred to multiple times in the letters of more than one chapter.

Letter numbers are given rather than page references, and the brief descriptions are centred on how the person relates to Britten and Pears.

For a full list which encompasses the editorial notes, please consult the Index.

AMIS, John (1922–2013)
Broadcaster and music critic; married for a time to violinist Olive Zorian (1916–65).
Letters 52, 53, 219, 248

ANSERMET, Ernest (1883–1969)
Swiss conductor; conducted first performances of *The Rape of Lucretia* and *Cantata Misericordium*.
Letters 191, 235, 245, 246, 252, 289

AUDEN, W.H. [Wystan] (1907–73)
Poet; collaborated with Britten in 1930s–early 1940s. Provided texts for *Hymn to St Cecilia*, *Cabaret Songs*, *On This Island*, *Our Hunting Fathers*, the GPO films *Night Mail*, *Coal Face* and *The Way to the Sea*, as well as a number of unrealised projects. Long associated with writer Christopher Isherwood, with whom he famously travelled to America in 1939, just before

the outbreak of war in Europe. He later lived with the poet Chester Kallman (1921–75) in New York.   Letters 2, 6, 12, 33, 66, 69, 96, 97, 156, 225, 228, 231, 345

BAKER, Margot
Friend of Pears's parents, Arthur and Jessie Pears.   Letters 9, 12, 16, 17, 18

BASS, Emmie – see TILLETT, Emmie

BEAN, Betty Randolph (1917–2002)
American publisher; Director at Boosey & Hawkes New York office. Travelled with Britten and Pears during their 1949 recital tour of the US.
                                          Letters 91, 93, 98, 109, 306, 307, 308, 311, 340, 343, 348

BEDFORD, Lesley – see DUFF, Lesley

BEDFORD, Steuart ['Stewy'] (b. 1939)
Conductor and pianist; assistant to Britten in 1970s. Conducted the first production of *Death in Venice*, including the premiere at the Aldeburgh Festival at Snape (1973) and at the Metropolitan Opera in New York (1974). Also conducted the first performances of *Phaedra* and the *Suite on English Folk Tunes 'A Time There Was …'*.   Letters 99, 340, 341, 343

BEHREND, Mary (1883–1977)
Arts patron, along with her husband, John 'Bow' Behrend. Their son, George, was employed as a driver by Britten and Pears. Dedicatee of String Quartet no. 2.
                                                                    Letters 48, 126, 128, 260

BEINUM, Eduard van (1901–59)
Dutch conductor. Closely associated with the Holland Festival, where he conducted the premiere of the *Spring Symphony*.   Letters 84, 86, 88, 125, 135, 158, 159, 164, 234

BERKELEY, Lennox (1903–89)
Composer; lived at the Old Mill at Snape, shared some of the time with Britten, 1938–44. Composed *Mont Juic*, a suite of Catalan dances, with Britten in 1937, in memory of Peter Burra (1909–37), a mutual friend of both composers and Pears. Dedicatee of the Piano Concerto.   Letters 2, 4, 7, 19, 40, 65, 66, 175, 216, 274, 278

BOSMANS, Henriette ['Jetty'] (1895–1952)
Dutch pianist and composer.   Letters 86, 89, 92, 109, 117, 125, 134, 135, 164

BRAIN, Dennis (1921–57)
Horn player, for whom Britten wrote the horn parts in *Serenade for Tenor, Horn and Strings* and *Canticle III: Still Falls the Rain*.   Letters 19, 68, 173, 192

BREAM, Julian (b. 1933)
Guitarist and lutenist; frequently accompanied Peter Pears. Gave the premieres of *Songs from the Chinese*, with Pears, and the *Nocturnal after John Dowland*, of which he was the dedicatee.

He would advise Britten on the mechanics of the instrument and edit performing versions of the scores.   Letters 208, 209, 211, 212, 213, 214, 215, 219, 225, 227, 228, 229, 230, 231, 232, 233, 234, 235, 236, 237, 248, 250, 251, 255, 256, 257, 258, 260, 262, 268, 276, 279, 281, 282, 288, 291, 303, 305, 306, 311, 343, 344, 345, 346, 347

BRIDGE, Ethel (1881–1960)
Violinist; married to composer Frank Bridge (1879–1941), Britten's teacher and mentor.
Letters 2, 18, 25, 26, 27, 28

BRITTEN, Barbara (1902–82)
Britten's eldest sister; worked as a nurse and health visitor.
Letters 17, 19, 30, 40, 46, 47, 55, 56, 58, 65, 70, 72, 76, 95, 99, 113, 114, 117, 128, 137, 175, 208, 288, 341

BRITTEN, Charlotte Elizabeth [Beth] (1909–89)
Britten's second older sister; married to Kit Welford (1911–73), a GP, with whom she had son, Sebastian, and daughters Sally and Rosemary [Roguey].
Letters 18, 35, 37, 43, 46, 48, 56, 58, 65, 70, 77, 79, 85, 89, 99, 101, 103, 105, 112, 113, 114, 121, 187, 210, 296, 297, 301, 341

BRITTEN, Robert (1907–87)
Britten's older brother; a teacher, married to Margery, father to John and Alan. Dedicatee of *Friday Afternoons*, written for his pupils to sing.   Letters 33, 113, 114

CAPLAN, Isador (1912–95)
Legal advisor to Britten and Pears. Joint dedicatee, with his wife, Joan, of *Owen Wingrave*.
Letters 92, 101, 109, 212, 231, 232, 315

'CLYTIE' the dachshund (1954–67)
The first dog acquired by the Britten–Pears household, from a litter bred by John Cranko. Mother of Jove. Her name (short for 'Clytemnestra') was typical of John Cranko's dogs, who all had classical names, and must also have been a tribute to Pears's teacher, Clytie Mundy.
Letters 192, 194, 196, 198, 201, 206, 209, 215, 220, 226, 227, 228, 231, 232, 242, 253, 256, 277, 279, 282

COLEMAN, Basil (1916–2013)
Producer and Director with the English Opera Group and the BBC; worked on *Billy Budd*, *Gloriana*, *The Turn of the Screw* and *Let's Make an Opera*.
Letters 146, 163, 184, 186, 215, 227, 230, 231, 232, 233, 238, 287, 290, 291, 302

COX, Peter
Took over as Administrator at Dartington College following the death of Christopher Martin in 1944. Later became first Principal of the College.
Letters 70, 71, 147, 148, 151, 152, 219

CRANBROOK, Fidelity, Lady [Fidel] (1912–2009)
Chairman of Aldeburgh Festival 1948–81; Countess of Cranbrook, married to Jock – John Gathorne-Hardy, 4th Earl of Cranbrook; their children were the dedicatees of *The Little Sweep*.   Letters 85, 101, 103, 114, 151, 180, 196, 199, 232, 238, 297

CRANKO, John (1927–73)
Choreographer, worked with Britten on *Gloriana* and *Prince of the Pagodas*, and as producer of *A Midsummer Night's Dream*; kept and bred dachshunds, providing Britten and Pears with their first, 'Clytie'.   Letters 186, 196, 199, 201, 238, 244, 247, 248

CROSS, Joan (1900–93)
Soprano who became Director of the Sadler's Wells Opera during the war, then a founder member of the English Opera Group as artist and producer; sang in first performances of *Peter Grimes* (as Ellen), *The Rape of Lucretia* (Female Chorus), *Albert Herring* (Lady Billows), *The Turn of the Screw* (Mrs Grose) and Elizabeth I in *Gloriana*. Dedicatee of Vol. 3 of the folk-song arrangements, including *O Waly Waly*, *The Foggy, Foggy Dew*, *The Plough Boy* and *Sweet Polly Oliver*.
          Letters 26, 35, 42, 43, 52, 56, 57, 60, 66, 71, 72, 75, 76, 77, 110, 115, 117, 130, 141, 146, 159

CROZIER, Eric (1914–94)
Writer and director; co-founder of the English Opera Group and Aldeburgh Festival; librettist for *Albert Herring*, *Billy Budd* (with E.M. Forster), *Saint Nicolas* and *Let's Make an Opera*; directed premieres of *Peter Grimes* and *The Rape of Lucretia*. Married to singer Nancy Evans.   Letters 62, 66, 70, 71, 79, 80, 81, 82, 99, 103, 113, 114, 122, 128, 143, 145, 248

CULLUM, Jeremy (1931–99)
Secretarial assistant and chauffeur to Britten and Pears.
               Letters 182, 185, 196, 199, 202, 206, 207, 208, 209, 210, 212, 214, 231, 232, 236,
               244, 253, 255, 256, 257, 262, 277, 278, 279, 282, 284, 287, 290, 297, 310

CURCIO, Maria (1918–2009)
Italian pianist and teacher; married to Peter Diamand.
               Letters 86, 87, 88, 94, 97, 100, 102, 124, 125, 138, 140, 163, 164, 190, 211, 215

CURZON, Clifford (1907–82)
Pianist; performed with Britten in piano works for four hands. Married to harpsichordist Lucille Wallace (1898–1977).   Letters 40, 45, 62, 70, 94, 100, 265

DIAMAND, Peter (1913–98)
Austrian arts administrator; Director of Edinburgh and Holland Festivals; married to pianist Maria Curcio.   Letters 83, 86, 87, 88, 94, 97, 100, 102, 107, 108, 114, 124, 125, 134, 135,
               138, 140, 157, 159, 163, 164, 190, 191, 195, 211, 215, 234, 256

DOUGLAS, Basil (1914–92)
Music administrator and agent. Worked for the BBC music department from 1936 to 1951, and was General Manager of the EOG from 1951 to 1957.
Letters 4, 13, 14, 17, 18, 85, 101, 139, 140, 146, 157, 184, 186

DUFF, Lesley (1907–87)
Soprano; sang with the English Opera Group, including in the premiere of *Albert Herring* (as Emmie). Mother of Steuart and David Bedford.   Letters 80, 89, 96, 98, 99, 106, 135, 137

DUNCAN, Roger (b. 1943)
Son of Ronald and Rose Marie Duncan. Dedicatee, with the Welford children, of *Noye's Fludde*.   Letters 192, 193, 194, 210, 212, 228, 232, 238, 240, 247, 261, 262

DUNCAN, Ronald [Ronnie] (1914–82)
Poet and dramatist; librettist for *The Rape of Lucretia*.   Letters 56, 72, 76, 193, 228, 232

DUNKERLEY, Piers (1921–59)
Friend of Britten who had also attended South Lodge School. Wounded and taken prisoner during the war, he was one of the dedicatees of the *War Requiem*, written after his death.
Letters 5, 55, 157, 158

EVANS, Nancy (1915–2000)
Mezzo-soprano; sang with the English Opera Group, including the premieres of *Albert Herring* (as Nancy) and Britten's version of *The Beggar's Opera* (as Polly), and alternating with Kathleen Ferrier in the title role for the first production of *The Rape of Lucretia*. Co-Director of the singing faculty of the Britten–Pears School at Snape Maltings. Married to the writer Eric Crozier.   Letters 81, 82, 89, 113, 114, 124, 125, 143, 145, 175

FERRIER, Kathleen (1912–53)
Contralto; sang in the premieres of *The Rape of Lucretia* (as Lucretia) and of *Canticle II: Abraham and Isaac*, of which she was the dedicatee (jointly with Pears).
Letters 50, 79, 82, 103, 140, 158, 159, 165, 166, 170, 181, 190, 291

FINEMAN, Gustaf
German concerts agent who acted for Pears.   Letters 164, 210, 211, 220, 251, 281

FISCHER-DIESKAU, Dietrich [Dieter] (1925–2012)
German baritone for whom Britten wrote *Songs and Proverbs of William Blake* and the solo baritone role in the *War Requiem*, both of which he premiered.
Letters 196, 197, 198, 201, 203, 281, 310

FORSTER, E.M. [Morgan] (1879–1970)
Writer; librettist for *Billy Budd* (with Eric Crozier); gave public lectures in the early years of the Aldeburgh Festival. Dedicatee of *Albert Herring*.
Letters 99, 106, 114, 121, 122, 132, 133, 134, 135, 145,
147, 151, 154, 170, 228, 231, 248, 261, 262

'GILDA' the dachshund (1965–80)
The third Britten–Pears dachshund, Gilda was given as a puppy to Britten as a gift from
Pears. When Miss Hudson retired as housekeeper, Gilda moved with her into 'Cosy Nook',
the cottage in the grounds of The Red House.   Letters 296, 297, 308, 309, 316

GISHFORD, Anthony [Tony] (1908–75)
Publisher; a Director at Boosey & Hawkes, who later moved to Faber Music.
                                      Letters 147, 148, 154, 172, 199, 238, 247, 268, 269, 270, 299

GRAHAM, Colin (1931–2007)
Stage director and designer; a key member of the English Opera Group, he produced/
directed the first productions of a number of Britten's operas, including *Noye's Fludde*, the
Church Parables, *Owen Wingrave* and *Death in Venice*.   Letters 287, 299, 302, 340, 343

GUTHRIE, Tyrone [Tony] (1900–71)
Opera and theatre producer, for the Old Vic and Sadler's Wells. Produced first production of
Britten's version of *The Beggar's Opera*.   Letters 33, 82, 103

HAREWOOD, George Lascelles, 7th Earl of Harewood (1923–2011)
Opera administrator, including Director and later Chairman of English National Opera
(formerly Sadler's Wells) from 1972 to 1995; co-founder of the English Opera Group.
Married to Marion Stein, with whom he had sons David, James and Jeremy.
                          Letters 110, 113, 130, 168, 169, 172, 174, 178, 181, 182, 184, 185,
                                198, 199, 212, 232, 236, 238, 245, 256, 265, 267, 279, 287

HAREWOOD, Marion – see STEIN, Marion

HAWKES, Ralph (1898–1950)
Britten's music publisher, Co-Director of Boosey & Hawkes in London.
                  Letters 8, 13, 15, 37, 52, 56, 60, 89, 90, 91, 92, 93, 94, 95, 96, 97, 98, 101, 104, 111, 114

HESSE, Prince Ludwig of Hesse and the Rhine [Lu] (1908–68)
German arts patron; married to Princess Margaret of Hesse, often hosted Britten and Pears
at their home, Schloss Wolfsgarten. Dedicatee of *Sechs Hölderlin-Fragmente* and, jointly with
his wife, of *Songs from the Chinese*.
                          Letters 194, 196, 198, 201, 202, 209, 211, 212, 239, 247, 249, 274, 276, 281

HESSE, Princess Margaret of Hesse and the Rhine [Peg] (née Campbell Geddes) (1913–97)
Arts patron; married to Prince Ludwig of Hesse, often hosted Britten and Pears at their
home, Schloss Wolfsgarten. Joint dedicatee, with her husband, of *Songs from the Chinese*.
                          Letters 194, 196, 197, 198, 200, 201, 202, 209, 211, 212, 239, 247, 249, 261, 274,
                                276, 279, 281, 315, 320, 321, 322, 329, 336, 337, 339, 342, 343, 344, 346

HOLLAND ROGERS, Iris (d. 1982)
Linguist; friend of Pears from childhood.   Letters 3, 7, 13, 17, 35, 37, 38, 40, 212

HOLST, Imogen [Imo] (1907–84)
Composer and conductor; Director of Music at Dartington then musical assistant to Britten from 1952 to 1964, collaborating with him on a number of publications as well as assisting in preparation of his scores. An authority on early music, and a key figure in the artistic development of the Aldeburgh Festival. Daughter of composer Gustav Holst. Dedicatee of Britten's Purcell realizations of the *Three Divine Hymns*, as well as (with Ninette de Valois) of the ballet *The Prince of the Pagodas*.
Letters 147, 148, 149, 150, 151, 152, 153, 155, 167, 171, 178, 180, 184, 186, 189, 194, 198, 209, 221, 227, 228, 231, 233, 234, 242, 259, 260, 277, 288, 290, 304, 309, 310

HUDSON, Elizabeth [Nellie, but always referred to as Miss Hudson] (1898–1982)
Cook and housekeeper to Britten and Pears at Crag House and The Red House. Her brother, George, worked as gardener at The Red House. Britten and Pears had the cottage 'Cosy Nook' built in the grounds of The Red House for her retirement.
Letters 124, 126, 144, 149, 158, 186, 196, 198, 201, 206, 209, 215, 216, 227, 231, 232, 250, 253, 281, 282, 308, 309

HURST, Helen (1887–1981)
Social worker; partner of Britten's sister Barbara.   Letters 17, 40, 76, 95, 99

ISHERWOOD, Christopher (1904–86)
Writer; dedicatee of *On this Island*. Long associated with W.H. Auden, with whom he wrote the plays *The Ascent of F6* and *On the Frontier* (for which Britten wrote the incidental music). He moved to New York with Auden in 1939, and later lived in California with the artist Don Bachardy (b. 1934).   Letters 2, 6, 28, 360, 361, 363

'JOVE' the dachshund (1956–after 1967)
The second dachshund at The Red House; son of Clytie.
Letters 201, 206, 209, 215, 220, 227, 228, 231, 242, 250, 251, 253, 277, 279

LAWRIE, James [Jimmie] (1907–79)
Chair of the English Opera Group board from 1950 to 1960. Dedicatee of *The Beggar's Opera*.
Letters 128, 139, 212, 215

LIER, Bertus van (1906–72)
Dutch composer and conductor.   Letters 124, 125, 157, 158, 159

LUDWIG, Johannes [Hans] (1904–96)
German architect, probably introduced to Pears and Britten by the Hesses. He worked on the Johanneskirche in Bruckmühl (1953–54) and the Paul-Gerhardt-Kirche in München-Laim (1953–56). Married to Belka Ludwig.
Letters 209, 213, 215, 237, 239, 255, 260, 274, 276, 278, 286

McCREADY, Michael
Physician and homeopathic practictioner often consulted by Britten and Pears in London.
Letters 171, 228, 236, 243, 247, 248, 252, 256, 265, 279

MALCOLM, George (1917–97)
Pianist, organist and conductor. Conducted the boys of the Westminster Cathedral Choir in the premiere of the *Missa Brevis in D*. Frequently performed at the Aldeburgh Festival throughout 1960s–70s.   Letters 219, 232, 240, 248, 260, 261, 283, 285, 286

MANÉN, Lucie (1889–1991)
German singer and teacher; Pears had singing lessons with her from 1965 onwards.
                                                                                       Letters 296, 298, 301, 302, 329, 338

MAUD, Humphrey (1934–2013)
Son of John Redcliffe-Maud (1906–82), a diplomat, and his wife Jean (1904–93); joint dedicatee, with his sisters Pamela, Caroline and Virginia, of *The Young Person's Guide to the Orchestra*.   Letters 79, 81, 98, 114, 238, 240

MAYER, Beata (1912–2000)
Daughter of Elizabeth and William Mayer. Dedicatee of the folk-song arrangement *The Ash Grove*. Married first to Dr Max Wachstein, with whom she had two daughters, Mukki and Monica, then to Wolfgang Sauerlander, an editor.
                                         Letters 8, 10, 17, 89, 91, 101, 225, 227, 306, 310, 311, 345, 348

MAYER, Elizabeth (1884–1970)
German-born translator and editor; with her husband William, long-term host of Britten and Pears at their home in Amityville, Long Island. Dedicatee of the *Hymn to St Cecilia*. Mother to Beata, Michael and Christopher.
        Letters 8, 16, 17, 35, 39, 59, 89, 90, 91, 92, 94, 95, 99, 101, 102, 103, 104, 114,
               117, 124, 210, 224, 225, 226, 227, 228, 229, 232, 303, 306, 310, 311, 345

MAYER, Michael (1916–2007)
Son of Elizabeth and William Mayer; worked as a hospital chaplain.
                                                                       Letters 26, 38, 101, 225, 227, 306, 311

MAYER, William (1887–1956)
German-born psychiatrist; dedicatee of the folk-song arrangement *Little Sir William*. Married to Elizabeth Mayer and father to Beata, Michael and Christopher.
                           Letters 8, 9, 15, 16, 17, 38, 39, 89, 90, 92, 93, 94, 97, 100, 101, 102, 104, 108, 227

MENUHIN, Yehudi (1916–99)
American-born violinist; travelled with Britten to perform at liberated concentration camps in Germany in 1945.   Letters 71, 72, 196, 197, 198, 199, 200, 201, 202, 214, 239

MITCHELL, Donald (b. 1925)
Music publisher and writer; edited *Letters from a Life*. After Britten's death, became Chair of the Britten Trust (later Estate). Married to Kathleen (b. 1916), head teacher at Pimlico School; they were joint dedicatees of *The Burning Fiery Furnace*.
                                                                       Letters 171, 305, 309, 341, 343

MUNDY, Clytie (née Hine) (1887–1983)
Australian soprano and singing teacher to Pears; settled in New York, and married John
Mundy (1886–1971), a cellist. Mother to Meg and John.
> Letters 89, 90, 91, 92, 93, 94, 95, 96, 97, 99, 100, 102, 114, 117, 225, 227, 228, 340

NEEL, Boyd (1905–81)
Conductor, including of the premieres of *Les Illuminations* and *Variations on a Theme of Frank
Bridge*. Director of the Boyd Neel String Orchestra.   Letters 1, 81, 134, 233, 365

NETTLESHIP, Ursula (1886–1968)
Choral conductor; Director of CEMA East Anglia; dedicatee of *A Ceremony of Carols*.
Britten and Pears stayed with her for a few months at her London flat in 1943.
> Letters 25, 30, 47, 48, 53, 62, 89, 92, 113, 219

NEVILLE-SMITH, Esther (d. 1955)
Friend of Pears through her husband, a Master at Lancing College. Commissioned *Saint
Nicolas* for the centenary celebrations at the School in 1948.
> Letters 19, 39, 65, 77, 101, 111, 129, 162

NICOLET, Aurèle (1926–2016)
Swiss flautist and teacher. Appeared often with Pears at the Bach Festival at Ansbach,
1950s–60s.   Letters 237, 239, 241, 283, 284, 285, 286

OLDHAM, Arthur (1926–2003)
Composer; assisted Britten as copyist from mid-1940s to 1950s, producing vocal scores for
publication, in exchange for lessons in composition.
> Letters 62, 65, 92, 94, 95, 99, 139, 149, 167, 188

PARKER, Barbara
Housekeeper at Crag House, 1947–49.
> Letters 79, 80, 85, 86, 88, 89, 92, 93, 94, 95, 96, 101, 104, 112, 113, 114

PERITON, Leslie (1908–83)
Accountant and financial advisor to Britten and Pears.
> Letters 64, 115, 133, 212, 214, 215, 238, 265

PHIPPS, Sue (née Pears) (b. 1931)
Agent to Britten and Pears from 1965; niece of Peter Pears. Married to Jack Phipps (1925–
2010), arts administrator, with whom she had son, Martin, a composer.
> Letters 236, 271, 288, 293, 297, 298, 303, 309, 310, 311, 320, 327, 342, 356

PIPER, John (1903–92)
Artist; founder member of the English Opera Group; from 1946 onwards, designer of the
first productions of many of Britten's stage works. Married to Myfanwy Piper, with whom he
was the joint dedicatee of the song cycle *Winter Words*.
> Letters 81, 128, 145, 154, 186, 236, 237, 238, 239, 244, 247, 248, 259, 269

PIPER, Myfanwy (1911–97)
Writer; librettist for *The Turn of the Screw*, *Owen Wingrave* and *Death in Venice*. Married to John Piper, and joint dedicatee, with him, of *Winter Words*.
                              Letters 128, 145, 236, 238, 244, 247, 269, 322, 343, 344

PLOMER, William (1903–73)
Writer; librettist for *Gloriana* and the three Church Parables.
                              Letters 168, 172, 180, 181, 303, 309, 311, 312

POTTER, Mary (1900–81)
Artist; lived at The Red House in Aldeburgh before Britten and Pears, then in 1957 exchanged it for Crag House, their home on the seafront. Later returned to live on The Red House site in 1963, where the Red Studio was specially built for her. Married to (and later divorced from) the writer Stephen Potter (1900–69), and mother to sons Andrew and Julian.
                              Letters 206, 208, 212, 220, 221, 297, 301, 305, 309

RANKL, Karl (1898–1968)
Austrian-born conductor; conducted *Peter Grimes* at Covent Garden in 1947–48.
                              Letters 114, 115, 180, 181, 183, 184, 188

REISS, Stephen (1918–99)
Art historian and administrator; Manager of the Aldeburgh Festival from 1955 to 1971, and of the English Opera Group from 1959 to 1961. Dedicatee of *A Midsummer Night's Dream*. Married to Beth Reiss.   Letters 189, 199, 212, 221, 224, 227, 228, 232, 234, 238, 247, 256,
                              262, 268, 277, 288, 290, 291, 297, 304, 306, 307, 309, 314

RICHTER, Karl (1926–81)
German conductor; often conducted performances by Pears at the Ansbach Bach Festival.
                              Letters 194, 197, 198, 200, 202, 203, 207, 208, 214, 237,
                              239, 240, 248, 275, 276, 278, 283, 284, 285

RITCHIE, Margaret [Mabel] (1903–69)
Soprano; member of the English Opera Group, sang in the premieres of *Albert Herring* (as Miss Wordsworth) and *The Rape of Lucretia* (as Lucia); dedicatee of Britten's realization of Purcell *The Blessed Virgin's Expostulation*.   Letters 21, 23, 34, 82, 103, 180, 183, 229

ROSTROPOVICH, Mstislav [Slava] (1927–2007)
Russian cellist; dedicatee and first performer of all of Britten's works for cello, and, jointly with his wife, the soprano Galina ['Gallia'] Vishnevskaya (1926–2012), of *The Poet's Echo*.
                              Letters 260, 268, 270, 287, 290, 296, 297, 302, 362

SACKVILLE-WEST, Edward [Eddy] (1901–65)
Writer and critic; wrote the radio play *The Rescue* for which Britten composed incidental music. Dedicatee of the *Serenade*.   Letters 33, 62, 69, 70, 147, 148, 151, 154

SLATER, Montagu (1902–56)
Writer; librettist for *Peter Grimes*. Joint dedicatee of *Ballad of Heroes* with his wife, Enid
(1903–88).   Letters 17, 18, 33, 44, 60, 62, 76

STEIN, Erwin (1885–1958)
Austrian musicologist and publisher; edited Britten's works for Boosey & Hawkes. Married
to Sophie Stein; father of Marion. Dedicatee of *The Rape of Lucretia*.
                            Letters 21, 40, 48, 52, 55, 62, 65, 68, 70, 92, 101, 109, 116,
                                              121, 124, 128, 133, 143, 164, 168, 199, 201, 243

STEIN, Marion (1926–2014)
Pianist, co-founder of the Leeds Piano Competition and closely associated with the development of the Aldeburgh Festival; married first to George Lascelles, Earl of Harewood
(with whom she had sons David, James and Jeremy), then later to Jeremy Thorpe.
                            Letters 40, 70, 133, 136, 137, 140, 164, 168, 174, 178, 182,
                                              184, 199, 212, 236, 238, 245, 256, 268, 287, 344

STEIN, Sophie (?1883–1965)
Married to Erwin Stein; mother of Marion.
                            Letters 40, 70, 101, 109, 113, 133, 140, 143, 164, 199, 201, 259, 260, 261, 262

STRODE, Rosamund (1927–2010)
Soprano; member of the Purcell Singers; took over as musical assistant to Britten from
Imogen Holst in 1964, and became the first Archivist of the Britten–Pears Library.
                            Letters 194, 277, 288, 294, 298, 305, 309, 318, 322

SWEETING, Elizabeth (1914–99)
Arts administrator; Manager of the Aldeburgh Festival from 1948 to 1955.
                            Letters 85, 95, 128, 137, 139, 149, 190, 262

THOMSON, Rita (b. 1934)
Nurse and carer for Britten in the 1970s and later for Pears in the 1980s.
                            Letters 340, 341, 342, 343, 344, 357, 358, 365

THORPE, Marion – see STEIN, Marion

TILLETT, Emmie (née BASS) (1897–1982)
Managing Director of concerts agency Ibbs & Tillett, who acted for Britten and Pears in
1940s–50s.   Letters 66, 72, 78, 85, 86, 108, 130, 188, 255

TIPPETT, Michael (1905–98)
Composer; fellow pacifist, imprisoned for refusing to participate in the non-combatant
duties assigned him as a conscientious objector. Composed the song cycles *Boyhood's End*
and *The Heart's Assurance* for Pears and Britten. Dedicatee of *Curlew River*.
                            Letters 47, 53, 66, 70, 139, 177

WEBSTER, David (1903–71)
General Administrator (i.e. Chief Executive) of the Royal Opera House, Covent Garden from 1945 to 1970. Britten composed a four-trumpet Fanfare for his farewell concert.
Letters 103, 114, 147, 151, 154, 155, 163, 164, 199, 201, 212, 250, 253

WELFORD, Beth – see BRITTEN, Beth

WELFORD, Rosemary [Roguey] (b. 1945)
Britten's niece, younger daughter of Beth and Kit Welford. Joint dedicatee, with Sebastian and Sally, and with Roger Duncan, of *Noye's Fludde*.   Letters 65, 79, 85, 89, 99, 301

WELFORD, Sally (b. 1943)
Britten's niece, daughter of Beth and Kit Welford. Joint dedicatee, with Sebastian and Roguey, and with Roger Duncan, of *Noye's Fludde*.
Letters 35, 37, 43, 46, 48, 52, 58, 65, 79, 85, 89, 99, 273, 274, 276, 278

WELFORD, Sebastian (b. 1939)
Britten's nephew, son of Beth and Kit Welford. Joint dedicatee, with his sisters Sally and Roguey, and with Roger Duncan, of *Noye's Fludde*.
Letters 35, 37, 43, 46, 48, 52, 58, 65, 79, 85, 99, 113

WEYMAR, Carl
German musician; founder and director of the Bach Festival at Ansbach.
Letters 203, 207, 237, 240, 278, 283

WOOD, Anne (1907–98)
Contralto who met Pears when they both sang with the BBC Singers in 1930s; first Manager of the English Opera Group.   Letters 109, 112, 122, 137, 184, 232, 250

WYSS, Sophie (1897–1983)
Swiss soprano; sang premieres of *Our Hunting Fathers* and *Les Illuminations*.
Letters 7, 15, 19, 34, 51, 65

List of Works

In this list we have included any work which is mentioned or referred to by Britten or Pears in the letters.

Letter numbers are given rather than page references, and the brief descriptions are centred on how the work relates to Britten and Pears. Opus or catalogue numbers have only been included where they are necessary to identify a work.

For a full list which encompasses the editorial notes, please consult the Index.

Britten Works

For Purcell realizations, see under Purcell *in* Works by Other Composers.

Albert Herring (1947)
A comic opera with a libretto by Eric Crozier (after a short story by Guy de Maupassant, *Le Rosier de Madame Husson*), dedicated to E.M. Forster 'in admiration'. The title role was written for Pears, and it was first performed at Glyndebourne on 20 June 1947, produced by Frederick Ashton and designed by John Piper.   Letters 79, 103, 163, 175, 180, 183, 331, 360

The Beggar's Opera (1948)
Britten's version of the 1728 ballad-opera by John Gay, dedicated to James Lawrie. First performed at the Arts Theatre, Cambridge, in a production by Tyrone Guthrie assisted by Basil Coleman, with Pears as Macheath and Nancy Evans as Polly Peachum, conducted by Britten on 24 May 1948.   Letters 82, 85, 94, 103, 183, 184, 203

Billy Budd (1951)
Opera with a libretto by E.M. Forster and Eric Crozier after the novel by Herman Melville. Commissioned by the Arts Council for the Festival of Britain, and dedicated to George and Marion Harewood. The role of Captain Vere was composed for Pears. First performed at Covent Garden, produced by Basil Coleman with designs by John Piper, and Britten conducting on 1 December 1951.   Letters 122, 132, 134, 138, 139, 141, 143, 145, 149, 151, 154,
157, 158, 163, 164, 167, 172, 198, 202, 290, 302

The Burning Fiery Furnace (1966)
Second of the three Church Parables.
Libretto by William Plomer adapted from the Book of Daniel, Chs 1–3. The role of Nebuchadnezzar was written for Pears, and Britten dedicated the work to Donald and Kathleen Mitchell. Performed without a conductor, by soloists, chorus and ensemble, the premiere, produced by Colin Graham, was given at Orford Church to open the Aldeburgh Festival on 9 June 1966.   Letter 301

Cantata Academica, Carmen Basiliense (1959)
For soloists, chorus and orchestra. Written to commemorate the 500th anniversary of the University of Basel in 1959, the text in Latin was compiled from the charter of the University by Bernhard Wyss. First performed in Basel by soloists including Pears with the Basler Kammerorchester and Kammerchor conducted by Paul Sacher on 1 July 1960.
                                                                              Letters 228, 232, 271, 364

Cantata Misericordium (1963)
For tenor, baritone, chorus and orchestra. The Latin text, based on the parable of the Good Samaritan, was by L.P. Wilkinson, Vice Provost of King's College, Cambridge. Dedicated to Fidelity Cranbrook, it was first performed by Pears and Dietrich Fischer-Dieskau with Le Motet de Genève and the Orchestre de la Suisse Romande conducted by Ernest Ansermet in Geneva on 1 September 1963.   Letters 268, 289

Canticle I: My Beloved is Mine (1947)
For high voice and piano, to a text by Francis Quarles. Written for a memorial concert given at Central Hall, Westminster for Dick Sheppard, founder of the Peace Pledge Union, where it was first performed by Britten and Pears on 1 November 1947.   Letters 79, 80, 351

Canticle II: Abraham and Isaac (1952)
For alto, tenor and piano, to a text from the Chester Miracle Play – Histories of Lot and Abraham. Composed for Pears and Britten to perform with Kathleen Ferrier, the joint dedicatee with Pears, and premiered by them at the Albert Hall in Nottingham on 21 January 1952.   Letters 212, 248, 260, 351

> *Britten's three further Canticles, III: Still falls the rain (1954, text by Sitwell), IV: The Journey of the Magi (1971, text by T.S. Eliot) and V: The Death of St Narcissus (1974, text by T.S. Eliot) are not mentioned in the letters.*

A Ceremony of Carols (1942)
For treble voices and harp. Partly composed on the MS *Axel Johnson*, on the return trip from the United States in March 1942. Dedicated to Ursula Nettleship, and first performed by the Fleet Street Choir at Norwich Castle on 5 December 1942.   Letters 40, 55, 187

A Charm of Lullabies (1947)
Cycle of songs for mezzo-soprano and piano to texts by William Blake, Robert Burns, Robert Greene, Thomas Randolph and John Philip. Dedicated to Nancy Evans. First performed on 3 January 1948 by the dedicatee, with Felix de Nobel accompanying.   Letters 82, 89

Church Parables: see
    Curlew River (1964)
    The Burning Fiery Furnace (1966)
    The Prodigal Son (1968)

Curlew River (1964)
First of the three Church Parables.
Libretto by William Plomer from the medieval Japanese Noh play *Sumidagawa*. The role of The Madwoman was written for Pears, and Britten dedicated the work to Michael Tippett. Performed without a conductor by the principal singers and a small chamber ensemble, the first performance, produced by Colin Graham, was staged at Orford Church on 13 June 1964.
Letters 284, 301

Death in Venice (1973)
Britten's last opera, with a libretto by Myfanwy Piper after the novella by Thomas Mann. Composed between December 1971 and March 1973, an ailing Britten delayed a heart valve operation in order to finish the score. Dedicated 'To Peter', the career-defining role of Aschenbach was composed for Pears. First performed at the Aldeburgh Festival, produced by Colin Graham, designed by John Piper and conducted by Steuart Bedford on 16 June 1973.   Letters 321, 323, 330, 336, 339, 340, 341, 342, 343, 344, 345, 351

Festival Te Deum (1944)
For treble, chorus and organ, a setting of Morning Prayer from The Book of Common Prayer. Written for the Centenary Festival of St Mark's, Swindon, and first performed there by the choristers and organist conducted by J.J. Gale on 24 April 1945.   Letters 66, 69, 70

First Suite for Cello (1964)
Premiered by the dedicatee, Mstislav Rostropovich, on 27 June 1965.   Letter 290

    The Second (1967) and Third (1971, rev. 1974) Suites for solo cello were both dedicated to and premiered by Rostropovich, but are not mentioned in the letters.

Folk-Song Arrangements
Britten published six volumes of folk-song arrangements in the 1940s–50s, and had been performing them with Pears in recital from the earliest days of their partnership. The individual songs were often dedicated to friends and fellow performers.

    The Ash Grove (1941)   Letter 96
    Vol. 1, No. 6. Dedicated to Beata Mayer.

The Bonny Earl o' Moray (1940)   Letter 96
Vol. 1, No. 3. Dedicated to Mildred Titley.

The Foggy, Foggy Dew (1942)   Letter 103
Vol. 3, No. 5. Dedicated to Joan Cross.

Heigh ho! Heigh hi! ['*Quand j'etais chez mon pere*'] (1942)   Letter 96
Vol. 2, No. 8. Dedicated 'to my young friends, Arnold and
Humphrey Gyde', the children of singer Sophie Wyss.

Little Sir William (1940)   Letter 48
Vol. 1, No. 2. Dedicated to William Mayer.

The Plough Boy (1945)   Letter 350
Vol. 3, No. 1. Dedicated to Joan Cross.

Sweet Polly Oliver (1945)   Letter 96
Vol. 3, No. 3. Dedicated to Joan Cross.

Gloriana (1953)
Opera with libretto by William Plomer after Lytton Strachey's *Elizabeth and Essex*.
Dedicated to Queen Elizabeth II and composed for the coronation year celebrations. The
role of Essex was composed for Pears, and the title role for Joan Cross. The first performance was conducted by John Pritchard at Covent Garden, produced by Basil Coleman with
designs by John Piper and dance choreography by John Cranko on 8 June 1953.
                                              Letters 170, 172, 178, 180, 181, 302

The Holy Sonnets of John Donne (1945)
For high voice and piano, to John Donne's texts. Composed for Pears (the dedicatee) and
Britten to perform together – premiered by them at the Wigmore Hall on 22 November
1945.   Letters 76, 213

I wonder as I wander (c 1940)
For voice and piano. Britten set this tune believing it to be a folk song, but it was in fact
written by the (at the time) living composer John Jacob Niles, who prohibited publication or
broadcast of Britten's version. However, Pears and Britten continued to perform it alongside
the folk-song arrangements throughout their recital career.   Letter 50

Les Illuminations (1939)
For high voice and string orchestra. Originally composed for Sophie Wyss, three of the
movements are individually dedicated – to Wulff Scherchen, Elizabeth Mayer and Pears.
First performed (complete) by Wyss with the Boyd Neel Orchestra at the Aeolian Hall in
London on 30 January 1940, it later became standard repertoire for Pears throughout his
career.   Letters 7, 51, 73, 79, 101, 164, 218, 245, 246, 324, 360

Let's Make an Opera – The Little Sweep (1949)
'An entertainment for young people' with libretto by Eric Crozier. First performed at the Aldeburgh Festival, produced by Basil Coleman and Stuart Burge, with designs by John Lewis, conducted by Norman Del Mar on 14 June 1949. Britten dedicated the score 'to the real Gay, Juliet, Sophie, Tina, Hughie, Jonny and Sammy – the Gathorne-Hardys of Great Glemham, Suffolk'.   Letters 123, 124, 125, 149, 154, 156, 232

Malaysian National Anthem (1957)
For military band. Commissioned by the Chief Minister of Malaysia in July 1957, but rejected by the Malaysian authorities and not performed in Britten's lifetime.   Letter 214

Mazurka Elegiaca (1941)
For two pianos. Dedicated 'in memoriam I.J. Paderewski', and played for the first time in the UK at the Cambridge Arts Theatre by Britten with Clifford Curzon on 25 April 1953.
Letter 37

A Midsummer Night's Dream (1960)
Opera with libretto adapted from Shakespeare by Britten and Pears. Dedicated to Stephen Reiss. The comic role of Flute/Thisbe (one of the mechanicals) was composed for Pears. First performed at the Aldeburgh Festival, produced by John Cranko with designs by John Piper, conducted by Britten at the Jubilee Hall on 11 June 1960.
Letters 236, 238, 242, 243, 248, 249, 253, 256, 258, 259, 261, 301, 302, 357, 358

Missa Brevis in D (1959)
For boys' choir and organ, to the Latin text of the Ordinary of the Roman Rite. Dedicated to George Malcolm and the boys of the Westminster Cathedral Choir, and first performed by them at Westminster on 22 July 1959.   Letters 236, 238, 239, 240

Motets for *Poet's Christmas* (BBC Radio, 1944)
Chorale (after an Old French Carol)
A Shepherd's Carol ('Oh lift your little pinkie')
Set to fragments from W.H. Auden's *For the Time Being: A Christmas Oratorio*.
Letters 69, 70

Nocturnal, after John Dowland: Reflections on 'Come, Heavy Sleep' (1963)
For guitar. Dedicated to Julian Bream, and first performed by him at the Jubilee Hall as part of the Aldeburgh Festival on 12 June 1964.   Letters 279, 282

Nocturne (1958)
Song cycle for tenor and ensemble. Like the earlier *Serenade*, it comprises an anthology of texts by different poets – Shelley, Tennyson, Coleridge, Middleton, Wordsworth, Owen, Keats and Shakespeare. Dedicated to Alma Mahler, it was first performed by Pears at the Leeds Festival with the BBC Symphony Orchestra conducted by Rudolf Schwarz on 16 October 1958.   Letters 222, 232, 243, 246, 249, 251, 252, 253, 254, 258, 289, 322

Noye's Fludde (1958)
Setting of the Chester Miracle Play as a 'community opera', for soloists, chorus, chamber ensemble and children's orchestra. The premiere was produced by Colin Graham with costumes (including animal headdresses for the children) by Ceri Richards, and staged at Orford Church as part of the Aldeburgh Festival conducted by Charles Mackerras on 18 June 1958.   Letter 236

O that I had ne'er been married (1922, rev. 1960s)
Song for voice and piano to a text by Robert Burns. The first public performance was given by Pears and Roger Vignoles as a TV broadcast on 29 November 1976, but had been recorded in May.   Letter 362

On this Island (1937)
Song cycle for high voice and piano, to texts by W.H. Auden. Dedicated to Christopher Isherwood, Britten composed it for the soprano Sophie Wyss and first performed it with her at Broadcasting House on 19 November 1937.   Letters 4, 358

Owen Wingrave (1969–70)
Opera with libretto by Myfanwy Piper after the story by Henry James. Pears played the role of General Sir Philip Wingrave, composed for him, and Britten dedicated the work to Joan and Isador Caplan. Britten's only opera specifically for television, it was first broadcast on 16 May 1971.   Letters 315, 333

Paul Bunyan (1941)
Operetta in two acts, written in Britten's American period, with a libretto by W.H. Auden. It was first performed by students at Columbia University in New York on 5 May 1941. Britten then revised it towards the end of his life, and it received concert performances in 1974 and a full production was staged at Snape Maltings on 4 June 1976.   Letters 8, 94, 337

Peter Grimes (1945)
Opera with libretto by Montagu Slater, based on characters from the narrative poem *The Borough* by George Crabbe. Commissioned by the Koussevitzky Music Foundation, 'dedicated to the memory of Natalie Koussevitzky'. The first of Britten's stage works with a title role written specifically for Pears, it was first performed at Sadler's Wells Theatre on 7 June 1945, conducted by Reginald Goodall, produced by Eric Crozier and designed by Kenneth Green.   Letters 17, 33, 43, 44, 45, 47, 48, 50, 52, 53, 56, 57, 58, 59, 68, 70, 71, 73, 75, 77, 93, 94, 96, 114, 189, 191, 212, 228, 231, 233, 235, 271, 303, 351, 359

'Four Sea Interludes' from *Peter Grimes*
Arranged for concert performance (with slightly adjusted endings), the Interludes have become one of Britten's most enduringly popular orchestral works.   Letter 93

Piano Concerto (1938, rev. 1946)
For piano and orchestra. Dedicated to Lennox Berkeley. Britten played the solo part himself at the premiere at the Proms with the BBC Symphony Orchestra conducted by Henry Wood at the Queen's Hall on 18 August 1938.   Letters 2, 6, 7, 8, 89, 92

The Poet's Echo (1965)
Song cycle for high voice and piano to Russian texts by Alexander Pushkin. It was first performed (incomplete) at Yerevan, Armenia, by the dedicatees, Galina Vishnevskaya and Mstislav Rostropovich, on 29 August 1965.   Letters 348, 358, 362

The Prince of the Pagodas (1956)
Ballet from a scenario by John Cranko. Britten dedicated the work to Imogen Holst and Ninette de Valois. It was premiered at the Royal Opera House, Covent Garden, in a production choreographed by John Cranko, designed by John Piper and conducted by Britten on 1 January 1957.   Letters 199, 201, 205

The Prodigal Son (1968)
Last of the three Church Parables.
Libretto by William Plomer after the Gospel of Luke 15: 11–32. The role of The Tempter was written for Pears, and Britten dedicated the work to Dmitri Shostakovich. Performed without a conductor by the principal singers and a small chamber ensemble, the first performance, produced by Colin Graham, was staged at Orford Church as part of the Aldeburgh Festival on 10 June 1968.   Letters 303, 305, 309, 311

The Rape of Lucretia (1946)
Britten's first chamber opera, with a libretto by Ronald Duncan after the play by André Obey. It was dedicated to Erwin Stein and first performed at Glyndebourne on 12 July 1946, with Kathleen Ferrier in the title role (alternating the rest of the run with Nancy Evans). The Male Chorus role was composed for Pears. The production was designed by John Piper, produced by Eric Crozier, and Ernest Ansermet conducted the Glyndebourne Opera Orchestra.   Letters 76, 77, 78, 90, 91, 98, 102, 110, 114, 130, 189, 191, 202, 228, 258, 350

Rejoice in the Lamb (1943)
For chorus and organ, to texts by Christopher Smart. Commissioned by Rev. Walter Hussey and first performed at St Matthew's Church, Northampton to mark the fiftieth anniversary of the church, conducted by Britten on 21 September 1943.   Letter 61

The Rescue (1943)
Incidental music for a radio melodrama by Edward Sackville-West (based on Homer's *Odyssey*). First broadcast on the BBC Home Service featuring Hedli Anderson, over two nights, 25 and 26 November 1943.   Letters 33, 41

Saint Nicolas (1948)
Cantata for tenor, chorus, string orchestra, keyboards and percussion, to a text by Eric Crozier, composed for the Lancing College Centenary, its official premiere, on 24 July 1948.

The work was first performed in public at the Aldeburgh Festival, with Pears in the title role, on 5 June 1948, with the Aldeburgh Festival choir and orchestra conducted by Leslie Woodgate.   Letters 79, 80, 82, 113, 114, 145, 220

Scottish Ballad (1941)
For two pianos and orchestra, dedicated to the husband and wife duo Ethel Bartlett and Rae Robertson, and first performed by them with the Cincinnati Symphony Orchestra conducted by Eugene Goossens on 28 November 1941.   Letters 33, 61, 309

Sechs Hölderlin-Fragmente (1958)
For voice and piano, to German texts by Friedrich Hölderlin. Dedicated to Prince Ludwig of Hesse on his fiftieth birthday. First public performance was a radio broadcast by Pears and Britten on 14 November 1958, actually recorded on 20 October 1958.
                                                    Letters 222, 227, 229, 230, 232

Serenade (1943)
Song cycle for tenor, horn and strings, to an anthology of texts by poets Cotton, Tennyson, Blake, Anon., Jonson and Keats. Composed for Pears to perform with horn virtuoso Dennis Brain, it was dedicated to the writer Edward Sackville-West and first performed at the Wigmore Hall on 15 October 1943, conducted by Walter Goehr.
                         Letters 35, 36, 37, 48, 68, 73, 93, 106, 146, 163, 195, 230, 232, 308, 351

Seven Sonnets of Michelangelo (1940)
Song cycle for tenor and piano to original Italian texts by Michelangelo. Dedicated 'to Peter', it was the first song cycle Britten composed expressly for Pears – they gave the first public performance together at the Wigmore Hall on 23 September 1942.
                                                    Letters 17, 25, 93, 163, 351

Sinfonia da Requiem (1940)
For full orchestra. Commissioned but later rejected by the Japanese government for supposed overt Christian content (the three movements are modelled after the Latin mass, titled Lacrymosa, Dies irae and Requiem aeternam). Dedicated 'to the memory of my parents'. First performed at Carnegie Hall by the New York Philharmonic conducted by John Barbirolli on 29 March 1941.   Letters 70, 93

Sonata in C (1961)
For cello and piano. Composed for Mstislav Rostropovich, the dedicatee, to play with Britten; they gave the premiere at the Jubilee Hall on 7 July 1961.   Letter 260

Songs and Proverbs of William Blake (1965)
For baritone and piano, to texts selected by Pears from Blake's *Songs of Experience, Auguries of Innocence* and *Proverbs of Hell*. Dedicated to Dietrich Fischer-Dieskau (inscribed by Britten 'For Dieter: the past and the future'), and premiered by him and Britten at the Jubilee Hall, Aldeburgh, on 24 June 1965.   Letters 290, 293, 294

Songs from the Chinese (1957)
For high voice and guitar, set to Arthur Waley's translations of Chinese poetry. Dedicated to the Prince and Princess of Hesse, the cycle was composed for Pears to perform with Julian Bream, and they gave the premiere at Great Glemham as part of the Aldeburgh Festival on 17 June 1958.   Letters 219, 228, 235, 248, 253, 307

Spring Symphony (1949)
For soprano, contralto and tenor solos, chorus and orchestra. Features an anthology of texts by Edmund Spenser, Thomas Nashe, John Milton, John Clare, George Peek, Robert Herrick, Richard Barnfield, William Blake and W.H. Auden. Dedicated 'to Serge Koussevitsky and the Boston Symphony Orchestra', the tenor solo was composed for Pears, who gave the first performance with Jo Vincent, Kathleen Ferrier, the Dutch Radio Chorus and Concertgebouw Orchestra conducted by Eduard van Beinum at the Holland Festival on 14 July 1949.   Letters 79, 89, 92, 94, 95, 99, 101, 103, 109, 110, 122, 125, 136, 253, 254, 257, 302

String Quartet no. 2 (1945)
Commissioned by and dedicated to Mary Behrend, in commemoration of the 250th anniversary of Purcell's death. Premiered by the Zorian String Quartet at the Wigmore Hall on 21 November 1945.   Letter 269

> *The First (1941) and Third (1976) String Quartets are not mentioned in the letters.*

Suite on English Folk Tunes 'A time there was …' (1974)
For chamber orchestra, 'lovingly and reverently dedicated to the memory of Percy Grainger'. First performed at Snape Maltings by the English Chamber Orchestra conducted by Steuart Bedford on 13 June 1975.   Letters 342, 344, 349

The Turn of the Screw (1954)
Opera with a libretto by Myfanwy Piper after the story by Henry James. The role of Peter Quint was written for Pears, and the work was premiered by the English Opera Group at Teatro la Fenice on 14 September 1954, produced by Basil Coleman and designed by John Piper. Pears played the role of Quint, and Britten conducted the EOG orchestra. Britten dedicated the work 'to those members of the English Opera Group who took part in the first performance'.   Letters 186, 189, 210, 212, 215, 238, 242, 244, 268, 269, 270, 284, 287, 289, 350

Variations on a Theme of Frank Bridge (1937)
For string orchestra, based around the theme from the second of Frank Bridge's *Three Idylls for String Quartet* (H 67). Britten dedicated the score to his mentor and teacher, Frank Bridge, as 'a tribute with affection and admiration'. First performed by the Boyd Neel String Orchestra, conducted by Boyd Neel, as a radio broadcast by Radio Hilversum, Holland, on 25 August 1937.   Letters 1, 66, 70

War Requiem (1962)
For soloists, chorus, orchestra, chamber orchestra, boys' choir and organ, to texts from the Latin mass for the Dead and the poetry of Wilfred Owen. Britten composed the solo vocal

parts to represent the British, German and Russian forces (for Pears, the baritone Dietrich Fischer-Dieskau and soprano Galina Vishnevskaya respectively). Dedicated to Roger Burney, Piers Dunkerley, David Gill and Michael Halliday, all friends of Britten whom he considered to be victims of conflict. Premiered on 30 May 1962 at the festival to celebrate the consecration of the new Coventry Cathedral (built alongside the old one which was bombed during World War II), by Pears with Fischer-Dieskau and Heather Harper (Vishnevskaya being prohibited from travelling to the UK by the Russian authorities), the Coventry Festival Chorus and City of Birmingham Symphony Orchestra conducted by Meredith Davies, and the Melos Ensemble conducted by Britten.

Letters 265, 266, 275, 276, 277, 287, 293, 300, 320

Winter Words (1953)
Song cycle of lyrics and ballads by Thomas Hardy for high voice and piano. Dedicated to John and Myfanwy Piper; Britten and Pears gave the first performance at Harewood House as part of the Leeds Festival on 8 October 1953, and thereafter it became a cornerstone of their joint recital repertoire.

Letters 349, 358, 362

The Young Person's Guide to the Orchestra (1945)
Variations for orchestra (with optional narrator's script written by Eric Crozier), based around a theme from Purcell's *Abdelazar* (Z 570/2). Dedicated to the Maud children (Humphrey and his sisters Pamela, Caroline and Virginia) 'for their edification and entertainment'. Originally composed for a Crown Film Unit educational film *Instruments of the Orchestra*, directed by Muir Mathieson, with a script by Montagu Slater. First performed as a concert piece by the Liverpool Philharmonic Orchestra conducted by Malcolm Sargent on 15 October 1946.

Letters 62, 93

Works by Other Composers

Various composers
Variations on an Elizabethan Theme 'Sellinger's Round' (1953)
Composite work for string orchestra, with the theme and six movements each by a different composer – Britten's fellow contributors were Imogen Holst (who arranged the Theme by Byrd), Arthur Oldham, Michael Tippett, Lennox Berkeley, Humphrey Searle and William Walton. It was first performed at the 1953 Aldeburgh Festival.

Letter 171

Arne, Thomas (1710–78)
A Favourite Collection of English Songs, sung by Mr Beard,
Miss Young, &c. at Ranelagh Gardens (1757)

Letter 363

Under the Greenwood Tree (1740)
Song from Shakespeare's *As You Like It*.

Letter 175

Bach, J.S. (1685–1750)

The majority of references to Bach's works in the letters relate to performances given or attended by Pears (for example, at the Ansbach Bachwoche).

The Art of Fugue [*Die Kunst der Fuge*]	Letters 202, 285
Brandenburg Concerto nos. 1, 3 and 4	Letter 214

We have listed the Cantatas in order of catalogue number rather than title.

Cantata *Bleib bei uns, denn es will Abend werden*, BWV 6	Letter 285
Cantata *Liebster Gott, wenn werd ich sterben?*, BWV 8	Letters 237, 241
Cantata *O Ewigkeit, du Donnerwort*, BWV 20	Letters 284, 285
Cantata *Ich hatte viel Bekümmernis*, BWV 21	Letters 200, 202
Cantata *Wer weiß, wie nahe mir mein Ende*, BWV 27	Letter 241
Cantata *Der Himmel lacht! die Erde jubilieret*, BWV 31	Letter 202
Cantata *O ewiges Feuer, o Ursprung der Liebe*, BWV 34	Letter 285
Cantata *Es ist dir gesagt, Mensch, was gut ist*, BWV 45	Letters 237, 241
Cantata *Nun ist das Heil und die Kraft*, BWV 50	Letter 285
Cantata *Jauchzet Gott in allen Landen*, BWV 51	Letters 198, 202
Cantata *Ich armer Mensch, ich Sündenknecht*, BWV 55	Letter 194
Cantata *Ich will den Kreuzstab gerne tragen*, BWV 56	Letter 203
Cantata *Gott der Herr ist Sonn und Schild*, BWV 79	Letter 241
Cantata *Unser Mund sei voll Lachens*, BWV 110	Letter 197
Cantata *Meinen Jesum laß ich nicht*, BWV 124	Letter 239
Cantata *Wachet auf, ruft uns die Stimme*, BWV 140	Letter 203
Cantata 160 *Ich weiß, dass mein Erlöser lebt*, BWV 160 Solo tenor cantata, now attributed to Telemann (TWV 1:877)	Letters 194, 202
Cantata *Gott, wie dein Name, so ist auch dein Ruhm*, BWV 171	Letter 197
Cantata *Schmücke dich, o liebe Seele*, BWV 180	Letters 284, 286
Cantata *Meine Seele rühmt und preist*, BWV 189	Letters 84, 194, 278

Pears was renowned for his interpretation of the Evangelist in the Bach and Schütz Passions.

Beethoven, Ludwig van (1770–1827)

Missa Solemnis (Mass in D major) (1819–23)   Letters 193, 222

Piano Trio in D major, op. 70, no. 1 'Ghost Trio' (1808)   Letter 135

Violin Sonata no. 9 'Kreutzer', op. 47 (1804)   Letter 71

Bellini, Vincenzo (1801–35)

I puritani (1835)
Opera which includes a famously high tenor part which Britten occasionally jokes about
Pears having to sing.   Letters 52, 103

Benjamin, Arthur (1893–1960)

Viola Sonata (1942)
'Quasi una fantasia'. Includes movements Elegy and Waltz-Toccata. Written for William
Primrose and performed at the 1950 Aldeburgh Festival by the dedicatee with the composer
at the piano.   Letter 131

Berg, Alban (1885–1935)

Songs selected from Sieben Frühe Lieder (1907):

Nacht, Die Nachtigall, Im Zimmer, Liebesode, Sommertage   Letters 52, 53

Wozzeck (1917–22)
Opera, based on the 1914 play by Georg Büchner.   Letters 92, 340

Berkeley, Lennox (1903–89)

Nelson (1951)
Pears sang the title role in a concert performance (with piano accompaniment) at the
Wigmore Hall, 14 February 1953.   Letters 175, 178

Four Ronsard Sonnets
Set 1 – for two tenors and piano (1952)
Commissioned by Pears, the songs were premiered by him with Hugues Cuénod and George
Malcolm, 8 March 1953.
Set 2 – for tenor and orchestra (1963)
Premiered at the Proms at the Royal Albert Hall by Pears with the BBC Symphony Orchestra
conducted by Berkeley, 9 August 1963.   Letters 274, 278

Ruth (1956)
Opera commissioned and premiered by the English Opera Group at Scala Theatre in
London conducted by Charles Mackerras on 2 October 1956.   Letter 216

Bizet, Georges (1838–75)

Carmen (1874)   Letter 14

Blomdahl, Karl-Birger (1916–68)
Aniara (1959)
Opera based on a poem by Harry Martinson, with a libretto by Erik Lindegren.   Letter 251

Bosmans, Henriette (1895–1952)
The Artist's Secret (c 1950)
For voice and piano with a text from *Dreams* by South African pacifist writer Olive Schreiner.
Dedicated to Pears.											Letter 135

Boughton, Rutland (1878–1960)
Concerto for oboe and strings (1936)
Written for the composer's daughter, Joy Boughton, who would also be the dedicatee of
Britten's works for solo oboe, including *Six Metamorphoses after Ovid* (1960).			Letter 1

Brahms, Johannes (1833–97)
Fest- und Gedenksprüche (1889)									Letter 248

Liebeslieder Waltzes (1869)										Letter 155

Sonata for clarinet and piano, op. 120 (1894)								Letter 219

Trio in E♭ major for Horn, Violin and Piano, op. 40 (1865)						Letter 179

Bridge, Frank (1879–1941)
Songs: *Adoration, Dweller in my deathless dreams, Go not happy day, Goldenhair, So perverse,*
When you are old & grey										Letter 53

Buxtehude, Dietrich (c 1637–1707)
Cantata (unidentified)											Letter 155

Coleridge-Taylor, Samuel (1875–1912)
The Song of Hiawatha (1899)										Letter 65

Copland, Aaron (1900–90)
Clarinet Concerto (1948)										Letter 93

Songs (unspecified)											Letter 248

Debussy, Claude (1862–1918)
Cinq Poèmes de Baudelaire (1887–89)									Letter 360

Proses Lyriques (1895)										Letter 360

Trois Ballades de François Villon (1910)   Letter 67

Trois Poèmes de Stéphane Mallarmé (1913)   Letter 67

Donizetti, Gaetano (1797–1848)
Emilia di Liverpool (1824)   Letter 365

Lucia di Lammermoor (1835)
Britten attended a performance of the Franco Zeffirelli production in February 1959, featuring
Joan Sutherland.   Letter 232

Dowland, John (1563–1626)
Awake, sweet love
Lute song from *The Firste Booke of Songes*, 1597.   Letter 323

Walsingham
Renaissance air arranged for lute.   Letter 343

Durey, Louis (1888–1979)
Images à Crusoe
For voice, flute, clarinet, celesta and strings. Britten played celesta in a performance
conducted by Reginald Goodall at the Wigmore Hall on 24 September 1942.   Letter 19

Easdale, Brian (1909–95)
The Sleeping Children (1951)
Chamber opera, the first to be commissioned by the English Opera Group,
who gave the premiere at the Cheltenham Festival on 9 July 1951.   Letter 103

Elgar, Edward (1857–1934)
The Dream of Gerontius (1900)
Oratorio for three soloists, chorus and orchestra. Pears was noted
for his interpretation of the title role.   Letter 314

Fall, Leo (1873–1925)
Die liebe Augustin (1912)
Operetta. Pears left after watching Act I of a performance in Cologne in 1951.   Letter 163

Flotow, Friedrich von (1812–83)
Martha (1847)
Opera to a libretto by Friedrich Riese.   Letter 178

Gerhard, Roberto (1896–1970)
Concerto for Piano and String Orchestra (1951)
Premiered at the Aldeburgh Festival, 16 June 1951, by Noel Mewton-Wood
with the Festival Orchestra conducted by Norman Del Mar.   Letter 161

The Duenna (1945–49)
Opera based on Sheridan's libretto, broadcast by the BBC in 1949
but not performed on stage until 1992.   Letter 161

Gluck, Christoph Willibald (1714–87)
Iphigénie en Tauride (1779)
Opera with a libretto by Nicolas-François Guillard.   Letter 142

Orfeo ed Euridice (1762, rev. 1774)
Opera with a libretto by Ranieri de' Calzabigi.   Letter 260

Grieg, Edvard (1843–1907)
Four Psalms (1906)
For solo baritone and mixed chorus.   Letter 248

Songs: *A Bird's Cry, Bright Night, By the Stream, The Hunter, To the Motherland, Wind & Wave*
                                                                          Letters 52, 53

Handel, George Frideric (1685–1759)
Acis and Galatea (1718)
Oratorio for four soloists, chorus and orchestra.   Letter 257

Messiah (1741)
Oratorio for five soloists, chorus and orchestra.
                    Letters 70, 81, 82, 96, 111, 112, 113, 139, 140, 175, 188, 192

Samson (1741)
Oratorio for soloists, chorus and orchestra.   Letter 43

Haydn, Joseph (1732–1809)
The Creation [*Die Schöpfung*] (1798)
Oratorio for five soloists, chorus and orchestra.   Letter 80

The Seasons [*Die Jahreszeiten*] (1801)
Oratorio for three soloists, chorus and orchestra.   Letters 39, 284, 311

Henze, Hans Werner (1926–2012)
The Emperor's Nightingale [*L'usignolo dell'imperatore*] (1959)
Ballet pantomime based on the Hans Christian Andersen fairy tale; dedicated to Prince
Ludwig and Princess Margaret of Hesse.   Letter 243

Kammermusik 1958
For tenor, guitar and eight solo instruments.   Letter 251

Holst, Gustav (1874–1934)
Four Songs for voice and violin (1917)   Letter 155

Fugal Concerto for Flute, Oboe and Strings (1923)   Letter 171

St Paul's Suite (1913)
For string orchestra.   Letter 148

The Wandering Scholar (1930)
Single-act opera with a libretto by Clifford Bax, originally premiered in 1934. An EOG production with Pears as Pierre directed by Eric Crozier was broadcast by the BBC on 5 January 1949. Britten then made a chamber orchestra reduction in 1951, which the EOG performed at the Cheltenham Festival, directed by Basil Coleman on 9 July 1951.
                                                                       Letter 103

Jacobson, Maurice (1896–1976)
The Lady of Shalott (1940)
Cantata for tenor, chorus and orchestra, set to the poem by Tennyson. Pears sang the tenor part (representing Lancelot) in a performance with the Etruscan Choral Society conducted by the composer on 11 May 1944. This concert was the first in which Pears sang with Kathleen Ferrier.   Letter 50

Janáček, Leoš (1854–1928)
Folk songs (unspecified)   Letter 191

Mládí ['Youth'] (1924)
For wind sextet.   Letter 191

On an Overgrown Path (1911)
15 miniatures for piano.   Letter 191

Lalo, Edouard (1823–92)
Le roi d'Ys (1888)
Opera.   Letter 14

Liszt, Franz (1811–86)
Piano Concerto no. 1 (1855)   Letter 70

Lucas, Leighton (1903–82)
Cassation in F
Dedicated to its first performers, the Roth Trio. Premiered at a British Council concert on 31 March 1950, where Pears was also singing.   Letter 135

Lutosławski, Witold (1913–94)
Paroles tissées (1965)
For tenor and orchestra. Dedicated to Pears and premiered by him at the Aldeburgh Festival with the Philomusica of London, conducted by George Malcolm, on 20 June 1965.
                                                                    Letters 288, 318

Mahler, Gustav (1860–1911)
Das Lied von der Erde (1909)
Symphony for alto, tenor and orchestra.   Letters 79, 80

Des Knaben Wunderhorn (1901)
Collection of settings of folk poems and tales by Arnim and Brentano, including *Rheinlegendchen* and *Um schlimme Kinder*.   Letter 175

Seven Last Songs [*Sieben Lieder aus letzter Zeit*] (1910)
Collection including the five *Rückert Lieder* (1901–2) with *Revelge* and *Der Tambourg'sell* from *Des Knaben Wunderhorn*.   Letter 175

Songs (unspecified)   Letters 52, 53

Symphony no. 4 (1901)   Letter 33

Massenet, Jules (1842–1912)
Manon (1884)
Opera.   Letter 14

Mendelssohn, Felix (1809–47)
Elijah (1846)
Oratorio for four soloists, chorus and orchestra.   Letter 46

Monteverdi, Claudio (1567–1643)
Il combattimento di Tancredi e Clorinda (1624)
Cantata for three soloists, strings and continuo.   Letter 155

L'Orfeo (1607)
Opera.   Letter 237

Morley, Thomas (1557/58–1602)
Come, sorrow, come
Lute song from Morley's First Book of Ayres (1600).   Letter 323

Mozart, Wolfgang Amadeus (1756–91)
Così fan tutte (1790)
Comic opera. Pears played Ferrando in the 1944 and 1945 Sadler's Wells production.
Letters 67, 73, 267

Don Giovanni (1787)
Opera. Pears often sang Don Ottavio's tenor aria 'Il mio tesoro' in his recitals with Britten in
the 1940s and 1950s.   Letters 4, 53, 193

Exsultate, jubilate (1773)
For soprano and orchestra.   Letter 118

Horn Quintet (1782)   Letter 211

The Magic Flute [*Die Zauberflöte*] (1791)
Opera. Pears played Tamino in the Sadler's Wells productions in 1943 and 1951.
Letters 33, 34, 96, 143, 144,145, 147, 197, 313

The Marriage of Figaro [*Le nozze di Figaro*] (1786)
Comic opera.   Letter 4

Misero! o sogno (1783)
Concert aria for tenor and orchestra. Remained part of Pears's repertoire through to the late
1970s.   Letter 53

Requiem in D minor (1791)
For chorus and orchestra.   Letter 325

Il seraglio [*Die Entführung aus dem Serail*] (1782)
Opera.   Letter 121

Symphony no. 35 'Haffner' (1782)   Letter 118

Musgrave, Thea (b. 1928)
Five Love Songs (1955)
For soprano and guitar.   Letter 359

Niles, John Jacob (1892–1980)
I wonder as I wander
Britten made an arrangement of John Jacob Niles's song, thinking it was a folk song, and asked
for permission once the error was discovered, but Niles refused, so Britten never published or
recorded his arrangement.   Letter 50

Offenbach, Jacques (1819–80)
Tales of Hoffmann (1881)
Pears alternated the role of Hoffmann with Henry Wendon in the Albion Operas Ltd
production in 1942.   Letter 16

Oldham, Arthur (1926–2003)
Love in a Village (1952)
Setting of Thomas Arne's ballad opera (1762). Premiered by the English Opera Group at the
1952 Aldeburgh Festival – Pears played Hawthorne.   Letter 167

Puccini, Giacomo (1858–1924)
La bohème (1896)
Opera. Pears sang Rodolfo in the 1944 Sadler's Wells production.   Letter 49, 50

Purcell, Henry (1659–95)
Details given are for Britten's realizations of the Purcell works mentioned in the letters.

The Blessed Virgin's Expostulation, Z 196
For high voice and piano. Britten's realization was first performed by the dedicatee, Margaret
Ritchie, with Britten at the piano, 1 December 1944.   Letters 82, 203

Chacony in G minor, Z 730
For string quartet or orchestra. Britten completed his realization in January 1948 and
conducted the Collegium Musicum Zurich at the premiere on 30 January 1948. His later
revision (in 1963) was first performed by the London Symphony Orchestra, with Britten
again conducting, at the Albert Hall on 12 September 1963.   Letter 93

Dido and Aeneas, Z 626
Opera. Britten's version was first made, in collaboration with Imogen Holst, for performance
by the English Opera Group at the Lyric Theatre, Hammersmith, on 1 May 1951, with
Nancy Evans as Dido. Britten and Holst then revised the realization in 1958–59, and it was
premiered by the EOG at Drottningholm in Sweden with Janet Baker as Dido on 16 May
1962. Pears sang Aeneas in Britten's broadcasts and recordings of the work.
Letters 140, 212, 228, 230, 231, 232, 234

Evening Hymn, Z 193
Third of the *Three Divine Hymns* for voice and piano, dedicated to Imogen Holst. Premiered
by Pears and Britten at St Matthew's, Northampton, on 19 October 1944.   Letter 60

The Fairy Queen, Z 629
A Masque for soloists, chorus and orchestra. Britten and Imogen Holst edited the score
together, and the scenario for concert performance was devised by Pears. Their version was
premiered at Snape Maltings as part of the Aldeburgh Festival, with Pears singing one of the
tenor solos and Britten conducting the English Chamber Orchestra on 25 June 1967.
Letters 60, 242

The Fatal Hour Comes on Apace, Z 421
[No details of a Britten realization of this song can be found, but Imogen Holst was known to have worked on an edition around 1953 – see list of works in Christopher Grogan (ed.), *Imogen Holst: A Life in Music* (rev. edn 2010)].   Letter 219

If Music be the Food of Love (third version), Z 379C
For voice and piano, the second from the collection *Seven songs from Orpheus Britannicus*. Pears and Britten premiered the realization at the Wigmore Hall on 21 November 1945.
                                                                              Letter 82

Job's Curse, Z 191
For high voice and piano. Britten's version was premiered by Pears and the composer at the Amsterdam Concertgebouw on 3 April 1948.   Letter 203

Mad Bess, Z 370
For voice and piano, the first from the collection *Six songs*. The realization was premiered by either Joan Cross (the dedicatee) or Pears and Britten at the Philharmonic Hall, Liverpool, on 17 November 1945.   Letter 203

Orpheus Britannicus
Britten edited and realized a number of songs from Purcell's two-volume collection (published 1698 and 1702). The individual songs mentioned in the letters are listed above.
                                                                        Letters 93, 203

Rossini, Gioachino (1792–1868)
The Barber of Seville [*Il barbiere di Siviglia*] (1816)
Pears played Count Almaviva in the 1943 Sadler's Wells production.   Letters 42, 50

Mosè in Egitto (1818, rev. 1827)
Opera.   Letter 309

Schoenberg, Arnold (1874–1951)
Pierrot Lunaire (1912)
Melodrama for voice and ensemble, using expressionist vocal technique (*Sprechstimme*).
                                                                              Letter 15

Schubert, Franz (1797–1828)
Adagio e Rondo concertante, D 487 (1816)
For piano and string trio.   Letter 256

Die Schöne Müllerin (1823)
Song cycle for high voice and piano, to poems by Wilhelm Müller. Pears and Britten first performed it in public together at the Wigmore Hall on 30 April 1944.
                                                             Letters 46, 47, 81, 234, 255

Shepherd on the Rock [*Der Hirt auf dem Felsen*] (1828)
For soprano, clarinet and piano.   Letter 82

Songs – for voice and piano:
   Die Allmacht, D 852 (1825)   Letter 175

   Am See, D 746 (c 1823)   Letter 53

   An die Musik, D 547 (1817)   Letter 175

   Auflösung, D 807 (1824)   Letter 53

   Dass sie hier gewesen, D 775 (?1823)   Letter 53

   Du bist die Ruh, D 776 (1823)   Letter 175

   Die Forelle, D 550 (1817)   Letter 17
   Britten made an arrangement for voice and small orchestra in 1942.

   Gretchens Bitte – Gretchen im Zwinger ('Ach! Neige'), D 564 (1817)   Letter 53

   Nacht und Träume, D 827 (?1822)   Letters 104, 120

   Nur wer die Sehnsucht kennt   Letter 310
   From the song cycle *Gesänge aus 'Wilhelm Meister'*, D 877 (1826)

   Vom Mitleiden Mariä, D 632 (1818)   Letter 53

   Der Winterabend, D 938 (1828)   Letter 228

   Songs (unspecified)   Letters 37, 315

Winterreise (1827)
Song cycle for voice and piano, to poems by Wilhelm Müller. Pears and Britten first performed it in public together at the Jubilee Hall as part of the Aldeburgh Festival on 3 July 1961 (having given a private performance at Harewood House a couple of weeks earlier). They later filmed a staged version at Snape Maltings for the BBC in 1970 (broadcast on 15 November 1970), in which Pears sings in costume and Britten plays but does not appear on screen.   Letters 196, 268, 272

Schütz, Heinrich (1585–1672)

The Christmas Story [*Weihnachtshistorie/Historia von der Geburt Jesu Christi*] (1664)
Oratorio for three soloists, chorus and orchestra.   Letter 281

St John Passion [*Johannes-Passion*] (1666)
For six voices and chorus.   Letter 294

St Matthew Passion [*Matthäus-Passion*] (1666)
For eight voices and chorus.   Letter 325

Seven Last Words from the Cross [*Die Sieben Worte Jesu Christi am Kreuz*] (1645)
Cantata for five voices, chorus and continuo.   Letters 146, 155, 166

Schumann, Robert (1810–56)
Frülingsnacht, no. 12 from *Liederkreis* (1840)
Britten made an arrangement for voice and small orchestra in 1942.   Letter 17

Spanisches Liederspiel (1849)
Song cycle for four voices and piano to texts by Emanuel Geibel after several Spanish poets.
Letter 155

Seiber, Mátyás (1905–60)
Pastorale & Burlesque (1942)
For flute and strings.   Letter 131

Sessions, Roger (1896–1985)
When Lilacs Last in the Dooryard Bloom'd (1970)
Commissioned for the American Bicentennial, Sessions sets a text by Walt Whitman
(1819–92) (written originally as an elegy on the death of Lincoln) in memory of Martin
Luther King and Robert Kennedy.   Letter 354

Smetana, Bedřich (1824–84)
The Bartered Bride [*Prodaná nevěsta*] (1866)
Opera with a libretto by Karel Sabina. Pears sang Vašek in the 1943–44 Sadler's Wells
production.   Letters 41, 75, 193

Vltava [*Die Moldau*] (1874)
Symphonic poem for orchestra.   Letter 17

Strauss, Richard (1864–1949)
Der Rosenkavalier (1910)
Comic opera with a libretto by Hugo von Hofmannsthal.   Letter 318

Sechs Lieder, op. 17 (1888)
For high voice and piano, to texts by Adolf Friedrich von Schack.   Letter 359

Stravinsky, Igor (1882–1971)
Oedipus Rex (1926–27, rev. 1948)
Opera-Oratorio, with a libretto by Jean Cocteau after Sophocles. Pears sang the title role in
Cologne with the West German Radio Symphony Orchestra, conducted by the composer, in
a performance and recording from 5 to 7 October 1951, and again twenty-five years later with
the Chicago Symphony Orchestra conducted by Georg Solti from 29 to 31 January 1976.
Letters 163, 164, 354

Suk, Josef (1874–1935)
Serenade (1892)
For string orchestra.   Letter 134

Tailleferre, Germaine (1892–1983)
Image (1918)
For flute, clarinet, celesta, piano and strings. Britten played celesta in a performance conducted by Reginald Goodall at the Wigmore Hall on 24 September 1942.   Letter 19

Telemann, Georg Philipp (1681–1767)
Suite in A minor, TWV 55:a2
For recorder (or flute), strings and continuo.   Letter 131

Tippett, Michael (1905–98)
Boyhood's End (1943)
Cantata for tenor and piano. Composed for and dedicated to Pears and Britten, it was central to many of their CEMA recitals throughout the 1940s and 1950s.   Letter 52

A Child of our Time (1941)
Oratorio for four soloists, chorus and orchestra. Pears was the tenor soloist at the premiere, with the London Philharmonic Orchestra conducted by Walter Goehr at the Royal Adelphi Theatre in London on 19 March 1944.   Letters 66, 70

The Heart's Assurance (1951)
Song cycle for tenor and piano to texts by Alun Lewis and Sidney Keyes. Commissioned by Pears, and premiered by him with Britten as part of the 1951 London Season of the Arts (part of the Festival of Britain) at the Wigmore Hall on 7 May 1951.   Letter 177

Verdi, Giuseppe (1813–1901)
Un ballo in maschera (1859)
Opera with a libretto by Antonio Somma, based on *Gustave III* by Eugène Scribe.
                                                                          Letter 159

Falstaff (1893)
Opera with a libretto by Arrigo Boito after Shakespeare.   Letter 195

Macbeth (1847)
Opera with a libretto by Francesco Piave after Shakespeare. Pears played the walk-on role of Il Re Duncano and sang in the chorus for the 1938 Glyndebourne production.   Letter 4

Rigoletto (1851)
Opera with a libretto by Francesco Piave after Victor Hugo's *Le roi s'amuse*. Pears sang The Duke of Mantua in the 1943–44 Sadler's Wells production.   Letters 33, 34, 35, 36, 37, 38

La traviata (1853)
Opera with a libretto by Francesco Piave based on *La dame aux Camélias*. Pears sang Alfred
Germont in the 1943 production at Sadler's Wells.   Letters 36, 37, 132

Vivaldi, Antonio (1678–1741)
Chamber concerto in G minor, RV 107
For flute, oboe, bassoon, violin and continuo.   Letter 131

Wagner, Richard (1813–83)
Die Meistersinger von Nürnberg (1868)
Opera. Pears sang David in the 1955 Covent Garden production.   Letter 202

Parsifal (1882)
Opera.   Letter 159

Walton, William (1902–83)
Façade (1921–27)
Entertainment for speaker and six players (often performed with two narrators), comprising
a recital of Edith Sitwell's poems with musical accompaniment by Walton. Pears recorded
the work with Sitwell and players from the English Opera Group in 1954.   Letters 15, 362

Wolf-Ferrari, Ermanno (1876–1948)
Le donne curiose (1903)
Opera with a libretto by Luigi Sugana after Carlo Goldoni.   Letter 309

Artworks

Letter numbers given in italics indicate that an image of the artwork is integrated in the letter text.

Beckmann, Wilhelm (1852–1942)
Wagner at his home in Bayreuth (1880)   Letter *221*

Blake, William (1757–1827)
St Paul Shaking Off the Viper (c 1803–5)
Purchased by Pears in 1949.   Letters 133, 134, 160

Bonington, Richard Parkes (1802–28)
Crypt of a Church
Purchased by Pears in 1950.   Letter 189

Constable, John (1776–1837)
Cloud study (18 April 1822)   Letter 160

[Portrait of Charles Golding Constable, the artist's younger son] (1835–36)   Letter 126

[Portrait of John Charles Constable, the artist's eldest son]   Letter 166

Stratford Mill, 1820   Letter 130

> **Misattributed to Constable**
> *Seascape*   Letter 160
>
> *Suffolk Landscape*   Letter 160

Cotman, John Sell (1782–1842), School of
Draining Mills at Crowland
Purchased by Pears in 1949.   Letters 134, 160

Fiore, Jacobello del (c 1370–1439)
Leone di San Marco [The Lion of St Mark] (1415)
The lion, the symbol of St Mark the Evangelist, sited in the Palazzo Ducale, Venice.
                                                                               Letter *330*

Frink, Elisabeth (1930–93)
Christ bound at the pillar (1952)   Letter 185

Gainsborough, Thomas (1727–88)
The Blue Boy (c 1770)
Portrait of Edward Ligonier, 1st Earl Ligonier (1740–82) (1770)
Portrait of German composer Carl Frederich Abel (1723–87) (c 1777)
All admired by Pears in the collections of the Huntington Art Gallery, California.
                                                                               Letter 359

Gore, Spencer (1878–1914)
The Haystacks (c 1913)   Letter 160

Green, Kenneth (1905–86)
Portrait of Britten (1943)   Letter 43

Grünewald (also Gothart Neithart), Mathias (c 1475–1528)
Isenheim Altarpiece (1512–16)
In the collections of Unterlinden Museum, Colmar, France. Provided the inspiration for Paul
Hindemith's symphony *Mathis der Maler* (1934).   Letters 87, *334*

Harth, Philipp (1887–1968)
Duck (undated)
Sculpture in bronze, acquired by Britten and Pears in 1963.   Letter 280

John, Gwen (1876–1939)
Study for *The Messenger*
Purchased by Pears in May 1954.   Letter 189

Piper, John (1903–92)
Loxford – Drop curtain for Albert Herring (1947)   Letters 160, 175

Potter, Mary (1900–81)
Boys at the Pool (1966)   Letter 301

Schwind, Moritz von (1804–71)
Die Morgenstunde (c 1860)
Admired by Britten in the collections of the Hesse Museum at Darmstadt. The figure at the
window strongly resembles Imogen Holst.   Letter *263*

Sickert, Walter (1860–1942)
Santa Maria della Salute, Venice (undated)   Letters 185, 250

Steer, Philip Wilson (1860–1942)
Harwich Estuary (1913)   Letters 185, 250

Stone, Reynolds (1909–79)
Pears and Britten bookplate (1970)   Letters 315, *317*

Tiepolo, Giovanni Battista (1696–1770)
The Investiture of Herold as Duke of Franconia (1751)
Fresco in the Kaisersaal at Würzburg, much admired by Britten and Pears.   Letter 316

Last Communion of St Lucy (1747–48)
Altarpiece at the Santi Apostoli in Venice.   Letter 305

Turner, J.M.W. (1775–1851)
Probably misattributed
Coastal Scene   Letter 160

Books, Poems and Plays

Auden, W.H. (1907–73)
For the Time Being: A Christmas Oratorio (1944)
A vast undertaking, Auden's 1,500-line Christmas story, presented as a series of dramatic monologues, was intended by the poet to be set to music by Britten in its entirety. However, it was far too extensive, and in the end Britten set only a couple of fragments for 'Poet's Christmas', a radio broadcast of poetry and music organised by Edward Sackville-West in December 1944.   Letters 66, 69

Austen, Jane (1775–1817)
Emma (1815)   Letter 52

Butler, Samuel (1805–1902) (ed. H.F. Jones)
Jones, H.F. (ed.) *The Notebooks of Samuel Butler* (1912)   Letter 289

Butts, Anthony (?1902–42)
Curious Relations
Semi-autobiographical comic novel, pseudonymously published under the name of 'D'Arfey' and edited by William Plomer.   Letter 125

de la Mare, Walter (1873–1956)
Love [Anthology] (1943)   Letter 112
With illustrations by Barnett Friedman; Pears gave Britten a copy for Christmas 1948.

Hardy, Thomas (1840–1928)
A Commonplace Day, Notebooks (1886)   Letter 207

Far from the Madding Crowd (1874)   Letter 361

Isherwood, Christopher (1904–86)
Mr Norris Changes Trains (1935)   Letter 28

Christopher and His Kind, 1929–1939 (1976)
A memoir, published by Farrar, Straus and Giroux of New York.   Letter 361

Maugham, W. Somerset (1874–1965)
Of Human Bondage (1915)   Letter 8

Morley, Robert (1908–92) and Langley, Noel (1911–80)
Edward, My Son (1947)
Play starring Robert Morley, produced first in the West End then on Broadway in 1948, where Meg Mundy (daughter of Pears's singing teacher, Clytie Mundy) joined the cast.

Letter 94

Natan, Alex
Primo Uomo: grosse Sänger der Oper (Great Opera Singers) (1963)   Letter 281

Richter, G.M.A.
Kouroi: Archaic Greek Youths: A Study of the Development of the Kouros Type in Greek Sculpture (London: The Phaidon Press, 1960). Acquired by Britten and Pears in January 1961.

Letter 262

Rousseau, Jean-Jacques (1712–78)
Confessions (1782)
Bought by Pears in October 1962.   Letter 272

Stein, Erwin (1885–1958)
Form and Performance (1962, posth.)
Completed after Stein's death by Britten (who wrote the Foreword), Pears, Donald Mitchell and Marion Stein.   Letter 243

Tennyson, Alfred, Lord (1809–92)
The Lady of Shalott (1833)   Letter 50

Waddell, Helen (1889–1965)
Peter Abelard (1933)
Historical novel.   Letter 52

Young, Arthur (1741–1820)
Travels in France and Italy during the Years 1787, 1788 and 1789
Published in 1792.   Letter 135

Films

Bergman, Ingmar (1918–2007)
The Virgin Spring ('Jungfrukällan')
Released 8 February 1960.   Letter 253

Billon, Pierre (1901–81)
Ruy blas
With a screenplay by Jean Cocteau adapted from the Victor Hugo drama. Opened in New York, October 1948.   Letter 94

Curtiz, Michael (1886–1962)
Casablanca (1942)   Letter 29

Ford, John (1894–1973)
How Green was my Valley (1941)   Letter 15

Hitchcock, Alfred (1899–1980)
Family Plot (1976)
Hitchcock's final film.   Letter 356

Marshall, George (1891–1975)
Destry Rides Again (1939)
Released in late December 1939.   Letter 9

Mathiesen, Muir (1911–75)
Instruments of the Orchestra (1946)
Crown Film Unit educational film for children, for which Britten composed the Purcell variations which became the concert work *The Young Person's Guide to the Orchestra*. It featured the London Symphony Orchestra conducted by Malcolm Sargent, and a script written by *Peter Grimes* librettist, Montagu Slater.   Letter 62

Select Bibliography

Note on primary sources at the Britten–Pears Foundation Archive

The published versions of Britten's letters to correspondents other than Pears have been cited where possible. Unpublished letters are included in the Bibliography. In addition to Britten and Pears's correspondence, key resources for this book were their office and pocket diaries, but any reference to Britten's journals up until 1938 is to the published edition. Concert, recital and opera programmes held in the Archive have also been consulted. Information about, and access to, this material can be found in the Britten–Pears Foundation online resources listed below.

Editions of Letters and Diaries

Letters from a Life: Selected Letters and Diaries of Benjamin Britten
  Volume One 1923–1939, ed. Donald Mitchell and Philip Reed. London: Faber and Faber, 1998
  Volume Two 1939–1945, ed. Donald Mitchell and Philip Reed. London: Faber and Faber, 1998
  Volume Three 1946–1951, ed. Donald Mitchell, Philip Reed and Mervyn Cooke. London: Faber and Faber, 2003
  Volume Four 1952–1957, ed. Philip Reed, Mervyn Cooke and Donald Mitchell. Woodbridge: The Boydell Press, 2008
  Volume Five 1958–1965, ed. Philip Reed and Mervyn Cooke. Woodbridge: The Boydell Press, 2010
  Volume Six 1966–1976, ed. Philip Reed and Mervyn Cooke. Woodbridge: The Boydell Press, 2012
Evans, John (ed.), *Journeying Boy: The Diaries of the Young Benjamin Britten 1928–1938*. London: Faber and Faber, 2009
Reed, Philip (ed.), *The Travel Diaries of Peter Pears 1936–1978*, Aldeburgh Studies in Music Volume Two. Woodbridge: The Boydell Press, 1999

Biography, Criticism and Other Relevant Studies and Sources

Bankes, Ariane and Jonathan Reekie (eds), *New Aldeburgh Anthology*. Woodbridge: The Boydell Press in association with Aldeburgh Music, 2009

Banks, Paul (ed.), *The Making of Peter Grimes: Essays and Studies*. Aldeburgh Studies in Music Volume Six. Woodbridge: The Boydell Press, 1996

—— (ed.), *Benjamin Britten: A Catalogue of his Published Works*. Aldeburgh: The Britten–Pears Library for the Britten Estate Limited, 1999

Barnes, Jennifer, *Television Opera: The Fall of Opera Commissioned for Television*. Woodbridge: The Boydell Press, 2003

Bennett, Moira, *Making Musicians: A Personal History of the Britten–Pears School*. Orford: Bittern Press, 2012

Blythe, Ronald (ed.), *Aldeburgh Anthology*. London: Snape Maltings Foundation in association with Faber Music, 1972

Bridcut, John, *Britten's Children*. London: Faber and Faber, 2006

—— *Essential Britten*. London: Faber and Faber, 2010

Britten, Benjamin and Peter Pears, Programme for Britten–Pears recital, 8 December 1949, Community Church Auditorium, New York, PG/1949/1208, Britten–Pears Foundation Archive

Britten, Benjamin and Imogen Holst, *The Story of Music*. London: Rathbone Books, 1958

Britten, Beth, *My Brother Benjamin*. London: Faber and Faber, 2013

Burrows, Jill, *The Aldeburgh Story*. Ipswich: The Aldeburgh Foundation, 1987

Campbell-Smith, Duncan, *Masters of the Post: The Authorized History of the Royal Mail*. London: Penguin Books, 2012

Carpenter, Humphrey, *Benjamin Britten: A Biography*. London: Faber and Faber, 1992

Carpenter, Humphrey, with research by Jennifer Doctor, *The Envy of the World: Fifty Years of the BBC Third Programme and Radio 3, 1946–1996*. London: Phoenix Giant, 1997

Cooke, Mervyn, *Britten and the Far East: Asian Influences in the Music of Benjamin Britten*, Aldeburgh Studies in Music Volume Four. Woodbridge: The Boydell Press, 1998

—— (ed.), *The Cambridge Companion to Benjamin Britten*. Cambridge: Cambridge University Press, 1999

Crozier, Eric, 'The Origin of the Aldeburgh Festival', *The Aldeburgh Festival of Music and the Arts Programme Book*, 1948, p. 6

—— 'Notes on Benjamin Britten', unpublished and undated typescript, Evans Crozier Papers, Box 5, Britten–Pears Foundation Archive

Crozier, Eric and Nancy Evans, 'Recalling the Art of Peter Pears', unpublished and undated transcription, Evans-Crozier Papers, Box 5, Britten–Pears Foundation Archive

Daunton, M.J., *Royal Mail: The Post Office since 1840*. London: The Athlone Press, 1985

Deutsch, Otto Erich (ed.), *Franz Schubert's Letters and Other Writings* (translated by Venetia Savile). New York: Vienna House, 1974

Evans, Peter, *The Music of Benjamin Britten*. Oxford: Clarendon Press, 1996

Ford, Boris (ed.), *Benjamin Britten's Poets: An Anthology of the Poems he Set to Music*. Manchester: Carcanet Press, 2013

Forster, E.M., 'George Crabbe: The Poet and the Man', *The Listener* 25 (29 May 1941), pp. 769–70

Garnham, Maureen, *As I Saw It: Basil Douglas, Benjamin Britten and the English Opera Group 1955–1957: A Personal Memoir*. London: St George's Publications, 1998

Gishford, Anthony (ed.), *Tribute to Benjamin Britten on his Fiftieth Birthday*. London: Faber and Faber, 1963

Greco, Stephen, 'A Knight at the Opera: An Interview with Sir Peter Pears', *The Advocate*, cclxxi (12 July 1979), pp. 37–9

Grogan, Christopher (ed.), *Imogen Holst: A Life in Music*, Aldeburgh Studies in Music Volume Seven. Woodbridge: The Boydell Press, 2010

Headington, Christopher, *Peter Pears: A Biography*. London: Faber and Faber, 1992

Herbert, David (ed.), *The Operas of Benjamin Britten*. London: Hamish Hamilton, 1979

Joint Property of Benjamin Britten and Peter Pears, The Red House, Aldeburgh Suffolk, Value for Insurance, Christie, Manson & Woods, LTD, November 1965, pp. 85–6, 91–2, Britten–Pears Foundation Archive

Keller, Hans, *Britten: Essays, Letters and Opera Guides*, ed. Christopher Wintle and A.M. Garnham. London: Cosman Keller Art and Music Trust and Plumbago Books, 2013

Kildea, Paul, *Selling Britten: Music and the Marketplace*. Oxford: Oxford University Press, 2002

—— (ed.), *Britten on Music*. Oxford: Oxford University Press, 2003

—— *Benjamin Britten: A Life in the Twentieth Century*. London: Penguin, 2014

Lees-Milne, James, *Diaries 1971–1983* (abridged and introduced by Michael Bloch). London: John Murray, 2007

LeGrove, Judith (ed.), *A Musical Eye: The Visual World of Britten and Pears*. Woodbridge: The Boydell Press in Association with the Britten–Pears Foundation, 2013

McGhee, Derek, *Homosexuality, Law and Resistance*. New York: Routledge, 2001

Mark, Christopher, *Britten: An Extraordinary Life*. London: ABRSM Publishing, 2013

Matthews, David, *Britten*. London: Haus Publishing Ltd, 2013

Mitchell, Donald and Hans Keller (eds), *Benjamin Britten: A Commentary on his Works from a Group of Specialists*. London: Rockliff Publishing Corporation Limited, 1952

Mitchell, Donald and John Evans, *Benjamin Britten: Pictures from a Life 1913–1976*. London: Faber and Faber, 1978

Morley, Peter, *A Life Rewound: Memoirs of a Freelance Producer and Director*. New Romney: Bank House Books, 2010

Palmer, Christopher (ed.), *The Britten Companion*. London: Faber and Faber, 1984

Pears, Peter, 'Hardy and his Poetry', autograph script for *Master Lesson*, BBC Radio 3, 17 September 1973, Pears's Writings, 5/G/H/1, Box 2, Britten–Pears Foundation Archive

Powell, Neil, *Benjamin Britten: A Life for Music*. London: Hutchinson, 2013

Rupprecht, Philip, *Britten's Musical Language*, Music in the 20th Century series. Cambridge: Cambridge University Press, 2001

—— (ed.), *Rethinking Britten*. Oxford: Oxford University Press, 2013

Schuttenhelm, Thomas, *The Orchestral Music of Michael Tippett: Creative Development and the Compositional Process*, Music since 1900 series. Cambridge: Cambridge University Press, 2014

Spalding, Frances, *John Piper, Myfanwy Piper: Lives in Art*. Oxford: Oxford University Press, 2009

Strode, Rosamund, *Music of Forty Festivals: A List of Works Performed at Aldeburgh Festivals from 1948 to 1987*. Aldeburgh: Aldeburgh Foundation and the Britten–Pears Library, 1987

Stuart, Philip, *Benjamin Britten, Performing and Performed: A Centenary Discography*. Unpublished discography (a copy is available in the Britten–Pears archive).

Thomson, Rita, unpublished letter to Peter Pears, 9 November 1976, Britten–Pears Foundation Archive

Thomson, Virgil, 'Music: Hand Work and Hand-Me-Downs', *New York Herald Tribune* (23 December 1941), 1941–43 Press Clippings, Britten–Pears Foundation Archive

Thorpe, Marion (ed.), *Peter Pears: A Tribute on His 75th Birthday*. London: Faber Music and the Britten–Pears Library, 1985

Tippins, Sherrill, *February House*. New York: Houghton Mifflin Company, 2005

Walker, Lucy, (ed.), *Benjamin Britten: New Perspectives on his Life and Work*. Aldeburgh Studies in Music Volume Eight. Woodbridge: The Boydell Press, 2009

—— *Britten in Pictures*. Woodbridge: The Boydell Press, 2012

Wallace, Helen, *Boosey and Hawkes: The Publishing Story*. London: Boosey and Hawkes Music Publishers Ltd, 2007

Weeks, Jeffrey, *Coming Out: Homosexual Politics in Britain from the Nineteenth Century to the Present* (revised and updated edition). London: Quartet Books, 1990

White, Eric Walter, *Benjamin Britten: His Life and Operas*, second edition edited by John Evans. London: Faber and Faber, 1983

Whittall, Arnold, *The Music of Britten and Tippett: Studies in Themes and Techniques*. Cambridge: Cambridge University Press, 1982

Wiebe, Heather, *Britten's Unquiet Pasts: Sound and Memory in Postwar Reconstruction*, Music since 1900 series. Cambridge: Cambridge University Press, 2012

Wright, David, *Faber Music: The First 25 Years 1965–1990*. London: Faber Music, 1990

Interviews

Recordings and transcriptions are held at the Britten–Pears Foundation Archive, Aldeburgh.

Cadbury-Brown, Jim, interview with Clare Howes, Church Walk, Aldeburgh, 19 October 2007

Collymore, Peter, interview with Stephen Lock, Britten–Pears Foundation, Aldeburgh, 16 June, 2008

Cullum, Jeremy, interview with Donald Mitchell, Chapel House, Horham, 20 August 1998

Strode, Rosamund, interview with Nicholas Clark, Britten–Pears Foundation, Aldeburgh, 11 December 2008

Thomson, Rita, interview with Colin Matthews, Church Farm, Aldeburgh, 12 December 2003

Films for Television

Contrasts: The Tenor Man's Story, Sir Peter Pears in Conversation with Donald Mitchell. Dir. Barrie Gavin. Central Television, first broadcast Central Television, 27 August 1985

A Time There Was … A Profile of Benjamin Britten. Dir. Tony Palmer. London Weekend Television, for *The Southbank Show*, first broadcast London Weekend Television, 6 April 1980. Transcript of soundtrack, Britten–Pears Foundation Archive

Websites

All last accessed, 30 June 2015

Bach Cantatas Website (BCW) http://www.bach-cantatas.com

BBC Genome – Radio Times archive http://genome.ch.bbc.co.uk

British Newspaper Archive (British Library/findmypast) http://www.britishnewspaperarchive .co.uk

Britten–Pears Foundation online archive catalogues and historical performances database http://www.brittenpears.org Research and Collections pages

Britten Thematic Catalogue http://www.brittenproject.org

Concert Programmes Project (CPP) database http://www.concertprogrammes.org.uk/

On This Day, 1950–2005. BBC News, 4 September 1957: Homosexuality 'should not be a crime'. http://news.bbc.co.uk/onthisday/hi/dates/stories/september/4/newsid_3007000/ 3007686.stm

Opera magazine online archive, 1950–2014 http://opera.archive.netcopy.co.uk

Royal Opera House performances database http://www.rohcollections.org.uk/performances. aspx

General Index

Page references refer to the text of the letters, except when they appear in italics, where they indicate editorial matter and notes.

Names or names of works followed by an asterisk (*) indicate entries in the Personalia and List of Works, where more detailed information can be found.

Britten and Pears are referred to as 'BB' and 'PP' throughout.